CW01084865

CHURCH HOUSE LIBRARY
ECTON HOUSE
NORTHAMPTON NN6 0QE

BOOK No _ _ _ 508 _ _ _ _ _ _ _

CLASS No _ _ _ B _ _ _ _ _ _ _

DATE added march 1993

HIGH CHURCH PROPHET

Bishop Samuel Horsley. Engraving by Henry Meyer (1813) after portrait by James Green. By permission of Carmarthen Museum.

HIGH CHURCH PROPHET

Bishop Samuel Horsley
(1733–1806)
and the Caroline Tradition in the
Later Georgian Church

F. C. MATHER

CLARENDON PRESS·OXFORD
1992

Oxford University Press. Walton Street. Oxford OX2 6DP

Oxford New York Toronto
Delhi Bombay Calcutta Madras Karachi
Petaling Jaya Singapore Hong Kong Tokyo
Nairobi Dar es Salaam Cape Town
Melbourne Auckland
and associated companies in
Berlin Ibadan

Oxford is a trade mark of Oxford University Press

Published in the United States
by Oxford University Press, New York

© F. C. Mather 1992

All rights reserved. No part of this publication may be reproduced,
stored in a retrieval system, or transmitted, in any form or by any means,
electronic, mechanical, photocopying, recording, or otherwise, without
the prior permission of Oxford University Press

British Library Cataloguing in Publication Data
Data available

Library of Congress Cataloging in Publication Data
Mather, F. C. (Frederick Clare)
High church prophet: Bishop Samuel Horsley (1733–1806) and the
Caroline tradition in the later Georgian church / F.C. Mather.
p.   cm.
Includes bibliographical references and index.
1. Horsley, Samuel, 1733–1806.   2. Church of England—Bishops—
Biography.   3. Anglican Communion—England—Bishops—Biography.
I. Title.
BX5199.H84M38   1992
283'.092—dc20
[B]   91-37372
ISBN 0-19-820227-X

Typeset by Best-set Typesetter Ltd., Hong Kong
Printed and bound in
Great Britain by Biddles Ltd,
Guildford and King's Lynn

TO PAT,
who always saw the best in
Horsley

Preface

SAMUEL HORSLEY, bishop in turn of St Davids, Rochester, and St Asaph and dean of Westminster, was described by Overton and Relton at the end of the Victorian age as 'the greatest figure in the Church since the death of Bishop Butler'. He was undoubtedly the ablest ecclesiastical statesman of the later eighteenth century, and also the most effective. Some aspects of his career entitle him to be seen as a national figure: his role as a scientist, editing the works of Newton and helping to plan the Royal Society's voyages of exploration; his assiduous attention to the business of the House of Lords during a critical period; his forthright stand on the great moral issues of the day, religious toleration, the abolition of the slave trade, and the impeachment of Warren Hastings.

On his own evaluation, however, his principal importance—'my public pretension, my pride, my glory'—lay in being a High Churchman. His career illustrates the persistence of a significant strain of Caroline Anglicanism, monarchical, episcopal, sacramental, and even its revival during the second half of the eighteenth century, notwithstanding the unfavourable climate of Enlightenment ideas and Industrial Revolution. What follows is not episcopal biography in the usual sense of the term, but a study of High Churchmanship, using Samuel Horsley as the point of reference. It will explore all aspects of his career, in the conviction that these are necessary to the understanding not only of the man but of the school, of which he was the foremost representative in his day.

I am indebted to the Leverhulme Trustees and to the University of Southampton for the year's leave in 1972–3 which enabled me to start work on this project. So many scholars have communicated information and ideas during the long process of completing it, which has been protracted by illness and commitment to work in other fields, that it is invidious to mention some rather than others. But I have particular pleasure in acknowledging the help of Dr John Oddy, who freely and generously made his doctoral thesis available to me, and read portions of my work relating to it. When the first draft of my book was approaching completion, Dr Jonathan Clark kindly furnished me with a proof copy of his *English Society*, which enabled me to take timely note of his important contributions to the study of Anglican political theory. Dr Grayson Ditchfield has likewise been particularly helpful in keeping me abreast of his studies in the history of Unitarianism, in supplying information, and in answering questions. Others who have corresponded with me or exchanged ideas in conversation include Miss Phoebe Ames, Mr Peter Bogan, Professor Owen Chadwick, Dr Tristram Clarke (Scottish Record Office), Mrs E. Cottrill and Mr R. T. Brown (The Drapers'

Company), Archbishop Couve de Murville, Dr John Ehrman, Professor Norman Gash, Bishop Alastair Haggart, Captain A. C. Horsley, Mrs B. L. Hough, the Revd Dr Gordon Huelin and Mr Arthur E. Barker (SPCK), Miss Eglantyne Jebb, Mr Colin McLaren (King's College, Aberdeen), the Revd David Mowbray (Broxbourne), the Revd C. E. Moxley, Dr Peter Nockles, Dr Edward Norman, Mrs Dorothy Owen, Miss Rosemary Rendel, the Revd K. A. G. Strachan, Mr Stanley Tongue (Shoreditch Public Library), and the Revd Dr A. R. Winnett. My old Southampton colleague, Charles Whitaker, placed his learning at my disposal in deciphering and interpreting Greek phrases in the documents.

My thanks are due to the seventh Earl Spencer for introducing me to the Poyntz papers, then at Althorp, to the Council of the Royal Society for admission to the Library and Archives, and to the Dean and Chapter of Westminster for granting me access to the historical records of the Abbey. I am grateful to the staff of the Department of Manuscripts in the British Library, to Dr Geoffrey Bill and his colleagues at Lambeth Palace Library, to the librarians of the Bodleian Library, Oxford, to the keeper of the archives in Cambridge University Library, and to Miss Elizabeth Poyser, archivist of the Archbishop of Westminster, for guidance to the manuscript collections in their custody; also to the county archivists of Chester, Lincoln, East Sussex, and Kent and the librarians and archivists of the National Library of Wales, the National Library of Scotland, Leeds City Reference Library, Manchester Central Reference Library, the Borthwick Institute in York, Chetham's Library, Manchester, the United Society for the Propagation of the Gospel, and Sion College, London for similar facilities, and to Dr Richard Sharp for the loan of a slide of Samuel Horsley from an etching by Dighton.

My greatest debt is to my wife Patricia, not only for typing the final draft, but for helping me with the research and placing her skill as an archivist at my disposal. Without her encouragement and conviction this book would never have reached completion. For the faults in it I am myself responsible.

F. C. MATHER

University of Southampton

Contents

Abbreviations

AAW	Archives of the Archbishopric of Westminster
Add. MSS	Additional Manuscripts
BL	Department of Manuscripts, British Library
Bodl.	The Bodleian Library, Oxford
CAB	Chapter Act Book
CH	Episcopal Chest Papers, SRO (CH 12/12/)
CH(J)	Bishop Jolly Kist Papers, SRO (CH 12/14/)
CRO	County Record Office
CUL	Cambridge University Library
DNB	*Dictionary of National Biography*
Gent. Mag.	*The Gentleman's Magazine*
HP	Horsley Papers, LPL MSS 1767–9
Jebb	H. H. Jebb, *A Great Bishop of One Hundred Years Ago: Being a Sketch of the Life of Samuel Horsley, LL.D., Bishop of St. David's, Rochester and St. Asaph, and Dean of Westminster* (1909)
JHC	*Journal of the House of Commons*
JHL	*Journal of the House of Lords*
LPL	Lambeth Palace Library
NLS	Department of Manuscripts, National Library of Scotland, Edinburgh
NLW	National Library of Wales, Aberystwyth
OCM	*Orthodox Churchman's Magazine*
ODCC	F. L. Cross and E. A. Livingstone, *Oxford Dictionary of the Christian Church* (1974)
pa.	parish registers
PL	Public Library
PP	Parliamentary Papers
Poyntz Letters	BL Althorp Papers, Letters of the Revd Charles Poyntz
PRO	Public Record Office
RO	Record Office
RS	The Royal Society
Sk.C.	Skinner (Boucher) Correspondence
SRO	Scottish Record Office, Edinburgh

Myth or Reality? The High Church Ideal in the Eighteenth-Century Church

THAT invaluable stand-by of the ecclesiastical historian, the revised *Oxford Dictionary of the Christian Church*, defines 'High Churchmen' as 'The group in the C. of E. which especially stresses her historical continuity with Catholic Christianity, and hence upholds a "high" conception of the authority of the Church, of the claims of the episcopate and of the nature of the Sacraments.' With these attributes, it may be added, went intense veneration for divine-right monarchy. Following what has long been the opinion of the majority of scholars, the definition accords to that school a 'host' of adherents in the seventeenth century, the age of the 'Caroline' divines, but claims that, after the Revolution of 1688–9, 'those who remained in the Established Church were excluded from ecclesiastical preferment as tainted with Jacobitism and for the most part fell into obscurity', only to be rescued by the Oxford Movement.[1] The name, which did not, in fact, gain currency until towards the end of the reign of William III,[2] has been allowed to have survived and flourished. C. J. Abbey and J. H. Overton wrote of the eighteenth century that 'from its first to its last year so called High Churchmen were abundant everywhere'. But the type had altered, and not for the better. The new High Churchmanship was 'an ecclesiastical toryism', persuaded of 'the unique excellence of the English Church, its divinely constituted government, and its high, if not exclusive title to purity and orthodoxy of doctrine'.[3]

This is to overstate the change. The deprivation of the Nonjurors did, indeed, bring a dilution of the intense spirituality and other-worldly outlook which was inherited from the bygone age of Donne, George Herbert, and the metaphysical poets, and could not easily be replaced in the comfortable and commonplace England of the late seventeenth century.[4] But politicization was no new thing. It was an abiding consequence of the union of Church and State established at the Reformation that churchmen must encompass their temporal objectives by collaboration with princes and statesmen. Thus the saintly Sancroftians worked with Clarendon and Rochester to promote

---

[1] *ODCC* 647.

[2] G. Every, *The High Church Party 1688–1718* (1956), pp. xiii, 1. In all instances the place of publication is London unless otherwise stated.

[3] C. J. Abbey and J. H. Overton, *The English Church in the Eighteenth Century* (1887), 51.

[4] Gareth Bennett, 'Thomas Ken (1637–1711), Bishop of Bath and Wells', in id., *To the Church of England*, ed. G. Rowell (Worthing, 1988), chap. v.

Church reform and hereditary succession to the throne by the systematic organization of the Crown's ecclesiastical patronage in the closing years of Charles II's reign just as deliberately as Francis Atterbury's party in the Canterbury Convocation worked with the Tories in the Parliaments of Anne.[5]

However much importance has been assigned to High Churchmanship as a form of political behaviour, sometimes indistinguishable from Toryism at the local level, this has been usually kept quite separate from High Church theology and High Church theory, which have not been allowed to count for much in eighteenth-century Church and society. For more than half a century, interpretation has been moulded by the judgements of the greatest of eighteenth-century English Church historians, the late Norman Sykes, who, while clearing the Georgian clergy of the heaviest charges of negligence, wrote firmly of 'the typical Latitudinarian churchmanship dominant in the century'.[6] In this study of the career of an influential late eighteenth-century bishop, his associates, and achievements, it will be argued that Sykes replaced one myth by another. The impartiality of his scholarship is evident from the fact that some of his episcopal biographies, those of Gibson and Wake in particular, do most to modify the impressions of his *Church and State in England in the Eighteenth Century*, but the impact of the latter has been such as to cause High Church writers of a later age to repudiate the eighteenth century. G. V. Bennett wrote of 'the critical change which came over English religious life between 1660 and 1740' and presented Tillotson as 'the father of the 18th century Church, aristocratic, urbane, latitudinarian, rational and unenthusiastic'.[7]

Under the microscope of the latest historical revision, Latitudinarianism has lost its cohesion and distinctiveness. No longer can it be viewed as a homogeneous block of clerical opinion: rational, informed by natural philosophy and science in opposition to patristic studies, sitting loose to church doctrines and favouring comprehension of Dissenters in the Establishment, Low Church, and politically Whig. The name first gained currency in Cambridge 'something before His Majesty's [King Charles] most happy return',[8] being used both then and for many years to come to denote the opinions of succeeding generations of churchmen, whose views had but little in common with one another. The earliest Latitudinarians were the Cambridge Platonists, Cudworth, Henry More, and others, who disseminated a curious mystical rationalism. John Spurr, however, in the most radical

---

[5] R. Beddard, 'The Commission for Ecclesiastical Promotions, 1681–84: An Instrument of Tory Reaction', *Historical Journal*, 10 (1967), 11–40; cf. G. V. Bennett, *The Tory Crisis in Church and State, 1688–1730* (Oxford, 1975), 92–3.

[6] Norman Sykes, *Church and State in England in the Eighteenth Century* (Cambridge, 1934), 425; cf. 268, 391.

[7] Bennett, *To the Church of England*, 75.

[8] John Gascoigne, 'Politics, Patronage and Newtonianism: The Cambridge Example', *Historical Journal*, 27 (1984), 3–9.

reappraisal, attaches the label to 'Commonwealth conformists', mainstream Anglicans who had held on to their preferments in Cambridge at the parliamentary visitation of 1644 by submitting to the visitors' terms, and afterwards with manifestly less effort conformed to the refurbished Episcopal Church of the Restoration. These riposted to the sneers of their more consistent brethren that they were 'traditours' or gentlemen 'of wide swallow', with the simple plea of necessity. Their most notable apologist 'S.P.' (probably Simon Patrick, later bishop of Chichester) observed in his *Brief Account of the New Sect of Latitude Men* (1662):

The greatest part of the men that seem to be pointed at under that name, are such whose fortune it was to be born so late, as to have their education in the University [of Cambridge] since the beginning of the unhappy troubles of this kingdom, where they ascended to their preferments by the regular steps of election, not much troubling themselves to inquire into the titles of some of their electors.

Individual Latitudinarians in the Restoration Church exhibited the positive qualities ascribed to the *genre*—interest in science (Joseph Glanvill and John Wilkins) and moral Christianity (Tillotson)—but collectively they were not more committed to these pursuits than other Anglicans nor closer to the Protestant Dissenters in their doctrines, though a sensitivity to their own chequered past made them more charitable and gentle towards the separated brethren as people and disposed to welcome their return.[9] Professor Aylmer, though critical of the minimalist interpretation of Latitudinarianism in general, concedes its applicability to the generation of divines whose formative years were in the 1640s or 1650s. Significantly these were also the men who received bishoprics from William III on the recommendation of Lord Nottingham in the early 1690s—Patrick and Stillingfleet, Fowler and Sprat, Tenison and Tillotson.[10] Bennett has noted in one of his posthumous essays that the younger Latitudinarians Patrick and Stillingfleet, so far from being rationalist opponents of the old learning, sought to reconcile reason not only with revelation in general but with the particular expression of it in the tradition of the Church. The latter's *Rational Account of the Grounds of the Protestant Religion*, published in various editions from *c*.1644, argued that the Fathers themselves admitted the claims of reason and that, while rational man had the duty to determine what is revelation, there could never be a conflict between a true formulation of the apostolic tradition and the claim of man to exercise his reason. In their insistence that the patristic writings must be given

[9] J. Spurr, 'Latitudinarianism and the Restoration Church', *Historical Journal*, 31 (1988), 61–82.

[10] G. E. Aylmer, 'Collective Mentalities in Mid-Seventeenth Century England, iv. Cross Currents: Neutrals, Trimmers and Others', Presidential Address, *Transactions of the Royal Historical Society*, 5th ser., 39 (1989), 1–22; cf. G. V. Bennett, 'King William III and the Episcopate', in id. and J. Walsh (eds.), *Essays in Modern English Church History in Memory of Norman Sykes* (1966).

a critical and discriminating use the Latitudinarians hardly went beyond the acknowledged Caroline divine Jeremy Taylor.[11] From this it must be concluded, contrary to widespread belief, that High Church divinity was not at the Revolution confronted by a rival and much updated system which was bound to overwhelm it. A capacity for sturdy survival and even for periodic reinvigoration remained in it.

The party which gathered in 1697 behind Francis Atterbury's call for a sitting Convocation was a politico-ecclesiastical party, not a theological one. Its leader grounded his plea principally on the constitutional claim that Convocation was a part of Parliament. But the debate both about the Convocation and within it was set in the framework of theological arguments affirming the independent spiritual authority of the clergy which, though they were mounted by fringe elements mainly but not exclusively Nonjuring, commanded enough support from the parish clergy outside that assembly to influence the responses of the more pragmatic party leaders in the dispute about Dissenters' baptisms in 1712–13.[12] As Dr Mark Goldie has shown, in correction of Bennett's biography, Atterbury himself incorporated in his *Letter to a Convocation Man* the Nonjuror argument that the Church is a society instituted for a supernatural end, and as such must have an inherent power of governing itself to that end.[13]

Out of the 'vitriolic debates between High and Low Churchmen which came to a head in the reign of Queen Anne' emerged, Dr John Gascoigne asserts, the new Latitudinarianism of Benjamin Hoadly which rested the theory of the State on some notion of a contract between the governing and the governed.[14] It also embraced a theological radicalism impatient of metaphysical dogmas. The advance of innovative ideology was most apparent in the University of Cambridge, where, from the turn of the century, Latitudinarian bishops like John Moore, bishop of Ely, had been using their college patronage to harness the natural philosophy of Isaac Newton, with its display of the argument from design, to their struggle against materialism and Deism. Thus, by the 1730s, the new science had become part of the staple round of undergraduate studies in the University.[15]

It would be wrong, however, to suppose that advanced Latitudinarianism quickly swept the board of its more traditional rivals. Hoadly's extreme Erastianism was unacceptable to both bishops and clergy. His sermon

---

[11] *To the Church of England*, chap. vii: 'The Latitudinarians'.

[12] Bennett, *Tory Crisis*, 152–6.

[13] Mark Goldie, 'The Nonjurors, Episcopacy and the Origins of the Convocation Controversy', in E. Cruickshanks (ed.), *Ideology and Conspiracy: Aspects of Jacobitism, 1689–1759* (Edinburgh, 1982).

[14] John Gascoigne, 'Anglican Latitudinarianism and Political Radicalism in the Late Eighteenth Century', *History*, 71 (1986), 22–38.

[15] J. L. Gascoigne, *Cambridge in the Age of the Enlightenment: Science, Religion and Politics from the Restoration to the French Revolution* (Cambridge, 1989), 149–79.

preached before King George I on 31 March 1717, denying that Christ had committed any independent spiritual authority to the Church, provoked a storm of clerical protest. In some respects High Church principles were still gaining ground under the first of the Hanoverian monarchs. Recruits came from an unexpected quarter. From Puritan New England a former rector of Yale and three other Congregational ministers sailed to the mother country in 1722–3 to obtain episcopal ordination, and returned to the colonies as SPG missionaries. Unsettled by readings from a library of books presented to Yale in 1714 by Connecticut's London agent, they came round to the conviction that episcopacy, working through apostolical succession, was of the *esse* of the Church. Curiously the writings which had done most to wean them from their erstwhile convictions were not mainly those of 'furious' High Churchmen, juring or nonjuring, but of moderate Anglicans, Patrick and Whitby,[16] Potter and Tillotson, Sharp and Scott.

Paradoxically, in the years when Atterbury's political High Church party was hurtling from power a spiritual High Churchmanship, concerned to restore primitive church order, was digging deeper roots. An advanced doctrine of Eucharistic sacrifice was propounded by John Johnson, vicar of Cranbrook, in a treatise entitled *Unbloody Sacrifice and Altar, Unvailed and Supported*, published in 1714–18. Johnson taught that the elements of bread and wine became in the Holy Communion the body and blood of Christ, not indeed in substance, as the Roman Catholics believed, but 'in power and effect', and that the service was therefore a 'proper' and propitiatory sacrifice based on the offering of those elements to God. In order to express this belief in action, he wished so to amend the Communion Office as to incorporate lost features of primitive liturgies, notably by the introduction of an oblation followed by an invocation of the consecrating power of the Holy Spirit after the recitation of Christ's words of institution. It was left to the Nonjurors to adopt Johnson's liturgical reforms.[17] Divines of his own Church at first attacked his views as popish. Within a few years, however, their hostility began to abate.[18] That Johnson's opinions enjoyed the acceptance of a minority within the Established Church in the early 1730s is indicated by the diary of the first earl of Egmont, which instances a friend named Dawney, a theoretical Jacobite with an Oxford upbringing, who communicated every Sunday 'at some church or other' in the neighbourhood. He told the earl (then Lord Percival) 'that the ancient Christians never assembled without doing it and thought their service otherwise imperfect'. He added that 'commemorating the death of Our Lord is not the principal business when we

---

[16] Bruce E. Steiner, *Samuel Seabury, 1729–1796: A Study in the High Church Tradition* (Athens, Ohio, 1971), 2–5.

[17] W. Jardine Grisbrooke, *Anglican Liturgies of the Seventeenth and Eighteenth Centuries* (1958), 71, 83–7.

[18] T. Brett, *The Life of the Rev. Mr. Johnson, Late Vicar of Cranbrook, Kent* (1748), pp. xxiv–xxvi.

communicate, but the offering up the elements to God'.[19] Johnson's work stood heir to a line of liturgical research, international and ecumenical in character, stretching well back into the seventeenth century.

From the other side of the Church, however, mysterious doctrines of the Eucharist came under sharp attack by advocates of the Latitudinarian cult of plainness, who regarded them as blocking the ordinary man's perception of the simple truths of Christianity, but their arguments did not pass unchallenged. Hoadly's *Plain Account of the Sacrament of the Lord's Supper* (1735) reduced the Communion rite to a simple memorial, but was promptly answered by Dr Gloster Ridley in 1736 and by Dr Daniel Waterland in 1737. Waterland wrote from a central Anglican position, but Ridley, who taught that 'the Lord's Supper instituted in memory of Christ's death was itself a Sacrifice as much as any of the Jewish Sacrifices were',[20] must be regarded as a High Churchman in the seventeenth-century tradition, though his teaching differed from that of Johnson and the Nonjurors.

For nearly twenty years after the Hanoverian succession, patronage worked on the side of conservative divinity and against the challenge of heterodoxy. Only a fraction of the Whig ascendancy which governed England during these years had any sympathy with Hoadly. These were the Old Whigs, a radical group which appeared soon after the Revolution of 1688, and angrily denounced Whig ministers for compromising fundamental principles in religion and politics in order to stay in office. Small in size, though greater in influence, they numbered no more than forty members of the House of Commons by the reign of George II. Their principal ecclesiastical adherents were Hoadly himself, Toland the Deist, and Matthew Tindal. Meanwhile Sir Robert Walpole dispensed Church patronage through Edmund Gibson, bishop of London (1723–48), whose settled policy was to see that all major posts went to clerics who were both firm ministerial Whigs in their politics and unquestionably orthodox in their theology.[21] He used his authority as 'ecclesiastical minister' to exclude from bishoprics theoretical Latitudinarians like Samuel Clarke, a notorious assailant of the doctrine of the Trinity, and Thomas Rundle, a critic of the received interpretation of the Old Testament text. So ardent a defender was he also of the independent spiritual authority of the Church that he threatened to refuse consecration to Rundle should his objections to the appointment be overborne.[22] William Wake, archbishop of Canterbury (1715–37), was a churchman of the same school, though less

[19] *Diary of the First Viscount Perceval, afterwards First Earl of Egmont* (Historical Manuscripts Commission, 1920), i. 191–2.

[20] *Four Sermons* by Gloster Ridley, LL B, Minister of Poplar and Lecturer of St Ann's, Middlesex (1736).

[21] T. F. J. Kendrick, 'Sir Robert Walpole, the Old Whigs and the Bishops, 1733–1736: A Study in Eighteenth Century Parliamentary Politics', *Historical Journal*, 11 (1968), 421–45.

[22] Norman Sykes, *Edmund Gibson, Bishop of London, 1669–1748* (Oxford, 1926), 134–6, 155–9, 265–72.

effective in exercising influence. He is chiefly remembered for his negotiations with doctors of the Sorbonne for reunion of the Anglican and Gallican Churches, and he firmly proclaimed his belief in the Catholicity of the Church of England.[23] His successor in the primacy, John Potter (1737–47), was a strict upholder of the authority of the Fathers of the first three Christian centuries, and claimed a divine origin for the distinction between bishops and lesser clergy.[24]

Linda Colley rejects the view that Tory High Church influences significantly affected church appointments after 1727 through the favour of Queen Caroline.[25] But there is some truth in it. The nomination of Thomas Sherlock to the see of Bangor in 1728 was important because it was the first step towards his becoming bishop of London twenty years later. His longevity and his exertions on behalf of the careers of other Tory churchmen like his brother-in-law Thomas Gooch, who entered on a succession of bishoprics in 1737, and Henry Stebbing, as well as of other staunch divines such as Charles Moss, bishop of Bath and Wells until 1802,[26] were among the strongest factors that ensured the projection of a patently strong and loyal Anglicanism into the second half of the eighteenth century. The type, however, was beginning to soften. Gooch, described by William Cole the antiquary as one who was 'bred up in the last century, under Bp. Compton, a single man of great decency & in the highest notions of Church discipline', disappointed his biographer by marrying for the third time at the age of 74,[27] thus breaking through what he deemed to be 'all the constant Practice of the Church in this matter'. Dr Colley's definitive survey reveals, however, much evidence of a persistent Tory-Anglicanisn at the parish level, which supplied such leaders as Sherlock with a following. In the House of Lords the terms 'Tory' and 'High Church' were used interchangeably to describe the opposition to Government as late as 1736.[28]

The several anti-clerical initiatives which came before Parliament in the 1730s, notably the Quaker Tithe Bill, which took the recovery of tithes out of the hands of the ecclesiastical courts and placed it under the JPs, revived in men of all schools of churchmanship the dying conviction that the Church of England was in danger under a Whig Government, but, as Stephen Taylor has pointed out, it was the Mortmain Bill of 1736 that did most to arouse the susceptibilities of old-fashioned Tory High Churchmen. Designed to 'prevent

---

[23] Norman Sykes, *William Wake, Archbishop of Canterbury* (Cambridge, 1957), i, chap. iv; cf. Lowther Clarke, *Eighteenth Century Piety* (1944), 3–4 for Wake's view of Anglican Catholicism, written in 1710.

[24] A. W. Rowden, *The Primates of the Four Georges* (1916), 119–20.

[25] Linda Colley, *In Defiance of Oligarchy: The Tory Party 1714–60* (Cambridge, 1982), 105.

[26] Edward Carpenter, *Thomas Sherlock* (1936), 312–17.

[27] BL Add. MSS 5828, Cole Papers, fos. 129–31, 'Some Account of Sir Thomas Gooch, Baronet, Lord Bishop of Ely'.

[28] Colley, *In Defiance of Oligarchy*, 107–9.

the alienation of land by dying persons to charitable uses . . . to the disherison
of their lawful heirs', it constituted 'a powerful attack on the whole concept
of corporate philanthropy, which was central to much anglican, especially
high church, piety'. Its attack on such charity as was channelled through
distinctively 'Church' corporations as Queen Anne's Bounty, the SPG, the
SPCK, and the Corporation of the Sons of the Clergy 'came close to a
personal attack on their faith'.[29]

Probably Walpole did not intend the breach with the Church of England,
which his tactical support of the attack on 'Church power' occasioned. He
had hoped to strengthen his position in the House of Commons by bidding
for the support of the Old Whigs, but instead he united Gibson and Sherlock
with the Tory lower clergy against the Tithe Bill. His tactlessness in not
consulting the bishops in advance drove them to an unusual act of defiance of
the State. They met and reached a unanimous decision to write circular
letters to their clergy, advising them to petition Parliament against the bill.
The measure was defeated in the Lords, and abandoned by the Government,
but Gibson was denounced as ringleader in the sedition, and forced out of his
position as 'ecclesiastical minister' in 1736. Historians have differed about the
significance of his departure. Kendrick thought that it marked the end of
ecclesiastical independence within the Whig system, claiming that the way was
clear 'for the Duke of Newcastle to manage the Church solely in the interest
of the government'.[30] Taylor has challenged this judgement, instancing
Newcastle's devout Anglicanism and anxiety to advance only clergy who
were orthodox in both theology and ecclesiology.[31] However, as Sykes
demonstrated many years ago, the duke had to share his church patronage
with powerful figures of a different persuasion, notably the king and the
archbishop.[32] At the highest levels in the Church it is difficult not to detect a
loss of strong leadership and a dilution of churchmanship after Gibson's fall.
The best that could be said of Herring, archbishop of York 1743–7 and
Canterbury 1747–57, was that he 'was by no means as colourless a person
as he was made out to be, but he was conservative and suspicious of
any proposals that might endanger existing arrangements, and excite
either clergy or laity'.[33] In revived comprehension schemes, conciliation of
Dissenters took precedence of defence of church principles. In 1748 the
liberal Presbyterian Samuel Chandler opened conversations for reunion on
terms which embraced abandonment of the Athanasian Creed and changing

[29] S. Taylor, 'Sir Robert Walpole, the Church of England and the Quakers' Tithe Bill of
1736', *Historical Journal*, 28 (1985), 51–77.
[30] 'Sir Robert Walpole, the Old Whigs and the Bishops'.
[31] 'Sir Robert Walpole, the Church of England and the Quakers' Tithe Bill of 1736'.
[32] Norman Sykes, 'The Duke of Newcastle as Ecclesiastical Minister', in R. Mitchison (ed.),
Essays in Eighteenth Century History (1962), chap. vii.
[33] J. S. Macauley and R. W. Greaves (eds.), *The Autobiography of Thomas Secker, Archbishop of
Canterbury* (Lawrence, Kan., 1988), 126.

the Thirty-Nine Articles 'into Scripture words'; in one account, discarding the Nicene Creed, kneeling at Communion, and the sign of the cross in baptism were also projected. The bishops who were first approached, Sherlock and Gooch, both High Churchmen, responded cautiously, but Archbishop Herring showed enthusiasm for the proposal, claiming that it was 'the impertinence of men thrusting their words into articles instead of the words of God, that have occasioned most of the divisions in the Christian Church from the beginning of it to this day'.[34]

With Herring at Canterbury, Hutton at York, the octogenarian Hoadly at Winchester, and Edward Chandler, an apologist for Quaker doctrines, at Durham, Latitudinarians of an advanced type reached the acme of their importance in the Church in the late 1740s and the 1750s, their influence being enlarged in Cambridge by the appointment of Edmund Law to be master of Peterhouse in 1756. It was claimed that when Hoadly died in 1761 he had 'lived to see the Nation become his converts and sons have blushed, to think their Fathers were his foes'.[35] It would be nearer the truth to say that he had outlived his strongest critics and to recognize that, even at its height, his influence among his fellow bishops and the mass of the clergy was by no means pervasive. A rough count based on the *DNB*, sermons, and other published sources indicates that not more than nine[36] of the twenty-seven English, Welsh, and Manx bishops at mid-century can be identified as liberal in politics or religion, while among the remainder were men conspicuously zealous for the doctrine and discipline of the Church of England. Lord James Beauclerk, a grandson of Charles II by Nell Gwyn, created bishop of Hereford as late as 1746, represented the most conservative strain. His sermon on the anniversary of the martyrdom of Charles I entirely repudiated the Great Rebellion as an act of 'apostasy', and dwelt emotionally on the attendant loss of the 'beauty of holiness'. He was not alone in applying the tenet of non-resistance to the existing Government.[37]

About that time, moreover, a turning point in English churchmanship occurred. Joseph Priestley, the Unitarian minister, took note of it in 1790: 'The body of the clergy seem to be more orthodox than they were in the last reign, and more bigotted. We see what a court and an establishment can do.'[38] The change in direction was already perceptible at the leadership level

---

[34] G. F. Nuttall (ed.), *Calendar of the Correspondence of Philip Doddridge, D. D., 1702–51* (HMC Joint Publication No. 26, with Northamptonshire Record Society; 1979), 266–7.

[35] Gascoigne, 'Anglican Latitudinarianism'.

[36] Herring (Canterbury), Hutton (York), Hoadly (Winchester), Chandler (Durham), Osbaldeston (Carlisle), Peploe (Chester), Mawson (Chichester), Lavington (Exeter), and Thomas (Peterborough).

[37] *Sermon Preached before . . . the Lords Spiritual and Temporal . . . in the Abbey Church Westminster . . . January 30th 1752* (1752).

[38] J. T. Rutt (ed.), *The Theological and Miscellaneous Works of Joseph Priestley* (1832), 50–1, Priestley to Lindsey, 22 Jan. 1790.

during the primacy of Thomas Secker (1758–68), the true significance of which has been disclosed by the sadly arrested work of the late Robert Greaves on the archbishop's manuscript autobiography. Previously viewed as firmly Protestant, mild and 'moderate towards' Dissenters but down on Roman Catholics, Secker has been presented by Greaves as a principal enemy of 'Low Church controversialists keeping the Hoadleian flag flying'. Emanating from a Nonconformist background, he shifted his views progressively in a traditional Anglican direction, and though pushed into the archbishopric of Canterbury by Newcastle and Hardwicke on Herring's advice, he ended his career in sharp riposte against Blackburne's *Confessional*, a Latitudinarian tract which anticipated Priestley by twenty-four years when it accused the bishops as a whole of conniving at the spread of popery and of getting every year themselves more like popish bishops.[39] Though his own convictions were moderate, Secker was respected by High Churchmen like Prebendary Berkeley, who intensely disliked his successor, Cornwallis.[40]

The revival of High Churchmanship itself began a few years before Secker went to Canterbury, and was influenced by Nonjuring writings. It was a projection from the activities of a cabal called Hutchinsonians, because they were followers of the minor philosopher John Hutchinson (1674–1737), who combined a mysterious veneration of the Hebrew language with a fundamentalist opposition to Newtonian science. After his death his disciples ranged themselves against the materialism of the philosophers of their time and the humanism of the Latitudinarian divines, but were not at first conspicuously Anglican in their loyalties. Hutchinson's original admirers included many Dissenters hostile to the constitution of the Church of England, and it was only later that two Anglican recruits, George Horne and William Jones (of Nayland), who had been drawn to the cause while students at University College, Oxford, imparted to the movement a strongly High Church and anti-Dissenting tone. Jones's biography of Horne ascribes the change in direction to the publication in 1751 of Bishop Robert Clayton's *Essay on Spirit*, an Arian treatise intended to promote alterations in the liturgy and very partial to Dissent.[41] This work, in fact, merely strengthened an existing estrangement between the Church of England and other Protestant communions evident in the previous year in the refusal of the bishops to support a collection in aid of the Protestants of Breslau.[42] Anglican coldness was mainly the product of resentment of the persecution of Episcopalians in Presbyterian Scotland and of quarrels over plans for comprehending the Dissenters in the Established

---

[39] Macauley and Greaves (eds.), *Thomas Secker*.
[40] BL Add. MSS 39, 311, fos. 244–5, G. Berkeley to 'my dearest friend', 13 Sept. 1769.
[41] William Jones, *The Works of George Horne, with Memoirs of his Life, Studies and Writings* (1809), i. 9–60.
[42] Nuttall, *Philip Doddridge* 336–8.

Church.[43] In preparing a reply to Clayton, Horne and Jones spent a month in the library of the latter's patron Sir John Dolben at Finedon, Northamptonshire, steeping themselves in its resources of divinity and ecclesiastical history. They made a particular study of the writings of the Nonjurors Charles Leslie and George Hickes, which imbued them with an enduring sense of the independent spiritual authority of the Church. Horne wrote of Hickes:

He shows the greatest knowledge of primitive antiquity, of fathers, councils, and the constitution and discipline of the church in the first and purest ages of it. This kind of learning is of much greater value and consequence than many now apprehend. What next after the Bible, can demand a Christian's attention before the history of the church, purchased by the blood of Christ, founded by inspired apostles, etc. etc .... Much I am sure is done by that cementing bond of the spirit, which unites Christians to their head and to one another and makes them consider themselves as members of the same body, that is as a church, as a fold of sheep, not as struggling individuals.[44]

Such opinions point forward to a kind of High Churchmanship more suitable to combating the ideals of a secularizing society than the old demand for privileges upheld by monarchical or parliamentary power. The Hutchinsonians, however, found no difficulty in reconciling their primitive view of church order with an extravagant loyalty to the Crown and constitution. Both Horne and Nathaniel Wetherell, master of University College, Oxford were renowned for sermons expounding the traditional doctrines of non-resistance, the latter in such terms as 'to have out-Filmered Filmer'.[45]

Hutchinsonianism never completely lost the obscurantist cosmogony imprinted upon it by its founder. As late as 1788 Horne, then dean of Canterbury, explained to a friend how essential it was for him to possess a copy of Catcott on the Deluge and that there was no difficulty in accounting for the quantity of water needed to produce a universal flood, as the earth was a hollow shell filled with water, and the fossils proved that the shell was at that time dissolved.[46] Increasingly, however, the apostles of the movement found a more credible function in defending traditional church order against continuing erosion. Two of their number, Dr Samuel Glasse, rector of Wanstead, and the Revd Charles Poyntz, incumbent of North Creake in Norfolk, turned their attention to reviving weekday festivals. Glasse wrote in 1788:

that yesterday being *Ascension Day* was observed in my parish at Wanstead, with due solemnity. We had full morning and evening service, a sermon and a Communion at

---

[43] Ibid. 281–2. By 1751 the treatment of Presbyterians in Anglican Virginia had become a bone of contention between Doddridge and Bp. Sherlock. Ibid. 353–4.

[44] Jones, *Horne*, i. 60–3.

[45] W. R. Ward, *Georgian Oxford* (Oxford, 1958), 205, 214–15.

[46] Poyntz Letters, Horne to Poyntz, 26 Apr. 1788.

which between 40 and 50 people attended. My congregation was above 200. The parish is not a large one. The workmen at the New Church adjoining, one and all laid down their tools and came to church.[47]

Thirteen years later at North Creake the curate was able to report that on the feast of the Ascension 'most of the farmers (I believe I may say all except old Mr. Blyth) attended me in the morning'. On All Saints Day double duty was done in the parish.[48]

The Hutchinsonians breathed the genuine spirit of religious revival. Their goal was Christian godliness combined with Christian order. In the early stages of the movement, at Oxford in the 1750s, Evangelicals like Haweis, Romaine, and James Stillingfleet were drawn to it as a compound of the most devout men in the University, only to be repelled, in Haweis's case by the discovery that the devotees anathematized Nonconformists and held what seemed to him an automatic view of the communication of grace through the sacraments.[49] The blend is illustrated by Horne's sermons and those of his friend George Berkeley, the son of the eminent philosopher of that name. Preaching at St Mary Magdalene's, Oxford on 12 December 1756, Berkeley delivered a forthright proclamation of the doctrine of justification by faith and a call to repentance and amendment of life. Among the dispositions which stood between men and Christ's intercession for them he listed the sin of schism and a refusal of 'His affectionate invitations to celebrate the Christian sacrifice'. Churchmen were reminded that their claims to advantage over Dissenters 'are conveyed unto us in a regular dispensation by the hand of bishops, priests and deacons: a sacred hierarchy constituted by the great Bishop of souls; and of whose uninterrupted regular succession (from the apostolic age to the present) we have as full evidence as that on which the canon of holy scripture is received'.[50] The evangelical tone in which these exhortations were delivered is shown by the climax of a sermon preached by Horne before the University on 1 March 1761, which made an eloquent appeal for immediate decision:

awake, thou Christian soul, and utter a song in praise of him who hath redeemed thee: awake, awake, put on the Lord Jesus thy strength, put on righteousness and holiness thy beautiful garments; shake thyself from the dust, and set thy affection on things above: the night is far spent, the day is at hand: cast off therefore the works of darkness, and put on the whole armour of light: arise, shine, for thy light is come, and the glory of the Lord is risen upon thee; arise, and stand up from the dead, and Christ shall give thee the light of life.[51]

[47] Ibid., Glasse to Poyntz, [n.d.] 1788.
[48] Ibid., W. Erratt to Poyntz, 16 June 1801; W. Wisey to Poyntz, 3 Dec. 1798.
[49] A. S. Wood, *Thomas Haweis 1734–1820* (1957), 46–7.
[50] Eliza Berkeley (ed.), *Sermons by the Late Rev. George Berkeley* (1799), no. 1.
[51] Jones, *Horne*, iv. 277.

It is not surprising that both Horne and Berkeley were accused of being Methodists, though they were both Catholic and sacramental High Churchmen.

The emergence of a distinctively Anglican Hutchinsonianism in the 1750s may be allowed to modify George Every's emphasis on the role of events occurring about mid-century in changing the character of English High Churchmanship. In his view it was the desertion of High Church piety by the Methodists and the few remaining Calvinists in the Church of England about that time that caused the High Church party to move away from defending heat and fervour in prayer, which they did at the time of the Bangorian controversy, towards the 'High and Dry' divinity which it reached at the close of the century.[52] It is suggested here that the transformation took place gradually over an extended time-scale. Not all Hutchinsonians shared the love of emotional Christianity displayed by some of their number, and the broad evolution was away from it. Berkeley's evangelical pulpit oratory packed his church at Acton with crowds from London, but he was criticized by Glasse in 1767 for a sermon which tended 'to coincide too nearly with the opinions of the Methodists, who seem to lay too little stress on the fruits of faith'.[53] Glasse himself trod the familiar paths of eighteenth-century benevolence, steeping himself in Sunday School work, the poor law, and prison administration.[54] George Horne's sermons in the early 1770s were quieter in tone than in a former period, while according to Nancy Murray, whose study covers the 1790s, those of the group as a whole were by then as effective when read as when heard. They were nevertheless well above the eighteenth-century norm for intensity and imagery.[55] The entente between High Churchmanship and Calvinism, exemplified by Horne's defence of the six Calvinistic Methodists expelled from St Edmund Hall in 1768 for praying and preaching in private houses and his collaboration with Evangelicals like Toplady to resist alterations in the liturgy and articles in 1772–3[56] lasted until the late 1790s, when Daubeny's attack on Wilberforce's *Practical View* sparked off two decades of controversy.

Hutchinsonians were the nearest thing to a coherent body on the High Church side of the eighteenth-century Church of England. Linked by ties of friendship and blood they formed a compact coterie, whose members corresponded and helped one another whenever possible. Though their numbers were few they exerted a large and growing influence in the Church during the first half of George III's reign. This was not merely due to the favour of a new court, appreciative of their Toryism. Crown preferments were slow to

---

[52] Every, *High Church Party*, 176–7.
[53] BL Add. MSS 39, 311, fos. 219–22, S. G. to Berkeley, 22 Oct. 1767.
[54] DNB xxi 421; also various letters in the Poyntz papers.
[55] Nancy U Murray, 'The Influence of the French Revolution on the Church of England and its Rivals, 1789–1802', D.Phil. thesis (Oxford, 1975), 45.
[56] C. J. Abbey, *The English Church and its Bishops, 1700–1800* (1887), ii. 125–7.

descend. Glasse became Chaplain in Ordinary to the king in 1772, Horne and Wetherell[57] obtained deaneries, but Horne alone became a bishop, and he was not raised to the bench until nearly the end of his long career. An occurrence preceding his earlier appointment to the deanery of Canterbury in 1781 shows how casual was the process of rewarding ecclesiastical friends of the Government. Lord North informed him through John Robinson, the patronage secretary of the Treasury, that he was to be made dean of Bristol. What followed is described by Jonathan Boucher, an intimate of the Hutchinsonians. North, he explained,

actually went to the King on purpose to ask for the Deanery of Bristol for Dr. Horne; but came away and forgot his errand: as he had done before when he went to ask for Mr. Jenkinson to be Secretary of War. In the meantime Mr. Hallam, a canon of Windsor got the Duke of Montagu to apply for him, and the King, thinking himself at full liberty instantly promised it. He has however since been informed of the accident and says that Dr. Horne shall soon have something as good if not a little better.[58]

The advance of the brotherhood was due more to its members' capacity to tread the lesser corridors of power for their own and their friends' advantage. In 1763 Glasse was intriguing with Berkeley to ensure a Hutchinsonian succession in the office of Steward of the Sons of the Clergy.[59] A decade later, Horne's first cousin William Stevens, a remarkable layman who combined a competence in theology with business interests in London hosiery-selling and the Cyfarthfa ironworks in Glamorgan,[60] began to carve out a position for himself and his circle in the Society for the Propagation of the Gospel. Joining the Barbados Committee in 1774, he became an auditor of the Society in the following year, and was soon active in proposing his friends—George Horne, John Frere, a Norfolk squire, and William Fowle— for membership. From 1778 to 1786 he and his associate Jonathan Boucher, an American loyalist refugee priest, were the most assiduous attenders at the small inner committee of the Society, which Stevens occasionally chaired.[61] The work of the SPG gave him intercourse with the most active of the bishops, especially with the archbishop of Canterbury, and led to his appointment in 1782, by Archbishop Cornwallis's influence, to the office of Treasurer of Queen Anne's Bounty, a post which brought him closer to the bishops who met at the Bounty offices in Dean's Yard during the abeyance of Convocation.[62] By his liberality with money and advice, Stevens attracted a widening

---

[57] Evidence that Nathan Wetherell became dean of Hereford in 1771–2 comes from the *Royal Calendar* for those two years.
[58] Locker Lampson MSS A.1/53, Boucher to John James, 18 Jan. 1781.
[59] BL Add. MSS 39, 311, fos. 133–4, Glasse to Berkeley, 9 May 1763.
[60] See Locker Lampson MSS B.3/25, 26, 56.
[61] Society for the Propagation of the Gospel, Journals, xx (1773–6), 72, 317, 410, 473–4; Committee Books, xlvii–l. Boucher, who was another ardent High Churchman, was under-secretary to the Society 1778–86. Journals, xxi 369; xxiv. 293.
[62] G. F. A. Best, *Temporal Pillars* (Cambridge, 1964), 123, 125–6.

entourage of influential friends who in 1800 founded a select dining club in his honour. By the end of the year it had twenty-four members, principally lawyers, clergy, country gentlemen, and merchants.[63]

The Hutchinsonians never lacked powerful connections. Berkeley was a protégé of Archbishop Secker,[64] Horne was a friend of Archbishop Moore,[65] but what was more remarkable was their willingness to pool their resources for the common good. John Parkhurst, a Hebrew lexicographer and also a clerical landowner with considerable estates at Epsom, exercised his patronage of the living of that place in favour of Samuel Glasse in 1782 and of Jonathan Boucher in 1785.[66] Charles Poyntz, whose sister Georgiana married the first Earl Spencer, was used by Berkeley and Jones of Nayland to enlist her support in favour of their schemes, while Glasse saw in him the means of harnessing even Whig political power to the welfare of the Church of England. When the Fox–North coalition took office, he wrote to Poyntz:

At length my worthy friend *Cincinnatus* is likely to be called from his *rustic* employment to be a burning and a shining light in the world: God grant you may become thereby a more able instrument of advancing His Glory, and the good of His Church. But hush! Not a word of that good Old Lady if you wish to be promoted. For these I apprehend are not the sort of folks that look upon her with a favourable eye.[67]

The only preferment Poyntz received was a place in the chapter of Durham cathedral, but even this enhanced his power to assist the aspirations of his friends to office.[68]

Historians have sometimes conveyed the impression that the Hutchinsonians were the only genuine High Churchmen left in the Church of England in the second half of the eighteenth century. This is mistaken. The country at large exhibited many different manifestations of a Church-conscious and Sacrament-conscious divinity which still needed to be brought together. Some were inheritances from the past, mature and declining. Others, like Hutchinsonianism, bore the stamp of revival. Provincial centres had their distinctive traditions. In Manchester the ritualistic churchmanship of the collegiate church, still conspicuous enough in 1748 to arouse criticism,[69] went into disintegration after the death in 1752 of the local Nonjuring bishop, who had been treated by the clergy with a respect denied to their distant Whig

[63] *Biographical List of the Members of the Club of Nobody's Friends* (1885).
[64] Jones, *Horne*, i. 40.
[65] Stevens wrote of the archbishop: 'His Grace goes to Bath next Wednesday for a fortnight and has a house in the square, where his friend the Bishop of Norwich has one likewise.' Locker Lampson MSS B.3/64, Stevens to Boucher, 9 Dec. 1791. It seems clear that Moore, if not actually a High Churchman, was surrounded by High Church influences.
[66] *DNB* xxi 421; xlii 310; Locker Lampson MSS B.3/20, Stevens to Boucher, 6 Sept. 1785.
[67] Poyntz Letters, S.G. to Poyntz, 'Easter Eve' [1783].
[68] Ibid., S.G. to Poyntz, 31 Oct. 1783; Berkeley to Poyntz, 2 Aug. 1789.
[69] J. Wickham Legg, *English Church Life from the Restoration to the Tractarian Movement* (1914), 19, 179–80.

Ordinary in Chester.[70] Some of its emotion was siphoned off into mysticism as with John Clowes, a pupil of the collegiate chaplain, John Clayton, who became a Swedenborgian in the 1770s.[71] Nevertheless an underground leaning to Nonjuring divinity remained with the Manchester clergy in 1797, when Thomas Garnett, next to the last of the bishops of the 'Orthodox British Church', circulated to seven of them a copy of the 'Litany and Prayers' of his own communion, and received the reply that the clergy 'all approve of the forms', but cannot introduce them into their respective churches without the consent of all the bishops.[72]

Collegiality was no doubt a factor in promoting a sense of clerical identity favourable to high views of the priesthood. As in Manchester, so also its influence was seen in Bath, where the Abbey Church and St John's Hospital maintained daily services late in the eighteenth century.[73] London clergy had a college of a different kind, a guild of parish priests founded in the seventeenth century to be an instrument for focusing clerical opinion. A meeting point for men of varying opinions, Sion College avoided committing itself to extreme positions of any kind, but the constant vigilance of its court over threats to the interests of its members and the security of the Established Church made it an arena into which the many High Churchmen of the metropolis were readily drawn.

Outside London and Westminster, where eighteen churches had either weekly communion or daily service, in some cases both, in the last thirty years of the eighteenth century,[74] the best performance was to be found in parts of the North and West, which had adhered to the king during the Civil War. These sustained in religion, as in other points of culture, a conservative practice, which was slowly giving way before the advance of industrialism. Out of sixty-six benefices in the rural archdeaconry of Salop making returns at Bishop North's primary visitation of 1772, thirty-eight mentioned celebrations of the Holy Communion more frequent than the Hanoverian standard of four per year, while forty-three recorded weekday services of some kind, often on saints' days or on Wednesdays and Fridays in Lent.[75] In towns some churches continued to hold services twice a day on weekdays throughout the year. Wigan still did so in 1778, as did St Nicholas, a chapel connected with the

[70] H. Broxap, *A Biography of Thomas Deacon, the Manchester Non Juror* (Manchester, 1911), 75–6.
[71] Chetham's Library MSS A.3/51–2, J. Clowes, 'Memoirs of the Author', intended for 'A History of the Commencement and Progress in Great Britain of the Lord's New Church'. See also cuttings from *Manchester City News* regarding St John's, Deansgate at Chetham's Library, Manchester.
[72] Bodl. Add. MSS D.30, Nonjuror Papers, fos. 26–7, F. Holmes to H. H. Norris, 11 Jan. 1837.
[73] Wickham Legg, *English Church Life*, 92–3.
[74] LPL Fulham Papers 82–4, dio. London Visitation Articles 1778; Guildhall Library, Diocese Book 1770–*c*.1812.
[75] Lichfield Joint RO B/V/5, dio. Coventry and Lichfield, pa. returns, 1772.

parish church in Liverpool. Newcastle upon Tyne All Saints and Newcastle St Nicholas followed the same practice in 1769. It may be significant that these churches were all situated in old corporate towns, traditionalism in religion in some way following a well-established communal life.[76]

Cornwall is a county in which the historian has found evidence of a 'notable strengthening' of the High Church outlook in the latter part of the eighteenth century and the opening years of the nineteenth. This has been shown to have been connected with a revival of interest in Cornish antiquities, and especially in the Celtic Christianity of the region. Pioneered by William Borlase about the middle of the century and stimulated by the discovery of the oratory of St Piran towards its close, the study led forward in John Whitaker's *Ancient Cathedral of Cornwall* (1804) to a nostalgic regret at the passing of medieval externals, such as vestments and incense.[77]

Despite a growing interest in antiquities among eighteenth-century clerics—for example Philip Bearcroft, Cole of Bletchley, and Bishop Douglas, all of them High Churchmen—history was important mainly as a court of appeal in current dialogue. During the second half of the eighteenth century the High Church tradition was involved in five main disputes, which helped to develop its strength and to shape its many-sided character.

First the quarrel with the Methodists over breaches of parish order and the holding of irregular services, with which was connected an attack on the 'enthusiasm' and moderate Calvinism of the Anglican Evangelicals. The two were joined in the crisis in the University of Oxford in 1768, when the expulsion of six students from St Edmund Hall for holding private devotional 'conventicles' was followed by a burst of controversy over pre-destination, assurance of salvation, and the value of good works done before justification. The Oxford Arminians, who led the assault on the Calvinists—notably Thomas Randolph, the Margaret Professor of Divinity, and Thomas Nowell, principal of St Mary's Hall—have been described as High Church-men.[78] They belonged to a species, not uncommon in the late eighteenth-century Church, which was donnish in manner, ostentatiously loyal to the Crown, zealous for the rights of bishops and clergy, and punctilious about conformity to statutes and articles of belief—'high', in fine, in the political sense—but hostile alike to emotionalism in religion and to the sacerdotalism of the Hutchinsonians and Nonjurors. The label 'High and Dry' does not misrepresent this type.

For many eighteenth-century churchmen, however, the reaffirmation of Catholic teaching concerning the Sacrament of the Lord's Supper against the

---

[76] Chester RO EDV/7/1/1–353, Visitation Articles 1778; F. C. Mather, 'Georgian Churchmanship Reconsidered', *Journal of Ecclesiastical History*, 36 (1985), 255–83.

[77] H. Miles Brown, 'The High Church Tradition in Cornwall, 1662–1831', *Church Quarterly Review*, 150 (1950), 69–80.

[78] Ward, *Georgian Oxford*, 241–3.

reductionism of the advanced Latitudinarians was a central task. This fact has been obscured by applying to the Eucharistic doctrine of the period criteria of Catholicity derived from the sensitive insights of the Oxford Movement. If, however, by the touchstone of objective presence, High Church sacramental theology of the Georgian epoch seems immature, the criterion of belief in a form of Eucharistic sacrifice yields a different conclusion. Three separate theories may be discerned, and the views of High Churchmen often combined more than one. The most extreme conceived of the Eucharist as a proper and propitiatory sacrifice, in which the bread and wine were themselves offered to God as symbols of Christ's oblation, begun not on the cross but when the rite was instituted at the Last Supper. Principally a Nonjuror tenet, this doctrine was nevertheless sustained in the Church of England through the mid eighteenth century by a small minority of obscure divines, notably Samuel Hardy, an elderly Suffolk rector, who pleaded for it in a work published as late as 1784.[79] After that time it underwent renewal, being disseminated in the new American republic by Samuel Seabury, who was consecrated bishop of Connecticut by the Scottish Nonjuring bishops,[80] and in England by Archdeacon Charles Daubeny, a Bath clergyman, who emerged as a leading High Church controversialist at the end of the century. In a volume of sermons mostly addressed to the congregation of the Free Church in Bath, opened in 1798, Daubeny maintained 'that the holy eucharist is not only a memorial of the passion and death of Christ for the sins of the world, but also of that offering of himself, his natural body and blood, which under the representation of bread and wine, he made to God at the institution of this holy ordinance'.[81]

A broader band of High Church opinion was by contrast content to affirm that the Eucharist was a commemorative or memorial sacrifice: one by which, in the words of Prebendary George Berkeley, Christians do not 'barely commemorate their Saviour's death', but also 'powerfully plead in the court of heaven the merits of his vicarious sufferings'.[82] This teaching, which was in line with the theology of the moderate Caroline divines of the seventeenth century such as Jeremy Taylor,[83] was expounded in the mid and later eighteenth century by Gloster Ridley and by the leading Hutchinsonians. As handled by the latter it had sacerdotalist implications hardly less pronounced than Johnson's doctrine of 'proper sacrifice'. In his *Essay on the Church* published in 1787 William Jones of Nayland observed of the Eucharist: 'This

---

[79] Wickham Legg, *English Church Life*, 71–3.

[80] Steiner, *Samuel Seabury*, 341–63.

[81] *Orthodox Churchman's Magazine*, 9 (1805), 59–66, reviewing C. Daubeny, *Discourses on Various Subjects* (quotation from 5th discourse, on Luke 22:19).

[82] Berkeley, *Sermons*, 89–105.

[83] For Taylor's doctrine of the Eucharist as an application and re-presentment of Christ's death see Jardine Grisbrooke, *Anglican Liturgies*, 25–7.

being the commemorative Sacrifice of the New Testament, it can be offered only by a priest; and all the world cannot make a priest.'[84]

There were many more eighteenth-century divines, however, who, while anxious to uphold the sacrificial character of the Sacrament of the Lord's Supper, took especial pains to guard against the suggestion that the Holy Communion service possessed any virtue of its own distinct from the one, sufficient sacrifice once offered on Calvary. This they encompassed by treating the Eucharist as a feast upon that sacrifice: a federal banquet in which the faithful communicant made a covenant with his God by doing symbolically what Jewish and pagan sacrificers had effected literally, namely consuming a portion of the victim slain. Of the three doctrines of Eucharistic sacrifice current in the Georgian Church, this was the most Protestant. Its antecedents lay outside the High Church tradition, being traceable to the seventeenth-century Cambridge Platonist, Ralph Cudworth.[85] Such teaching, however, was conservative when compared with Hoadly's *Plain Account*, which reduced the Sacrament to a plain memorial.

According to Bishop Cleaver preaching in 1787 the notion of a feast on a sacrifice was that which 'obtained the most general suffrage amongst the divines of our Church' before Hoadly propounded the doctrine of bare memorial half a century earlier, but it was the latter that was gaining hold upon the minds of the public in his own day. This, however, was not for want of efforts to set it back. Waterland's early attack on Hoadly's sacramental theology in the *Review* (1737) had been followed by William Warburton, another central churchman, in a published sermon which attracted attention in 1755 and later in a book, *A Rational Account of the Lord's Supper*, issued from the press in 1761. It led him into a sharp exchange over Eucharistic doctrine with John Butler, prebendary of Winchester, who defended the teachings of his patron, Hoadly.[86] Warburton was sufficiently Protestant to distinguish his doctrine of a feast upon a sacrifice from the thesis that the Eucharist was itself a sacrifice commemorative of that made on the cross. The 'thing done' and the 'commemoration of the thing done' could 'never be an action of the same kind'.[87] As the eighteenth century drew nearer its close, strict High Churchmen entered the lists, embellishing the doctrine with features of their own. George Croft, a clerical headmaster who was later to become an active leader of the 'Church and King' party in Birmingham, put it forward in a 5 November sermon in Oxford in 1783, in which he set out to disclose elements of truth in almost every Roman Catholic doctrine and prac-

---

[84] W. Jones, *Essay on the Church* (Gloucester, 1787), 21–2.
[85] Darwell Stone, *A History of the Doctrine of the Holy Eucharist* (1909), ii. 315–6.
[86] John Butler (attrib), *Superficial Observations upon the Bishop of Gloucester's Rational Account of the Sacrament of the Lord's Supper* (1761).
[87] Warburton, *Rational Account*.

tice, including the sacrifice of the Mass and the name of 'altar'.[88] Cleaver's two sermons before the University of Oxford on 25 November 1787 and another on 28 November 1790 took a most exalted view of the Sacrament, annexing to the due use of the latter 'as a Feast on a Sacrifice' the privileges of pardon and sanctification. He maintained that the rite was 'in its most obvious signification sacrificial', meaning that it was a 'representation', in the sense of a making present, the sacrifice of the death of Christ. An ardent advocate of patristic studies, he recalled with relish ancient titles for the Communion—'The Christian *Sacrifice*, the Christian *Passover*, the Christian *Oblation*, the *Eucharist*, etc.'.[89] George Pretyman, bishop of Lincoln, influential as a former secretary and friend of the Younger Pitt, was a High Churchman of a drier kind. In his *Elements of Christian Theology*, first published in 1799 for the use of ordination candidates, he contented himself with reaffirming Waterland. The two sacraments were 'federal acts', not 'barely external rites'.

A prolonged controversy over Prayer Book revision was the third main dispute in which High Churchmanship developed its identity. One of the outstanding tasks of the Church of England after the Glorious Revolution was to amend Cranmer's historic liturgy in such fashion as to bring it into line with current needs. Attempts to achieve this through a Commission of Divines appointed in 1689 and through Convocation achieved little before 1714, but individual churchmen returned to the consideration of the problem at mid-century, when John Jones, vicar of Alconbury, published in 1749 his *Free and Candid Disquisitions relating to the Church of England*, proposing the sort of alterations which had been advanced in 1689 to win back Dissenters.[90] The issue was kept alive in the late 1750s and early 1760s in the annual Hutchins Sermons on the liturgy of the Church of England delivered in Bow Church on St Mark's Day under the will of a London goldsmith. Here the conservative case was put by High Churchmen like Henry Stebbing and Gloster Ridley. Some of the proposals advanced were relatively uncontroversial, such as shortening the morning service and matching collects, epistles, and gospels,[91] but the extreme Latitudinarian tendency of much of the reform movement was displayed by Samuel Clarke's revision which proposed the entire omission of the Athanasian and Nicene Creeds and the rephrasing of all specifically Trinitarian formulas. Hutchins lecturers also had to meet Puritan objections

[88] *Sermons by the Late Rev. George Croft* (Birmingham, 1811), i. 15–30.
[89] W. Cleaver, *A Sermon on the Sacrament of the Lord's Supper...25 November 1787* (Oxford 1790); *A Sermon on a Discourse of Our Lord in the Sixth Chapter of St. John's Gospel...25 November 1787; A Sermon Preached before the University of Oxford...28th of November 1790* (Oxford, 1791).
[90] J. H. Overton and F. Relton, *The English Church from the Accession of George I to the End of the Eighteenth Century, 1714–1800* (1906), 208, 211–12.
[91] *A Sermon Preached in the Parish Church of St. Mary-Le-Bow on Monday, April 26, 1755, in Pursuance of the Last Will of Mr. John Hutchins, Citizen and Goldsmith of London: By Thomas Ashton, A.M., Rector of St. Botolph, Bishopsgate, and Fellow of Eton College* (1756).

to the liturgy in general as 'confessedly taken from the Roman Breviary and Missal' and to the practice of kneeling at Communion.[92] To the first charge Stebbing replied in 1760 that 'when we separated from Rome we preserved what was right even in the popish liturgy itself'.[93]

But the face of the enemy was changing. By the end of the first decade of George III's reign the Latitudinarians had lost their battle for the soul of the Church of England. John Gascoigne has supplied an explanation of this in terms which link theology with politics. In the mid eighteenth century, he maintains, when the main threat to the existing order appeared to come from those who looked back to the almost sacerdotal conception of monarchy associated with the Stuarts, it was natural that the dominant voices in the Established Church should emphasize the rational, unmystical aspects of Christianity. However, by the late eighteenth century, when the main ideological enemies of Church and State were basing their attack not on tradition and sentiment but on an appeal to reason, it was not surprising that the Church's major spokesmen no longer placed such stress on a rationally constructed natural theology but rather turned more and more to those aspects of revealed religion which they regarded as transcending human reason.[94] On this hypothesis it would be reasonable to expect the shift in the balance of opinion to occur, not with the change of monarch in 1760, but with the formation of the Society of the Supporters of the Bill of Rights in 1769.

Those who would claim for theology a momentum of its own might take refuge, however, in an older and simpler explanation, namely that Latitudinarianism overreached itself. Two years after 1769, following the lead of Francis Blackburne, a Latitudinarian in the line of Hoadly and Edmund Law, a petition requesting the abolition of compulsory subscription to the Thirty-Nine Articles by clergy and graduates, signed by 250 persons at the Feathers Tavern in London, was sent to the House of Commons. When Parliament, fearful that the disaffection might spread from the Church to the State, rejected the petition, a small but intellectually distinguished band of signatories, strongly connected with the Cambridge colleges, departed from the Church of England, leaving the Latitudinarian movement to a new generation of Cambridge divines—Paley, Hey, and Richard Watson, who sustained an Indian summer of Christian rationalism within the Established Church in the last two decades of the eighteenth century. Of these only one became a bishop, held for the rest of his career to a poor Welsh see, and, as Gascoigne has pointed out, frustration of worldly ambition may have played a

---

[92] In a Hutchins sermon of 1763, advising delay in reforming the liturgy, the future bishop, John Butler, referred to the 'objections which have been made to the posture of kneeling at the Sacrament'. *Sermon on the Liturgy of the Church of England* (1763).

[93] *On the Liturgy of the Church of England: A Sermon . . . by Henry Stebbing Junr. D. D. Chaplain in Ordinary to His Majesty; and Preacher to the Honourable Society of Gray's Inn* (1760).

[94] Gascoigne, *Cambridge*, 238.

part in causing Latitudinarian clerics of the later generation to turn, as
Richard Watson did, first to ecclesiastical and then to political reform.[95]

In their fall from power the Latitudinarians helped to forward the ambitions
of another dissident group, led from outside the Church of England while still
commanding fringe support within it. Though only about ten Anglican clergy
left the Church after the Feathers Tavern petition foundered, they were men
of sufficient calibre to transmit to the Unitarian Rational Dissenters the
powerful critique of the established order in Church and State which they
derived from Anglican Latitudinarianism.[96] Moreover the petition itself
touched off by example a campaign by these Dissenters to remove the obligation imposed on Nonconformist ministers to subscribe the doctrinal articles of
the Church of England in 1772–3. The demand was conceded in 1779,[97] and
the Dissenters braced themselves for two further attacks on the Established
Church in the following decade. One was upon its fundamental doctrines; the
other, upon its privileged position as an establishment, merged with the
secular struggle for political liberties and civil rights which radicals conducted
in England before and during the French Revolution. High Churchmen led
the Anglican counter-offensive in both disputes, which made up the number
of the five in which they were prominently involved during the second half of
the century. Their incidence, coming on top of those which had gone before,
produced a crisis of identity for English High Churchmanship dating from the
later 1780s. The best of the High Churchmen had never approved of the
label. George Horne saw 'High Church' as 'a name invented, according to Mr
Leslie, under which the Church of England might be abused with greater
security'.[98] Moreover, as a synonym for intolerant Toryism battling against
Whig oligarchy, it had lost most of its meaning with the breakdown of the old
two-party system early in the reign of George III. Dissent, however, and its
Liberal allies in Parliament used it with little discrimination, passing their
confusions to the historian. Priestley applied it in 1787 to a group of Anglican
activists in Birmingham, who wanted to exclude books of suspect divinity
from the subscribers' library.[99] During the parliamentary debate on the royal
Proclamation against Seditious Meetings, Charles James Fox identified it with
the political reaction against the French Revolution: 'It was the High Church
spirit, and an indisposition to all Reform, which marked more than anything
the temper of the times.'[100] In a polemic styled *High Church Politics* published
in 1792 the Dissenter Samuel Heywood ascribed to it the counter-agitation
against repeal of the Test and Corporation Acts and the subsequent attack

[95] Gascoigne, 'Anglican Latitudinarianism'.
[96] Ibid.
[97] Peter D. G. Thomas, *Lord North* (1976), 148.
[98] Jones, *Horne*, i. 335.
[99] Rutt (ed.), *Priestley*, i. 2. 5–6.
[100] Quoted from the *Manchester Herald*, 26 May 1792.

on Priestley's house. There was need of a new role-definition of High
Churchmanship just as there was need of a new Tory party. Samuel Horsley,
bishop of St Davids, did much to provide it. We must retrace our steps to
explain how he came to undertake the task and how he tackled it.

2

The Child of his Time

GREATER London in the 1730s was an almost continuous built-up sprawl from Limehouse in the east to Mayfair in the west, in places three miles broad from north to south, and still growing. Despite its immensity, and a population of some 600,000 inhabitants, quite unparalleled anywhere else in Britain, the capital was made up of a number of self-contained communities, each with its own peculiarities, which did not appreciably lessen until the closing decades of the century.[1] 'Charing Cross', wrote Defoe, 'is a mixture of Court and city; Man's Coffee-house is the Exchange Alley of this part of the town, and 'tis perpetually throng'd with men of business, as the others are with men of play and pleasure.'[2] Socially the district had passed its best. The noblemen's palaces which once fringed the Strand as far as Temple Bar had been demolished in the property boom of 1660–*c.*1690, and replaced by streets of smaller houses for City merchants and tradespeople. Four of the London markets, not including Covent Garden, were established in the vicinity during the reign of Charles II, and the frontages along the Strand were occupied by shops and taverns. By early Georgian times gentility had retreated westwards to the fashionable squares of St James, Soho, and Mayfair, but Charing Cross had vestiges of grandeur. Northumberland House, a mansion then belonging to the duke of Somerset, looked down upon it, and the Royal Mews, where the coaches of state were set up, spread expansively to the north, covering part of the site of the present Trafalgar Square. If variety is the key to vitality, Dr Johnson correctly remarked to Boswell that 'the full tide of human existence is at Charing Cross'.[3]

Close to this spot, in St Martin's Place, by the church of St Martin-in-the-Fields, the future bishop Samuel Horsley was born on 15 September 1733. He was baptized in that church on 8 October.[4] Like the place of his birth, Horsley's career presented arresting contrasts. Though he would emerge at the close of the century as the leading High Churchman on the bench, professing a theology which was unfashionable in the England of his age, his background was by no means detached from the central experiences of the national life. He had a foothold in the camp of change as well as in that of

---

[1] M. D. George, *London Life in the Eighteenth Century* (1976), 77–8.
[2] D. Defoe, *A Tour through the Whole Island of Great Britain, 1724–26* (1966), 365.
[3] Quoted from G. E. Mingay, *Georgian London* (1975), 11.
[4] Westminster PL 419/13, p. 41, pa. St Martin, for date of birth and baptism. *DNB* xxvii. 383–6, for place of birth.

conservation, and while his greater proclivity to the latter cast him for his greatest influence during the conservative reaction which occurred in Britain in the age of the French Revolution, his connections with the former supplied him with a breadth of interests in public affairs unparalleled among his episcopal contemporaries and an acute perception of the strength as well as of the weakness in his opponents' position. These qualities were uncommon among advanced High Churchmen, such as the English and Scottish Nonjurors, who were reserved and intensely dogmatic, but they won him respect from men who disagreed with him profoundly. After he had spoken against Lord Stanhope's 1789 bill to annul the statutes imposing religious observance, the radical peer paid him the tribute: 'The right reverend and learned prelate had argued clearly and ably. He could understand his meaning distinctly, he could ascertain in what they agreed, and knew at a glance the exact point on which they separated.'[5]

The ambivalence was present at the outset. The bishop had Dissenting blood in his veins. His father, the Revd John Horsley, who was lecturer in the parish of St Martin, had been educated for the Nonconformist ministry at Edinburgh University, whence he graduated on 14 February 1723[4].[6] At that time familial relationships existed at Edinburgh between students and their professors, who often supplemented their incomes by accepting into their houses as boarders the sons of parents who could afford to pay for the privilege.[7] Among those who did so was William Hamilton, professor of divinity from 1709 and later principal. This practice, useful in supplying scholastic and moral supervision in a non-collegiate university, led to the marriage of John Horsley to William Hamilton's daughter Anne, the mother of Samuel. Anne Horsley died before her son was 3 years of age, and was buried at St Martin's on 25 February 1735[6],[8] but it is unlikely that the intellectual influence of William Hamilton, a mildly liberal Presbyterian who, in the words of the *Caledonian Mercury*, 'taught such principles of benevolence and rational doctrine as made a lasting impression on the young clergy',[9] did not extend to his son-in-law, or pass through him to his daughter's son. Moreover, the Hamilton family sustained an interest in Samuel's development. At the age of 17 he was the favourite grandson of Mrs Hamilton, who received a report upon him from William Cleghorn, a professor of moral philosophy at Edinburgh, when he visited the Horsley household in Hertfordshire.[10] Thirty-five years later his uncle Robert Hamilton (d.1787),

[5] *Parl. Reg.* xxvi (1789), 260.
[6] *A Catalogue of the Graduates in the Faculties of Arts, Divinity and Law of the University of Edinburgh* (Edinburgh, 1858), 195.
[7] D. B. Horn, *A Short History of the University of Edinburgh* (Edinburgh, 1967), 61.
[8] Westminster PL 419/13, p. 70, pa. St Martin.
[9] *Caledonian Mercury*, 28 Feb. 1788. Hew Scott, *Fasti Ecclesiae Scoticanae* (Edinburgh, 1915), i. 146, for William Hamilton's career and family.
[10] Jebb, 11–12.

an anti-Calvinist minister of the Kirk, who also became professor of divinity at Edinburgh, offered encouragement and advice in his controversy with Dr Priestley.[11]

The Revd John Horsley's father, an earlier Samuel, was likewise a supporter of Nonconformity. This Samuel Horsley, who married Ruth Davison in St Giles, Cripplegate in 1694,[12] was a man of substance, living in the fashionable quarters of the West End. From 1731 to 1734 he had a property in Axe Yard next to Downing Street, Westminster, on which he paid £26. 10s. per annum in poor-rate, and afterwards moved to Chelsea, where he died on 4 July 1735. There can be little doubt that he was the same Samuel Horsley, who, in the years 1721–9, while still in his fifties, resided more splendidly in Brewers' Yard, Westminster, assessed for a £50 per annum poor-rate, with the earl of Lincoln as a neighbour. By his will, proved on 7 July 1735, was bequeathed £5,070, exclusive of an unspecified residue, 'together with all and singular my plate and Kings Towells, clocks and watches, medalls and all and singular such gold and silver coin as shall be in her [his wife's] possession (as her own) at my decease' and also such household goods 'as she shall make choice of for her own use'. Certain benefactions conditional on the want of issue of his son's marriage throw light upon his habits—£500 and a share of the interest on the trust fund of £3,000 from which it was to be taken to 'a certain Charity School whereof John Copeland Esquire, Samuel Travers merchant, George Baker Haberdasher and Edward Bliss dyer are managers and which is in Zoar Street in or near Crovell Lane in Southwarke'; the same amount to 'the Public Hospital near Hyde Park Corner set up for the relief of the lame, sick and needy'; also to 'the Governors of Saint Thomas's Hospital in Southwarke'. Instructive as to the elder Samuel's religious sympathies was the like provision for 'the poor and necessitous objects of or belonging to a certain Religious Society or Congregation of Protestant Dissenters in Westminster (whereof the Reverend Doctor Edmund Calamy was late minister or pastor and whereof the Reverend Mr. Samuel Say is now minister or pastor)'. Its significance was enhanced by a further, immediate bequest of £10 to Samuel Say, provided that he 'shall and do remain, abide and continue minister or pastor of the said Religious Society or Congregation of Protestant Dissenters in Westminster aforesaid to the time of my decease', in default of which the sum was to go to his successor.[13] The Long Ditch Meeting House, Princes Street, Westminster, where this congregation assembled,[14] was a Presbyterian chapel, and the Presbyterians stood on the Rational, not on the

---

[11] HP 1767, fos. 9–10, Hamilton to Horsley, 7 Jan. 1785.
[12] Guildhall Library MS 6419/11, pa. St Giles, Cripplegate, licence 4 Sept. 1694, wedding Sept. 1694.
[13] PRO, Probate (PCC) 11/672, 73–6; pa. St Margaret, Westminster, E.337–55.
[14] G. E. Evans, *Vestiges of Protestant Dissent* (Liverpool, 1897), 141–2; J. Evans, *Dissenting Congregations in England and Wales, 1715–29* (photog. repro. 1958, Dr Williams's Library).

Evangelical side, of the chasm which opened in English Dissent during the eighteenth century. It would be wrong to infer that, at this early stage in the development, any fundamental departure from Christian orthodoxy characterized their position. As Jeremy Goring and his co-historians of English Presbyterianism have pointed out, the 'movement' among liberal Dissenters remained, until quite late in the century, an Arminian revolt against Calvinism rather than an Arian rebellion against the Trinity.[15] Moreover, at first, the issue was scarcely one of doctrine at all, but of freedom to interpret the Bible. Edward Calamy III, who ministered at Long Ditch for twenty-nine years down to 1732, preached a modified Calvinism known as 'the Middle Way', but upheld the right of private judgement against ecclesiastical definitions and formulations.[16] It seems reasonable to suppose that Bishop Horsley's grandsire was a layman of similar cast of mind—tolerant, benevolent, and given to good works. Though there is nothing to suggest that he was himself unorthodox, he was quite undeterred by the heterodoxy attaching to the new minister Samuel Say,[17] when he arrived in 1734, from including that divine in his will.

Uncertainty surrounds the earlier history of the family and the source from which its wealth was derived. A table of genealogy drafted by Mrs Le Fanu Robinson, a great granddaughter of the Revd John Horsley by the youngest son of his second marriage, bears the remark that its members were descended from the Horsleys of Long Horsley, Northumberland gentry of lengthy pedigree.[18] The bishop had a coat of arms, but it is probable that the immediate antecedents of Samuel Horsley, the elder, had risen through trade. Alexander Gordon stated in the *Dictionary of National Biography* in 1891 that the latter was the second son of William Horsley of Broxbourne, Hertfordshire, who died on 10 February 1709.[19] He was briefed by Mrs Robinson whose paper, mentioned above, affirms that there 'are many Horsleys buried at Broxbourne, Herts., who were from the early 17th century merchants or in trade in East of London'. A recent enquiry by the present writer failed to disclose any Horsley tombs at Broxbourne, but the parish register of that place records the burial, on 15 February 1709[10], of Thomas Horsley 'from London'.[20] A corresponding entry in the register of St Giles, Cripplegate refers to an interment at Broxbon (*sic*) on the same date, but

---

[15] C. G. Bolam, J. Goring, H. L. Short, and R. Thomas, *The English Presbyterians* (1968), esp 21–2.

[16] Ibid. 127–33.

[17] Ibid. 198.

[18] HP 1767, fo. 233, identified by material supplied by Miss P. Ames. For the Horsleys of Long Horsley see J. C. Hodgson, *History of Northumberland* (1904), esp. vol. vii.

[19] *DNB* xxvii. 383–6.

[20] Hertfordshire CRO, pa. Broxbourne, burials, 15 Feb. 1709/10. I am indebted to the Revd David Mowbray, vicar of Broxbourne, and to Mr E. W. Paddick for help with my investigations at Broxbourne.

identifies the subject as William Horsly (*sic*), Draper.[21] Almost certainly this was a prominent City tradesman, whose decease in the country, to which he had either repaired or retired, was deemed worthy of remembrance in his home parish. There were many Horsleys in seventeenth-century London, but the archives of the Drapers' Company bear reference to one William Horsley, who seems to have been the father of the elder Samuel.[22] The son of Samuel Horsley of Ware in Hertfordshire, *pistor*, that is baker, he was baptized at Ware on 6 March 1643[4].[23] Coming to the City of London to seek his fortune, he was apprenticed to Edward Roberts in 1659 and made free of the Drapers' Company on 31 July 1667 by reason of his apprenticeship. He quickly joined the flight from the City to the West End which, led by the aristocracy and their dependants earlier in the century, was greatly intensified by the Fire. There were positive advantages, in terms of escape from regulation and local taxes, to be gained from operating outside the City, and William Horsley not only settled in the Strand but remained there for about twenty years, adding the trade of cheesemonger to that for which he had been trained.[24] In the grand jury list at the Westminster quarter sessions on 6 October 1681 his name appears in connection with the parish of St Martin-in-the-Fields as: 'Cheesemonger, Citizen and Draper of London, who hath been a trader there fourteen years, and is well known amongst all the neighbourhood, and hath served in several Public Offices in the Parish, and of unspotted Credit'.[25] About the year 1688 he returned to the City, and was listed in the poor-rate book for the parish of St Margaret Lothbury from then until 1704.[26] His parentage of Samuel Horsley of St Margaret, Westminster cannot be proved. It may be deduced, however, partly from the recurrence in the family of certain Christian names such as Samuel and the more distinctive feminine Puritan name, Mercy; more surely from the character of William Horsley's family during his later residence in St Margaret, Lothbury. In the Marriages, Births, and Burials Assessments for 1695 William Horsley is shown living in the parish with his wife Elizabeth and children Thomas and Mercy.[27] By that time Samuel was married, and might be expected to be

[21] Guildhall Library MS 6419/13, vols. 1702–11.

[22] Except where otherwise stated, the biographical information about William Horsley was supplied by Mr R. T. Brown, education officer of the Drapers' Company, from the records of the Company.

[23] Hertfordshire CRO, pa. Ware, baptisms.

[24] Evidence from the quarterage books of the Drapers' Company tallies with that of poor-rate ledgers and highway rate books of pa. St Martin-in-the-Fields, which show a William Horsley residing in High 'Streete' in 1669 and in the 'Strand' in 1683. Westminster City Reference Library, F. 1112, 3671. He was no longer there in 1691. Ibid., F.1170, 1173.

[25] J. C. Whitebrook (ed.), *London Citizens in 1651, being a transcript of Harleian MS. 4778* [1910], 33.

[26] Guildhall Library MS 4352/2, St Margaret, Lothbury, vestry minutes etc., 1677–1717. This again corroborates the testimony of the quarterage books.

[27] Corporation of London RO, 1695 Assessment according to the Act for Taxing Marriages, Births and Burials, XLIX, ii.

living under his own roof, but his will, proved in 1735, mentioned a brother, Thomas, and a sister, Mercy, married to Thomas Estwick. Mercy was likewise the name of a sister of William Horsley the draper as also of his mother.[28] Perhaps it was from her that the Puritan strain in the family descended.

It was the Revd John Horsley, however, who relinquished Nonconformity for the Church of England. According to Calamy he conformed about the time of the accession of George II in the company of seven other Dissenters, all, with the exception of Isaac Maddox—later bishop of Worcester, whose change of allegiance came, in fact, four years earlier in 1723—obscure men. This leakage followed a steady trickle of manpower into the Establishment, which had been in progress for several years, and reflected the decline in Old Dissent from the second to the fourth decades of the eighteenth century. Those who seceded included figures as distinguished as the philosopher-bishop Joseph Butler, who abandoned Presbyterianism about 1714, and Thomas Secker, afterwards archbishop of Canterbury, who made the decisive break on entering Exeter College, Oxford in 1721. Calamy mentioned more than thirty names in all.[29] Prominent among them were younger men, who ought to have supplied the Dissenting ministry of the future. The transfer of allegiance was perhaps partly a social phenomenon. With the old Presbyterian hopes for comprehension in a modified English Established Church ship-wrecked in 1689, able and ambitious scions of a third generation of Non-conformity must have considered well whether the points on which their grandfathers stuck were relevant enough to the conditions of a new age to be allowed to debar them from promising careers in the existing establishment. But theological factors were paramount, notably the dissatisfaction engendered among many Dissenters by the divisions and disturbances over doctrine and credal authority, which rent their communions. Chief among these was the Salters' Hall dispute of 1719. Originating in an appeal from Exeter where a small group of Arian ministers jangled with their orthodox brethren the controversy, which came before the General Body of London Ministers of the Three Denominations, turned on whether a declaration in favour of the orthodox doctrine of the Trinity should be issued or whether silence should be maintained, where Scripture was not self-evidently clear. The advocates of latitude carried the day, but by a majority of only four, and at the expense of provoking a backlash among the defeated minority, who subscribed a declaration of their own, and sent out advices contrary to those of the General Body.[30] Calamy observed that those who joined the Church of England in George II's reign were mostly of the party which 'complained

---

[28] Hertfordshine CRO, pa. Ware, baptisms, 31 Oct. 1641, 6 March 1643; burials, 19 Dec. 1664.

[29] Edmund Calamy, *An Historical Account of My Own Life* (1829), ii. 500–6. See also DNB xxxv. 298–9 (for Maddox) and ODCC, 214–15 (for Butler).

[30] Bolam *et al.*, *English Presbyterians*, 155–65.

much' of the 'spirit of imposition working among the Dissenters', that is they belonged to the more liberal wing, and this fits with the little that is known of the tradition of John Horsley's family. It is anomalous, as Calamy also notes, that their zest for freedom should have thrown them into a Church which prescribed for its clergy a full set of doctrinal articles and a liturgy that imparted further teaching on matters of faith.[31] There is a difference, however, between a living authority and a dead one, and to Dissenters who tended towards the Middle Way, or even towards Arminianism, it may well have appeared that the Established Church, stripped in 1717 of the coercive jurisdiction of Convocation, was a more lenient taskmaster than a Nonconformity in which militant Calvinists indulged a craving to define.

That is not to say that the recruits from Nonconformity adopted a Latitudinarian indifference to points of church order. Secker and Maddox, as bishops, led the attack in the Lords in 1748 on a clause designed to incapacitate all clergy ordained by Scottish bishops from exercising their ministry. Maddox was a High Church Whig, like his friend Edmund Gibson, who set him to write a 'Vindication' of the Elizabethan church settlement in reply to Neal's *History of the Puritans*. Though mild and amicable towards non-Anglican Protestants and a keen practitioner of charitable work in hospitals, his particular preference was for the episcopally organized and emotional Moravian Brethren, and he supported an Act of 1749 for the more distinct recognition of their status.[32] The Horsleys continued on terms of particular friendship with members of this group. Isaac Maddox and the Revd Richard Biscoe, another Dissenting convert who became chaplain to George II, were trustees under the will of Samuel Horsley of Westminster,[33] and Maddox presented John Horsley to the rectory of Newington Butts, Surrey, a peculiar in the gift of the bishop of Worcester, to which the young Samuel succeeded near the end of Bishop Maddox's career.[34]

The Revd John Horsley took the early education of his eldest son into his own hands, though an early nineteenth-century historian of Hertfordshire records hopefully that Samuel also received some instruction at Westminster School, while not being on the regular foundation.[35] The bishop's father was of scholarly and philanthropic bent, for in his will he left to Samuel 'all my printed books and manuscripts' and to the poor of Thorley, a Hertfordshire parish, of which he was rector from 1745 until his death in 1777, the sum of £5, to be distributed, 10s. apiece to six poor men and the remainder to other

[31] Calamy, *My Own Life*, 506.

[32] C. J. Abbey, *The English Church and its Bishops, 1700–1800* (1887), II. 69–70; *DNB* xxxv. 298–9; Calamy, *My Own Life*, 506; Beilby Porteus, *Works of Thomas Secker*, i. *Review of the Life and Character of Archbishop Secker* (1775), pp. xli–xliii.

[33] PRO Probate 11/672, fos. 73–6.

[34] *DNB* xxvii. 383–6.

[35] Ibid.; R. Clutterbuck, *The History and Antiquities of the County of Hertford* (1815), I. 43.

poor persons.[36] Of his theological opinions nothing is known; probably they were similar to those of his old friend and patron Isaac Maddox. Personal correspondence preserved in Lambeth Palace Library, however, throws much light on the affairs of the family which he sired.

John Horsley remarried after the premature death of Samuel's mother. His second wife, like his first, was a Scotswoman, Mary, the daughter of George Leslie of Kincraigie,[37] who bore him three sons and four daughters. John, the eldest son of the second marriage, became an impecunious writer, translating Racine's plays.[38] George, the second son, joined the service of the honourable East India Company.[39] Francis, the youngest, was a merchant, operating both in the Far East and in the West Indies; he acquired property in Grenada but, before French depredations in the Revolutionary War damaged his interests there, switched back to the Eastern hemisphere. His fortunes were closely linked with those of the Palmer family, which also possessed large holdings in Grenada in the 1780s, and likewise turned its attention eastwards later in the decade.[40] Francis's sister Mary married William Palmer, JP of Nazeing, who was High Sheriff of Essex in 1804,[41] and became the mother of John Horsley Palmer, a notable governor of the Bank of England.[42] The other three sisters—Anne, Sarah, and Elizabeth—lived unmarried into the early decades of the nineteenth century.[43]

The young Samuel Horsley grew to manhood in the company of his stepbrothers and stepsisters at Thorley. Worth £210 a year,[44] it was a comfortable living by mid eighteenth-century standards, especially when held in plurality with Newington Butts and a lectureship at St Martin's, and the children of the parsonage enjoyed an easy intimacy with the clerical squire. Much later in life Anne Horsley, writing to her brother Francis about Thorley Hall, invited him to 'retrace again the times when Mr. Roper carried us in turn on his head, set you on the table to dance an Hornpipe or smiled with his truly kind & benignant countenance over the delights of plum pudding, custard & apple pie with which his hospitable board was so often loaded for the gratification of his happy guests from the Parsonage. Such plum pudding I shall never eat again but the relish of it still remains in my mouth, & the

[36] PRO Probate 11/1037 (John Horsley).

[37] Inscription on memorial tablet to John Horsley, Thorley parish church, Herts.

[38] HP 1768, fos. 5–9, A. to F. Horsley, 20 Dec. 1785.

[39] PRO Probate 11/1037 (John Horsley).

[40] Ibid.; HP 1768, A. to F. Horsley, various letters from Dec. 1785 to Aug. 1788, esp. fos. 13–20, 5 Nov. 1786; fos. 69–71, 8 July 1795.

[41] Inscription on memorial tablet, Nazeing parish church, Essex; HP 1768, fos. 117–21, A. to F. Horsley, 7 Mar. 1804.

[42] *DNB* xliii. 144.

[43] Inscription on tombs of Elizabeth and Sarah Horsley in Thorley churchyard. HP 1768, fos. 112–15. Ann Horsley was writing under that name from Shepperton until Mar. 1806.

[44] HP 1768, fos. 117–21, A. to F. Horsley, 7 Mar. 1804. The same letter states that the value had risen to nearly £600 p.a. by the time of writing.

reverend owner of the mansion must ever live in our grateful remembrance.'[45] The Horsleys and their relatives the Palmers formed a closely knit family, the members helping one another, in Quaker manner, in business and in personal difficulties—'the fraternity at large', as Elizabeth dubbed them.[46] The religious tone of the household was unobtrusive but sincere. Occasional reminders of Puritan Dissenting past surfaced in the correspondence, as when sister Anne, commenting on her brother Francis's escape from pecuniary mishap through the timely help of William Palmer, expressed to him her belief in a particular providence: 'The ways of Providence are deep & inscrutable, & if any set of people have more particular reason than others to adore & depend on them, it is our Family. How have our most sanguine hopes been exceeded, & the cruse of oyle and barrell of meal supplied in the hour which most threatened its diminution.'[47]

Her piety, however, was entirely practical and undogmatic. When her stepbrother Samuel, then archdeacon of St Albans, entered into contest with the Unitarian Joseph Priestley over the respective claims of Unitarianism and Trinitarianism to constitute primitive Christianity, she commented unsympathetically: 'As it is a subject far above me to decide upon the merits of, I shall not trouble myself or you in Trinitarian or Unitarian discussion. A great deal of learning appears in both the combatants & all I can say about it is that they are very kind in helping each other to display it. Much good may the dispute do them both. It will never do me any.'[48] Elizabeth and Sally Horsley were more appreciative of their brother's public exertions, but their sympathies hardly extended beyond a distaste for Whigs and politically minded Dissenters common in England at the end of the eighteenth century.[49] The roots of Samuel's theologically developed High Churchmanship cannot easily be traced to his family.

His public career was curiously slow to mature. Atterbury, Gibson, Wake, Hoadly, Secker, and many lesser figures on the bench had become bishops, deans, or professors before they reached mid-century. Horsley, though a graduate of two universities, held a fellowship in neither, and did not win high ecclesiastical preferment until his middle fifties. The obstacle was not want of connection. He enjoyed a succession of influential patrons, while his friend Bishop Samuel Hallifax, though merely the son of a Nottinghamshire apothecary, was appointed to a chair of Arabic at Cambridge at the age of 35.[50] A serious handicap, however, was the lack of continuity which marked his earlier years. Only after protracted trial and error did he discover his true

   [45] Ibid.
   [46] HP 1768, fos. 163–8, E. to F. Horsley, 25 Jan. 1790.
   [47] HP 1768, fos. 1–2, A. to F. Horsley, 3 Apr. 1785.
   [48] HP 1768, fos. 13–20, A. to F. Horsley, 5 Nov. 1786.
   [49] HP 1768, fos. 155–62, E. to F. Horsley, 14 Mar. 1789; HP 1769, fos. 24–31, Sarah to F. Horsley, 24 Jan. 1790.
   [50] J. and J. A. Venn, *Alumni Cantabrigienses* (Cambridge, 1922), i. 2. 290.

vocation. For long it appeared likely that the Bar rather than the Church's ministry would be his goal. Though attendance at university was by no means the indispensable preliminary to enrolment at the Inns of Court, the Inns themselves, in a bid to shore up the social standing of their profession, were beginning in the 1750s and 1760s to attach more importance to a university background than they had accorded to it forty years earlier.[51] At Cambridge the earnest study of the common law of England dates only from about 1788, the year in which a professorship in the subject was conferred on Edward Christian of St John's.[52] But Trinity Hall was a law college, teaching civil law, a discipline adapted to the needs of practitioners in the church courts and the court of Admiralty, but, for want of anything better, serving as preliminary background for common lawyers too. Here it was that the youthful Samuel Horsley was admitted as a pensioner on 24 October 1751.[53] The bachelor's degree in civil law, called the LLB, was in low repute. During the first half of the century only half a dozen students or even fewer presented themselves for it in the course of a year, and though the numbers rose after 1750 to a limited extent recipients were as often aspiring country parsons as intending barristers. The statutes prescribed as a qualification membership of the university for six complete years, but a decree of the heads of houses dating from 1684 commuted the minimum period of residence to nine terms, that is one term less than was required of a bachelor of arts. For this reason, and also because the single exercise demanded of entrants in lieu of an examination was so much easier than the Latin disputation conducted in Arts, the LLB became a soft option, ideal for wealthy loungers whose need for gainful employment lacked urgency. In practice, students intending to graduate went down after residing three years and returned at the end of another three to keep an act and take their degree,[54] while a large proportion of university men did not bother to claim the qualification.[55] Samuel Horsley cannot have wasted his time. He was elected a scholar in 1753,[56] at a time when scholarships, though less competitive than they later became, were usually decided by some kind of oral examination.[57] On 25 January 1755 he was admitted to the Middle Temple.[58] Two years later he returned to Trinity Hall, with the enhanced status of fellow commoner, which would enable him to dine with the fellows, and in 1758 he took his LLB.[59]

[51] Paul Lucas, 'Blackstone and the Reform of the Legal Profession', *English Historical Review*, 77 (1972), 456–89.
[52] Christopher Wordsworth, *Scholae Academicae* (repr. 1968), 145.
[53] Venn and Venn, *Alumni Cantabrigienses*, i. 2. 410.
[54] D. A. Winstanley, *Unreformed Cambridge* (Cambridge, 1935), 57–60.
[55] Lucas, 'Blackstone and the Reform of the Legal Profession'.
[56] Venn and Venn, *Alumni Cantabrigienses*, i. 2. 410.
[57] Wordsworth, *Scholae Academicae*, 343–4, 346–7.
[58] *Register of Admissions to the Honourable Society of the Middle Temple* (1949), I. 348.
[59] Venn and Venn, *Alumni Cantabrigienses*, i. 2. 410; *DNB* xxvii. 383–6.

As an education, this fell far short of the best that Cambridge at the height of her eighteenth-century scientific glory could offer. It was true of the eighteenth century, as it has been claimed of the late seventeenth,[60] that, though a student would attend some professorial lectures in the university, the main part of his teaching took place in the college under the close supervision of the tutor. In those days Trinity Hall was a cramping environment. Its library was described by a visiting German scholar in 1710, Zacharias Conrad von Uffenbach, as 'like the hall itself, that is, very mean, consisting only of a few law books'.[60] Tutorial instruction was provided by, at the most, two clerical fellows, their ten lay brethren being absent for the greater part of the year.[62] Intellectual benefit cannot be measured, however, solely in terms of preparation for a degree. In the phrase of John Wallis, a Cambridge critic of the early seventeenth century, a man could 'divert'.[63] Much more than Oxford who continued to base her teaching on the Aristotelian trivium of logic, grammar, and rhetoric, mid-century Cambridge, the heritor of Newton and Bentley, offered to enquiring minds a grasp of the new exact and experimental sciences. Mathematics, astronomy, rigorous criticism of classical texts, chemistry, were there to be tapped in some of the colleges, notably Trinity, Clare, and Corpus for Newtonian studies. A student whose tutor was not versed in them would need the enthusiasm to go out and look for them, but the means of finding were not obscure. Lectures at Trinity Hall in 1766 on Cicero's *De Officiis*[64] may have been merely an exercise in old-fashioned rhetoric, but professors of the new philosophy, even when they did not lecture, got students to come and consult them, or conveyed their learning in published form.[65] At that time an undergraduate educated himself by reading, and Waterland's *Advice to a Young Student*, published 1706–40, suggested supplementary forms of guidance when it prescribed in the following order the aids to the study of the classics: 'Consult *Dictionaries, Lexicons, Notes*, Friends or Tutor.'[66] Eleven new textbooks of natural philosophy were published at Cambridge in the period 1720–50. Observatories over the great gate of Trinity and at St John's whetted the appetite for astronomy. When a bishop of Lincoln could write in 1750 that 'Mathematics and Natural Philosophy are so generally and so exactly understood, that more than twenty in every year of the Candidates for a Bachelor of Arts Degree are able to demonstrate the

---

[60] R. J. White, *Dr. Bentley: A Study in Academic Scarlet* (1965), 39.

[61] J. E. B. Mayor (ed.), *Cambridge under Queen Anne, Illustrated by Memoir of Ambrose Bonwicke & Diaries of Francis Burman and Zacharias Conrad von Uffenbach* (Cambridge, 1911), 163.

[62] D. A. Winstanley, *The University of Cambridge in the Eighteenth Century* (Cambridge, 1922), 266–7.

[63] White, *Dr. Bentley*, 44–5.

[64] Wordsworth, *Scolae Academicae*, 13.

[65] Ibid. 77–8.

[66] Ibid. 331.

principal Propositions in the *Principia*',[67] it is improbable that Horsley, who was later to distinguish himself as a mathematician, was not stirred to interest in the subject by his experiences as an undergraduate at Cambridge.

The environment was not, however, conducive to the growth of High Church principles. Unlike Oxford, which steered a course of Toryish in-dependence until 1772, when Lord North was elected Chancellor, Cambridge was scrupulously loyal to the first two Hanoverian kings and was brought within the Whig hegemony. The duke of Newcastle was its Chancellor for twenty years from 1748, and strove through chosen agents to maintain an influence in the colleges. At mid-century attitudes towards religion were marked by flippancy and agnosticism,[68] and Trinity Hall was noted for its conformity to the spirit of the age. The ten non-resident fellows, who constituted the great majority of the society, were practising civilians or even Members of Parliament. They resided only during the twelve days of Christmas, when they spent their mornings auditing the accounts and their evenings in sumptuous feasting. Thus, as Winstanley observes, 'the ordinary Fellow of Trinity Hall in the eighteenth century was far less "donnish" and far more a man of the world than the Fellows of other colleges'. According to a contemporary description the society was 'always composed of people of the best families and fortunes'.[69] Politically the college was rent by a struggle in 1756–7 caused by the efforts of the master, Dr Edward Simpson, a judge in the consistory court of London, to manipulate appointments in the Leicester House interest, but this was virtually over by the time that Horsley returned to Trinity Hall as a fellow commoner, and Newcastle's leadership was soon acknowledged by the master.[70] There is no reason to suppose that Horsley was involved in the dispute, but his enhanced status in so select a community marked a rise in his social position.

In eighteenth-century Cambridge fellow commoners were synonymous with bucks—undergraduates normally of the usual age and distinguished only by their rank, their unruly arrogance, and their privileges. On Horsley, however, the distinction must have been conferred by reason of his maturity, perhaps through influential contacts in the legal world established while he was at the Middle Temple. One can but conjecture as to the use he made of his time there. The Inns of Court were then in a decadent state, having abandoned the collegiate life and educational system at the end of the seventeenth century.[71] At best law students were, like Thurlow, put out to read in the offices of

[67] Ibid. 73. The observatory at Trinity College was established in Jan. 1705–6 for Roger Cotes, first Plumerian Professor of Astronomy, by the then master, Dr Richard Bentley, himself a classicist. Ibid. 245.

[68] Michael Grant, *Cambridge* (1966), 133.

[69] Winstanley, *University of Cambridge*, 266–7.

[70] Ibid. 268–81.

[71] W. Holdsworth, *A History of English Law*, xii (1938), 15–17.

attorneys or solicitors, and to pick up what they could of legal procedures by hanging around the courts in Westminster Hall.[72] At the Middle Temple by the 1730s it was possible to compound all the obligations of a student, including the formalities of residence, for the sum of £38. 6s. 2d.[73] It is unlikely, however, that the struggling son of a country parson with a large family would have chosen to waste the opportunity of acquiring some professional expertise. Probably, therefore, Samuel did study for the Bar in London for about two years. He was never called, but an early observation of cases in progress may well have laid the foundation of the skill in debate which he afterwards displayed in the House of Lords.

The decision which changed the course of Samuel Horsley's career was taken by the time that he had completed only three of the five years necessary to qualify for the Bar. Perhaps it was taken after two, and accounts for his decision to return to the University to take his LLB, for while a degree was not necessary in the law, it was expected of a clergyman hoping for preferment in the Church of England.[74] He was made a deacon on 16 July 1758 and priested only two months later, on 24 September, at the hands of Zachary Pearce, bishop of Rochester, acting for the bishop of London.[75] Pearce, a former vicar of St Martin-in-the-Fields, was Samuel's godfather, and as such may be expected to have made his imprint on the young man's theological outlook. His own views were a blend of the liberal and the orthodox. Joint editor of a collection of essays known as the *Freethinker*, published in 1718, he sought to rescue freethinking from the odium which the Deists had brought upon it, and wrote in vindication of miracles. Though not a High Churchman of the Tory kind—he was commissioned to write a defence of Walpole's arrest of Bishop Atterbury—he won the esteem of Dr Johnson,[76] and belonged to a large centre group insufficiently recognized by historians which combined a concern for the preservation of traditional Christian belief and church order with an accommodating temper which enabled its members to come to terms with the Hanoverians. It was from such a stable that Horsley, too, emerged. Less than four months after his ordination, he was instituted on 18 January 1759 to the rectory of St Mary, Newington Butts, a Canterbury peculiar in the deanery of Croydon, worth between £170 and £200 a year, which his father obligingly vacated in his favour.[77]

---

[72] R. Gore Browne, *Chancellor Thurlow* (1953), 7.

[73] Holdsworth, *English Law*, vi (1937), 489.

[74] Of 31 deacons made in the diocese of Exeter in 1702 only one was a non-graduate. A sample taken from Archbishop Herring's visitation returns for York diocese in 1743 yields only 13 non-graduate clergy out of 163. A. Warne, *Church and Society in Eighteenth-Century Devon* (Newton Abbot, 1969), 37.

[75] LPL VB.1/11, Archbishop's Act Book 1773–85, fos. 14, 247, dispensations for plurality, 22 Jan. 1774, 30 Nov. 1779.

[76] Abbey, *English Church*. ii. 63–6; Bennett, *Tory Crisis*, 259.

[77] LPL VB.2/11, Archbishop's Institution Act Book 1758–77, fos. 11–12, 18 Jan. 1759. For the real value of the living *c.*1760 see Canterbury Diocesan Book or Speculum 1758–68 (LPL VC.IV/6, fo. 56).

Despite its proximity to London, Newington was a rural parish. Market gardening and fruit-growing, notably the cultivation of peaches, were its outstanding occupations. The process which was to turn it by the end of the century into a fashionable suburb was only just beginning, but in 1763 Cornelius Van Mildert, a London distiller, whose son was the famous early nineteenth-century bishop of Durham, was chosen as rector's warden. Social control cannot have been easy in a parish of scattered hamlets, where there was an abundance of common land, some of it enclosed in 1769 to be let for the benefit of the 'numerous and expensive poor' with which the community was burdened.[78] Nevertheless, the new rector reported to his Ordinary soon after he was instituted that he knew of no parishioners who professed to disregard religion or commonly absented themselves from all public worship on the Lord's Day. Sectaries of all denominations were to be found, but not in considerable numbers, and the few Quakers did not refuse to pay to the parson his legal dues. The conduct of public worship was, by the standards of the age, exemplary: services twice a Sunday with two sermons, Sacrament monthly with thirty to forty communicants and on the great festivals, prayers every Wednesday and Friday and on all holy days throughout the year.[79] The robust condition of the Established Church in Newington was not entirely due to Horsley. There had been a vigorous High Church tradition in the parish earlier in the century. William Taswell, rector from 1698 to 1731, was rebuked by a Quaker apologist for publishing a pamphlet claiming his tithes on the ground that he belonged to the Melchizedecian priesthood, 'that old exploded notion of Lesley'[80] (that is Charles Leslie, the Nonjuror). In his time Dr Sacheverell had been elected to a lectureship in the parish during his imprisonment,[81] an action which suggests that the rector's convictions were shared by the more important of his flock. It is not improbable that the young Samuel Horsley's own strict churchmanship was assisted to mature by the environment of the place. At first, he threw himself energetically into its affairs. 'I have resided constantly upon my cure and in the house belonging to it ever since I have been in possession of the living', he informed the archbishop at the visitation of 1759–61. 'I have no curate.' 'I catechiz'd every Wednesday and Friday during Lent as the former ministers of this parish us'd to do.'[82] The results of his exertions were apparent in 100 candidates for confirmation on 23 March 1760. Soon afterwards he relaxed his grip on the parish, appointing a succession of curates to do the work. In April 1766 his

---

[78] *L.C.C. Survey of London* (1955), xxv. 82, 89; R. W. Bowers, *Sketches of Southwark Old and New* (1902), 487–92; LPL MS 1134/6, Archbishop Secker's Visitation Articles 1759–61, St Mary, Newington; Southwark PL MS 1534, St Mary, Newington, Vestry Book 1740–70, for nomination of C. Van Mildert.

[79] Archbishop Secker's Visitation Articles, St Mary, Newington.

[80] Thomas Johnson, *The Rector Corrected, Being an Answer to William Taswell... wherein his Objections against the Quakers... are Reduced to Four Heads* (1722) (Southwark PL).

[81] Geoffrey Holmes, *The Trial of Doctor Sacheverell* (1973), 256.

[82] Archbishop Secker's Visitation Articles, St Mary, Newington.

absence enabled the Easter vestry meeting to snatch the appointment of both the churchwardens. Although he retained the living until 1793, he sent his nominations to the position of rector's warden through the post in the later stages of his incumbency.[83]

Samuel Horsley's non-residence could at first be excused by his obligations to his father, who combined responsibilities at St Martin's with the care of a country parish in Hertfordshire valued at about £200 a year.[84] We have the testimony of a later rector that he was signing the register at Thorley in 1764.[85] The archbishop's Speculum for the years 1758–68 records that he took up lodgings in St Martin's, also to assist his father.[86] It seems probable that his change of abode betokened a shift in his interests away from parish work and towards the intellectual pursuits which could be more easily conducted in the metropolis. On 9 April 1767 he was elected a fellow of the Royal Society.[87] For someone of his background this was a less surprising honour than it would be today. At that time more than 70 per cent of the fellows were not scientists in the sense of being experts in natural philosophy or mathematics but men of broad general education.[88] Within the fostering environment of the Society, however, Horsley slowly advanced from the latter category into the former. His earliest publication, which appeared in the year of his election, was an exercise in apologetics, though the mode of argument was scientific.[89] It endeavoured to vindicate against the mechanistic cosmology of the Deists the notion that a series of fresh impulses from the Creator was needed to sustain the circulation of the planets in the solar system. Three years later, however, the Clarendon Press printed his restoration of the *De Inclinationibus* of Apollonius of Perge—a reconstruction from hints in the writings of a later Greek commentator, of a lost treatise by an eminent Alexandrian geometer of the third century BC. This was a small but lasting contribution to mathematical knowledge.[90] Socially, too, the period was one of significant advancement. If, as Professor G. F. A. Best has observed, becoming tutor to the scion of a noble house was 'the standard short-cut to high preferment for clergymen of middle-class background',[91] Horsley now

---

[83] Southwark PL MSS 1534, 1544, St Mary, Newington, Vestry Books 1740–70, 1788–1816.

[84] About £210 in 1770. LPL VB.I/11, Archbishop's Act Book 1773–85, fo. 247, dispensation for plurality, 30 Nov. 1779.

[85] *Gent. Mag.* 76 (1806), 1095–6.

[86] LPL VC.IV/5, Canterbury Diocesan Book 1758–68, fo. 393.

[87] The Record of the Royal Society of London (1940), 421.

[88] 71% in 1770. H. Lyons, *The Royal Society 1660–1940* (Cambridge, 1944), 341.

[89] *The Power of God, deduced from the Computable Instantaneous Productions of It in Solar System etc.* (1767).

[90] Sir Thomas Heath, writing in 1921, described Horsley's restoration of the treatise as 'much the most complete'. T. Heath, *A History of Greek Mathematics* (Oxford, 1921), II. 190. J. E. Hofmann, *Classical Mathematics* (1960), 152, called it 'noteworthy research'.

[91] G. F. A. Best, 'The Mind and Times of William Van Mildert', *Journal of Theological Studies*, NS, 14 (1963), 355–70.

adopted it. In November 1767 he was incorporated at Christ Church, Oxford in order to become tutor to Heneage Finch, Lord Guernsey, the eldest son of the third earl of Aylesford, who commenced his studies there in the same month.[92] Nine years later he acknowledged his pupil's family as his patrons by giving his only son the name Heneage, that of successive earls of Aylesford. The connection continued into the closing years of Horsley's life, when in 1801 a clergyman from Sevenoaks solicited the help of the fourth earl, Horsley's former charge, to procure his favourable intervention as bishop of Rochester in a non-residence case at Burham.[93]

It would be rash to draw strong inferences from it about Samuel Horsley's early convictions in politics or religion. In an age of shifting political alignments and low-key theological dialogue, acceptance of patronage could mean relatively little in terms of ideological commitment, and Horsley was a man of strong independence. The 'Aylesford Finches' were traditionally Tories, involved in High Church machinations at the end of Anne's reign and proscribed by the Hanoverians from 1716. Like many younger Tories impatient of perpetual exclusion, however, the third earl took advantage of the relaxed political tensions after the collapse of the 1745 rebellion to establish links with powerful Whig politicians. He became a supporter and friend of George Grenville, voting against the subsidy treaties of 1755 and against repeal of the Stamp Act in 1766. An aura of old-fashioned independent Toryism remained attached to him in 1762, when he ran for a short while as a candidate in the 'Old Interest' at the cancellarial election at Oxford, but his son, Horsley's pupil, who sat, first for Castle Rising and then for Maidstone, during the years 1772–7, gave general support to Lord North's Government in the seventies, as did most of the parliamentary connection built up by the late George Grenville.[94] The future bishop's own connections, however, were by no means limited to a single circle of like-minded persons. Robert Lowth, bishop of Oxford, a noted authority on Hebrew poetry, was to do more than anyone else to place Samuel Horsley on the higher echelons of power in the Church of England. Lowth's politics, however, were not those of the Finches, while his theological position differed in almost every significant respect from that which Horsley was eventually to reach. Lowth's 'Father in God' was the notorious Latitudinarian Bishop Hoadly, his friends were among the Cavendish family and the Rockingham Whigs, his outlook was materialistic and humanistic, concerned, as his celebrated controversy with William

---

[92] J. Foster, *Alumni Oxonienses*, 2nd ser. i (Liechtenstein, 1968), 694; G.E.C., *Complete Peerage* (Gloucester, 1982), i. 366.

[93] National Register of Archives, Report 10782 (1964) on Packington Hall (Warwickshire) MSS, family letters. This collection was extensively damaged by fire in Nov. 1979.

[94] Bennett, *Tory Crisis*, 166–7; R. Sedgwick, *The Commons, 1715–54* (1970), ii. 32–3; Sir L. Namier and J. Brooke, *The History of Parliament: The House of Commons 1754–1790* (1964), i. 313, 340, ii. 424–5; L. M. Wiggin, *The Faction of Cousins* (Yale, 1958), 266; J. Tomlinson (ed.), *Additional Grenville Papers, 1763–65* (Manchester, 1962), 231 n. 6; Ward, *Georgian Oxford*, 219.

Warburton reflects, with ancient literature as an expression of a former society rather than as evidence of the providence of God.[95] His paths and Horsley's crossed, perhaps at Christ Church, certainly in the Royal Society, where the two overlapped as members of the Council.

[95] B. Hepworth, *Robert Lowth* (Boston, 1978), esp. chap. i.

3

Man of Science and Liberality

How long Horsley was in Oxford is a matter for conjecture. His pupil was created MA on 16 June 1770, this marking the red-carpeted termination of a three-year undergraduate career. Two years later he was in Parliament, sitting for a pocket borough.[1] The tutor retained a connection with Christ Church for some time, receiving a DCL on 18 January 1774,[2] but the Royal Society displaced the University of Oxford as the principal arena of his activities. On 30 November 1771 he was elected to the Council of that learned body. As William, earl of Dartmouth and Robert Lowth, bishop of Oxford, were chosen at the same time,[3] it is probable that he was already within the circle of the latter. Even so his determination to rise further by his own efforts could scarcely have been more evident. He was assiduous in his attendance at Council meetings and was soon involved in the corporate research of the Royal Society. In the minutes of the Council on 23 July 1772 it was:

Ordered that the Hon. Mr. Cavendish, the Revd. Mr. Horsley, the Astronomer Royal, Dr. Franklin and the Hon. Mr. Barrington be a Committee for considering some experiments which are proposed to be made for measuring the attraction of hills and mountains; and that they have power to draw upon the Treasurer for what money they think expedient and necessary.[4]

The project arose from a paper by the Astronomer Royal, Nevil Maskelyne, arguing for an experimental measurement of the deflection of a vertical plumb-line by the attraction of a mountain mass. To be included with scientists of the eminence of Henry Cavendish and Benjamin Franklin in the directorate was a meaningful distinction, for despite the implication of a remark by Sir Henry Lyons he was not there as secretary of the Society. Moreover, although the actual experiment was eventually carried out by Maskelyne on a mountain in Perthshire called Schiehallion, with success which brought him the Copley medal,[5] Horsley had a responsible part in the preliminary surveys. At a Council meeting on 21 January 1773, 'it was recommended from the Committee for examining the attraction of mountains

---

[1] G. E. C., *Complete Peerage* (Gloucester, 1982), i. 366.

[2] *DNB.* xxvii. 383–6.

[3] RS Journal Book, xxvii (1771–4), fo. 138.

[4] RS Minutes of Council, vi (1769–82), fo. 145. Horsley's attendances at full Council may be verified from this record.

[5] H. Lyons, *The Royal Society 1660–1940* (Cambridge, 1944), 190–1. Horsley was not yet secretary when the Committee was appointed.

and ordered by Ballot, that the sum of £15. 15s. be paid to Mr John
Greenwood of Worcester, who assisted Mr. Horsley in some admeasurements
in Wales, out of the ballance of His Majesty's donation'.[6]

The decade after the conclusion of the Seven Years War witnessed a
renaissance of geographical discovery. English navigators, of whom the most
famous was Captain Cook, took up where the Tudors had left off in exploring
the South Seas, but there were also expeditions with a strongly scientific
purpose into other areas. In 1773 the Royal Society persuaded the Admiralty
to send two ships *Racehorse* and *Carcass* under the command of Captain the
Hon. Constantine John Phipps, into the Arctic regions to find a passage round
the North Pole to the East Indies and make observations both naturalistic and
astronomical. The young Nelson took part as a midshipman. The directions
and scientific instructions for the hazardous voyage through the icebergs were
drawn up by the Council of the Royal Society,[7] and Samuel Horsley was
among those who submitted papers which were delivered to the commander.
When the Observations of the expedition were written up, he detected an
error in the calculations made by the nautical astronomer Israel Lyons from
his quadrant readings on a rocky island. In a paper published in 1774 he
showed how this mistake upset the reckoning of the gain of the pendulum in
latitude 79°50′, and pointed out that the claim made in Phipps's account of
the voyage to have established a figure of the earth nearer to Sir Isaac
Newton's computation than any others hitherto made, rested upon some
outdated Newtonian assumptions as to the elliptical shape of the meridians.[8]

Though worded with studied courtesy, this intervention can scarcely have
endeared its author to Phipps (later Lord Mulgrave) and his friend Joseph
Banks, a distinguished promoter of scientific expeditions.[9] By that time,
however, Horsley had already risen to be one of the two secretaries of the
Royal Society. He was chosen on 30 November 1773.[10] His election was a
victory for the scientific fellows in their efforts to raise standards in their
branch of learning. Previous secretaries for about a decade and a half had
been librarians or archivists, and the drive towards scientific excellence had
come mainly from energetic presidents such as the astronomer earl, the
second Lord Macclesfield, and his successor Lord Morton. The initiative had

---

[6] RS Minutes of Council, vi, fo. 163.

[7] Lyons, *Royal Society*, 190; *Concise DNB* (Oxford, repr. 1969), i. 1039.

[8] *Remarks on the Observations made in the Late Voyage towards the North Pole for Determining the Acceleration of the Pendulum in Latitude 79°50′. By Samuel Horsley, LL.D., Sec. RS In a Letter to the Hon Constantine John Phipps* (1774); W. R. Dawson (ed.), *The Banks Letters* (1958), 669.

[9] Lyons, *Royal Society*, 187–90. It may be more than coincidental that Mulgrave was to take a leading part against Horsley in the dissensions which broke out in the Royal Society in 1783–4. On one occasion he intervened in a debate to stop him from citing his evidence. RS Miscellaneous Manuscripts, i, undated document, fo. 31, probably of 27 Feb. 1784. For particulars of the dissensions see below, pp. 50–52.

[10] *The Record of the Royal Society of London* (1940), 337, 342.

slackened under the antiquary James West, who followed Morton as president in the years 1768–72.[11] Horsley exerted himself to revive it. Even before he became secretary he was authorized to refurbish the library, which was found to be 'exceedingly defective in the most usefull and curious books in the different branches of Mathematics and Natural Philosophy, of the last two centuries; and is far from being complete in those of a later date'. The sum of £25 was voted to him by the Council on 24 June 1773 to spend on 'such old Mathematical and Astronomical Books as shall fall in his way and are proper to be added to the library'.[12]

Outstandingly the most important contribution of his secretaryship, however, was the proposal which he laid before Council on 21 December 1775 to 'publish, by subscription, a compleat edition of all the works of Sir Isaac Newton, with notes and comments, in five vols. in quarto', for which he already claimed to have the patronage of King George III. Newton's basic contribution to natural philosophy had long been available in the *Philosophiae Naturalis Principia Mathematica*, first printed for him by Halley in the summer of 1687. This ran through its second and third editions in 1713 and 1726 respectively, and was well known to Cambridge undergraduates in a simplified form through textbooks. But the great mathematician had also left behind him a heterogeneous collection of papers on various aspects of his subject—fluxions, the species and magnitude of curvilinear figures, optics, and lunar theory, as well as items of scientific correspondence. It was in the attempt to collate this wider range of material in a five-volume work, using hitherto unpublished manuscript sources for the purpose, that the originality of Horsley's mammoth undertaking lay.

As Newton was the most illustrious of the former presidents of the Royal Society, this was a project deemed worthy of corporate encouragement. It was:

resolved unanimously, that the said undertaking is highly honourable to this nation, and of the greatest importance to Science; and that Dr. Horsley be earnestly requested to proceed in it ... [and] that he have leave to inspect all papers preserved in the archives of this Society, as well the minutes of the Council and the Committee as the papers read at the meetings of the Society from its first institution, to the present times; and that the Librarian be directed to furnish him with all such papers as he shall call for in his custody, at the times appointed for the Librarian's attendance in the reading room.

There was, however, a grudging note in the reception which suggested that already all was not well in the relations between Horsley and his colleagues. It was contained in the proviso 'that it be understood that Dr. Horsley is to peruse these papers in this House of the Society; and upon no pretence to remove any of them from thence without special leave from the President and

---

[11] Lyons, *Royal Society*, 181, 185–90.
[12] RS Minutes of Council, vi, fo. 178.

council'.[13] However appropriate it might have been for a stranger, this was a curious restriction to lay upon a secretary. It was relaxed in June 1777 to the extent of allowing him to take into his own possession the original papers from which the *Commercium Epistolicum* was compiled, but he was compelled to execute a bond to return them after three months.[14]

Whether justified by previous experience of him or of other borrowers, the limitation on the use of manuscripts must have interposed a serious impediment to Horsley's work, for side by side with it he had resumed the labours of a country parson. In January 1774 his former pupil's father presented him to the rectory of Albury near Guildford, worth about £200 per annum in real value.[15] There at the age of 41 he married for the first time, his bride, Mary Botham, being the daughter of the previous rector, whose death had left her an orphan in the parsonage. She bore him two children: a son Heneage born on 23 February 1776 and later a daughter Harriott who died in infancy. His marriage was extremely happy but sadly brief, ending with his wife's death in August 1777. This left him with at first two small children to bring up. He was eventually able partly to off-load his burden by remarriage to Sarah Wright, a protégée of his first wife who had been in her service.[16] She, unfortunately, was a woman hampered by health poor from the beginning and slowly deteriorating. In 1786 he had to take her to Hastings for the sea-bathing in order to remedy 'that nervous disorder with which she is afflicted'.[17] These distractions were the more severely felt in that the long years of bachelorhood and heavy concentration on learned pursuits had induced in him a certain rigidity. When he was vicar of South Weald in 1785, his sister wrote:

The doctor is, I believe, still at Weald & does not return to town till after Christmas. Heneage grows a very fine boy & is as entertaining as can be imagined. His father has got a one horse chaise in which he drives himself, his wife and little son with great success, & has yet met with no sinister accident, which I own I thought rather to be apprehended from his short sight, & still more from his great absence, a circumstance not unlikely in my mind to have carried himself, his family & the Chaise into a ditch, while he was soaring among the stars or settling some mathematical difficulty.[18]

He, nevertheless, kept his head, and managed to preserve a calm, bucolic, eccentric routine, combining exercise with scientific investigation. His sister continued:

---

[13] Ibid., fos. 292–3.
[14] Ibid., fos. 326–7.
[15] *DNB* xxvii. 383–6; LPL VB. 1/11, Archbishop of Canterbury's Act Book, 1773–85, fo. 14, dispensation, 22 Jan. 1774.
[16] *DNB* xxvii. 383–86; Jebb, 21 ff.
[17] HP 1768, fos. 147–50, E. to F. Horsley, 11 Nov. 1786.
[18] Ibid., fos. 5–9, A. to F. Horsley, 20 Dec. 1785.

He was taking great pains to persuade Sister Betty this summer to let him come and fetch her over to Weald, Mrs. Horsley at the same time assuring her he would be careful. 'Oh yes, Aunt', says Heneage. 'You may depend upon it there's no danger, for we drive quite Mathematic[ally], for if we are to go a new road, my Papa always goes there before to look at it, & if there's a hill or a turning we always strike up a sticke in the middle & take a view of it.[19]

Even so his ecclesiastical responsibilities increased when Bishop Lowth, on becoming bishop of London in 1777, made him his domestic chaplain. Unlike his more notorious contemporaries in the eighteenth-century Establishment, he was careful not to increase his pluralities at the parish level. He gave up Albury when he was instituted to Thorley, his father's old rectory, in 1779, and surrendered Thorley on appointment to the vicarage of South Weald in Essex in 1782.[20] But as his practice was to reside for at least part of the year upon these benefices the problems of conducting mathematical research at the Royal Society's headquarters in London cannot have been inconsiderable.

It is a tribute to his determination that the Newton project advanced so rapidly.[21] The illness of his first wife occasioned a brief initial delay, exacerbated by the difficulty of finding a draughtsman competent to fashion the complex woodcuts needed for Newton's text. Thomas Bewick, the celebrated wood-engraver, claimed to have executed the task in 1778 on the recommendation of Horsley's friend and fellow mathematician Charles Hutton, for whom he had done similar work. But Horsley's letter to his printer in September 1777 implies that there had been a change in a former arrangement:

I hope that you will sometime tomorrow receive my copy of the *Arithmetica Universalis*, which is to be the first tract in my first volume ... You will set Mr. Gilbert about the figures immediately, and let the printing go on with as much expedition as possible. I would wish that my subscribers should have their first volume before next Midsummer; it will be a very large one.[22]

About this time an important breakthrough occurred in his researches. Though a limited number of Sir Isaac Newton's works had been published by his friends during his own lifetime, the great bulk of his mathematical papers had remained intact in his hands until his death together with other drafts on scientific and religious subjects. Most of this agglomeration of priceless manuscripts, largely composed of notebooks and loose sheets, passed even-

---

[19] Ibid.

[20] *DNB* xxvii. 383–6; LPL VB. 1/11, Archbishop's Act Book 1773–85, fos. 247, 315, dispensations in plurality, 30 Nov. 1779, 8 Apr. 1782.

[21] Except where otherwise indicated the following information and quotations concerning Horsley's study of Newton's works are taken from D. T. Whiteside (ed.), *The Mathematical Papers of Isaac Newton*, i–vii (Cambridge, 1967–76), esp. i, pp. xv–xxxvi.

[22] Ian Bain (ed.), *Thomas Bewick: My Life* (1981), 76. I owe this reference to Professor A. G. Howson.

tually into the possession of the earls of Portsmouth by the marriage of the son of the first earl to Catherine Conduitt, a granddaughter of Newton's stepsister Hannah. There it remained, its whereabouts known to scholars from 1757 onwards but its contents not yet public knowledge. As Dr D. T. Whiteside has explained, it was Horsley who made 'the first careful record we have of Newton's manuscript'. After some initial difficulty in gaining access to the papers, as the second earl was reluctant to allow the privacy of his estates to be invaded, he went down to Hurstbourne Park in Hampshire, and on 15 and 16 October 1777, assisted by William Mann Godschall, he compiled a Catalogue, preserved in the Keynes MSS at King's College, Cambridge. Later in the month between the 20th and the 26th he returned to make a closer examination of some of the mathematical papers, and to explore other parts of the collection. Evidently, he intended to print portions of the deposit, for he interpolated slips of paper among the manuscripts which he inspected, assessing their fitness for publication. On 9 July 1778 he presented a report on the documents to the Council of the Royal Society. The basis of this was a selective list of nine of the most important items.

First among these was a large fragment of a work on geometry, containing 'a very learned discourse upon the origin, the object & the progress of that science, observations on the works of the Greek geometers and an essay towards the restitution of Euclid's prisms'. Second, a discourse on prisms, which the compiler took to be part of Newton's great work on geometry. Third, a discourse showing the greater brevity of the geometric over the algebraic method in solving problems. Fourth, a paper entitled 'Regula Fratrum', embodying a rule for conducting algebraical computations in ambiguous cases already given in the published *Arithmetica Universalis* (1707), but recommended for printing on account of its elegant examples. The fifth item was a letter to Dr David Gregory, describing Newton's method of finding the roots of equations by sliding-rules; the sixth, correspondence between Newton and Gregory, establishing the claim of the former to be the inventor of the quadrature of binomial curves over that of the latter. The seventh was a third letter to Dr Oldenburgh, giving Newton's opinions on the division of angles and the possibility of a quadrature of the circle. Item eight was a construction of equations above the fourth degree by a eulical parabola; nine a fragment of a geometrical treatise on the principles of fluxions. The Council resolved 'that the printing of these papers may be of great use to Science and that their thanks be returned to the Earl of Portsmouth, for his obliging and liberal communication of them'.[23] The failure to thank Horsley must have seemed pointed.

When Horsley's long premeditated Latin edition of Newton's works, the *Opera Omnia*, appeared in five volumes during the years 1779–85, it drew to

---

[23] RS Minutes of Council, vi, fos. 346–50, from which the foregoing report is taken.

but a limited extent on the Portsmouth collection. Certain texts previously derived from copies, notably that of the *Geometrica Analytica*, were improved by collation with the manuscript, and selections from Newton's correspondence with Oldenburgh were imported into the fourth volume, but the original plan of the edition was not radically changed. By his rejection of material which modern scholars have judged valuable, Horsley laid himself open to a charge of myopia,[24] but has been defended on the grounds that the discovery of the Hurstbourne material came too late to permit of its evaluation in time for inclusion in an edition which had already been advertised to subscribers.[25] This is probably true, though, if Horsley had been more single-minded in his vocation, he could have pressed steadily on with the task in successive publications. A more convincing *apologia* is that contemporary opinion was ill-equipped to appreciate the value of the technical parts of Lord Portsmouth's papers. More than a hundred years later a catalogue of the manuscripts produced by a Cambridge University syndicate attracted minimal attention from scholars, and it was not until historians began to appreciate the value of the study of manuscripts as a means of arriving at exact knowledge that the importance of the unpublished papers was admitted. Horsley's book competently fulfilled the demand, as it was understood in the eighteenth century, for an accurate compendium of Newton's basic writings,[26] and his Catalogue remains, in the words of a modern authority, 'invaluable as a check on the not wholly productive efforts of later cataloguers'.[27] His contribution to mathematical scholarship, if not outstandingly original, was important, and Brougham's later dismissal of him as 'a mere amateur, and a somewhat feeble amateur in all essentials' and of his edition of Newton as being 'as signal a failure as any on record in the history of science',[28] is as superficial as it is unkind.

A portion of Newton's writings which Horsley is said to have shunned is that concerned with religion. The belief stems, no doubt, from the contrast between the manifest orthodoxy of the latter and the former's rejection of the Trinity. Lord Keynes recounts how when Horsley was asked to inspect a box of Newton's papers 'on esoteric and religious matters', he 'saw the contents with horror and slammed the lid'. But the story has been shown to be apocryphal. Horsley studied certain of the theological papers at Hurstbourne, and probably helped Charles Hutton to pinpoint the location of this material for his *Mathematical and Philosophical Dictionary*.[29] It is likely that his familiarity with Newton's interests in biblical criticism, shown in the papers, as well

[24] Whiteside (ed.), *Newton*, vii. 691.
[25] Ibid. i, p. xxvi.
[26] Ibid., pp. xxvii–xxviii, xxxii–xxxiii.
[27] Ibid., p. xxvi.
[28] *Lives of Men of Science*, quoted in C. R. Weld, *History of the Royal Society* (1848), 166–7.
[29] Whiteside (ed.), *Newton*, i, pp. xxvi (n. 32), xxvii, xxviii (n. 35).

as with the latter's published *Observations upon the Prophecies of Daniel, and the Apocalypse of St. John*, did much to stimulate his own exertions as a critic of the Bible and as a student of Old and New Testament prophecy later in his life.

The Newton project and the secretaryship of the Royal Society placed the Horsley of the 1770s at the centre of the intellectual landscape of an age which historians of ideas, notwithstanding certain reservations, have learned to label 'the English Enlightenment', for as John Gascoigne has observed, veneration for Newton was the hallmark of that phenomenon.[30] In explaining the survival of Newton's reputation so long after his death, historians such as Margaret Jacob[31] and Gascoigne have lately emphasized the use of his ideas made by Latitudinarian divines to strengthen their appeal to natural theology based on the argument from design. But Anita Guerrini's study of a circle of Tory and High Church Newtonians in Edinburgh and Oxford at the end of the seventeenth century and the beginning of the eighteenth has questioned whether 'Newtonianism' was a coherent ideology outside the realm of science. The seminal importance of Newton's contributions to the methods of science and the content of scientific knowledge made him appear as all things to all men.[32] Horsley's case strengthens this view. There is no observable connection between his decision to edit the works of Newton and his own affiliations in religion and politics, which were High Church. He shouldered the burden partly for the sake of science itself and partly to build up his own reputation. The treatise on the solar system[33] nevertheless won him a position in the more popular theological Newtonianism dating back to the Boyle lecturers, Bentley and Derham, which was less closely related to Newton's texts[34] and served mainly to cement the 'holy alliance' of science and religion that distinguished the English Enlightenment from its Continental counterpart.

At his prime, moreover, Horsley was not devoid of liberality in other branches of learning. He took a scientific attitude to the study of history. This showed itself as early as 1770, when, while still a tutor at Christ Church, he mapped out a programme of study for his stepbrother George, then a civil servant of the East India Company at Bombay, who was eager to improve his mind. In a long letter preserved in the Bodleian Library he warned him:

The mere knowledge of the facts of history & its dates, where such a prince was born, what Bishop crowned him, what lady he married, who poisoned him, & when and how,

---

[30] J. L. Gascoigne, *Cambridge in the Age of the Enlightenment* (Cambridge, 1989), 147.

[31] M. Jacob, *The Newtonians and the English Revolution, 1689–1720* (New York, 1976).

[32] A. Guerrini, 'The Tory Newtonians: Gregory, Pitcairne and their Circle', *Journal of British Studies*, 25 (1986), 288–311.

[33] See above, p. 38.

[34] For the diversities in Newton's following see R. E. Schofield, *Mechanism and Materialism: British Natural Philosophy in an Age of Reason* (Princeton, 1970).

is a very useless and contemptible pursuit. To make history a rational and manly study, it must have reference either to politicks or philosophy; & for this reason it must begin from the very beginning of things. At least a man should have some general knowledge of antient times before he comes to modern history.

This was fourteen years before the German critic Herder started to publish the *Ideen zur Philosophie der Geschichte der Menschheit* tracing an ascending process of civilization in the history of the nations. It was into such a pattern of progress that Horsley fitted the historical influence of Christianity. His brother was told to:

observe that the very great difference between the Christian religion & the superstitions of former ages has made the state of the human mind in countries equally civilized & in other respects similarly circumstanced very different in the ages that preceded Christ & those that have followed his nativity.

The period from Constantine the Great to the extinction of the Western Empire was 'highly interesting' to us 'because the decline of the Roman Empire was the beginning of things as they now are'. It was totally neglected, because it lacked a stylist such as Livy or Tacitus to record it. Gibbon had not yet started to publish the *Decline and Fall*. To those who knew Latin, Sigonius' *De Imperio Occidentali* was to be recommended, but it would be 'proper to know something of the Eastern Emperors that fall within this period'.

Samuel Horsley's own chosen field of historical writing—modern history which then included the medieval period—established a link with the most celebrated of the French *philosophes*. Before he became involved in the scientific work of the Royal Society, his chief preoccupation was with editing 'Mr. Voltaire's essay upon general history from Charlemagne to the present time'. He declared that he knew 'no book so proper to be put into the hands of beginners as a clue to direct their enquiries if it were cleared of some gross mistakes'. The critical brain, much more contemptuous of the 'lamentable labours of our Lawrence Echard & the continuators of his wretched work', revealed in 1770 no trace of the conservative, ecclesiastical sentiments which affected his later career. He agreed with his brother's strictures on the Oxford style of education, in Latin and Greek languages with 'a little school divinity', remarking: 'it is certainly calculated to form a monk, not a gentleman, a statesman, a philosopher or a merchant.' His interpretation of the history of Italy in the medieval period, which he thought should begin with Sigonius' *De Regno Italia* was libertarian in spirit, showing sympathy not with the papacy but with 'the great and generous efforts of the Italian republics for the recovery of their liberty & independence'.[35]

---

[35] Bodl. Engl. Misc. *c*.690, W. J. Palmer Correspondence 1794–1852, fos. 44–7, S. to G. Horsley, 20 Feb. 1770.

Horsley's career as an academician reached its close before the first volume of his 'Newton' issued from the press. At the anniversary meeting of the Royal Society on 30 November 1778 he relinquished the secretaryship, and his name was immediately dropped from the Council.[36] His displacement after so short a tenure cannot have been unattended by resentment. It accompanied a change in the presidency, when, partly to regain royal favour, after an embarrassing dispute with George III about the shape of lightning conductors, Sir John Pringle retired, and was replaced by Joseph Banks, a friend of the king. Banks was only 35 years of age, ten years younger than Horsley. A wealthy landowner, who had accompanied Phipps and Cook on voyages of exploration, he was a student of natural history, a discipline hitherto less cultivated in the Royal Society than mathematics and astronomy,[37] but encouraged by 'the growing fashionableness of agricultural improvement among the upper classes'.[38] It would not have been surprising if the prospective editor of Newton's works had resigned in a huff, even if he had not been ousted. After his retirement the Council and its new officers continued to treat him with the same cold correctness as before. In June 1779 he was allowed to borrow again the two-foot reflecting telescope, but only 'on giving the usual receipt'.[39] In January 1781 he wrote privately to Banks in anticipation of an official application to borrow certain manuscripts of Sir Isaac Newton from the Society and for leave for Basire to engrave two drawings, his intention being not to delay the printing of his edition of Newton's works. Banks's reply was polite but guarded. He saw no reason why the manuscripts should not be lent, 'but must enquire into precedents, and follow them'. As a 'a well-wisher of his work', he would 'give all the assistance he can with propriety'.[40]

Banks was an energetic, honest, and successful president, but the tight rein on which he ran the Society induced a rebellion which gave Samuel Horsley a brief opportunity to stage a come-back. The explosion burst on 20 November 1783, when Council under pressure from Banks passed a resolution forcing the resignation of Dr Charles Hutton, professor of mathematics at Woolwich Military Academy, from the office of the Society's foreign secretary.[41] This action was not wholly unwarranted, for complaints of neglecting correspondence had been received against him from abroad.[42] Unable to defend himself in Council, Hutton appealed to the Society at large, where his friends gathered majorities at two successive general meetings in favour of thanking

---

[36] *Record of the Royal Society*, 337, 342; RS Journal Book, xxix (1777–80), 289–90.
[37] Lyons, *Royal Society*, 193–4, 197–9.
[38] Gascoigne, *Cambridge*, 283.
[39] RS Minutes of Council, vi. 383.
[40] Dawson (ed.), *The Banks Letters*, 430.
[41] RS Minutes of Council, vi. 53a.
[42] RS Misc. i, fos. 28, 29, extract Bennet to Turton, 2 July 1783, Statement of Proceedings; Weld, *Royal Society*, 154–5.

him for his services and exonerating him from the charges. The second of these gatherings was packed with 'sympathetic strangers', of whom Samuel Horsley nominated two.[43] Horsley did not begin the agitation in support of his friend, but he quickly took charge of it, and turned it into an attack on the entire administration of the Royal Society during Banks's presidency, alleging infringement of chartered rights, interference with freedom of elections, and mismanagement of the Committee of Papers.[44]

His most active support was drawn from fellow mathematicians—Maskelyne, the Astronomer Royal, and Francis Maseres—who saw in the ousting of Hutton so much evidence that Banks cared nothing for mathematics and wished to replace it by natural history. There can be little doubt that a subject bias lay behind the controversy, for while Horsley and Maskelyne claimed that the glory of the Royal Society rested on mathematics, Banks replied: 'These gentlemen might easily be informed that however respectable Mathematics as a Science may be, it by no means can pretend to monopolise the praise due to learning. It is indeed little more than a tool with which other sciences are hew'd into form.'[45] The venom and vindictiveness with which the dispute was conducted have led others to conclude that Horsley's object was to oust Banks in order to take his place in the presidential chair. Historians of the Royal Society, notably Sir Henry Lyons and C. R. Weld, have blamed him for extending a quarrel which could have ended with the exoneration of Hutton.[46] This is scarcely just, for the president and Council had shown no disposition to compromise with the wishes of the majority in the general meeting, and there was, therefore, no means of procuring the reinstatement of the foreign secretary than by further pressurizing his opponents. Moreover the violence of the debate was not restricted to one side. Horsley had been repeatedly interrupted by calls for the question and the clattering of sticks when he attempted to state his evidence against Banks for the blackballing of prospective fellows.[47]

But he made serious errors which lost him the battle. One great mistake was when he foolishly allowed himself to be provoked by a sneer of Lord Mulgrave (formerly Captain Phipps) into threatening to lead a secession from the Society, describing the mace on the table as 'that toy'.[48] The day ended in a hands down victory for Banks, who won his vote of confidence by 119 votes to 42, and a muzzling resolution against the dissidents was carried.[49] Discountenanced by the general meeting of the fellows, the malcontents appealed

[43] RS Misc. i, fo. 42, 27 Nov. 1783; Journal Book, xxxi (1782–5), fos. 265, 268–9, minutes of general meetings, 11–18 Dec. 1783.
[44] Weld, *Royal Society*, 160.
[45] RS Misc. i, fo. 46a.
[46] Lyons, *Royal Society*, 213; Weld, *Royal Society*, 160–1.
[47] *An Authentic Narrative of the Dissentions and Debates in the Royal Society* (1784), 55–60.
[48] Ibid. 64–6.
[49] RS Journal Book, xxxi, fos. 270–1.

to public opinion. In March 1784 they published an anonymous pamphlet, *An Authentic Narrative of the Dissentions and Debates in the Royal Society*. This was a capital error, certain to alienate scholars by challenging their competence to regulate their corporate affairs. When on 25 March Maty tried to present this volume, packed with the speeches of himself, Horsley, Maskelyne, and others to the Royal Society, the initiative resulted in their utter discomfiture and a complete and lasting triumph for the president, who was allowed to propose his own candidate for the Society's secretaryship in place of Maty.[50] It marked the irreversible end of Horsley's career in the Royal Society.

[50] For various pieces of evidence of the Royal Society meeting on 25 Mar. 1784 see RS Journal Book, xxxi. 371–2, 409–10; Weld, *Royal Society*, 165; and RS Misc. i, fo. 46a.

CHURCH HOUSE LIBRARY
ECTON HOUSE
NORTHAMPTON NN6 0QE

BOOK No _ _ _ _ _ _ _ _ _

CLASS No _ _ _ _ _ _ _ _ _

DATE added _ _ _ _ _ _ _ _

4

An Image Refashioned!
Defender of the Faith

IT was to be expected that contemporaries would interpret the conflict in the Royal Society in terms of the political battle in the House of Commons which so nearly coincided with it, for in both a leader deep in the confidence of the king was fighting for his authority against a challenge from below. Dr Lort, a prebendary of St Paul's cathedral, observed that the opposition in that learned body, of which he believed Horsley to be the head, stemmed 'merely from that levelling spirit and impatience of all government which infects the present age'.[1] It was a curious setting for a man who was to become known to his critics as one of 'three reactionary intellectuals' preferred to bishoprics by the Younger Pitt.[2] A narrowing of his outlook to conservative, ecclesiastical matters was apparent by 1787 to his liberal-minded friend William Windham, who found it repellent.[3]

Professor W. R. Ward has written of 'a new harshness' injected into the religious scene in the reign of George III, as 'many independent politicians' and vested interests long in opposition, threatened by the innovative forces of the time, 'threw in their lot with the court'.[4] This furnished part of the explanation of the change in Horsley, but with him, as with certain Roman Catholic devotees of the European Enlightenment in its early stages,[5] the rapid growth in the pace of ideas, encroaching upon inherited religious convictions (which were thus forced to develop a hard protective crust), counted for much more.

The transformation went back to the restructuring of his career in the later 1770s, when, as his commitments to the Royal Society slackened, promotion in the Church started to come his way. Robert Lowth, on becoming bishop of London in 1777, appointed him to be his domestic chaplain. Four years later he made him archdeacon of St Albans.[6] Horsley's attachment to the Church was never free from self. In March 1782, when Lord North's Government was slipping from power, he asked for ministerial help to obtain the master-

---

[1] C. R. Weld, *History of the Royal Society* (1848), 169.
[2] J. C. D. Clark, *English Society 1688–1832* (Cambridge, 1985), 230.
[3] Jebb, 32.
[4] W. R. Ward, *Religion and Society in England 1790–1850* (1972), 21.
[5] See below, pp. 308–9.
[6] *DNB* xxvii (1891), 383–6.

ship of the Temple, and though this was refused,[7] he succeeded in obtaining from Lowth the prebend of Cadington Major in St Paul's cathedral in August 1783.[8] The principal consequence of his changed position, however, was not that his private interest was tied to the Church but that his public duties came to include responsibility for instructing the clergy in doctrine. This turned his combative mind into theological channels, unleashing it upon the main religious controversies of the day. Preaching as bishop's chaplain in St Paul's cathedral on Good Friday 1778, he proclaimed in forthright terms the mystery of redemption, and ventured to correct, charitably but firmly, the excesses of the Calvinistic Evangelicals on the one hand and those of the Rational Dissenters on the other. Arbitrary predestination and philosophical necessity fell alike under the hammer in a bid to assert the case for a Providence working through moral choice.[9] This teaching was High Church in the sense that it was in line with the emphasis of the best of the seventeenth-century Caroline divines from Hammond and Richard Montague to Beveridge and Bull, on free grace,[10] but its chief current significance in the evolution of Samuel Horsley's religious outlook was that it marked his first open breach with the Enlightenment. The thrust of his attack was on predestinarians 'versed in Physics', a reference to Joseph Priestley, whose *Doctrine of Philosophical Necessity Illustrated*, published in the previous year, followed in the steps of David Hartley, the mid eighteenth-century psychologist who applied the science of Isaac Newton to the working of the human mind, physiologically understood and determined.[11] Devoted though he remained to Newton's mathematics, Horsley was never a consistent Newtonian. He drew back abruptly when science started to encroach on the freedom of God's dealings with the soul.

Later developments induced in Horsley a more dogmatic and distinct High Churchmanship. After loss of office in the Royal Society he found intellectual satisfaction in the literary circle of Dr Samuel Johnson. He was on visiting terms with Johnson as early as March 1782,[12] and afterwards joined the select conversational club which the Doctor established in December 1783 to meet three times a week at the Essex Head tavern off the Strand. Johnson's clubs transcended party. He formed them to obtain the psychological help of challenging company, and while he assured Goldsmith of his belief that those who disagreed upon a capital point could yet live in friendship together,[13] the divisions themselves were sharp. Horsley was sometimes called on to mediate

---

[7] BL Add. MSS 38,309, Liverpool MSS, fo. 47, Jenkinson to Horsley, 20 Mar. 1782.

[8] G. Hennessy, *Novum Repertorium Ecclesiasticum Parochiale Londiniense* (1898), 18.

[9] Horsley, *Providence and Free Agency: A Sermon Preached April 17th 1778* (1778).

[10] P. E. More and F. L. Cross, *Anglicanism* (1962), 307–16.

[11] Basil Willey, *The Eighteenth Century Background* (1946), 136–54, 178–81.

[12] G. B. Hill, *Johnsonian Miscellanies* (Oxford, 1897), i. 106–7.

[13] W. Jackson Bate, *Samuel Johnson* (1978), 200 n., 366, 584; G. B. Hill (ed.), *Boswell's Life of Johnson*, iv (Oxford, 1934), 254.

between conflicting views of divinity. Samuel Parr, an advanced Whig Latitudinarian, tells of a debate he held with Johnson on the origin of evil: 'It called forth all the powers of our minds. No two tigers ever grappled with more fury; but we never lost sight of good manners. There was no Boswell present to detail our conversations. Sir, he would not have understood it. And then, Sir, who do you think was the umpire between us? That fiend Horsley.'[14] Entry into the Johnsonian fellowship helped the latter to sustain friendly contacts with other Foxite Whigs. He enjoyed a peculiar intimacy with William Windham, with whom he shared mathematical and other scholarly interests.[15] But it was with Johnson himself that he most nearly coincided in religion, and the evolution of his opinions may have been assisted by contact with the Doctor's loyal old-fashioned Tory Anglicanism, for the two men were very close.[16]

The event which did most to prompt the evolution of Horsley's opinions, however, and to stimulate the growth of a High Church theology during the decade was the Trinitarian controversy with Priestley (1783–90). This was a largely unexpected occurrence. The doctrine of the Trinity, though fundamental to the Thirty-Nine Articles and the Creeds, had been under attack in England for about a hundred years, first by the Socinianism vigorously propagated in the latter half of the seventeenth century and later by the followers of the advanced Latitudinarian cleric Samuel Clarke, whose *Scripture Doctrine of the Trinity* published in 1712 adopted an Arian position.[17] Clarke was answered in 1719–23 by Waterland but, although the controversy simmered for the rest of the century, the traditional position was progressively undermined by the eighteenth-century retreat from the appeal to antiquity, as Scripture interpreted by human reason alone was not considered a sufficient proof of the Athanasian construction. Even among those who professed to be orthodox themselves, a generous tolerance of the views of those of a different opinion came, as Sykes insisted,[18] to be observed.

The return to stringency in the 1780s was signalled by the imparting of a new depth to the controversy, as the doctrine of the Trinity became the touchstone of the teaching authority of the Anglican Church and of its standing in the community. Priestley sounded the call to battle in a book entitled *A History of the Corruptions of Christianity*, published in 1782. In it he aimed on the one hand to rescue the Christian religion from the sneers of

---

[14] W. Derry, *Dr. Parr* (Oxford, 1966), 174.

[15] Jebb, 29–32; Sir L. Namier and J. Brooke, *The History of Parliament: The House of Commons, 1754–1790* (1964), iii. 648–50.

[16] Parr, when approached to write an epitaph of Johnson, suggested that William Scott and Bishop Horsley might be approached with greater propriety on account of their greater intimacy with Johnson. Derry, *Dr. Parr*, 170.

[17] Norman Sykes, *From Seldon to Secker* (Cambridge, 1959), 165–7.

[18] Norman Sykes, *Church and State in England in the Eighteenth Century* (Cambridge, 1934), 348.

fashionable unbelief which he had encountered on his visit to Paris in 1774 and in Lord Shelburne's circle[19] by showing that the objects of attack were not part of the true and original Christian faith, but were introduced into it in the early Christian centuries by admixture with a different culture. There can be little doubt, however, that he was also deeply concerned to subvert the English Established Church from within by undermining the credibility of her formularies and practices. The method pursued in this well-documented two-volume work was historical. All aspects of the Catholic religion, which had survived in the post-Reformation Protestant churches, were treated as corruptions of the primitive faith. This thesis was applied in turn to the history of opinions regarding saints and angels, the condition of the departed, and the doctrine of the Lord's Supper, but the first part, dealing with the evolution of Christian teaching about the person of Christ was the one which attracted most attention. In it Priestley argued that the faith of the apostolic Church was Unitarian but that, responding to Platonic influences, Christian thinkers of the second and third centuries AD began to attach a separate divinity to Christ by personifying the Logos, originally no more than an attribute of the single Godhead. It was not, however, until the Council of Nicaea in AD 325 that the supremacy of the Father over the Son was abandoned, and a full Trinitarian belief accepted. The practical implications of the theme were pressed home in the General Conclusion, which threw down a challenge both to 'unbelievers', especially Edward Gibbon, the sceptical historian of the Roman Empire, who was taken to task for reprobating Christianity in general instead of discriminating between the genuine article and its corruption, and to the advocates for the present civil establishments of Christianity, notably Bishop Hurd of Worcester, a stiff and orthodox prelate, high in the royal favour, who had been publishing his sermons preached at Lincoln's Inn.[20] The bishops were exhorted to take in hand the relief of those of their clergy who were 'distressed with the obligation to subscribe what they cannot believe, and to recite what they utterly condemn'.[21]

Within the Established Church morale was sufficiently low to render an authoritative reply imperatively necessary. As Professor G. F. A. Best has observed: 'By the end of the War of American Independence, the people who mattered in English church and state were becoming aware that the structure and quality of their society were undergoing drastic change: change mainly, they feared, for the worse.'[22] Bishop Hurd wrote in November 1781: 'There is a madness among us that threatens to be universal, especially if this war

---

[19] Rutt (ed.), *Priestley*, i. 1, Memoirs, 198–9; cf. Willey, *Eighteenth Century Background*, 171.

[20] *Sermons Preached at Lincolns Inn between the Years 1765 and 1776 ... By Richard Hurd, D. D., Bishop of Lichfield and Coventry* (1785); cf. C. J. Abbey, *The English Church and its Bishops, 1700–1800* (1887), ii. 223–6.

[21] J. Priestley, *An History of the Corruptions of Christianity* (Birmingham, 1782), i. 467–8.

[22] G. F. A. Best, *Temporal Pillars* (Cambridge, 1964), 137.

continues. The state of the Church I could weep over, if tears would do any good.'[23] The reasons for the unease were broad and social, related to the upsurge of agitation and riot which occurred in a defeated and demoralized country experiencing the distortions of fundamental economic change. But Priestley in his treatise had touched a nerve where churchmen in particular were sensitive—the withdrawal of unorthodox clergy from the Established Church after Parliament's rejection of the Feathers Tavern petition. Priestley played this up in his *History*, claiming that in the last six months he had heard of five fresh instances of clergymen who had abandoned their prospects in the Church of England on account of becoming Unitarians.[24]

Samuel Horsley's answer to Priestley in his visitation charge to the clergy of the archdeaconry of St Albans, delivered on 22 May 1783 and published later in the year,[25] was to some extent a bid to steady the clergy and to arrest the drain. Scholarly and polemical, though wanting in original merit, it was well designed to achieve its end. The author's theological exposition proceeded in three stages. The first was an ostensibly convincing demonstration that his opponent's use of Scripture and patristic writings, notably those of Athanasius, Epiphanius, Origen, Eusebius, and others, to prove that the faith of the earliest Christians was Unitarian, was based on unnatural constructions and improbable inferences. The argument of the second was that the Platonic concept of the Three Principles was much older than Platonism, and was found in other branches of pagan religion, such as the Persian and Chaldean theology and 'the Roman superstition in a very late age'. It was thus to be regarded not as a corrupting influence on Christianity but as a primitive and independent revelation of the divine. The case was weakened by the admission that an early popular belief in a trinity featured 'even in the abominable rites of idolatrous worship'. In the third section, however, combating the notion that the post-apostolic Christians became Arians, Horsley scored a notable point from Priestley by turning the evidence of Athenagorus, which the latter had cited, against him.

The charge triggered a controversy which occupied the presses intermittently for six years. This was to do more than anything else to raise Horsley to the status of a national figure, but paradoxically he did not seek it. When in the autumn of 1783 the Unitarian leader replied to the charge in his *Letters to Dr. Horsley*, inviting the latter to enter into controversy with him, the response, published in the following summer, was a crushing rebuff:

When at the request of the clergy of my archdeaconry, I published the discourse, in which I had given them my thoughts of your late attack on the doctrine of the Trinity,

[23] F. Kilvert (ed.), *Memoirs of the Life and Writings of Richard Hurd* (1860), 144: Worcester to Balguy, 13 Nov. 1781.
[24] J. Priestley, *An History of the Corruptions of Christianity* (Birmingham, 1782), i. 469 n.
[25] Horsley, *St Albans Charge 1783* (1783).

it was not at all my intention to open a regular controversy with you upon the subject. I cannot think that you have redde [*sic*] my publication with so little discernment, as not to perceive in it a design of quite another kind, which yet, I fear, I shall find it difficult to avow in explicit terms, without giving an offence, which, were it possible, I would avoid.... My attack ... was not so much upon the opinions which you maintain, however I may hold them in abhorrence, as upon the credit of your Narrative; and if I have succeeded in overthrowing that, which the judgment of the learned must decide, I am not at all obliged to go into new arguments upon the main question.[26]

The most charitable explanation of these remarks, which might otherwise seem to betray insufferable arrogance is that by 'the main question' he meant the theological question of the truth of the doctrine of the Trinity. Few could doubt that, as an archdeacon, he had the right, indeed the duty, to instruct his clergy in an article of belief judged necessary to salvation without justifying his teaching to a Nonconformist minister. Nevertheless, by devoting his charge to the review of a work claiming to be of historical scholarship and by afterwards publishing it, he had laid himself open to the obligation to see the academic argument through. This he accepted in practice, though with manifest re-luctance, for the treatise which contained his disclaimer took up substantive points made by his adversary in his *Letters* in a manner which showed that its author had no reason to fear further debate. It was Priestley, however, who continued to force the pace, revelling in the publicity. In the autumn of 1784 he published new *Letters*, indicting the archdeacon of St Albans with mis-representing his arguments, falsifying ancient history, and impugning the character of a Church Father. For nearly eighteen months Horsley did not reply, but then in quick succession came his sermon at St Mary, Newington at Christmas 1785 and his Remarks on Dr Priestley's *Second Letter* in the ensuing spring.[27] Priestley's riposte was out in Birmingham before the middle of June,[28] but it was not until 1789 that Horsley proclaimed his intention of winding up the controversy by republishing his previous contributions in a single volume, which, while it contained supplemental disquisitions answering Priestley's third set of letters, ostentatiously ignored his four-volume work on *Early Opinions concerning Christ*.[29]

Horsley's delays indicate that he had been hard pressed, forced to reread, to reconsider. H. H. Jebb's view that he 'completely vanquished Priestley', though widely accepted,[30] will not withstand a study of the literature. It echoes the extravagant claims advanced by the bishop's partisans after his death, claims which drove Thomas Belsham to redress the balance with a review of the controversy in 1811. How far it is from the truth is clear from

[26] *Letters from the Archdeacon of St. Albans in Reply to Dr Priestley* (1784), 1–2.
[27] Horsley, *Tracts in Controversy with Dr Priestley* (Gloucester, 1789), Preface, pp. viii–x.
[28] Rutt (ed.), *Priestley*, i. 1. 389.
[29] T. Belsham (ed.), *Priestley's Tracts in Controversy with Bishop Horsley* (1815).
[30] Jebb, 44–5; cf. J. H. Overton and F. Relton, *The English Church 1714–1800* (1906), 255.

the fact that at the end of the debate Priestley could instance eleven serious historical points[31] on which he claimed (not always with justice) to have received no satisfactory answer. Equally unwarranted is the dismissal of Horsley's scholarship by Priestley and his admirers. Priestley's indictment of his opponent: 'I appeal to all the learned world whether any man, pretending to scholarship, ever undertook the study of a question of literature less prepared for it, or acquitted himself so wretchedly in it',[32] may be treated as polemical. Elsewhere he admitted that it was not Horsley's ability and learning that he questioned so much as his ingenuousness;[33] to a friend he confessed: 'As I wish to be well guarded in what I say to this antagonist, I wish for your keenest eye over it.'[34]

A modern biographer of Priestley has written, however: 'Horsley did not attempt to answer Priestley's arguments or to assess the validity of the historical method. Instead, he set out to destroy the authority of Priestley's name which had risen high in the public esteem through what were now called "lucky" scientific discoveries.'[35] Nothing could be further from the truth. The judgement that Horsley evaded the main question between himself and Priestley cannot be sustained. The greater part of his published correspondence with him was devoted to strengthening his case that there was no significant change in the doctrines of the Church from apostolic times to the post-Nicene era. The interminable discussion of the authenticity of the Epistles of Irenaeus and Barnabas, of the veracity of Origen, of the meaning of the word 'idiotae' as used by Tertullian, of the antiquity of the Nazarenes and the Ebionites, of whether a church of Hebrew Christians existed at Aelia after the days of the Emperor Hadrian, far from being mere intellectual showmanship, derived from this same central purpose. Few scholars today would admit the validity of Horsley's contention. Priestley was right to claim that an important change in the Church's teaching regarding the person of Christ and the Trinity took place in the second and third centuries AD under Platonic influences, though not in portraying it as a corruption. W. H. C. Frend has lately shown that Christian Platonists of Alexandria, Clement and Origen, brought in Plato to support scriptural orthodoxy against the Gnostics.[36] Horsley displayed great ingenuity, unswerving self-confidence, and much erudition, testing the validity of Priestley's application of the historical method by a diligent comparison of patristic texts.[37] Hence, though

---

[31] Belsham (ed.), *Priestley's Tracts*, 472–83: Second Letter to the Bishops.

[32] Ibid., pp. iii–viii.

[33] Priestley, *Letters to Dr Horne, Dean of Canterbury* (Birmingham, 1787), 4.

[34] Rutt (ed.), *Priestley*, ii. 47–8, Priestley to Belsham, 4 Dec. 1789.

[35] F. W. Gibbs, *Joseph Priestley: Adventurer in Science and Champion of Truth* (1965), 172.

[36] W. H. C. Frend, *The Rise of Christianity* (1984), 368–81.

[37] For example the Greek and Latin texts of the Epistle of Barnabas, his purpose being to rebut Priestley's allegation that the orthodox passages had been interpolated. Horsley, *Remarks on Dr Priestley's Second Letter to the Archdeacon of St. Albans* (1786), 6–8.

he was no more successful than his predecessors in resting the doctrine of the Trinity on Scripture, and did not even attempt to do so, he re-established the case for Trinitarian orthodoxy on a reputable scholarly foundation, and was hailed as victor by a receptive Anglican clientele bent on backlash against a century of doctrinal innovation.

A feature of the dispute which has generally escaped notice is its contribution to the revival of a positive High Church theology. This was of two kinds. Firstly the argument, because it was historical in character, restored the appeal to tradition as an arbiter of belief. Both sides were compelled to cite pre-Nicene patristic texts in their support. Samuel Horsley was not himself a distinguished student of the Fathers. He relied heavily upon evidence about them drawn from secondary sources—on Bishop Bull's *Defensio Fidei Nicenae* (1685) and J. L. Von Mosheim's *De Rebus Christianorum ante Constantinum* (1753). But the dispute with Priestley quickened an interest in ecclesiastical history, which developed from a sense of the importance of the later Roman period in European history present in his mind in 1770, and led him to commend it to others. His charge to the clergy of St Albans (1783), in which he opened the attack, contained an exhortation 'to the younger members of the priesthood' to read not only Bull, but the ecclesiastical historians Eusebius, Socrates 'Scholasticus', Sozomen, and Theodoret. 'From ecclesiastical history', he added, 'the student learns what the faith of the church hath at all times been; and he is enabled to separate the pure doctrine of the first age from all later innovations: a matter at all times of the highest moment; but of particular importance in the present juncture, when the whole opinion and learning of the Unitarian party is exerted, to wrench from us the argument from tradition.'[38] Horsley's message was taken by others. Horne acknowledged his influence, in the published version of a sermon preached in Canterbury cathedral on 1 July 1786 on the need to contend for the defence of Trinitarian churches 'by Scripture and history, reason and argument'.[39] Bishop Cleaver's book-list, printed in 1791 for the use of younger clergy and divinity students in the diocese of Chester, was prefaced by an exhortation to the study of the 'earliest Fathers'.[40] It was in this climate that Martin Routh, a young fellow of Magdalen College, Oxford, where Horne was president, turned from editing classical texts to plan a collection of patristic writings, which, when it began to appear twenty-six years later, won international repute as the *Reliquae Sacrae*.[41]

Secondly the debate was important because it provided Horsley with the opportunity to proclaim his attachment to the High Church doctrine of apostolic succession of the ministry. The occasion arose when Priestley

---

[38] Horsley, *St. Albans Charge 1783*.
[39] G. Horne, *The Duty of Contending for the Faith* (Oxford, 1786).
[40] W. Cleaver, *List of Books* (Oxford, Chester, and Manchester, 1791).
[41] R. D. Middleton, *Dr. Routh* (Oxford, 1938), 104–16.

in *Letters*, replying to the initial attack upon him, took exception to the archdeacon's use of the term 'conventicle' to describe the chapels where he and his fellow Unitarians officiated, riposting that 'our places of worship are as legal as yours'.[42] This claim had a certain validity now that Parliament in 1779 had removed the obligation of Dissenting pastors to subscribe the doctrinal parts of the Thirty-Nine Articles imposed by the Toleration Act. Horsley, in redefining his position, was obliged to take higher ground. His Letters of 1784 explained that it was Priestley's 'spiritual authority', not 'the authority which derives from human law', that he wished to question. His antagonist was heavily asked to:

bear with the prejudices of a churchman, who, when he reviews the practice of the primitive ages; when he ponders Our Saviour's parting promise to be always present with the Apostles, . . . when he connects it with the history of the first ordinations, and with the great stress laid upon the bishop's authority, by Clemens, the fellow labourer of St. Paul, by Ignatius, the disciple of St. John, and by the whole church for many ages allows himself to be easily persuaded, that the authority of the commission, under which he acts, is something more than meer [*sic*] human legislation can convey.[43]

However long he may have held these opinions, the curtailment of the legal privileges of the Church of England had brought them to the front of his mind, but so, as he confessed in the tract taking leave of the Trinitarian controversy, had his thoughts on 'the various disorders and distractions, which I had seen in my own country within the compass of my own life arising from the irregular zeal of self constituted teachers of religion'. His further remarks went on to show that the weapon which he had employed against Priestley had been girded in the conflict with teachers of a different kind from the learned Socinian Doctor—those who had 'torn' the unity of the Church, disturbed 'tender consciences' with 'groundless scruples', and driven 'melancholy tempers' to 'insanity', who had abused 'the simplicity of the vulgar', and from whose exertions 'the state hath lately been endangered, and the protestant cause disgraced, by a combination of wild fanatics, pretending to associate for the preservation of the reformed religion'.[44] These allusions to Methodism, Evangelicalism, and the recent Gordon riots point to a social factor as well as a political one, in the evolution of Horsley's theological opinions, but both were inseparable from the spiritual. Priestley was warned that 'true religion' had itself been injured 'by attempts to inflame devotion on the one hand, and by theories fabricated to reduce the mystery of its doctrines on the other'. [45] Hence the need of a criterion to distinguish good from bad teachers of

---

[42] J. Priestley, *Letters to Dr. Horsley in Answer to his Animadversions on the History of the Corruptions of Christianity* (Birmingham, 1783).
[43] Horsley, *Tracts*, 291–4: Seventeenth Letter to Dr Priestley, entitled 'The Archdeacon Takes Leave of the Controversy', 15 June 1784.
[44] Ibid.
[45] Ibid.

religion. Glimpses of a receding liberality may be snatched from his deduction
in 1784: 'I lean the more to the opinion that the commission of a ministry,
perpetuated by regular succession, is something more than a dream of
cloystered gownsmen, or a tale imposed upon the vulgar to serve the ends of
avarice and ambition.'[46]

In the second half of the decade the pace of the Trinitarian controversy
quickened, as other orthodox churchmen began to rally behind the archdeacon in defence of the Established faith. Bishop Hurd, the king's favourite,
was one of the first to praise him.[47] On Trinity Sunday 1786 the dean of
Canterbury (Horne) delivered in his cathedral an eloquent devotional discourse on 'the Trinity in unity', exhorting the congregation 'to serve, worship
and adore, Father, Son, and Holy Ghost, as the only true and living God'.
Some weeks later, preaching at the primary visitation of Archbishop Moore he
alluded darkly to Priestley's prophecies of the impending fall of Trinitarian
churches. A footnote to the published version paid tribute to Dr Horsley to
whom 'the thanks of the Church of England' were due 'for his sensible,
learned and judicious writings in her defence'.[48] One of the preachers of the
King's Chapel in Whitehall, William Purkis, devoted his Commencement
Sunday sermon in Cambridge on 2 July 1786 to the text from Colossians 2. 8:
'Beware lest any man spoil you through philosophy and vain deceit, after the
tradition of men, after the rudiments of the world, and not after Christ.'[49]
Printed copies were presented to bishops and other great men.

This drove Priestley to his boldest defiance yet. In the following year
he published *Letters* to candidates for ordination studying at Oxford and
Cambridge, urging them to petition Parliament for the removal of compulsory
subscription to articles of belief and for a reform of the liturgy, and in default
of this to renounce their matriculation subscription and to throw up their
careers. He added offensively: 'if you are sensible that they ought not to bow
down and worship Mary, on the authority of the church of Rome, neither
ought you to worship the Son of Mary on the authority of the church of
England.'[50] This insolence caused the Anglican counter-offensive to intensify
greatly. The threat to the allegiance of entrants to the Church's ministry was
taken particularly seriously. An anonymous reply to Priestley's *Letters* was
published in 1787 from 'An Undergraduate', though Lindsey ascribed it to
the president of Magdalen.[51] There was an address on the subject in the same
year in the popular style later associated with Jones of Nayland by 'One who is

[46] Ibid.
[47] Kilvert (ed.), *Hurd*, 15: Hurd to Balguy, 19 Oct. 1784.
[48] Horne, *Contending for the Faith*.
[49] W. Purkis, *The Influence of the Present Pursuits in Learning...* (Cambridge, 1786).
[50] J. Priestley, *Letters to Dr. Horne... to the Young Men who are in Course of Education at the Universities...* (Birmingham, 1787).
[51] *Letter to Dr Priestley...* (Oxford 1787); see MS note on flyleaf of copy held by Dr Williams's Library.

not LL.D., F.R.S., Ac. Imp., Petrop. R. Paris, Helm. Taurin, Aurel Med. Paris, Harlem, Cantab., America et Phil. Socius; but a Country Parson'.[52] Other men of note who plunged into the Trinitarian controversy at that time included John Parkhurst, the learned Hutchinsonian Hebraist, and Pretyman, bishop of Lincoln. Two Roman Catholic apologists, Geddes and Barnard, also took up the cudgels with Priestley, but the phalanx arrayed against him consisted mainly of High Churchmen of various kinds, finding a new identity in the cause and looking to Samuel Horsley as an example. The campaign brought him to the acme of his career. Though the Unitarianism which he had combated had revolutionary implications for the State, the influences which told in his favour were more ecclesiastical than political. He owed his preferment first to a prebend in Gloucester cathedral on 19 April 1787, and in the following year to the bishopric of St Davids, primarily to Lord Chancellor Thurlow, who had been much taken with his *Letters* to Dr Priestley, and had observed that 'those who defended the Church, ought to be supported by the Church'.[53] But another powerful influence working for him in the closet was that of Richard Hurd, bishop of Worcester, who had marked him out for distinction as early as October 1784, along with Travis, the author of a reply to Gibbon's *Decline and Fall of the Roman Empire*, on the grounds of their services to the restatement of 'old truths'. As one whose views had been pilloried by Priestley in the *Corruptions*, Hurd had every personal reason to be grateful to Horsley, as well as a conviction that Church and State had been brought low by the perpetual obtrusion of 'old and new nonsense' on the public.[54]

Confirmation of the new bishop's election took place on 6 May 1788; five days later he was consecrated at Lambeth Palace by Archbishop Moore, assisted by Porteus, bishop of London, Hallifax, bishop of Gloucester—an old friend—and Edward Smallwell, bishop of Oxford.[55] A modestly endowed Welsh see, valued at £900 in 1762,[56] it was not among the glittering prizes of the Church. Its influence depended on what the tenant made of it. Nevertheless, distinguished churchmen had occupied it in the past, including the High Church William Laud and George Bull. Horsley's principles now stood in line of succession from theirs, and he was consumed by determination to put them into effect. It must be seen how well he succeeded.

---

[52] *Letter to the Rev. Dr. Priestley* (Bath, 1787).
[53] *Gent. Mag.* 76/2 (1806), 987–90.
[54] Kilvert (ed.), *Hurd*, 154: Hurd to Balguy, 19 Oct. 1784.
[55] LPL VB. 1/12, Archbishop's Act Book 1786–98, fos. 88–9.
[56] See below, p. 177 and n. 60.

5

The Church in Danger!

OUTSIDE a narrow ecclesiastical élite the controversy with Priestley had made little stir. The conservative *Critical Review* was slow to notice it, and when it did so, focused upon the debating styles of the opponents.[1] By contrast, in his early years at St Davids, the bishop moved to the centre of a national conflict, in which passions were aroused on either side. The issue turned on the limits of religious toleration which the Glorious Revolution had signally failed to define. Through the middle decades of the eighteenth century, English Dissenters had rested broadly satisfied with a compromise which gave them freedom to worship in their chapels, liberty to run schools, and a good deal of practical power at the local level while theoretically they were denied the full rights of citizenship by the operation of the Test and Corporation Acts. Acquiescence was never complete, and from the time of the Middlesex election crisis of 1768 a new restiveness started to carry them back into the camp of enemies of the Establishment which they had occupied until the 1730s. A recent study of electoral behaviour by Dr J. A. Phillips has discerned a long-term withdrawal of Dissenting support from administration candidates in parliamentary elections from 1768 onwards.[2] The first attack, which spanned the 1770s, was on the outworks of establishment–notably on compulsory subscription of the Thirty-Nine Articles at the English universities and on the requirement that Nonconformist ministers and schoolmasters should subscribe the doctrinal, as distinct from the governmental, articles. These were matters which concerned principally the Rational or anti-Trinitarian Dissenters rather then the Dissenting community as a whole, but as Dr Grayson Ditchfield has lately shown in a substantial and important article,[3] they provoked, together with sundry proposals directed against observance of national fasts and the financial interests of the Church of England, a controversy of sufficient moment to divide the Church, the universities, and Parliament, and to stimulate a revived debate over relations between Church and Dissent and the precise legal status of the latter.

Religious rebellion engendered new alignments on the conservative side during the period of Lord North's ministry. While the bishops in the House

---

[1] *Critical Review*, 62 (1786), 265–72.

[2] J. A. Phillips, *Electoral Behaviour in Unreformed England: Plungers, Splitters and Straights* (Princeton, 1982), 292 ff.

[3] G. M. Ditchfield, 'The Subscription Issue in British Parliamentary Politics 1772–79', *Parliamentary History*, 7.1 (1988), 45–80.

of Lords remained almost unanimously loyal to Church and Government in the divisions over the Dissenters' Relief Bills of 1772 and 1773, regardless of their theological convictions, a High Church minority developed in the Commons under the leadership of Sir Roger Newdigate, an old-style Tory of impeccable church principles sitting for the University of Oxford. From the spring of 1776 onwards a popular Anglicanism also took shape out of doors, as the London press filled with subscription lists of those anxious to alleviate 'the Distresses of the Clergy of the Church of England in North America'.[4] Thus, as Jonathan Clark has made us aware,[5] the assault of the Socinian Dissenters on the Anglican citadel, and the defensive reaction of the latter, were both inextricably interwoven with the main political struggles of the period.

The subscription controversy ended in 1779 in a compromise which satisfied neither side, and when the Nonconformists took up the cudgels again towards the end of the following decade, it was for extended objects and on a broader base. In December 1786 the wealthy laymen of the London Committee of Deputies of the Three Denominations formed a larger Committee to Conduct the Application to Parliament for the repeal of the Test and Corporation Acts.[6] This was not the appeal of a weak and underprivileged sect. In the second half of the eighteenth century Dissenters were holding 'office with hazard' in a large number of corporations, no longer circumventing the tests by occasional conformity but ignoring them with impunity. In an age when, in Paul Langford's phrase, religion 'was in some measure a matter of class',[7] the tests stood out not as the cause but as a badge of inferiority of an urban mercantile élite, separated from the court aristocracy by a gap which may have widened during George III's reign,[8] but was certainly rendered more intolerable by the growing wealth which the Industrial Revolution and the expanding network of overseas trade placed in its hands. The Younger Pitt's pursuit of 'Commonwealth' goals and of trading policies favourable to the middle classes supplied the immediate incentive to men of this stamp to assert their claims to equal citizenship regardless of denomination.[9]

The Application Committee of 1786–7 was controlled by substantial merchants and professional men. Edward Jeffries, an eminent surgeon at St

---

[4] G. M. Ditchfield, 'The House of Lords in the Age of the American Revolution', in Clyve Jones (ed.), *A Pillar of the Constitution: The House of Lords in British Politics 1640–1784* (1989), chap. viii.

[5] Clark, *English Society*, chaps. 4 and 5.

[6] Ursula Henriques, *Religious Toleration in England 1787–1833* (1961), 59, gives the date of the first meeting of the Application Committee as 29 Dec. 1786.

[7] Paul Langford, *A Polite and Commercial People: England 1727–1783* (Oxford, 1989), 73.

[8] See R. W. Davis, *Dissent in Politics 1780–1830: The Political Life of William Smith, M. P.* (1971), 40–4, 46–7.

[9] Clark, *English Society*, 340–1; Robert Hole, *Pulpits, Politics and Public Order in England 1760–1832* (Cambridge, 1989), 122–4.

Thomas's, was the chairman. Some like Sir Henry Hoghton and Capel Lofft were well-connected gentlemen, while Henry Beaufoy, who came from a Quaker family, was probably a member of the Established Church when he joined the Committee.[10] In Parliament the Dissenters could anticipate support from outside their ranks. Though only nineteen MPs actually belonged to the three older Nonconformist bodies in the period 1754–90, Ditchfield has calculated that as many as 135 members of the House of Commons voted in favour of repeal of the Test and Corporation Acts in 1787 and/or 1789. Fifty-eight of these voted for it in the divisions of both years. These were not Dissenters but friends of Dissent: liberal-minded MPs or members sitting for large open constituencies where Dissent was strong. They were not a party but were drawn in almost equal proportions from the supporters of Pitt, from genuine independents, and from committed adherents of the Whig opposition. The petitioners had powerful friends. Ex-Prime Minister Shelburne was believed to be 'secretly the first mover' in their enterprise,[11] and had Pitt thrown his current Treasury weight behind the cause, enough wavering votes might have been influenced to secure success.

According to the archbishop the prime minister was at first undecided.[12] He had enjoyed Dissenting support in the general election of 1784, and individual repealers like Henry Beaufoy and William Smith stood behind his administration afterwards. It is not certain what tipped his mind against the application, but 'Church' pressure was a main factor. Archbishop Moore wrote to Pitt:

Having received the 'Case of the Protestant Dissenters with Reference to the Corporation and Test Acts' from the Chairman of their Committee, I thought it my duty to convene the bishops who are in town, in order to take it into consideration. I have the honour to transmit herewith the result of their meeting and to request your permission to wait upon you for half an hour on the subject of this intended application to Parliament on any day and at any hour most agreeable to you after Friday next.[13]

The primate, it would seem, had acted independently. He had not, as it has been claimed,[14] been persuaded by Pitt to convene the meeting. Persuasion flowed the other way. At the gathering, which was held at the offices of Queen Anne's Bounty Board in Dean's Yard, Westminster on 10 February 1787, the prelates showed that, notwithstanding the demise of Convocation, they could act together when church interests were threatened. Of sixteen bishops

---

[10] Davis, *Dissent in Politics*, 44–5.

[11] G. M. Ditchfield, 'The Parliamentary Struggle over the Repeal of the Test and Corporation Acts, 1787–1790', *English Historical Review*, 89 (1974), 551–77; see esp. 552 for letter from Moore to Eden, 9 Mar. 1787, stating from knowledge that Lansdowne (formerly Shelburne) was behind the application.

[12] Ibid. 552.

[13] LPL Moore Papers, viii, fos. 36–9, Moore to Pitt, 12 Feb. 1787.

[14] Henriques, *Religious Toleration*, 60, following Samuel Heywood, *High Church Politics* (1792), 13–14.

present, including the two archbishops, fourteen gave an opinion in favour of maintaining the tests. Latitudinarian opposition was confined to two: Richard Watson, bishop of Llandaff and Jonathan Shipley, bishop of St Asaph. The balance reflected a greater strictness in men recently appointed to the bench. Eleven of the majority grouping were introduced to it while Lord North was prime minister, a time of gathering resistance to rebellion overseas and Dissenting agitation at home. Watson, in the other camp, is the exception that proves the rule, for he was elevated during the short-lived ministry of Lord Shelburne. Nearly a half of the English and Welsh bishops who absented themselves from the meeting—five out of eleven—were appointed before 1770. They included the three veterans of the Newcastle era: Ashburnham, bishop of Chichester, nominated in 1754, Egerton of Durham, 1756, and Beauclerk of Hereford, 1746,[15] though the absence of the last must have been accidental.

Anglican opposition to repeal had not only to be stated. It had also to be justified, for the London Dissenters had gone about their business in a moderate and conciliatory way, not raising a dust but circulating their *Case* to Cabinet Ministers and leading Oppositionists, and interviewing others.[16] The *Case* itself employed reasonable arguments which appealed to the age's creed of benevolence. Hostile churchmen had no time to prepare an answer, for Beaufoy's repeal motion was debated in the Commons on 28 March. A republication of Thomas Sherlock's *Arguments against a Repeal of the Corporation and Test Acts*, managed by the Hutchinsonian High Churchman George Horne, dean of Canterbury, had to suffice for the moment. The emergency passed. Pitt's defection ensured the defeat of the motion by 176 votes to 98, and the Church of England was given two years to prepare against the next attack on the Acts. Horne was determined that the opportunity should not be lost. 'Our artillery should be always ready,' he wrote to his archbishop; 'and it will never be served with more alacrity than when Your Grace shall condescend to direct it.'[17] There is evidence in Archbishop Moore's Papers of a collective attempt, under his leadership, to produce a convincing reply to the *Case*. Gathered in one of the volumes[18] are about a dozen drafts, extracts, and papers bearing upon the points raised in the Dissenting Committee's apologetic. Most of the documents were not signed, but the the the title 'Bp. of B. and Wells' appears with a slight variation on two of them. Charles Moss, bishop of Bath and Wells, was a protégé of Sherlock.

The documents throw light on the reasons for 'Church' opposition to repeal. A recurring theme figures in the subtitle of one: 'The Admission of

---

[15] My calculations from report enclosed in Moore to Pitt, 12 Feb. 1787. LPL Moore Papers, viii, fos. 36–9.

[16] Henriques, *Religious Toleration*, 59–60.

[17] Ibid.; LPL Moore Papers, viii, fos. 5–6, Horne to Moore, 30 Mar. 1787.

[18] LPL Moore Papers, viii, fos. 7–70, miscellaneous papers re attempted repeal of tests 1787.

Dissenters to Civil Office is inconsistent with the safety of a national church.'
'Dissenters of whatever denomination', this proceeded, 'cannot but wish to
transfer the offices and revenues of the Church to their own party, and what
they wish they will endeavour to effect.' An allusion to the differences between Churchmen and Dissenters 'in the most essential articles of religion'
indicates a High Church standpoint in the paper but elsewhere in the drafts
a more secular defence of the tests was adumbrated. The constitutional
argument was advanced in a draft which was worded: 'By the Church in this
question is not meant the clergy ... By the Church is meant one branch of
our excellent constitution, established for the religious benefit of the subjects
of this realm.' Pleas of this kind were entered largely to meet specific points in
the Dissenters' *Case*, but also to gain broad support in Church and Parliament. The chief instigators appear to have been strict Anglican traditionalists
but the movement which they led was 'High Church' only in the broad sense
of being strong for the Church of England.

Samuel Horsley fits readily into the former category, but evidence of his
participation in the first phase of the anti-repeal campaign is not readily
available. Samuel Heywood's *High Church Politics*, a Dissenting polemic,
which misleadingly pinned the entire blame for the Anglican counter-
offensive against the Dissenters on what he called 'the high church party', and
fastened upon Horsley as its archetype, taxed him with the authorship of a
Review of the Case of the Protestant Dissenters, the most successful of the
Anglican replies to the demand for the removal of the Test and Corporation
Acts. But the *Review*, though written in 1787, was not published until 1790.[19]
The new bishop's first public intervention in the debate about religious liberty
was on a subject tangential to that of repeal of the tests.

On 18 May 1789, ten days after the House of Commons had overthrown a
renewed application from the Protestant Dissenters for repeal by the narrow
margin of 20 votes, the Lords gave a first reading to a curious bill, introduced
by Lord Stanhope, 'for relieving Members of the Church of England from
sundry heavy Penalties and Disabilities, to which by laws now in force they
may be liable; and for extending Freedom in Matters of Religion to all
Persons (Papists only excepted); and for other purposes therein mentioned'.
The two initiatives were independent of each other, sharing only a common
root in the movement to commemorate the centenary of the Glorious Revolution. Stanhope's measure did not propose to touch the Test and Corporation Acts. Its author, the Younger Pitt's brother-in-law and until then his
not undiscriminating supporter, was an aristocratic reformer moved by broad
principles and warm enthusiasms. His 1789 proposals were both less and
more radical than repeal of the tests. The provisions of the bill did not
concern themselves with admitting to political power anyone who did not

---

[19] Heywood, *High Church Politics*, 2.

enjoy it already. Their purpose was merely to place the freedom of worship accorded to most Protestant Dissenters in practice by the Toleration Act of 1689 on a firm basis of legal right, to remove various religious constraints, which were no longer generally enforced, from members of the Established Church, and to pave the way for the eventual liberation of loyal Roman Catholics from oppressive penal laws. Thus it was proposed to attack the 1662 Act of Uniformity and to remove a long string of statutory provisions, dating from Tudor and early Stuart times, which imposed fines for non-attendance at church, forbade the eating of meat on days of fasting and abstinence, penalized Catholic families for sending their sons and daughters abroad to be educated at Jesuit academies, and generally enforced the rites and ceremonies of the Church of England. The bill expressly excluded 'Papists' from its benefits, leaving it to future legislation to draw a line between these and other English Catholics; it had no crumbs for the Unitarians labouring under special legal disabilities.[20]

What rendered the proposal alarming to conservative Churchmen was not its enactments, but the general theories underlying it, and the fact that it was introduced so soon after the close defeat of repeal. The theories were written into the preamble, and further enunciated by Stanhope in his parliamentary speeches. Two principles were expounded in the former. The first was that no person should 'in any Case' be liable to penalty, or to be sued 'in any Ecclesiastical or other Court', for not attending divine service, for keeping servants of a religion other than that of the Church of England, for not observing fasting rules or conforming to the rites and ceremonies of the Church of England, 'any Statutes or Laws to the contrary hereof in any wise notwithstanding'. This would abrogate, or could be made to abrogate by a future redefinition of the saving clauses, the residual constraints of both the statute and the canon law on religious observance. Bishop Hallifax was quick to seize on the threat to the canons.

The second principle was an almost unlimited right of private judgement and liberty to proselytize. The preamble proclaimed that all except papists should have:

free Liberty to exercise their religion, and by speaking, writing, printing and publishing . . . to investigate religious subjects, and by preaching and teaching to instruct Persons in the Duties of Religion, in such Manner as every such person respectively shall judge the most conducive to promote Virtue, the Happiness of Society, and the Eternal Felicity of Mankind.[21]

As the archbishop pointed out, this could be construed as a charter for infidels. Bishop John Warren of Bangor adverted to Henley's chapel in the

---

[20] G. M. Ditchfield, 'Dissent and Toleration: Lord Stanhope's Bill of 1789', *Journal of Ecclesiastical History*, 29 (1978), 51–73.
[21] Ibid.

East End, where blasphemy was preached for many years, adding that, were the latitude given which was proposed in the bill, there would be a chapel of this sort in every street.[22]

Archbishop Moore lobbied strenuously against the bill. He tried to persuade the Lord Chancellor that it should be rejected at the first reading, but apparently without success. When it came up for second reading in the Upper Chamber on 9 June, four of the bishops spoke against it. Of the speeches against, Horsley's was the most moderate and also the most effective. The bishop's personal relations with Stanhope were long-standing and good. They had corresponded about scientific matters in the Royal Society years, and Stanhope had patronized Horsley's project for publishing the works of Newton in 1775. In 1792 he sent him a copy of his own tract upon the *Rights of Juries*, which Horsley, in return, described as 'excellent'.[23] Probably neither of them wished to break the friendship, and this seems the principal explanation of the flattering distinction which Stanhope drew in his favour when commenting on the episcopal contributions to the Lords debate. It also governed Horsley's approach. The last of the bishops to speak, he acknowledged that there were laws on the statute book which ought not to be there, but he objected to the bill on the grounds that 'it would rudely tear up the foundations of the Church of England, and as the destruction of an ally must naturally affect the interests and existence of the principal, it might tend to destroy the very being of the English Constitution'. He commended the Act of Elizabeth I lessening the penalty for non-attendance at church to one shilling, on the ground that 'if a law inflicted a penalty less in amount than a man of the lower class would spend, if he did not go to church, it was, in his mind not a severe law', for, if labourers did not spend their Sundays in church, they would spend them in a worse place, 'and in the exercise of a less useful employment'. Horsley accepted Stanhope's principle, which he had reiterated during the debate, that the right of private judgement in religious matters was inalienable, but he distinguished between holding opinions and acting upon them, stating that in the latter sphere the magistrate had the duty to intervene. Present law enforced no particular conformity to the Established Church but only to the worship of God in general. The magistrate 'had no right to punish what was merely sinful, but only that which was detrimental to society'. Hence, however, he must punish atheism and contempt for the Christian religion.[24] It would be too much to say that Horsley's speech killed the bill, which, in its ill-considered form, had no chance of passing the House of Lords. But it won from the *Gentleman's Magazine* praise for its enlightenment.

[22] *Parl. Reg.* xxvi (1789), 254–7.
[23] Stanhope Papers, Horsley to Stanhope, 2 Feb. and 18 July 1773, 10 and 17 Dec. 1775, 27 Oct. 1792. I am much indebted to Dr Grayson Ditchfield for drawing my attention to this material.
[24] *Parl. Reg.* xxvi (1789), 258–60.

The basic arguments against the bill did not differ from those employed by other prelatical opponents, but the engagement of utilitarian criteria, the qualified acceptance of liberal values, the citation of Blackstone on the risk attendant upon the indiscriminate repeal of ancient laws,[25] rendered them more palatable to the generation.

Horsley's next intrusion into the struggle over religious liberty was a great deal less felicitous. After the failure of Stanhope's proposals at their second reading in the Lords, interest swung back to the repeal of the Test and Corporation Acts. The slender majority against Beaufoy's second motion on 8 May 1789, though due more to the propitious time of the year when the vote was taken than to any increase in the Dissenters' strength,[26] encouraged their Committee to redouble its efforts. A new form of organization was adopted. Local associations, modelled on those of the economical and parliamentary reformers in 1780, spread through the country during the summer and autumn, and county meetings were promoted. This innovation, which coincided with a Whig politicization of the repeal cause at the parliamentary level, was connected in its later stages with the forthcoming general election.[27] When, on 13 January 1790, the Jeffries Committee resolved upon renewing their application to Parliament for repeal of the tests in the ensuing session, a proposal was made to link these associations by delegacy with the London body, and the local committees were advised to apply to their MPs 'to give their attendance and support' when the repeal motion was brought forward. Though the intention to impose pledges on candidates was expressly repudiated, steps were taken to compile a central record of the replies, and the London Committee recommended that the Protestant Dissenters should 'shew a particular and marked attention, at the ensuing General Election, to the interests of such Candidates as they believe to be well affected to civil and religious liberty'.[28]

It was in the context of these manœuvres that Bishop Horsley's notorious letter to the clergy of his diocese, instructing them how to cast their votes, acquired significance. In itself it was scarcely more than a move, though a heavy-handed move, in eighteenth-century interest politics at the local level. In March 1787 J. G. Philipps, Whig member for Carmarthen borough, was pressed by the minister of the Dissenting congregation in Lammas Street, backed by several prominent members of his congregation and burgesses, to support the motion for repeal. Probably he needed little urging, for he was a follower of Fox. By his vote he made enemies of the Church party among his constituents, and when, two years later, the Pittite member for the county, Sir

---

[25] Ditchfield, 'Dissent and Toleration', 64.

[26] Ditchfield, 'Parliamentary Struggle', 568–9.

[27] Ibid. 572–3; Davis, *Dissent in Politics*, 48–9; Henriques, *Religious Toleration*, 63.

[28] Dr Williams's Library, Odgers MSS 93 H.4, Jeffries to chairmen of local Dissenting committees, 13 Jan. 1790 and appendages.

William Mansel, who had discredited himself with the administration, withdrew his candidature for the next election, and began to canvass for the
borough seat in opposition to Philipps, Horsley, who had since arrived as
bishop of the diocese, threw his weight behind him.[29] His letter, taken from
the Frend Collection, Cambridge University Library, ran as follows:

Reverend Sir,
   Sir William Mansell has declared himself a candidate to represent the borough of
Carmarthen in the next Parliament. I cannot refrain from declaring that he has my
heartiest good wishes. Mr. Philipps the present member has received the thanks of the
Dissenters for the part he took in the late attempt to overthrow our ecclesiastical
constitution by repeal of the Corporation and Test Acts. By this it is easy to guess what
part he is likely to take in any further attempt for the same purpose. I hope that I shall
not have the mortification to find a single clergyman in my diocese who will be so false
to his own character and his duty to the Established Church as to give his vote for any
man who has discovered such principles.

I am, Reverend Sir,
Your affectionate Brother
and Faithful Servant,

Abergwilly, August 24th 1789

A true copy   Samuel St. David's[30]

   This is a suspicious document. Though a further copy has been entered
editorially in the contemporary *Parliamentary Register*, and R. B. Barlow claims
to have transcribed one from the Edward Jeffries (?Odgers) Manuscripts at Dr
Williams's Library,[31] no original appears to have survived, and it is, therefore,
impossible to be certain to whom it was sent. As the Carmarthen borough
franchise was vested in about 100 burgesses, some of whom were not resident, it was presumed that the letter was circulated for the benefit of those
clergy of St Davids diocese who had a vote in the borough election. It was
quite unsuccessful in defeating the Philipps influence in Carmarthen at the
1790 election,[32] and, falling into the hands of the Dissenters and their Whig
allies, was magnified by them as a counterblast to the charges of constitutional
innovation which were levelled against them for trying to force through repeal
by repeated pressure on an unwilling legislature. By it Horsley's own reputation was tarnished for posterity. Oldfield in his history of the boroughs
described the bishop's interference as 'illegal and unconstitutional',[33] but it is

[29] 'The Cwmgwili Manuscripts', *Transactions for the Carmarthenshire Antiquarian Society*, 26
(1936), 26–7, 64–6; cf. Sir L. Namier and J. Brooke, *The History of Parliament: The House of
Commons 1754–1790* (1964), i. 462–3; iii. 109, 275.
   [30] CUL Add. MSS 7886, fo. 243, copy to William Frend, 24 Aug. 1789.
   [31] *Parl. Reg.* xxvii, 149 n.; R. B. Barlow, *Citizenship and Conscience* (Pennsylvania, 1972), 266
and n. 91. Both state that the letter was addressed to the clergy of the diocese of St Davids. I have
been unable to trace a copy in Odgers MSS.
   [32] Namier and Brooke, *Commons*, i. 462–3; iii. 109, 275.
   [33] T. H. B. Oldfield, *An Entire and Complete History, Political and Personal, of the Boroughs of
Great Britain* (1792), iii. 15.

difficult to see why constitutionally a prelate might not do with his clergy what lay peers did regularly with their tenants. The incongruity with his spiritual view of the episcopal function can scarcely be denied.

The bishop of St Davids' principal claim to distinction as the defender of the Test and Corporation Acts was literary in form. On 5 February 1790 was published *A Review of the Case of the Protestant Dissenters with Reference to the Corporation and Test Acts*. This tract was composed in the opening months of 1787, when the Protestant Dissenters first circulated their *Case*, but suppressed when the House of Commons voted down Beaufoy's repeal motion on 28 March. It eventually appeared anonymously, but was publicly ascribed to Horsley, who made no attempt to disclaim it.[34] His ebullient, sarcastic style of polemic pervaded it, and the title-page of the original edition in the British Library has been inscribed by an unknown hand, 'By Bishop Horsley, as I understand'. The evidence of his authorship is not absolutely conclusive, given a difference in the argument from what he wrote elsewhere. The differences may be explained, however, by the fact that he was not putting forward his whole positive case for the tests but replying to the attacks of his opponents on them. The book was skilfully written. The nine points of the *Case* were grouped by the author under three heads, which were so weighted as to facilitate an overall victory. His three categories were:

1. Grounds of Claim.
2. Religious Grounds of their Position (meaning criticisms of the tests derived from Christian obligation).
3. Political Reasons.

Priority was at once assigned to the last of these. It was explicitly stated that 'the main thing in question is the justice and propriety of one of those great measures of the State respecting the Church, in which, so long as religious ordinances are not profaned, nor the conscience of the individual persecuted, political expedience must overrule all other considerations'. The underpinning premiss identified the principal object of the Test and Corporation Acts as 'the securing of the Civil Constitution against the factious attempts of discontented parties' to force their way into office, and conceded that 'the security of the reformed episcopal church of England' was but 'one subordinate object, as a means of the principal'.[35] In keeping with the purposes of a work which was aimed at a broad spectrum of conservative opinion, the argument stayed well within the normal framework of eighteenth-century assumptions concerning liberty and property. The right of private judgement

---

[34] *Letter from the Rt. Hon. Lord Petre to the Rt. Reverend Dr. Horsley, Bishop of St. Davids* (1790), 5, stated that the *Review* was 'publicly received as coming from your Lordship's pen', and proceeded to reply to it as such. Cf. Heywood, *High Church Politics*, 2, referring to Sir Henry Englefield's challenge to Horsley to deny the authorship, which the latter failed to take up.

[35] *A Review of the Case of the Protestant Dissenters* (1790), 1, 4–5.

within just limits was defended, but the Test and Corporation Acts were said not to infringe it, as civil incapacities 'carry no infamy', except when imposed by a court for crime.[36]

To the Dissenters' claim that repeal of the tests would in no way affect the Established Church was opposed the familiar Warburtonian argument that the Acts constituted a necessary protection for the Church's established status. Insisting that establishment itself rested on other laws, which ratified the Thirty-Nine Articles, prescribed the use of the liturgy, appointed tithes, and defined the power and privileges of the hierarchy, Horsley drew a distinction in language which the eighteenth century could well understand: 'The Establishment is not made, but it is guarded by them [the test laws]: just as a Gentleman's property is not made, but it is guarded by his park-fence and by his garden wall.'[37] The language in which he expressed himself sometimes sounded extreme and reactionary, but his argument was at bottom defensive. Thus the *Case*'s plea that modern Dissenters were friends of the public peace in Church and State, was met by reference to suspicion aroused by late publications that 'the principles of a Nonconformist in religion, and a Republican in politics, are inseparably united'.[38] At one point he appeared to commend Queen Anne's defunct statute against occasional conformity, but merely for the purpose of demonstrating the illogicalness of the Dissenting contention that the laws should be repealed because the tests were means insufficient to their end. 'If a fence is weak', he answered, 'it should be strengthened.'[39]

Five days later Horsley endeavoured to carry the war more deeply into enemy territory by replying to four letters in favour of repeal which appeared in the Whig *Gazetteer*, one of the most widely circulated London morning newspapers, on 9 February 1790.[40] Of the four correspondents, one was Hollis, the republican; the other three wrote under pseudonyms. It was with feigned apology that the bishop approached the editor. He would be brief, and would confine himself to the principles on which the question was to be debated. In fact, his letter ran to about 1,800 words, and was mainly concerned to turn the arguments of the four back on their authors.

The contentions which Horsley employed against his opponents in this letter were broadly the same as those which appeared in the *Review*, but there was one important difference. In both cases the nub of the matter was the need to preserve an Established Church. But while in the latter, establishment was defended as an integral part of the civil constitution which the State in

---

[36] Ibid. 24–5.
[37] Ibid. 52–3.
[38] Ibid. 29.
[39] Ibid. 50.
[40] R. L. Haig, *The Gazetteer 1735–1797: A Study in the Eighteenth Century English Newspaper* (Carbondale, Ill., 1960), 167, 196, 211.

promote the happiness and welfare of the whole community and each of its members, Horsley argued that a Christian believes that the problem had been solved by divine intervention:

He believes that the powers, knowledge, and will of the man were rendered perfectly commensurate, proportionate and harmonious with each other, and with the divine will, by the union of the only begotten eternal Word with the Human Nature in the person of Our Lord and Saviour Jesus Christ, who instituted a society into which all men were then, have been since, are now and may be for ever hereafter until the end of the world admitted upon the conditions by him then declared and appointed. He believes that the same Lord Jesus Christ hath been, is, and will be ever hereafter present, by His Holy Spirit, unto the end of the world with this Society, of which he is forever the head and king. That all power both in heaven and earth hath been given and is actually exercised by him since his Ascension into heaven: That the Holy Scriptures have been authoritatively given under the influence of His Spirit; that they are to be so received as the law of the kingdom and the rule of our faith and practice, and are so to continue until his coming again. That all kingdoms and states in the world are to be regarded as the provinces of this great and universal kingdom, to which all men owe their first and highest allegiance; but especially Christians, to whom the Saviour King hath been proclaimed and by whom he hath been solemnly acknowledged.

These principles bear a close resemblance to the ideas expressed in Edmund Burke's *Reflections on the Revolution in France*. There was the same determination to view the State as something higher than 'a partnership agreement in a trade of pepper and coffee', and to see particular states as 'municipal corporations of that universal kingdom'.[44] Curiously the bishop's paper was written at the very time when Burke was beginning to turn his mind to composing the *Reflections*, but as that classic was not published until November, it seems almost certain that Horsley reached his conclusions independently of Burke. They agreed especially that the unity of Church and State was the linchpin of this divinely constituted order. Horsley's allegiance here was not to the liberties of the clergy, though he asserted these with great force elsewhere, but to the traditional Anglican concept, handed down by Hooker, of a single society which was both Church and State. Thus he continued:

With such principles, and such views, the Christian must regard the intimate and inseparable union of religious and civil government as the grand desideratum with respect to human happiness. He sees them it is true in many instances greatly at variance and their union but very imperfect in any; yet he perceives that magistrates can have no just rights, nor subjects an true rule of obedience, unless such an union is considered as somewhere really existing, so that all our various forms of government may be referred to the only one perfect form and regarded as tending thereto.[45]

---

[44] Burke's phrases. *Reflections on the Revolution in France* (Penguin edn.; Harmondsworth, 1969), 194–5.
[45] HP 1767, fos. 198–203, 'Thoughts upon Civil Government'.

The identification of the interests of the Church of England with those of the State was likewise the theme of the nationwide campaign of public meetings to protest against repeal of the tests which came to a head in February 1790. The SPCK set the tone of the protest in the first of seven resolutions passed at its general meeting in Bartlett's Buildings on the first of the month, affirming that 'the repeated attempt of the Dissenters to obtain a repeal of the Corporation and Test Acts must give great uneasiness to all true friends of the Established Church', the test being 'a wise and necessary provision of the Laws for the common security of the civil and ecclesiastical constitution, the interests of which in this realm are inseparably connected'.[46] Support was forthcoming from a range of classes and corporations, whose privileges were under attack in the changing world of the late eighteenth century, and which rushed to make common cause with the clergy in their rearguard action against assailants. The duke of Newcastle was involved, and the earl of Aylesford presided over a numerous meeting of the nobility, gentry, and clergy of the county of Warwick. County meetings were held in Nottinghamshire and Yorkshire, and also in Suffolk, where the resolutions were signed by 'upward of 1200 gentlemen, clergy and freeholders'. The Common Hall of the borough of Leicester and the Common Council of the City of London likewise met to pass resolutions, and contrary to local protocol the borough-reeve and constables of Manchester convened a meeting of members of the Established Church to oppose the Dissenters' application to Parliament. A similar procedure to the last was adopted by the mayor and corporation of Southampton, while the mayor and principal inhabitants were involved in an anti-repeal meeting at Maidstone. Other assemblages with the same purpose were held at Barnstaple, Coventry, Bolton, Gloucester, and Tewkesbury.[47]

The extent of the opposition to repeal in the country has doubtless been obscured by the successful propagandist use made of the term 'High Church' by Whigs and Dissenters to portray their opponents.[48] In effect the upsurge was a broad conservative movement, provoked by the insistence of the Dissenting demand and enhanced by the lengthening shadow of events in France, not the work of a faction. The clergy who supplied the movement with leadership did so in numbers too large to admit of their being classed as a single 'Church' party. Two hundred and thirty-four clergymen of the archdeaconry of Chester signed resolutions in favour of retaining the tests, and 60 per cent of their brethren in the archdeaconry of York lent support to the

---

[46] SPCK Minutes, vol. xxx (1787–91), fos. 288–91.

[47] A. H. Lincoln, *Some Political and Social Ideas of English Dissent, 1763–1800* (Cambridge, 1938), 261–7; *Leicester Journal*, 12 and 26 Feb. 1790; Archibald Prentice, *Historical Sketches and Personal Recollections of Manchester*, intro. by Donald Read (1970), 2–3; A. Temple Patterson, *A History of Southampton 1700–1914*, i (Southampton, 1966), 67.

[48] See esp. Heywood, *High Church Politics*, 4–5.

cause. A closer inspection of the lists reveals a heterogeneity of ecclesiastical traditions. The Manchester signatories included, in addition to the fellows of the High Church Collegiate church, Cornelius Bailey, priest in charge of St James's, 'a rank Methody', Samuel Hall of St Ann's, who had incurred suspicion of Latitudinarianism by omitting the Athanasian Creed from the service to please the Presbyterians, and John Clowes of St John's, a disciple of Swedenborg.[49] Fifteen clergy of the parish of Leeds signed a letter of 15 January, proclaiming the Test and Corporation Acts to be 'a salutary provision for the security of our established constitution, in both its civil and religious branches'. Of these, Peter Haddon, the vicar, was a scholar and a gentleman firmly attached to the constitution. Miles Atkinson, the lecturer, was a loyal Evangelical, once active in the Elland Society; Richard Fawcett, one of the curates, was a young Cambridge graduate, earnest for sound Christian doctrine but generous in disposition. William Sheepshanks was a somewhat lazy protégé of the influential High Church bishop, Pretyman, Joseph Whiteley, curate of the chapelry of Beeston, a scholar of distinction, and Joseph Swain, curate of Farnley, an exponent of what Norman Sykes called 'practical Christianity', given to supporting charities, a man whose exertions may be said 'to have caused many a widow's heart to sing'.[50] Together these constituted a not untypical set of eighteenth-century clergy.

Undoubtedly, however, the campaign had a High Church core. This was more evident in some places than in others, according to the local traditions. In Manchester, where the Collegiate Church had long been a focus of loyalism, the 'public meeting' of members of the Established Church held in the Hotel on 3 February to oppose repeal of the tests was ineffectively packed and clumsily controlled, by a group of virulent Tories, breathing the spirit of Dr Sacheverell. The outlook of these men was exhibited not so much by the resolutions passed, which were moderately worded and designed to capture the support of uncommitted churchmen who attended the gathering,[51] as in the propaganda put out by the activists before and after the meeting. A poster advertising the event ended with the words: 'Remember, who trampled upon, and made shipwreck of both Church and State, in the last century, and guard against a repetition of the like dreadful scene.'[52] This was followed by a satirical handbill which ran:

---

[49] *Manchester Mercury*, 23 Feb. 1790; *Leicester Journal*, 26 Feb. 1790. The York percentage is calculated upon a total given by citations to the archdeacon's visitation, 19 Apr. 1790. Borthwick Institute, York, Y/V/CB.17.

[50] *Leicester Journal*, 19 Feb. 1790; cf. R. V. Taylor, *Biographia Leodiensis* (Leeds, 1865); *Practical Sermons of the late Rev. Miles Atkinson, A. B., Vicar of Kippax etc. . . . To which is Prefixed a Short Memoir of the Life and Character of the Author* (1812).

[51] 'Facts respecting a Meeting at the Hotel, Manchester, the 3rd day of February 1790.' Manchester Central Reference Library MSS f.1790/1/M. For a different version, blaming the Dissenters, see handbill signed 'T.S.', 12 Feb. 1790. Ibid. 1790/1/D. and E; *Manchester Mercury*, 9 Feb. 1790.

[52] Bill, 'To the Members of the Church of England'. Manchester CRL f.1790/1/A.

And it came to pass in the thirtieth year of the reign of King George the Third, who was anointed King over Great Britain, that the sect of people, called Dissenters (who prospered in the land) conspired together and said, Let us chuse out from among ourselves a King, Governors, Rulers, and men of cunning devises;

And let us depose, dethrone, and put to death, this King, as we did his predecessor, Charles the Good, and let his name be no more heard among us.

And let us chuse priests of our own tribe, and give them the inheritance of the priests of Luther, and whoever will not become as one of us, and take 'the Solemn League and Covenant', let him be cut off from an inheritance in the land, and his possessions shall be unto us for a spoil.

And, moreover, we will deny Christ, and confess Arius, Socinius [sic], and Pelagius, and we will entirely overthrow the Britannic constitution; These things will we do, and many more, to make our names famous throughout the earth.

Now the rest of their Acts, and how they were discomfited, are they not to be found in the Chronicles of the Hotel, in Manchester.[53]

A hostile chronicler claimed that 'a Junto, calling themselves... a Committee' endeavoured to control entrance to the Hotel room, refusing to open the doors even to Churchmen likely to oppose them, while admitting their own supporters by the back-stairs. Elsewhere it was stated, however, that the local Protestant Dissenters intruded in large numbers, and this may have played a part in causing the organizers to rush the proceedings indecorously. The borough-reeve was interrupted while reading the advertisement, and a set of resolutions was proposed *en bloc*, and declared carried, amidst the confusion which arose when Anglican speakers were silenced as they endeavoured to protest against the procedure. Some of the clergy, who had attended as a body in their gowns and cassocks to lend official sanction to the occasion, joined in the clamour to eject the Dissenters. The malcontents withdrew to the Bull's Head, where under reforming leadership they passed resolutions not against the Test and Corporation Acts but against the way in which the 'Church and King' men had called and conducted the meeting.[54]

Conservative High Churchmanship also gave a decided lead in the West Midlands. In Birmingham the head against repeal was taken by two Anglican clergymen who worked in close collaboration: Spencer Madan, the rector of the traditionally High Church St Philip's, and George Croft, headmaster of Brewood School in Staffordshire, soon to become lecturer at St Martin's. Croft, who defended the Test Laws in a sermon preached at St Philip's on 3 January, had once delivered an apology for Roman Catholic teachings on church order and sacraments.[55] The anti-repeal meeting of the Warwickshire nobility, gentry, and clergy on 2 February had for its president the zealous

---

[53] Ibid., f.1790/L/B.
[54] For sources see above, n. 51. Prentice, *Manchester*, 3.
[55] *DNB* xxxv 291; *Gent. Mag.* NS 7 (1837), 205–7; Croft, *Sermons* (1811), i. 15–30.

fourth earl of Aylesford, a peer of impeccable High Church lineage and a former pupil of Samuel Horsley.

Horsley was accused by his opponents of igniting the whole campaign. The pseudonymous 'Liberius' of Berkeley near Frome wrote in the *Gazetteer*: 'Dr Horsley has sounded the high church bell, and the *quondam* Mayor of Southampton has answered it.' He also accused him, in a blistering personal attack, of 'only supporting the Church for the revenue of it', and aligned him with 'a worldly establishment that would tyrannize over reason and conscience—over philosophy and the Bible'.[56] It is a mark of the bishop's restraint that he allowed such calumnies to pass unnoticed.

The claim that he launched the counter-offensive is an exaggeration stemming from an overestimation of the importance of his letter to the clergy of St Davids. The movement developed spontaneously in reaction to the attempts of the Nonconformists at their various meetings to appeal for the support of Anglicans in their quest of repeal. The Leeds clergy acted first, to rebut the suggestion of a Dissenters' meeting at Wakefield that many of the Established clergy acknowledged as a grievance the perversion of the Sacrament to a merely civil purpose.[57] The response was transmitted across the country by the simple device of printing the notices and resolutions of successive assemblages in newspapers.[58] But Bishop Horsley did have a share in the initial triggering action. The SPCK at its meeting on 1 February resolved that the thanks of the board be returned to the bishops of St Asaph and St Davids for the good part they had taken in this business. Hallifax and Horsley were both High Churchmen, though of different types. It was ordered that the anti-repeal resolutions of the meeting, which Hallifax chaired and Horsley attended, should be printed in the public newspapers and published in the Society's next annual report[59] so as to produce the widest effect.

The decisive defeat of repeal when Charles James Fox proposed it in the House of Commons on 2 March 1790 was not primarily due to Anglican exertions outside the House. The huge adverse majority—294 votes to 105—which settled the question for thirty-eight years, and cast a shadow over associated attempts to extend religious toleration in the ensuing years, was the result partly of deepening fears of events in France and partly of the Foxite political complexion which the repeal campaign had assumed. A factor of considerable importance in producing the inflated attendance of members opposed to the motion was that Pitt by reaction had ordered a Call of the House on the day before the debate took place. Nevertheless, concern for

---

[56] *Gazetteer*, 25 Jan. 1790.

[57] *Leicester Journal*, 19 Feb. 1790.

[58] See decision of Warwickshire meeting to send its resolutions to London, Birmingham, and other country papers. Ibid. 12 Feb. 1790.

[59] SPCK Minutes of General Meetings and Committees, xxx, fos. 288–91.

the security of the Established Church was strongly vociferated by speakers against repeal, whose ranks embraced conservative Whigs like Burke and former independents such as Philip Yorke as well as committed Pittites.[60] These sentiments were influenced by the extremism which had become apparent in the Dissenting camp.

Historians have long recognized a distinction between the moderate and pragmatic laymen of the metropolis who launched the campaign against the Test and Corporation Acts, and the more extreme advocates of repeal based in the provinces. They have noted that the objectives of the latter encompassed attacks not only upon the tests but on the liturgy and revenues of the Church of England.[61] Such aspirations have been viewed merely as isolated menaces darkening the backcloth of the repeal struggle in its later stages. The Frend correspondence in Cambridge University Library, however, provides evidence of a sustained movement against orthodox Protestantism, and especially the Anglican form of it, conducted by a group of Unitarian intellectuals, drawn from the ranks of former clergy of the Establishment. Priestley, a Dissenter, was its prophet, but Theophilus Lindsey, an ex-Anglican who ministered to the Essex Street chapel in London, was the chief organizer. A knot of active Unitarians found its focus in the University of Cambridge, where William Frend, fellow and tutor of Jesus College, was the most notable of those still resident. His contacts included the former fellows of Jesus, Robert Tyrwhitt and Gilbert Wakefield, but chiefly R. E. Garnham of nearby Bury St Edmunds. Others held ministerial charges in provincial towns of the North and West, where 'free enquiry and the doctrine of the true worship of God' was reported to be 'making its spread pretty rapidly' in 1789, however much it failed to thrive in the South 'under the baleful shade of a metropolitan cathedral'.[62] At Chowbent near Wigan the 'young Mr Toulmin', and in Bath a pupil of Thomas Belsham, used their congregations as a base from which to spread the principles of the unity of God.[63]

Lindsey and Frend were heavily involved in the final stages of the struggle for the repeal of the tests. Frend distributed to the heads of houses in Cambridge 'a valuable work of Bishop Horsley on the liberty of conscience', while he and Henry Musgrave, another Cambridge resident, were active in the cause of abolishing the slave trade.[64] But the Unitarian leaders had their own distinctive interests which occupied most of their attention during the repeal years and gathered momentum afterwards. The first was the propagation of Unitarian beliefs preparatory to the formation of the Unitarian Society in February 1791. This was the responsibility of Lindsey, assisted by

[60] Ditchfield, 'Parliamentary Struggle', 565–9.
[61] Henriques, *Religious Toleration*, 59; Ward, *Religion and Society*, 22.
[62] CUL Add. MSS 7886, fo. 149, T. Lindsey to W. Frend, 14 Nov. 1789.
[63] Ibid., fo. 156, Lindsey to Frend, 14 July 1790.
[64] Frida Knight, *University Rebel* (1971), 104–5.

his agents in the provinces to whom he sent tracts in bulk for distribution.[65] 'Pray mention to him (i.e. Mr Tyrwhitt)', wrote Lindsey to Frend on 14 July 1790, 'that I am this very day sending to Bath three dozen of his Two Discourses, to a young man, formerly pupil of Mr Belsham's, very lately settled there as dissenting minister.' At that time twelve Lancashire ministers of the Wigan district, including Toulmin, joined forces to establish a monthly journal of a popular kind designed to further their own plan and to combat 'the multitude of gospel magazines etc etc etc which fall into the hands of the common people'.[66]

It was not just Methodism but the traditional system of belief founded upon the King James Bible and the Book of Common Prayer that the Unitarians wished to subvert. They viewed themselves as being engaged in carrying to completion the half-accomplished tasks of the sixteenth-century Reformers, and held the past in contempt. Garnham wrote to Frend: 'Heretics you find have not been quite idle. They have pretty well turned that portentous monster of orthodoxy, St Lewis'[67]—a reference probably to the bishop of Norwich, Lewis Bagot, who had harried the Unitarian sympathizer Le Grice.[68] They set themselves the task of producing a new translation of the English Bible. Priestley unfolded the main plan to Bretland in May 1789, observing that 'my part is the Hagiographa, Mr Dobson engages for the prophecies, Mr Lindsey for the New Testament, & Mr Frend for the historical books'.[69] Garnham, who undertook the Epistles, worked in harness with Frend, the two exchanging advice on the most suitable renderings for their respective assignments while Gilbert Wakefield laboured independently on a translation of the New Testament which he was about to publish in March 1790. An inner 'conclave' was bound to secrecy,[70] on account of the widespread interest in biblical translation, aroused in Cambridge by the writings of John Symonds, professor of modern history, whose *Critical Observations on our Present Version of the Gospels and the Acts of the Apostles* appeared in 1789. The Unitarians had to face scholarly rivalries and the hostility of university conservatives like Thomas Kipling, the Margaret Professor of Divinity, who 'harangued away against any new translation of the bible; perhaps having got scent of a certain design, or moved by Dr Symonds's work and tending towards it'.[71]

[65] CUL Add. MSS 7886, fo. 165, Lindsey to Frend, 14 Feb. 1791, reporting the 'respectable commencement of the New Society' on Wednesday; cf. Knight, *University Rebel*, 86, 111.

[66] CUL Add. MSS 7886, fo. 156, Lindsey to Frend, 14 July 1790.

[67] Ibid., fo. 79, R. E. Garnham to Frend, 13 Jan. 1790.

[68] G. M. Ditchfield, 'Anti-Trinitarianism and Toleration in Late Eighteenth Century British Politics: The Unitarian Petition of 1792', *Journal of Ecclesiastical History*, 42 (1991), 39–67.

[69] Knight, *University Rebel*, 97–8.

[70] CUL Add. MSS 7886, fo. 79, Garnham to Frend, 13 Jan. 1790; Ibid., fo. 82, do. to do. [n.d.], observing *inter alia* that 'Mr. Tyrwhitt's discovery must be a conclave secret'; Ibid., fo. 153, Lindsey to Frend, 18 Mar. 1790.

[71] Ibid., fo. 148, Lindsey to Frend, 10 Aug. 1789.

The second and the most provocative of their objectives was to force a revision of the Book of Common Prayer. In this they received the help of the duke of Grafton, a retired prime minister of rakish reputation, who had made a belated atonement for his sins by attaching himself to Lindsey's chapel in Essex Street. During the summer of 1788 a treatise entitled *Hints etc. submitted to the Serious Attention of the Clergy, Nobility and Gentry, Newly Associated* was published anonymously by a 'Layman', credibly identified as the duke. This was a bid to enlist the help of the Proclamation Society, lately formed by Wilberforce to promote the reformation of manners, in the cause of Prayer Book reform. It was argued that the mass of the people would never be converted to a proper sense of duty until their betters returned to regular church-going, from which they were deterred by the 'offensive, ill-founded and unscriptural' character of parts of the Anglican liturgy. Dissemination of the tract was blocked by High Churchmen. Rivington's, the publishers, who also acted for the SPCK, declined to promote the sales.[72] In the following March, Lindsey who was publisher and director of the Unitarian book service, began to show an interest in it as much for the purpose of inducing its illustrious author to 'come forth as a reformer' as because of its particular content, and during the year 1789 a revised second edition of the book appeared under different auspices.[73] A desire to rid the liturgy of its Trinitarian components continued to interest members of the group in the ensuing year. Garnham wrote to Frend in April 1790: 'The Norrisian Professor maintains the Athanasian Creed to be a hymn. We will do all we can to make it an old song.'[74]

Conservative Anglicanism, stigmatized by its opponents as 'High Church', bestirred itself against the efforts of the Unitarians on all fronts. During the summer of 1789 William Cleaver, newly bishop of Chester, toured Lancashire, Westmorland, and the northern deaneries of Yorkshire, 'charging against Socinianism'. Lewis Bagot, bishop of Norwich, whom Lindsey dismissed as 'a dealer in pious frauds', joined Kipling in disparaging the idea of a new translation of the Bible. George Horne presided as dean over the 'metropolitan cathedral' which cast its shadow on the prospects of Unitarianism in southern England.[75]

The role of force in the counter-offensive was less than in the standard account, which highlights the destruction of Priestley's house and laboratory near Birmingham and other acts of violence by 'Church and King' mobs in Manchester and elsewhere. Such outrages found little countenance at the highest level. 'A churchman lives not in the present age so weak', declared Samuel Horsley, 'who would not in policy, if not in love, discourage, rather

[72] Ibid., fo. 146, do. to do., 6 Mar. 1789.
[73] Ibid., fo. 147, do. to do., 13 Mar. 1789.
[74] Ibid., fo. 81, Garnham to Frend, 22 Apr. 1790.
[75] Ibid., fos. 148, 149, Lindsey to Frend, 10 Aug. and 14 Nov. 1789.

than promote, anything that might be called a persecution of the Unitarian blasphemy . . . Persecution is the hot-bed, in which nonsense and impiety have ever thrived.'[76] The Unitarians were answered by hard evidence and by a divinity which plugged the gaps in their own. One of the most effective contributions to the debate was the reply to the *Hints*, published in 1790 under the title *An Apology for the Liturgy and Clergy of the Church of England*, written by 'A Clergyman'. Some, at Cambridge, attributed it to the late bishop of St Asaph, Samuel Hallifax, others to 'two prelates', but Gilbert Wakefield charged Horsley publicly with the authorship, and he never denied it.[77] Perhaps he wrote it in collaboration with Hallifax, his close friend. The style closely resembled that displayed in his earlier encounters with Priestley. With considered insolence the treatise first demolished Grafton's pretensions to adorn his cause:

You were doubtless aware that, whatever the colour of your life may be, when you condescended to take upon you the form and habit of an author you were under a necessity of foregoing every other mark of distinction that may belong to you. The community of letters, you want not to be informed, is a perfect Republic; and no rewards are assigned, in that society, but to those, who are found, after a severe and impartial examination, to have deserved them.[78]

This was harsh, but not gratuitously so, for deflation was a necessary part of the exercise, a main object of which was to staunch the claims of Socinianism to high social and academic influence.

The remainder of the *Apology* made some serious and telling points against the *Hints* and the religious outlook which lay behind it. The work had little difficulty in demolishing the claim that it was the offensive and unscriptural character of Anglican worship that kept the 'fine world' away from church; it was rather 'because they care not for any service'.[79] It was not against all liturgical reform, conceding that 'a few things may be found in our Ritual, which, with advantage to the symmetry and beauty of the whole, might perhaps be altered or removed', but firm objection was raised in it to the proposal to amend or modify the Athanasian Creed and other parts of the liturgy which inculcated the same teaching. The Trinity alone was not all that was at issue. The author quickly passes to a critique of the philosophy underlying liturgical reform, namely the endeavour to bring down the doc-

---

[76] Horsley, *Tracts in Controversy with Dr. Priestley* (Dundee, 1815), 455, quoted from Ditchfield, 'Anti-Trinitarianism'. I am grateful to Dr Ditchfield for drawing my attention to this quotation. But see below, p. 168, for the allegation that Horsley persecuted Unitarians in his own diocese.

[77] Gilbert Wakefield, *An Address to the Rt. Rev. Dr. Samuel Horsley, Bishop of St. Davids, on the Subject of an Apology for the Liturgy and Clergy of the Church of England* (Birmingham, 1790), 'Advertisement' and 43; cf. John Symonds, *Observations upon the Expediency of Revising the Present English Version of the Epistles in the New Testament* (Cambridge, 1794), ii.

[78] Horsley (attrib.), *An Apology for the Liturgy and Clergy of the Church of England* (1790), 3.

[79] Ibid. 8–10.

trines delivered in the Scriptures 'to the level of our comprehension, under pretence of forming what some are pleased to call a *rational* system of religion', involving 'the rejecting of every article peculiar to revelation' and the substitution of 'a cold and cheerless set of meagre opinions, yielding no comfort to the mind of man either in life or in death'.[80] Against this were upheld the claims of mystery:

I am far from contending, there are not many things in the sacred books, and particularly in the doctrines now mentioned, which we cannot explain; which elude our most anxious enquiries, and refuse to be brought under the test of our severest reason ... On subjects of this mysterious nature, it is not expected that we comprehend, but that we believe; where we cannot unriddle we are to learn to trust; where our faculties are too weak to penetrate, we are to check our curiosity and adore.[81]

The *Apology*'s case against the revisionists did not lack substance. Under cover of updating they were changing content. Garnham's letter to William Frend shows how, in the new translation of the Bible, the text was to be amended to eliminate all suggestion of mystical union:

In my turn let me consult you for a good translation of 'Christ's abiding in us & we in him'. My idea of the signification of the phrase is that of a friendly connection, as between members of the same family, which figurative language seems to be used even with respect to the Deity, John xiv. 23, 'we will take up our abode with him'. May then μένειν ἐν υἱῷ be rendered to continue in *intimacy with* the Son, μένει ἐν ὑμῖν he continueth in intimacy with you? The term of *dependence* or *reliance* will not I think so well suit in the latter instance? I shall be obliged to you for a good reading.[82]

Stimulated by the exchange with the Anglicans, Unitarian activities continued to expand during the early years of the French Revolution. They were closely linked in supporting personnel with the radical political societies. The formation in 1791 of the Unitarian Society for Promoting Christian Knowledge on the Principle of the Unity of God gave a focus to the cause. It was followed in 1792 by an appeal to Parliament to remove the specific disabilities still bearing upon Unitarians, namely the Blasphemy Act, 1697, and the seventeenth section of the Toleration Act, 1689, which debarred them from benefiting from the provisions of that statute. These laws were no longer enforced, but, as Fox explained to the House of Commons, they provided legitimation for general backlash against Socinians.[83] Politically, the campaign to remove them was the epilogue of a broader struggle for religious liberty. The main body of political Dissent leagued under the Standing Committee of Protestant Dissenters watched it from afar for its bearing on the prospects for

---

[80] Ibid. 68–9.
[81] Ibid. 66–7.
[82] CUL Add. MSS 7886, fo. 82, Garnham to Frend [n.d.].
[83] *Parl. Reg.* xxxiii (1792), 24.

repeal. The Unitarian activists waited to be prompted by Charles James Fox and their friends in Parliament. Lindsey, Tayleur, and other Unitarians exerted themselves to collect about 1,600 signatures for a petition presented by Fox to the Commons on 8 March 1792.[84] On 11 May he moved to introduce a bill to repeal or amend the Blasphemy Act and a string of statutes penalizing religious dissent from the reign of Edward VI to the Marriage Act of George II.[85] Leaving the Test and Corporation Acts untouched, it was broader than Stanhope's bill, and gave something to the more extreme dissidents of all kinds: to Unitarians, Roman Catholics, and Quakers, and even to Jews. But the time could scarcely have been less ripe. The launching of the Association of the Friends of the People by Charles Grey and the liberal Whigs during the preceding month had dealt a deadly blow to the unity of the Whig party, and had encouraged the Government to bid for the support of the right wing.[86] Fox's motion was defeated by a majority of 79,[87] and legality was not granted to the profession of Unitarianism until 1813.

As the battle over the Unitarian petition was conducted in the House of Commons, Bishop Horsley was not directly involved in it, but his friends in the country were stirred to action in the preparations for meeting it. Early in 1792 it was claimed that Priestley had seen 'a printed paper . . . from some High Church men, inviting all that wish well to the establishment to unite against the efforts that are making against it by Socinians, Republicans, Deists etc.'.[88] The phraseology suggests that this may have been a prospectus of the Society for the Reformation of Principles, a notable turning point in High Church journalism, which can be seen as, in part at least, a response to the petition of the Unitarians.

Viewed in its entirety the drive to enlarge the toleration of Protestant Dissenters beyond the boundaries of the 1689 Act encountered little success in the late 1780s and the 1790s. The struggle was important chiefly for the impact which it made on the character of the contestants.[89] To the Anglican side it imparted a deeper theological colouring. Because the challenge to the confessional state was spearheaded by Socinianism, a radically different doctrinal system to that of the Established Church, the question at issue quickly extended from how much freedom men should enjoy to the truth of what they believed. The attacks mounted by the more extreme Unitarians, not only upon the doctrine of the Trinity, but on the broad foundations of the

[84] *Parl. Reg.* xxxii (1792), 38–9; H. McLachlan (ed.), *Letters of Theophilus Lindsey* (Manchester, 1920), 70–1; Barlow, *Citizenship and Conscience*, 286.

[85] *JHC* 47 (1792), 787–9.

[86] F. O'Gorman, *The Whig Party and the French Revolution* (1967), 82–90; John Ehrman, *The Younger Pitt: The Reluctant Transition* (1983), chap. vi, *passim*.

[87] *Parl. Reg.* xxxiii (1792), 17–40.

[88] Barlow, *Citizenship and Conscience*, 286, quoting letter from Lindsey to Tayleur, 15 Feb. 1792, reproduced in McLachlan, *Letters of Theophilus Lindsey*.

[89] For the effect on the Unitarians see Ditchfield, 'Anti-Trinitarianism'.

Anglican type of Protestantism, rebounded in the Church of England in a retreat of some of its members from the loose accommodating liberalism of the 1760s and 1770s into a distinctive Prayer Book Anglicanism which enjoined subscription to the Articles, and trod the *via media* between arid Latitudinarianism and Methodist exuberance. This was the note struck by the *British Critic* in the 1790s. Though moderate and restrained, it was a step in the High Church direction.

6

Protecting the Weakest

THE positioning of Samuel Horsley in the history of religious toleration presents today a curious paradox. He was the hammer of the Protestant Dissenters in their efforts to remove the Test and Corporation Acts. But he was also the foremost, and decidedly the cleverest, of those Anglican clergy who sought to extend the freedom of Christian bodies more oppressed than the Dissenters. At approximately the time when he was fighting Lord Stanhope's bill for general religious liberty and the Nonconformist bids to repeal the tests, he intervened decisively in support of exertions to promote the relief of English Catholics and to mitigate the penal laws against Scottish Episcopalians. Ulterior motives have been invoked to explain the discrepancy. Dr Dominic Bellenger has argued recently that Anglican tenderness towards Roman Catholics at the time of the French Revolution was not so much a genuine act of toleration as a political move to assert the 'gravitas' of the national church and to erect a counterpoise to impiety and infidelity.[1] Doubtless these considerations weighed. When contemporary standards are substituted for ours, however, no inconsistency may of necessity be perceived between forwarding religious liberty on some fronts and restraining it on others.

However widespread their aversion to persecution, few eighteenth-century Englishmen shared the conviction of John Locke that religious belief was irrelevant to civil co-operation, and that the magistrate should, therefore, practise an unlimited toleration. At first the Toleration Act of 1689 was seen by more than 80 per cent of the parish clergy as no more than a passing indulgence to a few scrupulous consciences.[2] Even towards the close of the eighteenth century, when toleration in the shape of freedom of worship, freedom to teach, and freedom to share in local government had been largely established in practice if not in law, all but a Latitudinarian and radical minority continued to distinguish between this and civil equality. The Younger Pitt, still in his reforming years, observed: 'I do not see any reason to consider the exclusion of the Dissenters more as a mark of infamy than any other distinction that upholds political government.'[3]

The churches defended by Horsley, however, still stood in need of basic

[1] Dominic Bellenger, 'The Émigré Clergy and the English Church, 1789–1815', *Journal of Ecclesiastical History*, 34 (1983), 392–410.

[2] Geoffrey Holmes, *The Trial of Doctor Sacheverell* (1973), 35.

[3] Ursula Henriques, *Religious Toleration in England 1787–1833* (1961), 70.

rights. Newman described the condition of the Roman Catholics under the penal laws: 'No longer the Catholic Church in the country; nay, no longer, I may say a Catholic community—but a few adherents of the Old Religion, moving silently and sorrowfully about as memorials of what had been.'[4] This assessment cannot be sustained today. By the leading Catholic historians of the present—Bossy, Aveling, and Eamon Duffy—English recusancy in the eighteenth century is viewed, in respect of size and strength, as 'a modestly successful Nonconformist sect',[5] with some 67,000 to 80,000 adherents in the closing years of Bishop Challoner's vicariate (*c.*1767–81),[6] expanding if at a rate less than that of the population as a whole. It was developing throughout the period a sizeable urban wing of merchants and professional men to offset the decline of the nobility, while priests trained in Continental seminaries were importing the learning and ideas of the European Enlightenment, bringing tensions which, if they displayed vitality, also foreshadowed, as the century drew to its close, the sharper conflicts of the Victorian age between Liberals and Ultramontanes.

If English recusants were not crushed by the penal laws, it would be wrong to assume that they were not disadvantaged by them. The laws themselves were both ancient and savage. By an Act of 1584, unrepealed though long in abeyance, Jesuits, seminary priests, and other kinds of priest remaining on English soil, were rendered liable to be hanged and quartered for treason. Further legislation of that period imposed on Catholics ruinous fines and a year's imprisonment for saying or hearing Mass. Heavy recusancy fines backed by the sanction of confiscation of property were prescribed for those who absented themselves from the parish churches. Statutes passed in 1606 in the wake of the Gunpowder Plot added an obligation to receive the Sacrament according to the Anglican rite and an oath repudiating the Pope's power to depose heretical rulers, refusal of which carried the crippling penalties of a praemunire. Recusants were also forbidden to travel more than five miles from their homes without licence from the Privy Council or from a Justice of the Peace. From 1629 they were subjected like foreigners to a double rate of taxation. By the second Test Act, 1678, they were debarred from sitting in either House of Parliament. The Glorious Revolution, which for the Protestant Dissenters ushered in an era of extended toleration, conferred upon them no relief, for it identified them with the fallen dynasty. Accordingly, from 1692 onwards Parliament superimposed upon the old penal code a new one characterized to a greater extent by modern scientific efficiency. Catholics were charged a double rate on the new annual land-tax, and every effort was

---

[4] Quoted from J. H. C. Aveling, *The Handle and the Axe* (1976), 253.

[5] E. Duffy, *Peter and Jack: Roman Catholics and Dissent in Eighteenth Century England* (Friends of Dr Williams's Library, Lecture 36; 1982), 3.

[6] J. A. Williams, 'Change or Decay? The Provincial Laity 1691–1781', in E. Duffy (ed.), *Challenor and his Church: A Catholic Bishop in Georgian England* (1981), 31.

made to thwart evasion of payment. They were also excluded from practising at the Bar. Notably savage was the Act of 1700 'for the further prevention of Popery', which incapacitated Catholics from purchasing land, and disinherited them to the benefit of their Protestant kinsfolk unless they took certain oaths and declarations. Their bishops and priests were made liable to life imprisonment for officiating and keeping a school, and the severity of the ban was increased by allowing the informer a reward of £100 for every conviction. This statute rivalled in ferocity those passed for the oppression of Irish landowners during the reign of Anne.

In England not all the penal laws were systematically enforced. By William III's reign they were intended to contain, not to crush, the Catholics.[7] The statutes forbidding the Mass were held in reserve for use in emergencies and times of unusually strong feeling. A crop of prosecutions and threatened prosecutions was launched against priests as late as 1767–71,[8] but the Mass was being celebrated in purpose-built chapels from about 1680 onwards, although caution was required for a century or more in the choice of sites and ceremonial. Not until 1792 did the Winchester Catholics venture to replace their small chapel in the garden of the presbytery by an elaborate Gothic church with a fan-vaulted roof and painted bosses.[9] Meanwhile, however, the rising prosperity of agriculture helped enterprising Catholic landlords to reduce the double land-tax to unimportance,[10] and Catholic lawyers overcame the prohibition of their practice in the courts by making a success, as did the Lincoln's Inn-trained Charles Butler, of the business of conveyancing.

The hostility of the Protestant population was a greater handicap to Catholics than the penal laws. Here and there this showed itself in sundry acts of discrimination against the humbler sort, such as the withdrawal of licences from papist alehouse keepers by local functionaries.[11] In times of excitement such as followed the Jacobite invasion in 1745 or attended the campaign of the Protestant Association in 1778–80, Roman Catholic chapels in the provinces were destroyed by mobs. But the Gordon riots were wholly untypical, resulting more from social tensions in an overcrowded metropolis than from hatred of the Pope's religion. The importance of the penal laws was that they symbolized, in Edward Norman's phrase, the 'Catholics' civil inferiority'.[12]

The prejudices which consigned them to isolation were only partly religious. Most English Protestants in the later eighteenth century would have agreed, it is true, that the Church of Rome was, historically and actually, not

---

[7] G. M. Trevelyan, *The English Revolution 1688–9* (1954), 160–1.

[8] W. J. Amherst, *The History of Catholic Emancipation 1771–1820* (1886), i. 83–5. Amherst claimed that the last prosecution of a priest under the penal laws was in 1771.

[9] Barbara Carpenter Turner, *Winchester* (Southampton, 1980), 151.

[10] John Bossy, *The English Catholic Community 1570–1850* (1975), 326.

[11] Duffy (ed.), *Challenor and his Church*, 37.

[12] E. Norman, *The English Catholic Church in the Nineteenth Century* (Oxford, 1984), 34.

only mistaken but corrupt. Archbishop Secker, than whom it would be difficult to find a more centrally placed Anglican, spelt out its impurities in *Five Sermons against Popery*, printed in 1772. These were the failure to affirm the supremacy of Scripture over tradition, transubstantiation, invocation of saints, worship of the Virgin Mary, Communion in one kind, compulsory auricular confession, the notion of the Mass as an offering of Christ's body, purgatory, indulgences, and all idea of an intermediate state between death and the Last Judgement. However, the theological case against Roman Catholicism would have carried less weight in an age which attached more importance to reason than to dogma, had it not been augmented by powerful cultural, social, and political factors. To the majority of its opponents popery was objectionable because it was authoritarian, because it was backward, and because it was different. The claimed 'independence of the Church on the civil power' seemed to the Georgian mind to portend a sacerdotal tyranny which the law would be unable to control. Hence an anonymous address to the Anglican archbishops and bishops, published in 1767, cited the case of a sick priest peremptorily recalled to York by his superior, and gave examples of the compulsory baptism of the children of mixed marriages.[13] The same treatise raised the spectre of the poisoning of Englishmen's minds by reactionary Jesuits expelled by the Catholic monarchies of Europe,[14] while the belief that Catholics held themselves free not to keep faith with their neighbours even in private transactions was a continuing source of suspicion.

Anti-Catholicism, usually restrained in its expression, continued as a feature of the English scene throughout the eighteenth century. Attempts to dampen it were the work of individuals. No irreversible current moved towards the relaxation of the penal laws. At times the tide even flowed in the opposite direction, as when in 1767 the House of Lords called for an exact return of papists throughout England. Nevertheless, certain influences operative in the middle and later years of the century reduced tension.

Of these the most important was the decline of Jacobitism and the collapse of the British Catholic monarchy. Not all Catholics had been Jacobites, except in the formal sense that their clergy prayed liturgically for the exiled Stuarts, while many, perhaps most, Jacobites were Protestants. But the unrelenting allegiance of James II and the Old Pretender to the Church of Rome, and the encouragement given to Jacobite plots and invasion projects by Catholic powers, created the impression of a treasonable association between Catholicism and the Stuart cause. By the accession of George III the connection

---

[13] *An Address to their Graces the Archbishops of Canterbury and York and the Right Reverend the Bishops of the Church of England* (1767).

[14] The Jesuits were expelled from Spain, Naples, and Sicily in 1767, but only a few of the Order were despatched to England at that time. Aveling, *The Handle and the Axe*, 313. The real cause of the English anti-Catholic outburst of the late 1760s and early 1770s must be sought elsewhere, probably in domestic and social factors.

had ceased to matter; soon afterwards it ceased to exist. The external threat from the Jacobites vanished after 1759, when the British navy frustrated Choiseul's plan for landings in England and Scotland in the interest of the Young Pretender.[15] Encouraged by the latter's conversion to Protestantism, which was made public in the same year, the English Catholics extricated themselves from the cause. On the death of the Prince's father, the titular James III, in 1765, the vicars apostolic, following a papal lead, ordered their clergy to pray for George III.[16]

The loyalty of the Catholics to the dynasty was revealed by the War of American Independence, when it was used as a counterweight to transatlantic republicanism. Sir John Dalrymple's success in raising Catholic troops in Ireland and his proposal to do the same in Scotland in return for a repeal of the penal laws set in motion the events which led to the passing of the Savile Relief Act of 1778 which removed the fierce proscriptions of the 1700 statute. It was endorsed by Lord North and his friends in the hope of inducing the Irish Parliament to grant comparable relief, which might have the effect of strengthening allegiance to the British Government in Ireland.[17]

The concession from expediency provided indirectly the catalyst of a sustained pressure from the Catholic side for further liberation. Professor Owen Chadwick has shown in a work of capacious insight how the European Enlightenment, so far from being a purely anti-Catholic movement, permeated Catholic colleges, and found expression in the utterances of bishops and professors, whose object was to modernize the Church for her own good.[18] In England it found its most self-conscious embodiment in the Cisalpines, a creative minority of Roman Catholic clergy and laymen bent on curtailing those features of their own religious system which distinguished them from Protestants. Their object was sincerely theological as well as aimed at the practical object of creating a climate favourable to the removal of anti-Catholic legislation. Liberal in temper and politically Whiggish, the group drew inspiration from the writings of Fr. Joseph Berington, a former professor of philosophy at Douai, dismissed from the post which he held in 1771, for teaching 'new-fangled' notions in contempt of scholasticism. Returning to England he continued to develop his ideas especially after 1778, when the Savile relief legislation provoked a backlash of criticism of Catholic intolerance. Zealous to correct the impression, he attacked the monastic orders, expressed doubts about clerical celibacy, and called for a vernacular liturgy. He committed himself to a belief in universal toleration, and in his *Reflections*,

[15] Claude Nordman, 'Choiseul and the Last Jacobite Attempt of 1759', in Cruickshanks (ed.), *Ideology and Conspiracy*, 201–17.

[16] Aveling, *The Handle and the Axe*, 254.

[17] R. K. Donovan, 'Sir John Dalrymple and the Origins of Roman Catholic Relief, 1775–78', *Recusant History*, 17 (1984), 188–96; cf. Maurice O'Connell, *Irish Politics and Social Conflict in the Age of the American Revolution* (Philadelphia, 1965), 108–10.

[18] Owen Chadwick, *The Popes and the European Revolution* (Oxford, 1981), chap. vi, *passim*.

published in 1785, introduced the representative principle into the govern-
ment of the Church, reducing the Pope to the role of head of the executive.
From 1782 a Committee of Cisalpine laymen, men of birth or affluence like
Charles Butler, the secretary, John Throckmorton, and Lord Petre, gathered
to advance the cause of relief. It could do little until 1788, when, following the
Protestant Dissenters' lead on repeal of the tests, it opened negotiations with
the Younger Pitt for a Catholic Bill. At the prime minister's request certain
Catholic universities of Europe were consulted about the disquieting doctrine
of the Pope's deposing and dispensing power, and gave reassuring answers. At
this point, however, the Committee made the fatal mistake of submitting to
the guidance of the eccentric libertarian, Lord Stanhope, who advised it to
bolster its case with a statement of principles, and prepared for the occasion
the Declaration and Protestation of the English Catholics. Imprudent in itself,
being laden with unnecessary denunciations of 'infallibility in the Pope' and of
the power of the clergy to absolve Catholics 'from any compact or oath
whatever', it was followed in June 1789 by the publication of a still less
prudent oath, also prepared by the Committee with Stanhope's assistance. In
order to benefit from the proposed relief, Catholics were to be described as
'Protesting Catholic Dissenters' to distinguish them from 'Papists', were to
assent to the Pope's powers being described as 'heretical', and were to deny
him 'any spiritual power or jurisdiction . . . that can directly or indirectly
interfere with . . . the constitution of this kingdom'.

This oath brought to a head all the mounting suspicions of the orthodox
clergy and laity which the former pronouncements of the Cisalpines had
provoked. On 21 October the English vicars apostolic condemned it by
encyclical without giving their reasons. The quarrel continued throughout
the following year, and penetrated every level of English Catholic activity,
especially the coincident appointment of two new vicars. When the Relief Bill
was eventually introduced into Parliament early in 1791, and the offending
terminology was modified by a committee in the Commons in April, the effect
was to divide the vicarial party down the middle. John Douglass, the new
London vicar, joined his colleague Talbot in accepting the proposals, while
Walmesley and Gibson continued to resist.[19]

It was clear that on the Roman question toleration could not proceed from
the steady acceptance of any single theory of political obligation such as was
once believed to have developed from the ideas of Newton and Locke and to
have been nourished by the Enlightenment. The intolerance of the foes of
intolerance proved too strong for that, and a decisive intervention from the
other side was required to provide a solution. In order to be effective this
needed help from outside the Roman communion, for the Catholics were

---

[19] The above account of the Cisalpine controversy is derived from Eamon Duffy,
'Ecclesiastical Democracy Detected', *Recusant History*, 10 (1970), 193–209, 309–31.

themselves too deeply sundered to agree upon it and too weak politically to persuade Parliament to accept it. That the assistance should have come from the Old High Church of the Establishment is less surprising than it may seem.

Most Anglican divines, whether High Church or Low, shared the general antipathy to Rome which characterized Reformed theology from the reign of Elizabeth I. Unlike most popular Protestantism, however, Anglican divinity of a high or central cast, taking its cue from Richard Hooker, conducted the quarrel with Romanism within a framework of agreed postulates. These included an acceptance of the need to prove historical continuity with the primitive Church, respect for episcopacy as an institution, appeal to historic sources later than the Bible, and often an admission from the Anglican side that some kind of universal primacy was warranted by tradition. With Laud and the seventeenth-century High Churchmen the Anglican apologetic had embraced appeals to the 'ecclesiastical constitutions' to affirm the equality of the patriarchs in the early Church, and while the Pope was accorded 'a primacy of order', a branch theory in which the 'Roman church and the church of England' appeared as 'but two distinct members of that catholic church which is spread over the face of the earth' was advanced by Laud.[20] Dialogues for resolving differences were conducted in an amicable spirit with the papal agent Panzani and an English Franciscan friar, Franciscus a Sancta Clara, and although these had no tangible effect, the quarrels between the French Church and the papacy at the end of the seventeenth century and the beginning of the eighteenth established new affinities between Anglicanism and a form of European Catholicism. During the reign of George I the Whig Archbishop Wake opened a negotiation with two rebellious Gallican divines supported by the Sorbonne, and some preliminary agreement was reached on points of church order before the French civil authorities intercepted the correspondence.[21] Concurrence in doctrine was always more difficult to attain, but even in the relatively Protestant later eighteenth century there was no want of reputable Anglican theologians willing to temper condemnation of the superstitions of the Roman Church with a recognition of its merits. Caught in the Romanists' dialectical trap, that the Anglicans must make up their minds whether the pre-Reformation Church was a true Church, in which case they should cease to protest against it, or not a true Church, whereupon they should desist to base their own claims to truth upon it, Secker wanted to have the question both ways: 'In one respect, as their [that is, the Roman Catholic] Church professed the fundamentals of christianity, it was, and is a true Church; and so far ours is derived from it. In another

[20] Norman Sykes, *Old Priest and New Presbyter* (Cambridge, 1966), 183.

[21] Norman Sykes, *William Wake, Archbishop of Canterbury 1657–1737* (Cambridge, 1957), i. Chap. iv provides the definitive account of the Gallican correspondence. This superb biography also deals with Wake's subsequent ecumenical encounter with Pierre Francois le Courayer, canon of St Geneviève in the 1720s.

respect, as it obscured and contradicted them by unjustifiable doctrines and practices, it was not a true church; and so far we protest against it.'[22]

George Croft, who was later involved in High Church politics in Birmingham, condoned even the corruptions by viewing them historically. In the curious context of a 5 November sermon preached in St Mary's, Oxford in 1783, he urged that 'even in many of their corruptions, we can trace the semblance of something good—the perversion of something originally laudable'. Thus in penance could be seen 'proper punishment' of offenders, in absolution and indulgences 'consolation administered to sincere repentance'. From transubstantiation could be learned 'the very great reverence paid from earliest times to the Holy Eucharist'. Infallibility could be tracked to 'the original purpose of referring to the decisions of public councils, what it was less safe to trust to the discretion of contending individuals'. 'Statues, pictures, and images, were at first only decorations, and not objects of worship' etc.[23]

It was, therefore, no presumption that the English Catholics, when they ran into difficulties over the 1791 Relief Bill, should have turned to the Anglican bishops for help. Charles Walmesley, the vicar apostolic of the Western District, an ultra-conservative, wrote to the archbishops of Canterbury and York, asking them to procure the suppression of the whole bill.[24] A month earlier, however, a more diplomatic proposal had emerged from the vicarial camp. The energetic and resourceful John Milner, a future vicar apostolic, still in the early stages of his career as pastor of the Catholics of Winchester, penned identical letters to the bishop of Salisbury, Shute Barrington, and to John Butler, bishop of Hereford, suggesting that Parliament might consider substituting for the present oath either 'the oath of allegiance appointed for the Roman Catholics of England in 1778' or 'that for those of Ireland in 1774'. He owed his introduction to Warden Huntingford of Winchester College, 'my respectable friend', as he called him. According to a footnote in Almon and Debrett the two oaths were 'in effect the same', but the latter was 'drawn with the greater accuracy', and it was for this, he admitted to Douglass, that he was working. With a contemptuous tilt at the Cisalpines of the Committee he told the Anglican prelates that, unlike 'the present lay formulary which bespeaks its authors to have been ignorant of theological matters', it had been drawn up by divines and sanctioned by the faculty of Sorbonne.[25]

Though the Irish oath provided in substance the solution which was

---

[22] *Five Sermons against Popery: By Thomas Secker LL.D.* (Windsor, 1827), from sermons printed at Dublin in 1772 for circulation in Ireland, 104–5.

[23] Croft, *Sermons*, i. 15–30.

[24] AAW, A ser., xliii. 79, Bp. Walmesley to Bp. Douglass, 31 May 1791.

[25] Ibid. 68, Milner to bp. of Salisbury, 2 May; 70, Milner to Bp. Douglass, 3 May 1791; *Parl. Reg.*, xxx (1791), 250 n.

adopted, it was Bishop Horsley who brought it forward when the revised bill came before the House of Lords. Roman Catholic historians from Bernard Ward to Eamon Duffy have assigned the credit for his mediation unhesitatingly to Cisalpine agency. Dr Duffy writes: 'Joseph Berington had never relished the phrasing of the oath, though he thought it basically acceptable. He now approached Douglass, and suggested that the bishop should sign a letter, drafted by Berington, to the Anglican Bishop of St. Davids, Samuel Horsley, asking him to intervene. Douglass agreed, and Horsley more than justified the trust.'[26] The view has manuscript support, for Berington observed to Douglass shortly after the event: 'I am sure you will own that the measure he [John Milner] so much extols, of writing to the bishop of St Davids, came at least from me; that I was the author of the Note; and that I procured it to be delivered into the bishop's hands.'[27] As an explanation, however, it is inadequate. The manner of Bishop Horsley's intervention suggests that he was acting not as the retained agent of one side in the dispute, but in response to the situation as a whole.

His relations with the Cisalpine party left much to be desired. He cannot have approved of Berington's *Address to the Protestant Dissenters*, urging cooperation between oppressed bodies against the Establishment, much less of the active collaboration with Stanhope in drafting the Protestation and the oath, while the fierce anti-clerical tone of such critics of the Apostolic Vicars as Alexander Geddes must have seemed to him nearer to republicanism than to the Reformed religion.[28] In his *Review of the Case of the Protestant Dissenters*, he allowed himself to become embroiled with the Catholics by some ill-chosen remarks on their current strength and readiness to honour their engagements. This led Lord Petre, the paymaster of the Catholic Committee, to launch a furious attack on the treatise.[29]

It has commonly escaped notice that the bishop's first move towards the 1791 Relief Bill was not to ease its passage through the Lords but to delay it and to remove control from the hands of the Catholic Committee. In his speech at the second reading on 31 May he was principally concerned to show that those Catholics who scrupled against the oath in its present form were 'not the Pope's courtiers, more than the gentlemen of the Roman Catholic Committee'. They were ready to renounce the doctrine that faith is not to be kept with heretics, to renounce as 'impious and unchristian' the belief that princes excommunicated by the Pope might be murdered by their subjects and to deny that they might be deposed. But they scrupled to apply the epithets 'impious, unchristian and damnable' to the deposing doctrine from respect for virtuous forefathers who had 'acquiesced in this error as a specu-

[26] 'Ecclesiastical Democracy', 320.
[27] AAW, A ser., xliii. 117, J. Berington to Bp. Douglass, 3 Sept. 1791.
[28] Duffy, 'Ecclesiastical Democracy', 309, 312–14, 317.
[29] *Letter from the Rt. Hon Lord Petre to the Rt. Rev. Doctor Horsley, Bishop of St. Davids* (1790).

lative doctrine, though they never acted upon it'. He drove the point home with an analogy designed to appeal to noblemen educated in the classics:

My Lords, I believe, your Lordships all believe, that there is no name under heaven by which men might be saved, but the name of Jesus Christ: nevertheless, my Lords, I should be very unwilling to assert, my Lords I would refuse to swear, that it is a matter of my belief that such men as Socrates, Plato, Tully, Seneca, and Marcus Antoninus, who were every one of them idolaters, are now suffering in the place of torment, and are doomed to suffer there to all eternity . . . My Lords, will not your Lordships permit the Roman Catholics to have the same tenderness for the memory of Bellarmen [*sic*] and Erasmus which your Lordships would feel for that of virtuous heathens?

It was part of Horsley's oratorical genius to use familiar idiom to commend ideas which were totally foreign.

Turning to a more serious objection of Catholics to the oath, the belief that it obliged them to deny the Pope's spiritual authority, Horsley had little difficulty in demonstrating that the words could mean nothing less. They demanded a renunciation of the 'ecclesiastical power' of 'foreign churches' when it encroached 'directly or indirectly' on the laws and constitution of the realm. The supremacy of the Pope not only interfered with the king's head-ship of the Church but, by invalidating all ordinations and consecrations not emanating from the authority of the See of Rome, disqualified the bishops from sitting and speaking in the House of Lords. The purpose of the argu-ment was to show that the Cisalpine party, which insisted equally on the spiritual authority of Rome, was by implication not less disaffected towards Government than the Catholics who boggled at the oath. Horsley's sym-pathies were firmly with the vicars, even on questions of canonical obedience. Referring to an encyclical requiring Catholics not to swear the doctrinal points before receiving the approbation of their ecclesiastical superiors, he told the House: 'I believe, were I a Roman Catholic, I should think it my duty to submit to it.'

When it came to devising a solution for the deadlock the bishop was undecided. He canvassed the case for substituting the 1778 oath for the existing one, but dropped the suggestion on the flimsy ground that a com-mittee of the Lords would not be unanimous on such a motion. His con-clusion, therefore, was that the bill was incurable. If, however, the Lords rejected it, he would pledge himself to bring in a new bill early next session which should not be pregnant with the mischiefs of the current proposal. Better still, the Lords should name a committee to revise all subsisting laws against the Roman Catholics and to frame a bill repealing those which might safely be repealed.[30]

It is difficult to explain this advice without inferring that he had some plan of his own to settle the Catholic question on what he described as 'a broad

[30] *Parl. Reg.* xxx (1791), 241–50.

and permanent basis'. Influenced, no doubt, by the desire to assert the *gravitas* of the national Church, even the *gravitas* of the See of St Davids, he was primarily concerned to bring tolerance to the English Catholics, provided that it could be done without placing them under the exclusive control of the unreliable Cisalpines, who might collude with the Dissenters against the Church, and accused their own bishops of 'usurpation of authority'. If he was influenced by anyone, it was by Milner, whose letter to the bishops of Salisbury and Hereford had almost certainly been shown to him. Milner himself claimed that 'he was chiefly guided by the arguments which I suggested in my letter to the bp of Salisbury'.[31] A comparison of Horsley's speech with the text of the letter suggests affinities which are unlikely to have been accidental. Milner had supplied the argument about respect for the opinions of ancestors, reminding the Anglicans of their own reverence for the Nonjurors:

The Church of England does not at present hold the doctrine in defence of which some of its most illustrious prelates, who at the time were the instruments and the victims of the Revolution, sacrificed every worldly hope. Yet it is presumed the divines of the present day would be cautious in swearing to a censure which would imply that the conscientious Sandcroft [*sic*] and the pious Kenn [*sic*] had lived and died in the possession of *impious and damnable tenets*.

It was Milner, too, who had raised the issue of spiritual authority and the papal supremacy, and had explained what Horsley repeated in the Lords, that both parties among the Catholics were at one in holding these doctrines. From him came the hint that the dissident Catholics would be in a worse plight if the bill passed in its existing form.[32] It was doubtless the source of Horsley's blood-curdling sentences about gaols and informers beginning: 'My Lords, if the party relieved by this bill should take the advantage which the law will give them against the other party, a horrible persecution may arise.'[33] The suggestion of the 1778 oath was also Milner's, but though Horsley did not push it to a conclusion, this was not contrary to the advice of the Winchester priest, who had left it to Parliament to decide whether any measure of Catholic relief should be granted at that time.[34] A letter to Douglass on 3 May shows that he cared more about gaining the Irish oath than about saving the Cisalpine Bill, which he deemed 'valuable more to lawyers than to the cause of religion'.[35]

When, however, despite Bishop Horsley's advice, the House of Lords was persuaded by Lord Grenville to grant it a second reading, Milner acted

---

[31] AAW, III B, 48, Milner to Bp. Douglass, 26 May 1800.
[32] AAW, A ser., xliii. 68, Milner to bp. of Salisbury, 2 May 1791.
[33] *Parl. Reg.* xxx (1791), 241–50.
[34] AAW, A ser., xliii. 68, Milner to bp. of Salisbury, 2 May 1791.
[35] Ibid. 70, Milner to Bp. Douglass, 3 May 1791.

promptly to obtain an acceptable compromise in committee, where the decisive battle would be fought. He wrote to the London vicar apostolic on 2 June:

What then I have most earnestly to request of Yr. Lordship is that you wd wait upon the Duke of Leeds & the Bishop of St. Davids, both of whom have spoken so handsomely of Yr. Lordship & of those who are connected with you & follow up the stroke by urging them to push for the Irish oath, & if that is impracticable to expunge not one or two of the most objectionable passages, but each one that Bp Walmesley objects to, that thus we may not have a doubtful oath but one that is clearly orthodox, & that there may not be one dissentient voice amongst us. Your Lordship needs no other introduction than yr business, no other recommendation than yr character. You might however take with you either the French bp or Mr Bray who is a very intelligent and honest man. All that wd be necessary wd be to send up a card with yr name, saying you shd be glad of a few minutes conversation on the bill that day to be committed. This was the clue Mr. Burke furnished me with, & I found it sufficient wherever I wished for an audience. The appearance of things is so much changed since the conference at Bath that I am confident the other Bps will when informed of the situation of affairs not only applaud but think the step I propose absolutely necessary . . . If however you cannot bring yourself to attempt the negotiation, I hope at least you will spur on Mr Bray & others to exert themselves that we may have as accurate an oath as possible, for this purpose. I cd wish that in addition to the two objections already stated, that about oaths might be more compleatly mended. I am sure it wd be carried if properly explained. I shd hope however that by due exertions the Irish oath might be carried.[36]

The oath applied to the Irish Catholics in 1774 was accepted by the whole House on 4 June, on the motion of Bishop Horsley. The chief credit for the action which was taken belongs to John Milner, who had been working towards it for about a month through his private contacts with the Anglican leaders. These included a new factor in Anglo–Roman relations, 'the French bp', J. F. de la Marche, bishop of St Pol de Léon, who had fled to England in April, and was being suggested by Milner to Bishop Douglass as a suitable link-man with the Protestant clergy and nobility as early as the beginning of May on account of his appeal to their charitable impulses.[37] Berington doubtless played a part in the negotiations but it was less important than he claimed. Significantly, he did not participate in the Catholic deputation which waited upon Horsley after the event to thank him for his services. This consisted of Bishop Douglass, James Barnard, and Milner.[38]

But Horsley's own role was crucial. Without his eloquent espousal of a discredited wing, the Catholics could have done nothing to amend their bill.

[36] Ibid. 84, Milner to Bp. Douglass, 7 June 1791.

[37] Ibid. 70, Milner to Bp. Douglass, 3 May 1791. For biographical particulars of La Marche see Dominic Aidan Bellenger, *The French Exiled Clergy in the British Isles after 1789* (Bath, 1986), esp. chap. vii.

[38] AAW, A ser., xliii. 96, Douglass, Barnard, and Milner [to Horsley etc.], June 1791.

They might not even have acquired sufficient unity to try, for the conflicts between the Orthodox and the Cisalpine parties continued to rage over questions of authority and faith for five years to come. His abandonment of the original bill at its second reading may have been partly designed to soften up the latter for concessions. He had one further service to perform. When Lord Guilford (formerly Prime Minister North), assisted by Lord Stanhope, grafted upon the new oath a clause accepting that by the Act of Settlement the succession to the throne stood limited to the Electress Sophia 'and the heirs of her body being Protestant', the apostolic vicars, mindful that it was not long since their clergy had prayed for the Pretender, sensed a fresh threat to their consciences. Horsley assured them that the compromising words were merely descriptive of an Act of Parliament and did not stand part of the oath itself. He declared to them that they were not being asked to pronounce 'on the justice or injustice of the Revolution' but merely to confirm their vicarial oath to defend the succession of the Crown against 'the descendants of the said James, and against all other persons whatsoever'. He told them that he was persuaded that the House of Peers upheld this construction, and that they might use his name in support of it. The Catholic deputation which visited him set out their account of his assurances in a letter,[39] thus using him as a constitutional guarantee.

In its agreed form the new oath softened the language in which the Pope's deposing authority was abjured, and replaced the capacious 'ecclesiastical power' by temporal or civil jurisdiction, power, superiority, or pre-eminence as the attributes to be renounced. It proved to be broadly acceptable, and the Act which embodied it became a landmark in the history of Roman Catholicism in England. The Relief Act of 1791 conferred on Catholics in general liberties which might otherwise have been confined to an unorthodox élite. These were limited in range. The gains were chiefly in freedom of worship—the right to open churches by a process of registration—and in the removal of professional disabilities. But Catholic chapels, where Mass was said, might not have bell or steeple, and the religious orders might not wear their habits in public. Perhaps, if Bishop Horsley's proposal of a revising committee for the penal laws had been taken up, the benefits might have been enlarged. But political emancipation would not have been included.

In addition to its immediate effect, the bishop's intervention had certain long- and medium-term consequences for England's relationship with the Roman Catholic Church. It contributed firstly to the restoration of diplomatic relations with the Holy See, officially abandoned in 1558, when the British ambassador was recalled to London. Resumption was gradual and halting, reaching consummation only in the twentieth century, with the establishment of the Apostolic Delegation in 1938 and the receipt of an Apostolic Pro

[39] Ibid.

Nuncio in 1982. But, as Fr. Gary Mooney has shown, a significant *rapprochement* occurred during the French Revolutionary and Napoleonic Wars and in the early peace years down to 1823.[40] It began in 1793 with the papal mission of Cardinal Erskine to Britain. From within the Curia, it was extended by Cardinal Consalvi, Secretary of State to Pius VII, who procured the admission of English consuls and diplomatic agents to the ports of the Papal States, and achieved a good working relationship with Castlereagh. However, Erskine's mission was of fundamental significance, being the first time since James II's reign that a representative of the Pope had been acknowledged at St James's. The incipient negotiations were conducted by Sir John Coxe Hippisley, an experienced agent of the British Government in Italy, acting unofficially at the Roman court. He was encouraged by Burke and by the Hanoverian prince, later duke of Sussex, who had himself visited Rome, and had made a favourable impression on the Pope and the Stuart Cardinal York, the second son of the Old Pretender. Strategic, economic, and political expectations encouraged the initiative. Vice-Admiral Lord Hood wanted to provision his fleet with fruit and vegetables drawn from the Papal States. Prince Augustus Frederick proposed a commercial treaty with the court of Rome. Hippisley himself urged the discontent in Ireland as a reason for conciliating the papacy. But Pius VI showed a becoming interest in the treatment of the *émigré* clergy and of English Catholics in Britain. He had not approved of the overbearing stand of the vicars apostolic on the 1791 bill, and thought that in future, Hippisley discovered, 'men of more liberal habits and of good families' should be appointed. He nevertheless angled for a further relaxation of the English penal laws. To win the sovereign pontiff to make civil and commercial concessions, Hippisley proposed a softening of the statute 13 Elizabeth I, which forbade the English Catholic clergy to communicate with Rome.[41] But for the more limited object of establishing a diplomatic mission, he made particular use of Bishop Horsley's speech on the Relief Bill of 1791. He wrote to Windham from Gensano on 24 August 1793:

I stated to the Cardinal Secretary in writing my own opinion on the subject, having read all the papers & having the Parliamentary Debates at hand. I made extracts of Mitford's, your own, Burke's, Fox's & other speeches, particularly, the Bishop of St. Davids, which the Pope read with much satisfaction. The result of these various communications, has been a preference to Erskine, & he has received ostensibly from the Pope permission to visit his family in Britain.[42]

He remained until 1801, and although the British Government at first insisted that his mission should not have a public character, he was received with full

---

[40] Gary Mooney, 'British Diplomatic Relations with the Holy See, 1793–1830', *Recusant History*, 14 (1978), 193–210.

[41] BL Add. MSS 37, 848, Windham Papers, correspondence of J. C. Hippisley, June–Sept. 1793.

[42] Ibid., fos. 84–106, Hippisley to Windham, 24 Aug. 1793.

diplomatic honours, and came to be recognized as 'Legate to His Holiness' at the English court.[43]

A further result of Samuel Horsley's intervention in the debate over the Catholic Relief Bill was to open a new phase in Anglo–Roman Catholic ecumenical encounter which, though brief in duration, bore valuable fruit in the treatment of the French *émigré* clergy. John Milner lost no time in using the connection with the bishop of St Davids to strengthen his own party in the internecine conflicts within his own communion. The change which took place in the English political atmosphere in the early 1790s empowered him to turn the tables on the Cisalpines. In the age of the Jacobites moderate Catholicism had been the brand most likely to allay the fears of its Protestant neighbours. But when the spectre turned Jacobin, conservatives in the Established Church could be most easily wooed with the argument that 'those who begin by "reforming" the Church end by destroying all social order'.[44] Milner projected an alliance with High Churchmen, for whom the appeal of orthodoxy was direct as well as indirect, if only the ground of controversy was selected with care. One facet of the Cisalpine controversy suggested a natural basis of agreement. Vacancies in two of the vicariates during 1790 had prompted John Throckmorton, a prominent member of the Catholic Committee, to publish, under the pseudonym of 'A Layman', a letter to the clergy of the districts involved, advocating both the election of bishops with the consent of the laity, and the replacement of missionary vicars by bishops in ordinary. This pamphlet, reissued in the following year, released a flood of controversial literature. The titles of two of Milner's rejoinders indicate the lines of his attack: *The Divine Right of Episcopacy*, published in 1791, and *Ecclesiastical Democracy Detected*, 1792.[45] Towards the end of 1791 he sent a copy of the former to Bishop Horsley, together with his English translation of the bishop of St Pol de Léon's *Pastoral Letter & Ordinances* to the clergy of his diocese.

Horsley replied sympathetically, but cautiously. He was not going to be drawn into a partisan alliance with the Catholic *outrés*, but made no secret of his preferences:

Upon my arrival in town the latter end of last month I found upon my study table your own tract upon Episcopacy, & the Bishop of Léon's charge, for both of which I beg you to accept my best thanks. Men like the Bishop of Léon, suffering for conscience's sake, of whatever particular denomination, present to the world an august and edifying spectacle.

I confess I have little apprehension that the conduct of genuine Roman Catholics, will ever give the legislature reason to repent of what has been done. I shall never give myself credit for the least share of political sagacity should the event disappoint my

[43] Mooney, 'British Diplomatic Relations', 196.
[44] Duffy, 'Ecclesiastical Democracy', 319.
[45] *DNB* xxxviii. 14–17.

expectation. I think this cannot happen, unless the democratic phrenzy should seize the majority of your people. But the consequence of that must be, that they would cease to be Roman Catholic, or they would be driven out of it. For the admirers of Civil Democracy will never long be quiet under ecclesiastical government of another form. Tho' a protestant Bishop I should little rejoice in the accession of such converts.

I am, Rev. Sir

Your very faithful and obedient serv^t

Samuel St Davids[46]

Upper Seymour Street
Jan 17 1792

If anyone was bent on making political capital out of the RC–Anglican connection, it was Milner, for he forwarded the letter to the London vicar apostolic, suggesting that the gist of it might be communicated to Dr Troy, the Catholic archbishop of Dublin, who might find it 'at once an encourage-ment & a hint to him in his present trying circumstances'.[47] Troy was a sturdy advocate of friendly relations with Dublin castle at a time when a democratic element among the Catholics of that city was being shepherded by Wolfe Tone into combination with the Presbyterians for full religious liberty and reform of Parliament.

St Pol de Léon, whom Horsley so much admired, was a forerunner of the mass immigration of clerical refugees from France. This began in August/ September 1792 with the deportation of ecclesiastics who had refused the civic oath. It has been estimated by Dr Bellenger in his authoritative study of the exiles that 1,500 of them were in England by the end of that period and 1,000 in Jersey. Many were destitute, and needed to be provided with the cheapest doss. Though their penury was often not lasting, being relieved by remissions from France, the number of refugees continued to rise and stood at a mean figure of 5,000 on the English mainland throughout the period 1793–1800.[48] Meanwhile the English colleges and convents in France and occupied Belgium transferred themselves to Britain, and were joined by some French monastic orders. Most of the French secular clergy returned to France in the opening years of the nineteenth century, when Napoleon was negotiating his Concordat with the papacy, and their long-term influence on the revival of English Catholicism is now thought to have been confined to a few parishes, chiefly sea-ports.[49]

At the time, however, they presented an acute problem of assimilation.

[46] AAW, A ser., xliv (1792–3), 7, Horsley to Milner, 17/20 Jan. 1792.

[47] Ibid., Milner to Bp. Douglass, 20 Jan. 1792.

[48] These figures are from Bellenger, *The French Exiled Clergy*, 3. Many more came to Britain for short periods. Dr Bellenger's meticulously researched 'Working List' contains nearly 7,000 names, including those of 36 bishops, but it is provisional. Ibid. 142–256.

[49] D. A. Bellenger, 'The English Catholics and the French Exiled Clergy', *Recusant History*, 15 (1981), 433–51, revising the heroic interpretation in Bernard Ward, *The Dawn of the Catholic Revival in England 1781–1803* (1909).

As Dr Bellenger has firmly shown, they were accorded a mixed reception. The heads of the Anglican establishment, notably the bishops, the cathedral chapters, and the ancient universities, at first fell over themselves to be helpful; the clergy as a group were well disposed. Dissenters, on the other hand, radicals, inferior clergy, and ordinary parishioners, were often hostile to the efforts to raise funds on their behalf. In Bellenger's view charity to the foreign clergy was 'politick', hence divisive. It rested upon the need to exalt them as a model of good citizenship and 'a bulwark against chaos'. The inspiration proceeded from Bishop Horsley's sermon to the Lords spiritual and temporal in Westminster Abbey on 30 January 1793, to mark the anniversary of Charles I's execution.[50] This is to claim too much. Planning and fund-raising in aid of the refugees was already well advanced when Horsley entered the pulpit of the Abbey. A national relief committee had been formed in London in September 1792 under the direction of John Eardley Wilmot. Though the launching meeting was heavily attended by those who were to support the later Reevesite Association, respectability as a philanthropic endeavour was guaranteed by the presence of Wilberforce. Local committees were established all over the country, and by the end of the year subscriptions amounted to £19,303. 16s. 11d.[51]

The bishop's sermon was but incidentally concerned with the *émigré* clergy; it was chiefly a eulogy of the British constitution. But in the final paragraph of a discourse running to twenty-eight printed pages, he allowed himself this set-off to his thrust against the British republicans:

We ought to mark those who cause divisions and offences. Nice scruples about external forms, and differences of opinion upon controvertible points, cannot but take place among the best Christians, and dissolve not the fraternal tie: None, indeed, at this season, are more entitled to our offices of love, than those with whom the difference is wide, in points of doctrine, discipline, and external rights—those venerable exiles the prelates and clergy of the fallen church of France, endeared to us by the edifying example they exhibit of patient suffering for conscience's sake: But if any enjoying the blessings of the British government, living under the protection of its free constitution and its equal laws, have dared to avow the wicked sentiment, that this day of national contrition, this rueful day of guilt and shame, 'is a proud day for England, to be remembered as such by the latest posterity of freemen', with such persons it is meet that we abjure all brotherhood . . . Miserable men! . . . It is our duty to pray God, if perhaps the thoughts of their hearts may be forgiven them.[52]

Given Horsley's Catholic proclivities, to say nothing of his acknowledged generosity, there is at least as good reason to suppose that the brief allusion to the exiles was made to enable them to benefit from the anti-Jacobin fever, as for thinking of it as a stick with which to beat the revolutionaries on either

---

[50] Bellenger, 'Émigré Clergy'.

[51] Margery Weiner, *The French Exiles 1789–1815* (1960), 56–9.

[52] Horsley, *Sermons* (1816), iii. 293–321.

side of the Channel. It was followed within three months by the king's letter directing collections in churches, which raised £41,314. 2s. 7½d. in aid of the exilic cause.[53]

Even among highly placed Anglican churchmen, however, support for the refugees began to waver from about 1794 onwards. There is some evidence that this was due to pressure from below. The city of Winchester was a centre of recurring friction, on account of the high proportion of immigrants to the total population, More than 680 French clergy lived in the King's House, the old royal palace, in November 1793, the number of residents rising to over 1,000 early in 1796, and a further 168 were distributed in private houses throughout the town. The pressure on the local economy was intensified by the presence of troops in the garrison.[54] Curiously, Warden Huntingford, who had previously done so much to encourage Milner and St Pol de Léon, was the first to draw the attention of the SPCK in London to the risk that Protestants might be converted. His letter received by the general meeting on 7 October 1794 was accompanied by the offer of £10 from collegiate funds to finance the supply of tracts against popery to parish ministers.[55] Huntingford's private correspondence in the Sidmouth Papers during the two preceding years, reveals a deep sympathy with the exiles, combined with a recognition that a clamour against them among the populace based on economic factors, notably the rise in the price of corn, was being 'wickedly and industriously propagated by some spirits'. He expressed concern to Addington, however, that the 'excessively indiscreet' benevolence of the Marquis of Buckingham in supplying his militia regiment quartered near Winchester with 600 pairs of gloves, made in a workshop opened by his Catholic wife for the refugees, had given the common people a handle of complaint.[56] In response to the warden's letter, the SPCK resolved to despatch to Winchester copies of three tracts from its catalogue.

Diplomacy continued to mark the Anglican approach when conflict was again brought to a head in Winchester at the close of 1795 by the actual proselytizing of Fr. Jacques Couvet, one of the French clergy lodging in the town. Concerted action was taken by a group of cathedral clergy, headed by Edmund Poulter, who was also a magistrate. Couvet was obdurate, and Thomas Rennell, a High Church prebendary who later became dean, raised the general issue of 'the conduct of the French Romish priests in that City' with the SPCK. The Society notified the archbishop, who arranged with the Home Secretary to have Couvet quietly expelled from the country under the

---

[53] Bellenger, 'Émigré Clergy'.

[54] Bellenger, *The French Exiled Clergy*, 4, 75. The civilian population of Winchester in 1801 is given as 6,194, plus about 2,000 military. Carpenter Turner, *Winchester*, 212.

[55] SPCK Minutes of General Meetings and Committees, xxxi (1792–5), fos. 278–9, 283–4.

[56] Sidmouth MSS 152M/C. 1792/F24, C.1793/F9, G. J. Huntingford to H. Addington, 24 Oct. 1792, 27 Oct. 1793.

Aliens Act. Meanwhile the bishop of Winchester instituted an inquiry by his diocesan chancellor Dr John Sturges, which averted the risk of a witch-hunt against the exiles. Horsley chaired the extraordinary meeting of the SPCK, which thanked the archbishop for the report of his action, but it is not known what he said.[57] Doubtless he shared the approval of the soft handling of the case.

Nevertheless, as the country settled to a long war of attrition against France, relations with a body of men belonging by nationality, though not by allegiance, to the enemy, continued to deteriorate. Jones of Nayland, as conservative a High Churchman as it would be possible to find, expressed the sentiments of many when he wrote to the widow of the bishop of Norwich in December 1797: 'We don't quarrel with Papishes, but I must own, my own opinion of them is not so favourable to them as in times past; because I cannot find that their late troubles have lessened their pride or mended any of their doctrines, so have not answered what I suppose to have been the purpose of divine providence against them.'[58] Evangelical Protestantism was gaining ground at both the middle-class and popular levels, and Catholicism was being discredited by rebellion in Ireland. In 1799–1800 the refugees found themselves at the receiving end of a new backlash of Protestant fury, more widespread than before. Milner reported to his bishop in April 1800 that the bishop of London, once a friend of the exiles, had 'paid a visit to Mons. Carron & threatened terrible things'. In Winchester, a city which had two immigrant convents, a stir developed in March over the recruitment of nuns and the risk that foreign priests might gather congregations. Trivial incidents were inflated into *causes célèbres*. A woman took the habit for three weeks, and then became a boarder at St Peter's House. The matter was reported to Poulter, the bishop of Winchester's brother-in-law. There was gossip about vows and engagements to which two other names were attached, and a French priest allowed half a dozen poor cottagers in the Forest of Bere to join him in Sunday prayers. Brownlow North, the diocesan bishop, shed his genial inertia, and wrote to the bishop of St Pol de Léon, expressing his determination that French clergy should not minister to English Catholics and that no nuns should take pensioners.[59] Thoroughly alarmed, Milner intervened to smooth things down, but when he found the Churchmen of Winchester turning to a political solution, he sensed an ulterior motive affecting himself.

In 1798 he had published the first edition of his *History . . . and Survey of the Antiquities of Winchester*, a work of lasting value but flawed both by multitudinous errors and a tendentiousness in handling later ecclesiastical devel-

[57] SPCK Minutes, xxxii (1796–9), fos. 6–7, 13–14, 25, 30–31; cf. *Annual Hampshire Repository*, i (1799), 127–50; F. P. Isherwood (trans.), *Banished by the Revolution* (Jersey Catholic Record; St Helier, 1972), 133–5.

[58] Horne MSS, D.6.I, W. Jones to Mrs G. Horne, 5 Dec. 1797.

[59] AAW III B, 28, 37, Milner to Bp. Douglass, 18 Mar. and 17 Apr. 1800.

opments which, in the light of the delicate position of Winchester Catholics, can be described only as imprudent. The chapter on the eighteenth century was full of animadversions on the Georgian bishops of Winchester, especially on Benjamin Hoadly, for whom he reserved his fiercest gibe. Of the latter's monument in the cathedral, he wrote:

The column against which it is placed has been cut away to a considerable depth, in order to make a place for it, evidently to the weakening of the whole fabric. Thus it may be said with truth of Dr Hoadley [*sic*], that both living and dying he undermined the church of which he was a prelate.[60]

Dr John Sturges, the chancellor, by then the chief surviving representative in the cathedral chapter of the waning Hoadleian tradition, undertook to answer Milner. His *Reflections on the Principles and Institutions of Popery* contrived to turn the issue from Latitudinarianism to the protection of Reformation Protestantism, of which Hoadly was presented as the last defender. The Cisalpine Catholic Joseph Berington joined him, attacking some of the abuses in his own communion. Milner struck back at enemies in both camps. He replied to Berington in the *Gentleman's Magazine*, seeking to divide him from Sturges on questions of establishment and politics.[61] To counter Sturges required more cunning, for he was a man of rank and consideration, a preacher to the king. He planned, therefore, to divide the Church of England by constructing a High Church–Roman Catholic alliance against Low Church Latitudinarianism. Correspondence with the apostolic vicar shows that he aimed to secure 'those bishops who are termed orthodox: particularly Dr Horseley [*sic*] & Dr Cleaver of Chester'.[62]

Accordingly his *Letters to a Prebendary*, printed in January 1800 as a full-length book, embodied a Letter on 'Hoadlyism', which examined the articles, the liturgy, and the homilies of the Established Church, to point the contrast between their plain doctrines and those of the Hoadlyites in four main areas: (1) The nature and form of the Church; (2) the sacraments; (3) the Christian mysteries; (4) the assent and subscription required to the Thirty-Nine Articles and the Book of Common Prayer. Hoadly's disciples, Balguy and Sturges, were shown to hold feeble doctrines of church authority, of miracle, and of real presence in the Eucharist; by contrast Cleaver's Oxford sermon on the Sacrament was cited with firm approval. As usual Milner went too far. He insulted the whole church at Winchester, quoting with relish a remark by Archbishop Secker that certain reviewers were only Christian 'according to the Winchester system: *secundum usum Winton*'.[63] Thus he came eventually to

---

[60] John Milner, *The History, Civil and Ecclesiastical, and Survey of the Antiquities of Winchester* (Winchester, 1801 edn.), 32–3.

[61] *Gent. Mag.* 69/2 (1799), 750–1; cf. 653–4.

[62] AAW III, 13, Milner to Bp. Douglass, 6 Jan. 1800; cf. 93, do. to do., Oct. 1799.

[63] John Milner, *Letters to a Prebendary* (Winchester, 1800), 252–7, n.3.

believe that the whole stir 'with ministry and parliament' against monasteries, French priests, etc. 'originates in the resentment of Messrs. Newbolt, Poulter, Dr. Sturges & a few of their friends at the unexpected attack which I had made upon their weak side in the article of Hoadlyism'.[64]

Newbolt, rector of St Maurice's, had influence with the MP Sir Henry Paulet St John Mildmay, who agreed to introduce a bill to tighten the restrictions on Roman Catholic convents and schools.[65] He unfolded its principles to the House of Commons on 22 May 1800. Convents were to be subjected to the Aliens Act. They were to be prohibited from recruiting new members and required to make annual returns to quarter sessions of their members, the pupils they taught, and the names and addresses of their parents. Magistrates were to inspect the schools. The bill had a slow and stormy passage through the Commons. Windham and Sheridan condemned it in scathing terms, while the independent Wilberforce thought 'the country should find its security in its morals, its manners, the mildness of its institutions, and its own religious institutions'.[66] Probably the measure would have been strangled at birth had not Pitt supported it. Catholics believed him to have urged that 'the church of Winchester is a respectable church, and attention must be paid to it'.[67] Minor concessions in committee detached Sheridan from the opposition, but the amended bill not only retained the ban on recruitment but left the convents dependent on royal licence which would expire one year after the expected termination of war with France. In this form it passed to the House of Lords, where it was read a second time on 10 July, and was immediately debated on the question for its commitment.

Bishop Samuel Horsley was then given his second major opportunity to abet Catholic relief. Milner, acting on the precedent of 1791, was responsible for enlisting his support. Hardly had the bill been announced in the Commons before he wrote to the London vicar apostolic: 'Does yr Lordship disapprove of my writing a long & confidential letter to the bishop of Rochester? He will certainly take some part or other in the business & perhaps it may be possible to gain him to the right side, as was the case in the affair of the oath.' Presuming upon the vicar's 'former conditional assent', he wrote to the bishop, making much of his own feelings on the Unitarian controversy, and giving him 'good reason to believe that if the present bill is supported by the bench of Bps, such support would be considered by the public as an implied approbation of Socinian principles'. He was capitalizing on the ideological dispute which his essay on Hoadlyism had raised. Similar letters went to Lord Chancellor Loughborough and other members of the Cabinet, playing up

[64] AAW III B, 115, Milner to Bp. Douglass, 27 Mar. 1800.

[65] According to Milner, Mildmay was indebted to Newbolt for winning over the corporation from Lord Temple's interest to his own. Ibid.

[66] *Parl. Reg.* xii (1800), 179.

[67] Ward, *Dawn of the Catholic Revival*; cf. Bellenger, 'Émigré Clergy'.

reports of Pitt's subservience to the church of Winchester and telling them that 'if his Majesty's ministers did uphold Dr Sturges and his friends in the present contest, it would appear to the whole nation that they abandoned the orthodox doctrine of the established church & favoured Socinianism'. Milner's imprudence in lecturing the Cabinet was rebuked by Douglass,[68] but the vicar apostolic followed his general lead. He had a long conference with Horsley at the deanery about an hour before that prelate went down to the House.[69]

Horsley led the opposition in the Lords to the commitment of the bill, moving that it stand committed to this day three months, which was tantamount to rejecting it. His speech was long, ponderous, and overwhelming, the effusion of a good mind slowing down. The case which he presented against the bill was, in a nutshell, that it was 'altogether unnecessary, dangerous, and unconstitutional'. After a preliminary saunter through the history of the penal laws, he proceeded to show, by reference to selected ancient statutes, that these already offered a quite sufficient security against proselytizing by the *émigré* clergy. In doing so he allowed himself a digression which displayed his sympathy with the Catholics, who at least had a religion worth propagating—one 'affecting the future interests of men, and furnishing means for the securing of those interests'—against the Socinians, who were thought 'the best of Protestants', yet whose religion consisted 'merely in negatives'. 'The man who puts the son of Mary upon a level only with the son of Sophronisca—who acknowledges in our Lord Jesus Christ nothing more than the Socrates of Jerusalem', he added contemptuously, 'will feel, I suppose, no more zeal for the propagation of the gospel . . . than I feel to propagate the dry moral of Socrates or of Marcus Antoninus.' Dr Bellenger has argued that his opposition to the bill was subordinate to the need to combat fashionable impiety and infidelity.[70] He was rising to Milner's bait. Moreover, the above-quoted remark was merely an aside. Turning to the 'express and principal object of the bill', the monastic communities, Horsley supplied the House with precise information of their numbers, nationality, and distribution: six settlements of monks and twenty-two convents of nuns, eighteen of which were English and only four French. He presented these largely in the praiseworthy guise of keepers of schools, cited at length the clauses of the 1791 Act regulating such schools, and damped down fears (which, he said, were principally responsible for the introduction of the bill) that the importation of convents would lead to a general reintroduction of monastic institutions. He also dealt with rumours of new professions of nuns, and though he had to be prompted by the Lord Chancellor when he thoughtlessly revealed details which might lead to prosecutions, he left with the House the impression, a

[68] AAW III B, 48, 57, 60, Milner to Bp. Douglass, 26 May, 6 and 21 July 1800.
[69] AAW, Bishop Douglass's Diary, ii (1800–12), fo. 38.
[70] 'Émigré Clergy'.

broadly correct one, that such professions had been few, and had been limited to nuns who were already probationers when their orders came to Britain.

It was clear that the bishop of Rochester had been heavily briefed with information about the monastic orders, probably by Milner, but it was when he came to the charge of unconstitutionality that he delivered his trump card. Speaking of the bill's preamble which enabled the king to license religious orders to perform Roman Catholic rites and ceremonies, 'any law or statute to the contrary notwithstanding', he observed in some such terms as these:

Had noble Lords considered what were the rites and ordinances of the Roman Catholics, and the enormous power this enactment gave the Crown? Penance was a rite and ordinance of Roman Catholics; and would his Majesty expose any of his subjects to corporal severities, which were sometimes ordered and inflicted among other acts of penance? Besides, the superiors of those religious institutions must have the authority of the Pope, by the medium of his bull, for sanctioning such discipline. Would they allow the Pope's bulls again to come into England, and give the King a suspending power, for such he would have with respect to all the various and express statutes that had been passed against the authority of the Pope in this country?

In a fuller account he talked of James II and appealed to a successor of one of the Seven Bishops, present in the House, to give him his support.

It is not obvious what to make of his concluding remarks that he would not object to the clauses of the bill obliging Roman Catholic schoolmasters to make an annual return of their pupils and the guardians of their pupils to quarter sessions, for he had no intention of separating them from the rest of the measure, which he wished to reject *in toto*. Probably a main aim was to safeguard his consistency in the event of similar action by others against Protestant Dissenting preachers and their schools, which he would feel obliged to support when it came before the House. Pretyman had been dunning the Government for such legislation in the preceding year, and early in 1800 Michael Angelo Taylor, MP for Durham, was known to be preparing a bill to subject itinerant preachers to the effective control of magistrates.[71] Horsley's remarks, however, were quite consonant with the general tenor of his speech. Singling out the question of schools enabled him to point the moral that much less was to be dreaded from the Roman Catholic monastic schools than from those of some of the Dissenters in which 'the doctrines of Jacobinism, sedition and infidelity, were but too frequently inculcated, to his certain knowledge'. In a time of crisis this was the most telling argument that could be used to win support for the Catholic exiles. It does not necessarily mean that the bishop's opposition to the bill was grounded on his desire to achieve social control of the English masses.

The bishop of Winchester (North) followed in the debate with a feeble defence of the bill. He claimed that it was necessary 'to quiet the apprehen-

---

[71] Ward, *Religion and Society*, 52.

sions and jealousies entertained hastily, and by persons of heated and intemperate minds'. Lord Grenville, the Foreign Secretary, gave powerful support to Horsley, whose motion he seconded. As the member of Government chiefly responsible for watching the conduct of the immigrants, he assured the House that that of the French *émigré* clergy had been for the most part unexceptionable.

Paradoxically, it was the Lord Chancellor, a friend of one of the promoters of the bill, who delivered the *coup de grâce* to it. Recognizing that in its present form it could no longer survive, he endeavoured to send it forward into committee. Ostensibly this was to explore the possibility of amending it, but his principal motive was to make mischief for Horsley. Blandly, he produced for the House a private letter which he had received referring to the theological controversy between Milner and Sturges. Almost certainly it was Milner's own. Admitting the unfairness of making the immigrant clergy the victims of a clash of opinions with which they were unconnected, he proceeded to deliver his own sentiments on the merits of the contestants. 'Milner', he observed, 'was full of the most studied aspersions on individual ministers of the Protestant Church, and the most irritable reflections and unfounded charges against its system and practice, while Dr. Sturges' publication was candid, temperate, and full of the liberal line of argument which it well became a Christian and a Scholar to adhere to.'

Horsley fell straight into the trap. He rose again, to debate the theological issue with the Chancellor. 'Dr Sturges had certainly written in very gentleman-like language; but he owned he wished the Chancellor of Winchester had held in mind the high station he had attained in the church, and shown more orthodoxy and more zeal for the discipline of our Protestant establishment. Mr Milner had used too many asperities against our established religion, and the practice of its professors and ministers; but ... '. Here Lord Hardwicke interrupted on a point of order. It was 'highly disorderly' to debate a criticism on a literary controversy wholly unconnected with the bill; besides, no peer was permitted to speak more than once in the same debate. The Chancellor upheld the second objection. Horsley was up and down in irate protest, but before a general cry of 'Order' drowned his voice, he managed to blurt out 'that he thought that Mr Milner had in many cases the advantage of the Chancellor of Winchester'.

Though his dignity was dented, he had won his case. After Lord Loughborough's revelation it seemed as though the House was being asked to legislate in pursuit of a 'literary controversy'. The bishop's motion to commit to 'this day three months' was carried on a division.[72]

How much was gained by the defeat of the bill is not easy to assess. In

[72] Account of debate compiled from *Parl. Reg.* xii (1800), 342–51 and much fuller version of Horsley's speech in *Parl. Hist.* xxxv (1800) 368–85.

practical benefit to the refugees very little. The French clergy, whose fortunes were indirectly involved in the outcome of the debate, mostly returned to their homeland in the two years following it. English colleges and convents, which were the specific beneficiaries, often remained in England, and established themselves as schools like Ampleforth and Downside or as seminaries like Stonyhurst and Ware. Down to the middle of the nineteenth century, however, the growth of monasticism in this country was slow and uncertain. Horsley did not succeed in reversing the tide of anti-Catholicism in Britain. It was, nevertheless, significant that the principle of toleration was applied to Roman Catholics by both sides during the debate. Horsley spoke of his country's 'natural proneness to toleration, as far as it could be allowed with safety to Church and state'; his brother bishop of Winchester praised the 'pure spirit of mildness and toleration', in which the Convents Bill was drawn.[73] This was gain on the attitudes which had lingered in conventional circles for most of the eighteenth century.

Toleration, however, still did not mean religious equality. Bishop Horsley's ideas were rooted in a characteristically eighteenth-century concept of establishment, which did not so much subordinate the body ecclesiastical to the body temporal as assume an indissoluble bond between them. This conviction set up a tension with the aspirations of Roman Catholics which drew him away from them in the closing years of his life. The rift was incipient in July 1800, when Lord Petre and Sir John Hippisley broached to the Home Secretary a plan for converting the English vicars apostolic into diocesan bishops. The Catholic Bishop Douglass sounded Horsley on this, and found him at one with his fellow bishops against it.[74]

The divergence widened over Catholic emancipation, a loose expression which is used by historians to cover changes ranging from the removal of the few residual penal laws to proposals to admit them to Parliament and high offices of State. When, under pressure of events in Ireland, the Younger Pitt put it to his Cabinet in a broad form, and was compelled to leave office in February 1801 by disagreement with his sovereign, Horsley came out against it. The London vicar apostolic wrote in his journal: 'The Bishop of Rochester tells me that he shall vote against it (All the Bishops will doubtless side with the head of their church).'[75] This was only part of the explanation. There was a two-way traffic between royal opposition to the grant of emancipation and ecclesiastical hostility to it. Archbishop Moore had exhorted the king to resist Pitt's proposals, and if George III needed no encouragement to comply with the request,[76] neither did the bishops need prompting by the example of the

---

[73] *Parl. Reg.*, 3rd ser., xii. 343, 347.
[74] AAW, Bishop Douglass's Diary, ii (1800–12). fo. 40.
[75] Ibid., fo. 57.
[76] A. D. Harvey, *Britain in the Early Nineteenth Century* (1978), 119–21.

monarch to oppose a reform which challenged the Church of England's Established status.

After Pitt's first ministry fell, the lead in favour of the Catholics passed to Lord Grenville. But the prelates in his group—Cleaver, Moss, and Vernon as well as Horsley—did not fall into line with their leader on emancipation.[77] When, after Pitt's return to office, Grenville presented a petition of the Irish Catholics, asking for the broadest range of public offices to be opened to them, Horsley opposed its going into committee of the House of Lords on 13 May 1805, helping to procure its rejection by 178 votes to 49:[78]

I hold that the Roman Catholics of this country are dutiful and loyal subjects of his majesty, and I think them as well entitled to every thing that can be properly called toleration, and to every indulgence which can be extended to them with safety to the principles of our constitution, as many of those who do us the honour to call themselves our protestant brethren; the Roman Catholics indeed differing less from us, in essential points of doctrine and in church discipline than many of them. But my mind is so unfashionably constructed that it cannot quit hold of the distinction between toleration and admission to political power and authority in the state . . . The statutes, which exclude them from offices of high trust and authority in the state, are not penal. Such exclusions are not penalties, and the relaxation of those statutes would not be toleration. It would be an indulgence of a very different kind.[79]

This was the distinction by which he had lived. In England, where Catholics were a strong minority, it had some credibility, but as the affairs of Ireland, a mainly Catholic country, were pushed to the forefront of politics, he started to perceive its limitations. A conflict arose in his mind between his love of consistent principles and his strong common sense. He began to waver between doctrinaire establishmentarianism and pragmatism. Inwardly he was less certain in his views than publicly he sounded. He lent private support to a plan under discussion in parliamentary circles in November 1804 for granting pensions to Irish Catholic ecclesiastics in return for their being appointed by the Crown. He wrote to Auckland: 'Is it not possible to do this without Parliament in the first instance? What I fear is that we shall find in Parliament a strong party that will be satisfied with nothing short of what they call emancipation.'[80] When the Irish petition reached the Lords six months later, his first thought was to allow it to go into committee in order to see whether something in it could be granted. Only during the debate was he moved to present blanket opposition by some remarks of Lord Redesdale, the Chancellor of Ireland, on the usurpations of title and tyrannical use of

---

[77] J. J. Sack, *The Grenvillites 1801–29* (Urbana, Ill. 1979), 105, 120.

[78] Harvey, *Britain in the Early Nineteenth Century*, 161.

[79] *Parl. Deb.*, 1st ser., iv (1805), 795–6.

[80] BL Add. MSS 34,456, Auckland MSS, fo. 148, Horsley to Auckland, 22 Nov. 1804; cf. HP 1767, fo. 148, S. to H. Horsley, 25 Nov. 1804.

excommunication by the Irish Catholic hierarchy.[81] His remarks to his son, four weeks before his death, with the pro-Catholic Talents administration in office, show how near he was to changing his view:

The Roman Catholics will be before us again this session. My mind was never so long unsettled upon any great question before. Something must be done; but what I am not prepared to say. I shall see Windham as soon as I get to town, and probably my friends Lord Spencer and Grenville; for I suspect there is really no great difference of opinion between us.[82]

The proposal which Lord Grenville's Government brought forward in 1807, to admit Catholics to the higher commands in the armed forces, was just the kind of emancipation which he might have supported. It involved no new principle, being merely an extension of the Irish Act of 1793.[83] But by that time Horsley was dead.

One of his last actions was to help to set aside a remnant of the penal code. In June 1806 he took part with the friends of the Prince of Wales in an appeal to the House of Lords against a Chancery decree which would have removed the child Mary Emma Georgiana Seymour ('Minney') from the custody of Mrs Fitzherbert. Minney, orphan daughter of Lord Hugh and Lady Horatia Seymour, had been placed by her mother in Mrs Fitzherbert's care, but guardians appointed under her father's will afterwards sued for her return to the family, partly because the foster mother was a Roman Catholic. Eldon, while Chancellor, granted their request, but when the Talents ministry took office, the House of Lords, under strong pressure from the Prince, reversed the decision, vesting the guardianship in the marquis of Hertford, head of the Seymour family, and his wife Isabella, who were willing to leave the girl with Mrs Fitzherbert. The case was fraught with political significance, but Horsley concentrated on the issue of Catholic disabilities. While admitting the general rule excluding Roman Catholics from the guardianship of the children of Protestant parents, he pleaded for an exemption in this case: partly because the bishop of Winchester (North) had undertaken to superintend Minney's religious education and partly—a point which indicates his uncommon insight into the child mind—because the act of tearing her away from Mrs Fitzherbert would engender in her a prejudice which would cause her eventually to join the Church of Rome.[84] It was a judgement characteristic of the tact used by Horsley when furthering Catholic causes.

---

[81] *Parl. Deb.*, 1st ser., iv (1805), 799–804.

[82] *Speeches in Parliament of Samuel Horsley*, ed. H. Horsley (Dundee, 1813), i, pp. ii–iii.

[83] Harvey, *Britain in the Early Nineteenth Century*, 194–5.

[84] HP 1767, fos. 151–2, Horsley to H. Horsley, 18 June 1806. For background details of this case see Bernard Falk, *The Royal Fitzroys* (1950), 231–2; Shane Leslie, *Salutation to Five* (1951), 35–6; A. S. Turberville, *The House of Lords in the Age of Reform 1784–1837* (1958), 201; Harvey, *Britain in the Early Nineteenth Century*, 161; *Parl. Deb.*, 1st ser., vii (1806), 669–71. These accounts contain discrepancies.

He was ever a true friend of Roman Catholics. His favour towards them did not only proceed from their value as allies against Revolution and unbelief. It was rooted in a sincere belief in toleration, as understood by conservative Churchmen of the time. Not less, however, did it arise from a sense of shared theological conviction which extended to many parts, though not to the whole, of the Roman system. His endorsement in the House of Lords of the Ultramontane position on canonical obedience, and Milner's public recognition from the Roman side that there were two different kinds of Anglicanism, were features of the co-operation which helped to define emergent 'orthodox' High Churchmanship and to fix its position in the Church of England in the three decades which lay ahead.

CHURCH HOUSE LIBRARY
ECTON HOUSE
NORTHAMPTON NN6 0QE

BOOK No _ _ _ _ _ _ _ _ _ _

CLASS No _ _ _ _ _ _ _ _ _

DATE added _ _ _ _ _ _ _ _

7

'A Free, Valid and Purely Ecclesiastical Episcopacy'

LIKE the English Catholics, the Episcopalians of Scotland suffered a denial of basic religious freedom for most of the eighteenth century. Like them also, they upheld a form of church order, a liturgy, and a system of belief which commended them to High Churchmen of Horsley's viewpoint. But there were significant differences in the character of the two denominations, and from these sprang dissimilarities in their external relations.

The Episcopals sustained a dramatic contraction under laws which were tightened against them in the middle years of the century. Roman Catholics advanced slowly from long-standing disabilities. The abolition of episcopacy in Scotland at the Glorious Revolution, and its subsequent replacement by the Presbyterian church system, was the work of an active minority, reluctantly supported by the Crown. Continued adherents of the old polity cannot be exactly counted, but it is recognized that their number remained large for many years afterwards. The leading historians of the Kirk have conceded recently that at the beginning of the eighteenth century Episcopalians enjoyed general support north of the Tay, where half the population of Scotland lived, and that many south of that river shared their outlook or were indifferent to the dispute.[1] Owing to the firm royalist control exerted over the Church through the universities and through lay patronage in the generation after the Restoration, more than half the clergy were disaffected to the Presbyterian settlement when it was imposed by the Scottish Parliament in 1690.[2] Because they enjoyed the support of most of the Scottish nobility and many of the lairds, they were often able to retain their parochial charges until they died. MacRae reports that no fewer than 133 did so as late as 1710,[3] and many more functioned in their own meeting houses. The episcopate itself went into obscure retirement after being disowned by the State, but a renewal of energy was discernible from 1705, when the consecration of bishops was resumed.[4] After a brief spell of official favour in the closing years of Anne's reign the Church passed, under the first two Hanoverian kings, into an era of legal

---

[1] A. L. Drummond and James Bulloch, *The Scottish Church 1688–1843* (Edinburgh, 1973), 15; cf. Bruce Lenman, 'The Scottish Episcopal Clergy and the Ideology of Jacobitism', in Cruickshanks (ed.), *Ideology and Conspiracy*, chap. ii, *passim*; Rosalind Mitchison, *A History of Scotland* (1970), 285.

[2] Lenman, 'Scottish Episcopal Clergy', 39.

[3] J. MacRae, 'The Liturgy of the Scottish Nonjurors: Its Sources and Editions', *Records of the Scottish Church History Society*, 3 (1929), 69–78.

[4] Ibid. 124, 181–5.

proscription, which, together with internal theological dissensions and local conflicts with an aggressive Evangelical Presbyterianism,[5] prompted a more or less continuous decline. The strength of the clergy fell to 125 by 1744 and to 53 by 1790. A press estimate of lay attachment made at the close of 1789 yielded a figure of only 30,000, perhaps one-fifteenth of the population of Scotland.[6]

A second difference, not less important for being superficially obvious, is that Scottish Episcopalianism was a Protestant communion, severed from the Church of England by no theologically incongruous or politically dangerous notions of supranational papal authority. Though bishops had returned to Scotland at the Restoration, Laudian ceremonial and the controversial Scottish liturgy of 1637 were not revived, and when, after the Act of Union, set prayers were introduced into Episcopal chapels, it was the English Book of Common Prayer that was favoured.[7] Episcopalians, therefore, were enabled to muster an earlier and broader support from Anglican churchmen south of the border for the redress of their grievances than Roman Catholics could ever command. They were the pivot of the aspirations of powerful ecclesiastics like Bishop Atterbury and Archbishop John Sharp to restore the fortunes of the Church of England after the Revolution by planting the English form of church government among Protestant churches elsewhere. Hence, during the Tory ascendancy of Harley and St John, in which Queen Anne's reign culminated, they received the backing of the High Church party for the protection of an Episcopal minister against Presbyterian oppression in 1711 and for the passing of a special Toleration Act tailored to their needs in the following year.[8] When Samuel Horsley and others returned to the defence of the Episcopalians just under eighty years later, they were acting upon good precedent.

By that time, however, the plight and the character of the Episcopal Church had changed radically. The toleration of its ministers embodied in the Act of 1712[9] presupposed their willingness to take the oaths of allegiance and abjuration of the Pretender, and to pray in their meeting houses for Queen Anne and the Electress Sophia. Most of them swallowed the abjuration oath in order to qualify themselves,[10] but they remained, in Dr Bruce Lenman's words, 'the most significant single group of men creating and transmitting

---

[5] John MacInnes, *The Evangelical Movement in the Highlands of Scotland 1688–1800* (Aberdeen, 1951), chap. ii, *passim*.

[6] Figures quoted by F. C. Mather, 'Church, Parliament and Penal Laws: Some Anglo-Scottish Interactions in the Eighteenth Century', *English Historical Review*, 92 (1977), 540–72.

[7] J. D. Lawson, *History of the Scottish Episcopal Church from the Revolution to the Present Time* (Edinburgh, 1843), 50–2, 190–3.

[8] A. Tindal Hart, *The Life and Times of John Sharp Archbishop of York* (1949), 283–4; Mitchison, *A History of Scotland*, 319–20.

[9] 10 Anne, c. vii.

[10] Bruce Lenman, *The Jacobite Risings in Britain 1689–1746* (1980), 130.

articulate Jacobite theology', while their flocks 'produced the vast majority of active participants in every single Jacobite rebellion from that of Claverhouse in 1689 to the final fling which died on the battlefield of Culloden in the Spring of 1746'.[11] Theirs consequently was the communion singled out by Hanoverian Governments for the harshest retribution. An Act of 1719[12] specifically directed against Episcopal ministers subjected them to six months' imprisonment for omitting the State prayers, and ordered the offending chapels to be closed for a like period. Services in private houses were brought under similar regulation. This statute was not continuously enforced,[13] but the Jacobite rebellion of 1745 provoked Acts which struck at the roots of the native Episcopal communion. That of 1746[14] required Episcopal pastors to produce proof to the magistrates that they had been ordained by bishops of the Established Churches of England and Ireland. It also deprived the laity of their civic rights for attending the services of unqualified ministers. Even the nobility were to forfeit their right to choose, or to serve as, Scottish representative peers if they attended twice in the year before an election. Offending commoners suffered a similar loss of the franchise and the right to be elected as MPs. Pastors who officiated unqualified incurred penalties up to transportation for life. A clause in the Act of 1748 for the disarming of the Highlands removed the loopholes in the law by which a few existing ministers had managed to qualify. All clergy ordained by Scottish bishops were banned from officiating, irrespective of when their letters of orders were registered.[15]

Unlike earlier statutes the post-1745 legislation was rigorously applied. In its final form it was not a frightened reaction against rebellion, but a part of a confident drive by the victorious British Government to change the way of life in the Highlands. In a persecution which lasted for about ten years Episcopal chapels which had escaped destruction by the duke of Cumberland's army in 1746 were closed. When a milder regime ensued from the closing years of George II's reign onwards into that of the king's successor, the communion emerged with a reduced, uncertain position, comparable to that of English Catholics, in which worship had to be conducted in semi-concealment, sometimes in private houses, and chapels could be shut at the whim of the local authorities. In these circumstances it faded from the recognition of its English sister.[16] The impressive muster of twenty English bishops, the entire complement present on the occasion, against the retrospective clause of the 1748 Act in committee of the House of Lords,[17] was the last expression of

---

[11] Lenman, 'Scottish Episcopal Clergy', 36.
[12] 5 George I, c. xxix.
[13] Lawson, *Scottish Episcopal Church*, 265–6.
[14] 19 George II, c. xxxviii.
[15] 21 George II, c. xxxiv; cf. *Parl. Hist.* xiv (1747–53), 277.
[16] Lawson, *Scottish Episcopal Church*, 291, 300–13; Mather, 'Church, Parliament and Penal Laws'.
[17] *Parl. Hist.* xiv (1747–53), 269–72.

general interest in episcopacy in Scotland before a quarter of a century of oblivion, punctuated only by the occasional comments of visitors. Visiting an English chapel at Montrose with Johnson in 1773, Boswell observed: 'Dr Johnson gave a shilling extraordinary to the clerk, saying, "He belongs to an honest church". I put him in mind that episcopals were but dissenters here; they were only tolerated. "Sir, (said he) we are here as Christians in Turkey." '[18]

Ironically, the most imposing episcopal churches perceived by Dr Johnson during his travels in Scotland were the English qualified chapels. These formed a rival episcopal denomination to that superintended by the Nonjuring bishops. Originally founded to minister to English residents in the sea-ports, they spread among Scotsmen, especially after the crippling legislation of 1746–8 had been laid upon the native Church. They were served by clergy ordained by English and Irish bishops, who occasionally visited them to confirm, but exercised no jurisdiction over them. The chapels were, therefore, virtually independent charges with power vested in the lay managers. The clerical body serving them was much smaller than that of Nonjuring churches—twenty-six in 1789—but lay adherents were more numerous in the larger towns and also more wealthy and influential.[19] Hence, those congregations which did exist presented a thriving image, contrasting markedly with the tenuous hold of the Scottish bishops' following even in the same towns.

Under these restrictive conditions the communion of the indigenous Scottish bishops changed from being a Dissenting segment of a national Church into a theological sect. In this the evolution of a distinctive Scottish liturgy played a major part. Though it had native roots in the antiquarian researches of Thomas Rattray, laird of Craighall,[20] the change was hastened by the proposals of a party among the English Nonjurors to introduce the 'usages': four amendments to the Prayer Book service designed to bring it into line with historic Catholic tradition. These were the mixing of water and wine in the chalice, commemoration of the faithful departed, invocation of the Holy Spirit to bless the elements of bread and wine, and an explicit offering of those elements to God the Father.[21] A beginning was made with the arrival of Bishop James Gadderar in Aberdeen in 1723 to deputize for Bishop Archibald Campbell. Both had been previously *episcopi vagantes*, actively engaged in the deliberations of the Nonjurors in England. One of Gadderar's first acts in Aberdeen was to order a reprint of the recently republished Laudian liturgy of 1637 for the benefit of his diocese. He encouraged his

[18] James Boswell, *The Journey of a Tour to the Hebrides with Samuel Johnson* (repr. 1948), 51. I owe this reference to the late Dr A. R. Winnett.
[19] Mather, 'Church, Parliament and Penal Laws'.
[20] MacRae, 'The Liturgy of the Scottish Nonjurors'.
[21] H. Broxap, *The Later Nonjurors* (Cambridge, 1924), 47.

clergy unofficially to vary the order of the parts in such a way as to accommodate it to Usager preferences.[22] Later the variations were incorporated in
the text. A characteristically Scottish sequence in which the intercessory
prayer for the Church, including her departed members, followed instead of
preceding the prayer of consecration appeared in the Ordinal prepared by
Bishop Robert Keith some time after 1743.[23] Rattray's *Ancient Liturgy of the
Church of Jerusalem*, published in 1744, imparted a 'primitive' and Eastern
quality to the revisions, which reached definitive form in the Scottish Communion Office of 1764.[24] The lead in introducing the new liturgy came from
a few scholarly bishops who persuaded a divided clergy and a still more hostile
laity of its value. Nevertheless, the Office became in due course the badge of
identity for a dwindling community which, in the generation after the Jacobite
rebellion of 1715, severed its last links with the Church of Scotland, and
forfeited the benefits of toleration which it might previously have gained by
using the English Prayer Book.

Detachment from civil society was also apparent in an assertion of the
clergy's independence of the civil power. This was affirmed as much against
the Pretender as against the Hanoverians. The momentum behind the successful movement to replace the collegiate system of episcopacy by diocesan
bishops in the 1720s came largely from the belief that the clergy had an
inherent right to elect their own diocesans. The change was resisted by
the Old Pretender and his agent Lockhart who exerted a control through
appointments to the college.[25] Two decades later in 1743 the Scottish bishops
surprised an English Nonjuror by acting synodically to make canons without
the licence of the self-styled James VIII and III.[26] When the Stuart cause
virtually collapsed after the disaster of Culloden, a younger generation of
Episcopalians started to ground their claim to respect less on their adherence
to the legitimate line of British kings and more on their descent from the true
Church of the King of Kings. In the published version of his sermon 'The
Nature and Extent of the Apostolical Commission', preached at the consecration of the American Bishop Seabury in 1784, John Skinner, co-adjutor
bishop of Aberdeen, viewed the Church as a divine society, drawing its
authority from Christ through the apostolic succession of its ministry. This
society he held to be by its original constitution 'independent of the state'. In
support of his claim he cited the testimony of Acts 4: 19, where two of the
apostles, threatened by the Jewish Sanhedrin, and commanded not to speak in
the name of Jesus, replied to their judges: 'Whether it be right in the sight of

[22] MacRae, 'The Liturgy of the Scottish Nonjurors'; cf. Broxap, *The Later Nonjurors*, 61.
[23] CH 1037, ordinal by Bishop Keith commissioned 1743 and inscribed by 'R. F.', 18 July
1757.
[24] MacRae, 'The Liturgy of the Scottish Nonjurors', cf. J. Dowden (ed.), *The Scottish
Communion Office 1764* (Oxford, 1922), *passim*.
[25] Lawson, *Scottish Episcopal Church*, chaps. xiv, xv, *passim*.
[26] Broxap, *The Later Nonjurors*, 245.

God to hearken unto you more than unto God, judge ye.' A footnote to the publication quoted with approval remarks of the English High Churchman Reeves to the effect that neither (law) books, nor reports, nor statutes could avail against the inherent power of the clergy, and ended by commending his own communion for venturing 'to show more regard to the *acts* of the apostles than to the acts of the British parliament'.[27]

The extreme anti-Erastianism of this address could not but provoke opposition in any Established Church, and it is not surprising that Bishop Lowth of London interpreted it as an attack on the English bishops for not consecrating Seabury.[28] Nevertheless, the shift of the emphasis in Episcopalianism away from Jacobitism towards a doctrine of ministry which English High Churchmen half-acknowledged, set in train reconciling influences between the two Churches. The consecration was itself a product of these, for the way was prepared for it by the High Church prebendary of Canterbury George Berkeley, who repaired to St Andrews in 1781 to place his son at the University and to promote his own scholarly intercourse with Principal Watson, the Hispanist. He stayed there for three years, developing fruitful contacts with Episcopal clergy like Strachan and George Gleig of Pittenween who invited him to officiate in their chapels.[29] Berkeley had a grand design in view. With American interests derived from his father Bishop Berkeley he sought to counter William White's plan of quasi-Presbyterian establishment propounded for the rebel colonies of North America. Using his familiarity with Gleig as an introduction, he approached Bishop Skinner on 9 October 1782 with a plan to pre-empt the ground by sending a bishop consecrated by and from the Scottish Episcopalians to serve without State recognition in America. He failed to convince the withdrawn and timid bishops in Scotland of the need to take so bold a step.[30] But when towards the end of the following year application was made to them to consecrate an American clergyman, Samuel Seabury, sent by the clergy of Connecticut who had tried and failed to obtain the episcopal order from the English bench, he was instrumental in removing their reservations.[31] After continuing hesitation and division the consecration of Seabury took place in Aberdeen on 14 November 1784. The Scottish bishops prepared a letter to the episcopal clergy of the state of Connecticut assuring them of 'the blessings of a free, valid and purely

[27] John Skinner, *The Nature and Extent of the Apostolical Commission: A Sermon* (Aberdeen, 1785).

[28] J. Skinner (of Forfar), *Annals of Scottish Episcopacy from the Year 1788 to the Year 1816* (Edinburgh, 1818), 57–65.

[29] W. Fraser Mitchell, *Bishop Berkeley's Grandson: His Séjour in Scotland and Literary Associates* (repr. from *University of Edinburgh Journal* (1935), in Dr. Williams's Library); cf. BL Add. MSS 39,312, fo. 31, Skinner to Gleig, 14 Oct. 1784.

[30] CH 1989, 1988, Berkeley to Skinner, 9 Oct. 1782, 21 March 1783; H. G. G. Herklots, *The Church of England and the American Episcopal Church* (1966), 90–2.

[31] CH 1998, Berkeley to Skinner, 24 Nov. 1783.

ecclesiastical episcopacy', and signed with Seabury a Concordat, by which he bound himself to 'take a serious view' of the Scottish Communion Office, and to 'introduce it by degrees into practice without the Compulsion of Authority on one side, or the prejudice of former custom on the other'.[32]

With the Seabury consecration, contacts between English Churchmen and the Nonjuring world multiplied. Berkeley remained in touch with Gleig, and introduced him to the archbishop of Canterbury in 1786.[33] The chief impetus came from the American refugee clergy Jonathan Boucher and T. B. Chandler, active not only in procuring Seabury's commissioning for Connecticut but in prompting a similar deed for Nova Scotia. Bishop Skinner, whose enthusiasm was thoroughly aroused, encouraged Chandler to open a correspondence with him about anything interesting to the cause of establishing 'a pure and primitive Episcopacy in the Western world', and the task was passed to Boucher.[34] With Chandler's help Boucher also established a communication with the English Nonjuring bishops, Kenrick Price at Manchester and William Cartwright at Shrewsbury. William Stevens, the broadly connected lay theologian, who had befriended Boucher, was privy to the correspondence which lasted for eleven years, from 1785 to 1796, embracing all the leading issues at stake between the Church of England and the Nonjurors.[35] In 1789 the bishop of Carlisle exchanged letters with Cartwright at the behest of Archbishop Moore.[36] During the 1780s, therefore, individual High Churchmen of the English Established Church acquired a sympathetic familiarity with fringe elements in Anglicanism saturated with Catholic beliefs. For the most part they were unable to concur with Scottish and Nonjuring divines in their disparagement of State authority in matters of religion or in the exclusive importance which they assigned to the liturgical 'usages'. But their awareness of apostolic ministry and Eucharistic mystery was heightened by the encounter.[37]

Samuel Horsley's interest in the affairs of the Scottish Episcopal Church came late, and was at first relatively casual. Though he was himself half Scottish, it was not, as H. H. Jebb suggested, 'always present'.[38] According to

---

[32] Herklots, *Church of England*, 95–9; cf. Bruce E. Steiner, *Samuel Seabury, 1729–1796: A Study in the High Church Tradition* (Athens, Ohio, 1971), *passim*.

[33] Mather, 'Church, Parliament and Penal Laws'.

[34] Skinner, *Annals*, 42–58; Mather, 'Church, Parliament and Penal Laws'.

[35] Bodl. Add. MSS D. 30, Nonjuror Papers, fos. 35–40, Cartwright to Chandler, 30 Aug. 1784, Cartwright to Boucher, 23 Apr. 1785, and subsequent letters.

[36] Ibid., fos. 92–4, Carliol to Cartwright, 16 June and 14 July 1789; BL Egerton MSS 2185, Letters to Bp. Douglas and his Son, i (1748–89), 175–80, 184–6, Cartwright to Douglas, 3 and 19 June 1789.

[37] Bp. Douglas was reminded of opinions which he had formed as 'a young man at Oxford' (*c.*1740), by studying the controversy among the Nonjurors, that the usages were 'of high antiquity', though 'matters which I cannot consider as essential'. Bodl. Add. MSS D. 30, Nonjuror Papers, fos. 92–3, Carliol to Cartwright, 14 July 1789.

[38] Jebb, 95–6.

the Victorian historian, J. P. Lawson, he was drawn by a long controversy in the *Gentleman's Magazine* in 1785–6, over the right of Nonjuring bishops to bestow mitres, to publish a letter over his own initials, admitting that he had been comparatively ignorant of the history and state of Episcopalianism in Scotland before it performed its service to Seabury.[39] Research has failed to uncover this letter, but, in writing to the Scottish clergy, he observed: 'Ever since it came to my knowledge that the merciful providence of God preserved to the present day, though in a state of great affliction, a remnant of the old Episcopal Church of Scotland, I felt the deepest concern in their sufferings, and the most earnest desire that they might obtain relief from the extreme severity of the penal laws.'[40]

Even then he moved cautiously. There is nothing to connect him with the intention formed by some of the clergy of the Church of England to do the Scottish Episcopal Church some service 'at a convenient season' which was notified to the Primus anonymously on 9 June 1785.[41] Boucher and Berkeley were the intermediaries between the archbishop of Canterbury and the Episcopals Skinner and Gleig in the negotiations for an appeal to Parliament to undo the penal laws. The continuance of the Episcopalian clergy in the Jacobite State prayers, even when adherence to the Pretender had ceased to be an article of faith, held up progress while Prince Charles Edward Stuart lived. But when he died in Rome on 31 January 1788, a sick and dissipated old man, Dr Abernethy Drummond, the recently elected bishop of Edinburgh, persuaded five of his six episcopal colleagues, nearly all the clergy, and the vast majority of laymen that as the Pretender's brother the Cardinal York had disqualified himself from the succession by contracting engagements to the Pope incompatible with the sovereignty of an independent State, prayers should henceforth be offered at services for the House of Hanover. Drummond had every intention that the submission should be followed by a bill giving relief from the penal laws. A private suggestion to the archbishop of Canterbury that the English bishops should corporately initiate the repeal met with no response.[42] Support came mainly from Scotland, where a handful of powerful magnates, notably Henry Dundas, the Treasurer of the Navy, and Ilay Campbell, the Lord Advocate, were recruited by the wealthy Abernethy Drummond.[43] Even this was poorly co-ordinated, and when the ending of the illness of King George III cleared the decks for action in Parliament, three of the Scottish bishops—Skinner, now the Primus, Drummond, and John Strachan—had to come to London to plead their own cause. When they arrived towards the end of April 1789 the time could scarcely have been less

[39] Lawson, *Scottish Episcopal Church*, 330.
[40] Quoted from Jebb, 96.
[41] Skinner, *Annals*, 62.
[42] Mather, 'Church, Parliament and Penal Laws'.
[43] Skinner, *Annals*, 84–5.

propitious. Their English friends did not expect them. Jonathan Boucher
made hasty preparations to introduce them to William Stevens and Jones
of Nayland, using the Hutchinsonianism of the latter to commend him to
Skinner.[44] The Church of England bishops were embarrassed by Henry
Beaufoy's imminent motion for repeal of the Test and Corporation Acts
which most of them were committed to resist, as the English Dissenters used
what they saw as the comparatively favourable position of the Episcopalians in
Scotland as an argument in favour of their own case.[45] Moreover, the clergy
of the English chapels in Scotland, uncertain as they still had reason to be, of
the kind of recognition which the Scottish bishops intended to seek from the
British Parliament, had been stirring doubts in the minds of English prelates
about the theological complexion of the denomination which they headed.[46]

Upon their arrival the three supplicants approached the English bishops
individually to explain their position. Stevens and Jones of Nayland vetted
their letter to the primate, and Jones procured them an interview. They were
careful to distinguish their case from that of the English Dissenters and
Scottish Catholics and to emphasize that they allowed their clergy to use the
Prayer Book service as an alternative to the Scottish Communion Office. But
the response was lukewarm. The most that the archbishop would promise was
to consider their business when the Beaufoy motion had been discussed.[47]
The evidence of papers in the Episcopal Chest shows that four other bishops
gave them audience.[48] Of these Horsley was the most forthcoming. He was
friendly but curious. Unlike most of his colleagues he addressed his visitors
in terms which recognized their episcopal character. To 'the Rt. Revd. Mr
Skinner,' he wrote on 2 May: 'The Bishop of St Davids presents his com-
pliments to Bishop Skinner and his associates and will be happy to have the
honour of seeing them on Monday next about noon, if it be consistent with
their own engagements. If not the Bishop will be at home at any other time
they will be pleased to appoint, except on the days of Mr Hastings' trial.'[49]
Skinner was invited to dine at the Horsleys' on 13 May.[50] When the bishops
attended, Horsley peppered them with questions and emerged happy to
find that they differed from the Church of England in no essential point of
doctrine or discipline; 'Whatever', said he, 'might have been your religious

---

[44] CH 1390, Boucher to Skinner, 28 Apr. 1789.

[45] See G. M. Ditchfield, 'The Scottish Campaign against the Test Act, 1790–91', *Historical Journal*, 23 (1980), 37–61 for a lucid explanation of the relationship of the tests question to Scotland; Mather, 'Church, Parliament and Penal Laws'.

[46] Ibid.

[47] Skinner, *Annals*, 97–9.

[48] Beilby Porteus (London), John Thomas (Rochester), Lewis Bagot (Norwich), and Horsley. John Douglas (Carlisle) and John Hinchcliffe (Peterborough) sent friendly replies to the solicitations of the Scottish bishops but did not see them. CH 1399, 1401, 1404.

[49] CH 1393, to Skinner, 2 May [1789].

[50] CH 1395.

tenets, as your political disaffection is removed, I think you entitled to toleration, as far as you ask it. But perhaps it may facilitate your business to let it be known, as I am now competent to do, that you do not essentially differ from our Church.'[51] The bishop of St Davids was not prepared to accept the religious professions of the Scottish Episcopalians on their own evaluation. The historian of the Scottish Communion Office writes:

At the time when efforts were being made for the repeal of the penal laws affecting the Scottish Church, Samuel Horsley, then Bishop of St. Davids, showed himself a warm friend to the cause of his oppressed brethren in Scotland. He was much interested in questions relating to the formularies of faith and worship in our Church, and prepared, with a view to nothing more than his own private satisfaction, a *Collation*, in four parallel columns, of the Communion Offices in the first Prayer Book of Edward VI, the Scottish Prayer Book of 1637, the present English Prayer Book, and the present Scottish Communion Office.[52]

The researches enjoined upon him by the task doubtless helped forward the evolution of the Catholic element in his liturgical and theological opinions.[53]

Horsley's moral support brought the Scottish bishops no practical assistance either from himself or from his colleagues for the bill which was brought forward on their behalf during the 1789 session. True to promise Dundas and some friends from Scotland made the principal exertions to gain them a hearing.[54] J. A. Park, a barrister and a protégé of Lord Mansfield, drafted the bill as their agent. Dundas undertook the arrangements for presenting it to the legislature. As originally proposed it was a sweeping measure, not only repealing the penal statutes of 1719, 1746, and 1748, but entitling Episcopal congregations to all the privileges of Queen Anne's toleration on conditions less exacting to themselves. Their pastors were to be required to subscribe a simple oath of allegiance to George III, an oath denying papal pretensions and the right of foreign princes or prelates to exercise ecclesiastical jurisdiction in Britain, but not the dreaded oath of abjuration of the Pretender prescribed by the 1712 Act, which would have involved them in an abnegation of their previous allegiance. Collectively the English bishops maintained a benevolent neutrality. Archbishop Moore, however, who for some years had been encouraging the Scots to hope for a less extensive indulgence at an appropriate time, advised Dundas to show the draft privately to his own legal adviser, Sir William Wynne. On Wynne's advice it was modified in such a way as to remove the suggestion that episcopacy in Scotland was being accorded a

---

[51] Skinner, *Annals*, 99.

[52] Dowden (ed.), *Scottish Communion Office*, 82–4. A copy of the Collation attested by Bishop John Skinner and dated London, 30 Mar. 1793, is in the Episcopal Chest (CH 1504).

[53] See below, p. 205.

[54] Lord Henderland introduced them to Lord Stormont with a commendation to Lord Mansfield. CH 1389, Henderland to Stormont, 2 Apr. 1789.

quasi-established position. The title was amended from an 'Act to prevent the Disturbing those of the Episcopal Communion in Scotland' to an 'Act for granting Relief to Pastors or Ministers, and other persons being or professing to be of the Episcopal Communion in that part of Great Britain called Scotland'. Moreover, it was provided that the Toleration Act of 1712 conferring 'privileges' should be added to those to be repealed. The archbishop remained uneasy. He would have preferred to have had a clause inserted into the bill debarring persons deriving their orders from Scottish bishops from being appointed to English livings. Although Wynne dissuaded him from insisting on this, he nervously probed the analogy of the preferment of a converted priest originally ordained by an Irish Catholic bishop. Aware, no doubt of the acute competition for livings faced by so many of the English clergy,[55] Moore had begun to cast anxious and curious eyes on rival hierarchies in the British Isles whose claims to ordain were impeccable.

In this atmosphere of uncertainty the Relief Bill foundered. Passing the Lower House with a few amendments, it was shelved without division at its second reading in the Lords on 6 July. Lord Chancellor Thurlow delivered the *coup de grâce* to what, though sponsored by a member of the Government, was a private bill. His stated objection, communicated to the Scottish bishops two or three days earlier, was to the proposed alteration of the oaths. Nevertheless, the bishops' offer, prompted by Lord Hopetoun, an Episcopalian nobleman, to delete this feature failed to save the measure. The English prelates did not raise a finger to prevent the defeat. Only three of them were in their places in the Lords when the disaster occurred. The primate was not among them; nor was Samuel Horsley.[56]

The bishop of St Davids must have been acutely embarrassed by his patron's stalwart resistance to a bill granting the toleration to which he stood committed, but there is no reason to believe that his absence was dictated by personal considerations. Older historians of Episcopalianism have assumed too readily that, being all along firmly and zealously dedicated to the cause, he prevaricated only because of Thurlow's known and sustained opposition. Thus William Walker's *Life and Times of John Skinner*, a book published in 1887, which strongly influenced H. H. Jebb's interpretation, affirmed that Horsley's objections to a clause subsequently proposed to admit Scottish clergy to English livings was governed simply by a desire to meet Thurlow's claim that the episcopacy of the Scottish bishops was not a 'legal' or 'regal' episcopacy. 'No-one knew better than Bishop Horsley', he wrote, 'how hollow and erastian this objection was, yet he laboured to show that there was in it an element of plausibility which would have great weight with the erastian

---

[55] P. Virgin, *The Church in an Age of Negligence* (Cambridge, 1989), 139.

[56] See Mather, 'Church, Parliament and Penal Laws' for above details of the progress of the application. Further particulars are from CH 1405, 1427, and LPL Moore Papers, vi, fos. 160–6. Cf. Skinner, *Annals*, 113–16.

minded legislators of the time.' The same work later interprets his giving
to the House of Lords 'the usual erastian explanation' of 'the distinction
between a spiritual and a legal episcopacy' as being 'to avert the great man's
wrath'.[57] This is a mistake resulting from the ascription of post-Tractarian
values to the later Georgian Old High Church. High Churchmen of the late
eighteenth century, of whom Horsley was by no means a unique example,
acknowledged the imperatives of establishment because it came naturally
to them to do so, but they also recognized a higher power resting in the
episcopal order, by virtue of its apostolic descent. It was because the re-
emergence of the Scottish hierarchy forced upon them, in a manner not
previously required, the need to discriminate between the two that the
struggle for repeal raised so many problems and hesitations in their minds.

Further unsuccessful bids were made by the Scottish Episcopalians to
secure their liberties in the next two years, but advances towards reaching
agreement were achieved. In the winter of 1789–90 the initiative in the
campaign was transferred from the authoritarian and intriguing bishop of
Edinburgh Abernethy Drummond to an elected committee of the Episcopal
Church acting through the Primus, Bishop Skinner, and its secretary, Roger
Aitken of Aberdeen, and working in conjunction with a small committee of
correspondence in London consisting of Hutchinsonian friends in the English
Church, William Stevens and George Gaskin, together with the lawyer, J. A.
Park.[58]

The bishops of the Church of England still controlled the pace of operations in Parliament, and were influenced towards making concessions by
the threats to religion in general. When Skinner returned home from a
conference in Perth in February 1790 he found a letter informing him that the
archbishop of Canterbury had pronounced in favour of legislation during the
current session, for the sake not only of the poor clergy who would be injured
by delay but also 'of those people who at present go to no Church at all, and
whose morals are consequently injured'.[59] But nothing could be countenanced
until the English Dissenters' move for the repeal of the Test and Corporation
Acts had been defeated. Even Horsley told Dr Gaskin that 'your bill must not
be received until that is disposed of'.[60] The decisive overthrow of Fox's
repeal motion on 2 March removed all excuse for further delay, and within a
few days the London correspondents were preparing a new bill to be introduced into the House of Commons by the Attorney General or Sir William
Dolben, MP for Oxford University. Difficulties continued over the problem of

[57] Wm. Walker, *The Life and Times of John Skinner Bishop of Aberdeen and Primus of the Scottish Episcopal Church* (Aberdeen, 1887), 119, 135.

[58] Mather, 'Church, Parliament and Penal Laws'; BL. Add. MSS 39,312, fos. 24–6, Gleig to Berkeley, 20 Nov. 1789.

[59] Skinner, *Annals*, 153–4.

[60] Ibid. 149.

recognizing the validity of Scottish episcopal orders in England. To please the English hierarchy the London correspondents planned to incorporate in their bill a clause enacting that no letters of orders from Scottish bishops should be admitted as qualifications for preferment in the Church of England.[61] The Scottish Committee objected to this on ecclesiastical, national, and practical grounds, and issued a strongly worded Representation against it on 18 March. The Committee asserted its Church's claim to 'that *divine Right* of Episcopacy to which the Scotch has an equal claim with the English Church', rejected the analogy with a clause in the Act of 1786 enabling the consecration of bishops for the American republic on the grounds that the Americans, unlike the Scots, were aliens. Fears were expressed that the clause would drive the most promising ordinands to seek ordination in England as a qualification for preferment in both countries, leading to a brain drain from Scotland, and would give a handle to the English chapels in that country to question the validity of Scottish orders.

The Scottish Committee accepted that in practice the patrimony of the English Church should be effectively confined to her own sons, but proposed an alternative clause, so worded as to avoid casting a slur on Scottish ordinations, and conceding as a quid pro quo that English bishops were to lose their right to ordain on Scottish titles, which would mitigate the nuisance of the qualified clergy to the native hierarchy.[62]

Faced by this conflict of opinion Dr Gaskin turned to Bishop Horsley for advice. He found him unsympathetic towards the Representation and unwilling to step out of line with other English bishops. His view, as described by Gaskin, was as follows:

The King, his Lordship observed, is, in a certain sense, the Head of the Church, and without his permission our Bishops are not to consecrate any Bishop, nor is any British subject, obtaining the Episcopal character without the King's permission, so far to be acknowledged a Bishop as that his Episcopal acts shall have a civil effect in the Established Church of England. It does not follow that because the same regard is not paid to the letters of orders of a Protestant Bishop in Scotland as to those of a Popish bishop abroad, therefore the validity of the former, in a spiritual or ecclesiastical sense, is in the least degree a doubtful point. But the fact is, that considering the Royal Supremacy in Britain, our Bishops think that they cannot introduce into their Church persons admitted to holy orders by a Bishop in Great Britain, to whose consecration, the King, in virtue of his supremacy, had not given his consent.

The furthest he would go towards meeting the wishes of the Scots was to suggest the addition of a clause that presentation to a benefice or call from a

---

[61] Ibid. 153–5.

[62] CH 1442, Representation on behalf of the Committee of Convention of the Scottish Episcopal Church, 18 Mar. 1790.

congregation in Scotland should not be deemed a legal title to receive orders from an English bishop.[63]

It is improbable that he assumed this position merely to humour Thurlow. The Chancellor's first objections to the Episcopal Bill had turned on altering oaths of State; only after Horsley's pronouncement did he add the charge that the Scottish bishops were seeking to enhance their authority by legislation. The bishop of St Davids may have been pandering to the Erastian doctrines of some of his colleagues. But a more likely explanation of his equivocation is that he was struggling to adapt the theory of establishment which he held throughout his career to his current awareness of a spiritually authentic episcopate which it would not easily fit. In his 'Thoughts upon Civil Government', written about a month earlier for a different purpose, he admitted an exception to the union of religious and civil Government in cases where Christ's will was declared in abrogation of the law of the land.[64]

John Warren, bishop of Bangor, was another late eighteenth-century High Churchman conscious of the same tension. But he proposed to resolve it in a different way. When Gaskin interviewed him for the London correspondents on 8 April, he was given the impression which he afterwards related to Bishop Skinner that the bishop not only 'sees your hierarchy in its true point of view' but was 'for having it explicitly acknowledged as to its inherent spiritual power, as is that of the American Bishops'. He wished to insert into the Scottish Relief Bill a clause modelled on the American Consecrations Act of 1786 which, while debarring the Scottish bishops and their clergy from ministering in 'any of his Majesty's dominions outside Scotland', gave them explicit legislative recognition as bishops, priests, and deacons.[65]

The correspondents failed to rally support for this clause,[66] and were thrown back on Horsley and his proposal to prevent English bishops from ordaining on Scottish titles. It was at this stage, late in the month of April 1790, that he emerged as the principal champion of their cause. His first exertions were directed towards collecting evidence of persons improperly ordained by prelates of the English and Irish Churches to officiate in Scotland. Skinner furnished him with a few examples—a Presbyterian schoolmaster sent to London by two gentlemen of Ellon to be ordained by an English primate in opposition to his own early ministry, a clergyman at Peterhead admitted by a bishop of Down and Connor, who was on holiday, to humour a schismatic congregation there.[67] Bishop Horsley's projected clause

[63] Skinner, *Annals*, 158–9.
[64] See above, pp. 75–6.
[65] Skinner, *Annals*, 167–8. Warren was believed to be more in the Lord Chancellor's confidence than any other English bishop. Ibid. 117.
[66] CH 1446, Skinner to Gaskin, 29 Apr. 1790.
[67] Ibid.

can have done nothing to reduce the hostility of the clergy and laity of the qualified chapels, who had come out openly against the bill at the beginning of the year. Nor was it calculated to appease Thurlow, who was believed to be acting under their influence.[68] Horsley, nevertheless, began to use his personal influence to soften the Chancellor's resistance. He spoke to him about it at the beginning of May, but 'found him so extremely uninformed upon the business, that he says it will take him too much time to make him understand it, to give us any reasonable hope of success this session'.[69]

Nearly a year elapsed before the contest was resumed. During that period Parliament had been dissolved, a general election held, and the new legislature successively prorogued for most of the second half of the year. But the opponents of the penal laws had not been wasting their time. When the campaign reopened in February 1791 five of the bishops in the House of Lords appear to have been acting together as a party of supporters, for they each received from the Scottish Primus an amended version of his appeal to the English prelates, treating them as privy to the plan of relief. It asked them to ensure that any clause disqualifying the Scottish clergy from holding English livings should not invalidate their orders in spirituals.[70] Except for the archbishop of Canterbury all were High Churchmen—George Horne, bishop of Norwich, John Douglas, bishop of Carlisle, John Warren, bishop of Bangor, and Samuel Horsley, bishop of St Davids. Douglas brought forth useful evidence of support for relief within the Presbyterian Church of Scotland,[71] but in energy and resourcefulness Horsley towered above his colleagues. To avoid offending Thurlow it was planned to begin this time in the House of Lords, where the marquis of Buckingham was appointed to introduce the bill in April,[72] and J. A. Park had a preliminary audience with the Chancellor on 7 April. He found him quite intractable. As soon as one of his objections to the measure was met, he moved to another. When this was reported to Dr Gaskin, the English correspondents repaired to the bishop of St Davids and the bishop of Norwich. Bishop Horsley remarked that he would go at once to the House of Lords and appoint a time to wait upon the Chancellor in private. What happened when they breakfasted together on the following day (9 April)[73] was described by the bishop in a letter to the bishop of Carlisle:

Upon conversing with the Lord Chancellor upon the case of the Scottish Episcopalians, I found he had great difficulties about dispensing with the abjuration oath. And

---

[68] Bishop Skinner firmly believed this to be the case, but there is no conclusive proof of it. Mather, 'Church, Parliament and Penal Laws'.
[69] Skinner, *Annals*, 177–80.
[70] CH 1449, Skinner to the English bishops with modified version, 9–10 Feb. 1791.
[71] CH 1452, Carliol to Skinner, 23 Feb. 1791.
[72] Mather, 'Church, Parliament and Penal Laws'.
[73] CH 1459, Park to Skinner, 10 June 1791.

his Lordship made objections, which, I confess, appeared to me to carry great weight. I send your Lordship a draught of a new bill. drawn by Mr. Park, upon a principle suggested by me. Your Lordship will perceive that the effect of it will be, to relieve such of them, as can persuade themselves to take the oaths, from the penalties to which they would still be subject, notwithstanding their oaths, by virtue of the ninth clause of the 19th of G.2 C.38 [the 1746 penal law]. And whenever the Cardinal York shall drop, as the abjuration oath will die with him, the relief of this bill will become compleat. The Bill leaves the delicate question of the validity of their orders quite untouched. If we can carry this bill I believe it will be the most that can be done for them.   I am, My dear Sir,

Your very faithful Servt
Samuel St. Davids[74]

The bishop omitted to say to Douglas what Park stressed to Skinner, that the 'first object of the Bill' was 'to relieve the laity from any penalty, which you will see is effectually done'.[75]

Horsley's dynamism was never more apparent. Having requested Park to draft a new bill, before he could comply he brought with him a bill of his own, to which the former had only to add a preamble.[76] In order to make sure of it, he sent it with a covering letter to Lord Kenyon, Chief Justice of the King's Bench and a close friend of the Chancellor.[77] The new bill proved to be no more acceptable to Thurlow than its predecessor. When Horsley presented it to him, he was treated, Lord Kellie observed, 'so strangely by the Chancellor that he did not chuse to speak to anyone upon the subject'.[78] But the bill received more widespread support in other quarters than any of its predecessors. It was approved by Lord Kellie, a leading friend of the Episcopal Church among the Scottish noble families, by Dundas, and by the marquis of Buckingham. Bishop Skinner though it 'unexceptionable', and 'a great body' of the English bishops expressed approbation of it when it was explained to them by the archbishop. Porteus, bishop of London, an associate of Hannah More and of Wilberforce, came out zealously in its favour, and, though Thurlow's resistance caused postponement to yet another year, Lord Kellie was confident that general opinion would carry it against the Chancellor in the following year.[79]

The prophecy was justified, but the battle in Parliament had still to be fought through. Meanwhile, the odds against the contenders lengthened, as the growing counter-revolutionary fever in the country impinged upon their

---

[74] BL. Eg. MSS 2186, letters to Bp. Douglas and his son, ii, fo. 30, Horsley to Douglas, 24 Apr. 1791.

[75] CH 1459, Park to Skinner, 10 June 1791.

[76] Ibid.

[77] Horsley to Kenyon, 24 Apr. 1791, in G. T. Kenyon, *The Life of Lloyd, First Lord Kenyon, Lord Chief Justice of England* (1873), 269–70; cf. 164–7, 235.

[78] CH 1459, Park to Skinner, 10 June 1791.

[79] CH 1461, Skinner to Kellie, 21 June 1791.

prospects. Gleig warned Horsley in September 1791 'that the late commotions at Birmingham and elsewhere' might 'make it imprudent to introduce any bill for our relief so early as in the next session'. The Episcopal clergy were being proletarianized by their opponents, who represented them 'as a set of uneducated, illiterate men', and their bishops as 'being capable of admitting into holy orders any contemptible creature who may offer himself a candidate'.[80] While the earliest objections to emancipation had been constitutional, concerned with oaths and the role of the House of Lords, the challenge henceforth became preponderantly social. The general character of the Episcopalians and their fitness to be tolerated was the principal issue to be determined when a new Relief Bill was presented to the House of Lords at the beginning of April 1792.

Bishop Horsley had supervised the drafting of the measure, insisting that it be cast in the form of his product of the previous year.[81] He also amended the statement of the political principles of the Scottish Episcopalians, known as the Representation, which was designed to be circulated among the members of the Upper House, removing features objectionable to Hanoverian Whiggery. He wrote to Dr Gaskin:

The omission of one short sentence in the 7th page of the Representation of our friends will I think obviate the scruple you suggested to me in the Vestry Room at Bow. I therefore return the proof-sheet with that correction. In truth had that sentence stood, avowal would at the worst have been this that tho' they ceased to be Jacobites, they continue to be Tories.

I am aware that the objection may still arise from the republican quarter. 'The principles which you avow are a sufficient security of your loyalty to the persons and the descendants of the Sovereign who you now acknowledge. But what security have we for your loyalty to the Act of Settlement [?]' If this objection should be made it must be met in debate & I think it will not be difficult to come over it ... The language we are to hold to the public on behalf of our friends, is 'These are their principles— Erroneous perhaps to some degree. But neither dishonourable to themselves nor dangerous to you'.[82]

Notwithstanding these precautions Thurlow still intrigued against the bill. He fastened upon the feature of it which the bishop of St Davids had done most to devise: its want of requirement that pastors should register their orders with a public authority. This, he maintained, would empower all sorts of people, such as the blacksmith of Gretna Green, to set themselves up as Episcopal ministers and celebrate marriages. He wanted to reintroduce the requirement to show ordination by the Established bishops of England and Ireland. This, he observed, was the only guarantee which he would accept that Episcopal

---

[80] BL Add. MSS 39, 312, fo. 128, Gleig to Horsley, 7 Sept. 1791.
[81] Mather, 'Church, Parliament and Penal Laws'; cf. CH 1487, relief bills.
[82] CH 1473, Horsley to Gaskin, 24 Feb. 1792.

ministers taught 'doctrines fit to be tolerated', and were properly qualified to perform baptisms and marriages, both of which Scottish law required them to do.[83]

The Scottish Churchmen fought back with every weapon at their command. Bishop Skinner and his associates whipped up the royal boroughs of Scotland to petition Parliament in favour of the Relief Bill. Five counties and ten boroughs complied, and four other Scottish constituencies, including the capital city of Edinburgh, sent instructions to their MPs to support the bill.[84] Though this movement created an impression of wider interest in the country which can only have helped, it was of secondary importance to lobbying and thrustful but conciliatory debate on the floor of the House of Lords. Samuel Horsley found these methods more congenial and took the leading part in them. He was assisted by other English bishops, by sympathetic Scottish noblemen, and by the presence in London of the Primus, Bishop John Skinner, one of the two delegates sent by the Scottish Committee to counteract expressions in the printed case which presented the Episcopalians as enemies of the constitution.

By these techniques the Lord Chancellor's resistance was slowly worn down. He was persuaded to forgo opposing the bill in principle at its second reading on 2 May. This enabled it to pass without division. Before the committee stage opened on 9 May Horsley negotiated a compromise which broke the deadlock of the last three years. Thurlow was persuaded to accept as sufficient evidence of the fitness of the Episcopalians to be tolerated a public declaration of religious principles which showed that they were close to the Church of England. The suggestion was floated by the bishop in his speech at the second reading when he asked that they be put on the same footing as English Dissenters (before 1779), who had qualified for toleration under the 1689 Act by 'subscribing a great many of the 39 Articles'. He induced the London Committee and other friends of the Scots to agree that a clause requiring the Episcopal clergy to subscribe the Articles should be added to the bill in committee. As a counterpoise to reassure the bishops of the Church of England, a clause inhibiting the Scots from taking 'any bene-fice, curacy or other spiritual promotion' in England, Wales, or Berwick-upon-Tweed was also prepared for insertion.[85]

The Act which received the royal assent on 15 June 1792[86] conferred upon

---

[83] Skinner, *Annals*, 195–9; *A Narrative of the Proceedings relating to the Bill . . . for Granting Relief to Pastors, etc. . . . of the Episcopal Communion in Scotland, by a Member of their Committee* (Aberdeen, 1792), 10–12, 22–3. Episcopal ministers were recognized as competent to baptize and to marry by the Scottish Toleration Act of 1712, and still performed marriages before the 1792 Relief Act.

[84] CH 1468, Gaskin to Skinner, 10 Feb. 1792; cf. CH 1467, Skinner to Lord Fife, 10 Feb. 1792; *Narrative*, 8–9, 10.

[85] Ibid. 23–6.

[86] 32 George III, c. lxiii.

the Scottish Episcopalians an imperfect toleration, though it was probably the
most that could be obtained for them at the time. It freed the laity from all
penalties and civil disabilities provided that they attended chapels where the
king was prayed for. The clergy gained an indulgence which was legally
conditional upon their taking oaths unacceptable to their consciences. They
could not even subscribe the Thirty-Nine Articles in the form required by
the statute without also swearing the oath of abjuration of the Pretender. But
they knew that in practice they enjoyed security from persecution, and had
been given grounds to hope that when Cardinal York, the last serious Stuart
claimant to the throne, died, the law would be changed to make their relief
absolute. Had Bishop Horsley lived until that event it almost certainly would
have been. But Horsley died in 1806, the cardinal in 1807. Not until 1871
was the clause requiring the abjuration oath repealed.[87]

Anxious, meanwhile, to correct sinister misrepresentations of the character
of his flock and to improve relations with the English Church, Bishop Skinner
proposed to a convention at Laurencekirk on 22 August 1792 that the
Episcopalians should voluntarily adopt the Thirty-Nine Articles 'with some
little variation in point of form' as a statement of their own beliefs, and require
future candidates for holy orders to subscribe them as such.[88] The clergy of
his own diocese, Aberdeen, declared synodically on 7 November following
that 'though various opinions may be, and always have been entertained in the
interpretation of some of those articles' they considered them to be agreeable to 'the word of God'.[89] Even those conservative Scottish bishops like
Abernethy Drummond and Andrew Macfarlane, who disliked the Calvinistic
tone of the Articles,[90] were disposed to go along with such a declaration on
the grounds that it would be particularly acceptable to the bishop of St Davids
and other English High Churchmen as 'a pledge of our appearing on their
side' in the battle for Christian orthodoxy 'against Arians, Unitarians, and all
the enemies of Christ'.[91] At a time when the reverberations of the Unitarian
petition had not died away, this was a reasonable expectation. In particular the
bishops of Scotland may have expected to be repaid for their doctrinal
allegiance by support for the endeavours which they had been making since
1791 to absorb the English qualified chapels.[92]

Union at Edinburgh was seen as the key to fusion in other parts of
Scotland, and Bishop Horsley was called in to advise. Proposals were aired
simultaneously, at the beginning of 1793 by the Scottish Primus and by the
rich vestrymen of the proprietorial English chapel in the Cowgate, where the

---

[87] By 34 & 35 Victoria, c. xlviii.
[88] CH 1380, report of Skinner's speech at Laurencekirk Convention, Aug. 1792.
[89] CH 1502, Declaration of Aberdeen Diocesan Synod, 7 Nov. 1792.
[90] CH(J).66, Drummond to Watson, 4 Feb. 1793.
[91] Ibid.
[92] Mather, 'Church Parliament and Penal Laws'.

laity were more favourable to unity with the Scottish bishops than their ministers, who sometimes held English livings in plurality with their Scottish charges, and did not wish to sever their connections with the law and discipline of the Church of England. Bishop Skinner planned to win over the dissidents by bringing up an Englishman to serve as bishop of Edinburgh. His choice alighted on Jonathan Boucher, the American exiled priest, who was first to be appointed to the cure of one of the Edinburgh chapels, and then made bishop. Boucher responded encouragingly to the suggestion when it was put to him privately by Skinner, though it was stipulated that he should use the Scottish Communion Office.[93] Many obstacles stood in the way of the scheme. It required the collaboration of the existing Scottish bishop, Abernethy Drummond, who was sincerely anxious for unity but hoped to bring it about in his own way. He was slow to adopt the suggestion that he should retire in favour of Boucher, but eventually agreed to invite the latter to visit Edinburgh, and conducted negotiations for terms of union with Sir William Forbes, the founder, and other vestrymen of the English chapel.[94] It was apparent, however, both to Drummond and the Primus that without open encouragement from the English hierarchy neither Boucher nor the qualified clergy would be ready to proceed with the plan. Boucher was disposed to angle for a stall in Carlisle cathedral to ensure his financial security before moving to Edinburgh.[95] It was to Archbishop Moore and the two High Church prelates, Douglas and Horsley (especially the latter), that the Episcopalians chiefly looked for support. Abernethy in his warm, well-meaning, and hasty manner wrote to solicit their interest in his efforts to bring about a coalition at Edinburgh. He found them strangely cold. The archbishop was 'Caution itself', and Horsley failed to reply.[96] This caused Bishop Skinner to suggest to Boucher on 20 February that he might take advantage of his 'habit of seeing the Bishop of St. Davids on an easy and friendly footing' to raise the matter with him privately. English High Churchmen who had served the Scots as their London correspondents during the relief struggle, namely Stevens and Gaskin, were enlisted by the Primus to gain the ear of sympathetic English prelates in the new cause.[97]

But St Davids was being solicited from the other side. Alexander Cleeve, minister of the new English Chapel of St George's, York Place, who orchestrated the opposition to the Scottish bishops' plan, saw him in London during the winter of 1792–3. On being shown the articles of union proposed

[93] Sk.C., Skinner to Boucher, 13 Feb. 1793.

[94] Sk.C., do. to do., 20 Feb. and 7 Aug. 1793; CH(J).66, Drummond to Watson, 18 Jan. and 8 Feb. 1794.

[95] Sk.C., Skinner to Boucher, 13 Feb. 1793.

[96] CH(J).66, Drummond to Watson, 11 Feb. 1793; Sk.C., Skinner to Boucher, 13 and 20 Feb. 1793.

[97] Sk.C., Skinner to Boucher, 20 Feb., 9 Mar. and 15 May 1793.

by Abernethy Drummond, the bishop reacted so strongly against 'what might be understood to imply a denial of the King's supremacy' that Cleeve was encouraged to launch an appeal some time later 'to the fountain head of decision in a cause like this' for a written opinion of the projected union which he intended to use to influence his colleagues.[98]

The letter caused acute embarrassment. It revealed the bishop's own uncertainty. 'I was really in no haste to answer it', he observed, 'lest upon a question of so much delicacy, I should advise ill, or, which would be much the same thing, give advice from which false conclusions might be drawn, by the one side or the other. But having lately had a correspondence with the Bishop of Salisbury [John Douglas] upon the subject, which has enabled me to make up my mind more perfectly than ever upon every part of the question, I have since ventured to give my opinion to Mr Cleeve.'[99] Horsley's reply to Cleeve was written from Carmarthen on 10 October 1793. Its content, deducible from an extract copied for the Edinburgh vestryman Lord Eskgrove, was wholly hostile to the plan of union at Edinburgh. His objections turned partly on the refusal of the native clergy to take the oath of abjuration, by which they were prevented from giving proof of their orthodoxy in the form prescribed by the Relief Act. Secondly, he warned against the proposed articles of union which because of their implications for the royal supremacy, could not be subscribed by an English cleric without risking the penalty of excommunication under the second and third canons.[100]

Twelve days later the bishop of St Davids sent his own paraphrase of the letter to the earl of Kellie, a nobleman in the opposite camp. This reiterated the ban on the subscription of articles seeming to deny the royal supremacy by English clergymen, but added a positive suggestion which was lacking in Cleeve's extract:

Nevertheless, since the late act of Parliament expressly gives permission to the laity of Scotland to attend the ministry of the clergy of Scottish ordination, provided only that the King and Royal family be prayed for by such clergymen in terms of the English liturgy, it is in my judgement the *duty* of the laity to return into the bosom of their indigenous Church. *They have no excuse for not returning.* And our English clergy, instead of dissuading the return of the Scottish laity to the communion of their own Church, ought to come away, & leave the Episcopalians of Scotland in the hands of their own Bishops, who, I dare say will manage their spiritual concerns very well. This

---

[98] NLS Acc. 4796, Fettercairn Papers, Box 122, Cleeve to Eskgrove, 31 Oct. 1793, with extract from Horsley.

[99] CH(J).66, extract from Horsley to Kellie, 22 Oct. 1793, in Drummond to Watson, 11 Jan. 1794.

[100] NLS 4796/122, extract from Horsley to Cleeve, in Cleeve to Eskgrove, 31 Oct. 1793.

[101] CH(J).66, extract from Horsley to Kellie, 22 Oct. 1793, in Drummond to Watson, 11 Jan. 1794.

is the substance of my opinion which I wish to be *known to all parties*, tho' I have some doubt whether it will please either.[101]

Either Bishop Horsley was saying different things to different men, or Cleeve had omitted an important part of his advice. The second alternative seems more likely than the first, for the section which was excluded would have weakened the influence of the qualified clergy over their flocks. The advice which he gave to the laity of the English chapels to make peace with the Scottish bishops sprang from genuine theological conviction, for he repeated it even more strongly to Bishop Abernethy Drummond in October 1799. Their separation was schism, and the English clergy by staying were 'guilty of fomenting schism'. He was ready to consider the interposition of an 'act of authority', by which he seemed to mean an Act of Parliament, if persuasion failed.[102]

In the short term the Horsley intervention set back the process of building a viable Church in Scotland from the disparate elements already present. All hope of cementing a scheme of local union at Edinburgh under a bishop from England was for the moment removed. Boucher was discouraged by the denial of English hierarchical support and the plan to consecrate him was abandoned in May 1794 amid fears of resistance by the Kirk and the populace to the bringing of a bishop from south of the border, exploited and even fomented, Skinner believed, by the malcontent English clergy.[103] But Horsley never abandoned the respect for a 'pure spiritual episcopacy' which he had allowed the Scottish bishops to possess, when speaking in the House of Lords at the second reading of the Relief Bill.[104] As an Established Churchman he did not completely identify with it, and never underestimated the problems of relating it to political episcopacy as it existed in England, in Ireland, and in the Scottish qualified chapels. Distrusting all quick and over-simplified solutions, he believed from the beginning that 'to be effectual the work must be gradual'.[105] He developed a close personal relationship with the Scottish Churchmen in the closing years of his life. In 1802 he admitted the young William Skinner, son of the Primus and himself a future Primus, to the diaconate at Rochester to serve his father's congregation at Aberdeen, thus making a special and symbolical exception to his general rule that English bishops should not ordain on Scottish titles.[106] Support for the Scottish bishops became an institutionalized component of Old High Churchmanship in England in the early decades of the nineteenth century, and Bishop Horsley

---

[102] NLS 4796/122, copy of Horsley to Drummond, 16 Oct. 1799.
[103] Sk.C., Skinner to Boucher, 7 Nov. 1793, 23 May and 9 July 1794, and 19 Mar. 1795.
[104] *Parl. Reg.*, 2nd ser., xxxiii (1792), 385–91.
[105] Boucher MSS B.3/68, Stevens to Boucher, 11 Sept. 1793.
[106] Sk.C., Skinner to Boucher, 20 Feb. and 23 July 1802.

played a special part in making it such. In 1805 he organized an appeal to his fellow bishops in aid of the legal expenses of the church in Banff. This was a precursor of the Scottish Episcopal Fund patronized by leaders of the Hackney Phalanx.[107] It was not, however, until 1840 that the diocesan authority of those bishops and the validity of the orders they conferred was legally recognized by Parliament.[108]

[107] Lawson, *Scottish Episcopal Church*, 364–5, 442–3. For subscriptions received for the Scottish Episcopal Church by 1811 from such High Churchmen as Martin Routh, Thomas Sikes, H. H. Norris, and Archdeacon Nares see BL Add. MSS 35,649, Hardwicke Papers, fos. 381–4, 'Memoir'.

[108] Lawson, *Scottish Episcopal Church*, 416–17.

8

Church Administration and Reform

THE place of Samuel Horsley in church reform needs to be set against a new stereotype. He has long been judged a good diocesan bishop—unusually good for the age in which he lived. His Edwardian biographer H. H. Jebb spoke of the untiring energy which he threw into all departments of a bishop's work. In the organization of his diocese, his visitation of remote parishes, his profuse hospitality, his care for the poorer clergy, his preparation for ordinations, and his restoration of the cathedral, he left a record which remains until today.[1] Of the eighteenth century, the official historian of Rochester diocese had already written: 'In Samuel Horsley, the last bishop of the century, the see of Rochester had an occupant of a different stamp to either of his immediate predecessors. A man of vigorous intellect and strong will, he combated the errors of the time, whether practical or doctrinal, with firmness and ability.'[2] One stain alone appeared upon his spotless mantle. 'He is said to have had the defects of his qualities', observed Overton and Relton, 'and to have been somewhat irritable and dictatorial; but lesser men might be content to be dictated to by such a giant.'[3]

Since these assessments were made, the criteria for judging him have hardened appreciably. Not only has the spread of democratic values engendered cynicism about great men. The furtherance of research, powerfully stimulated by the late Norman Sykes, has yielded a more variegated pattern of responsibility in the exercise of ministry by bishops and their clergy. Universal condemnation of the eighteenth-century Church, such as threw Horsley's activity into relief, is no longer fashionable, and a more recent generation has begun to discover movements of church reform in progress long before the Reformed Parliament went to work. What is called the third church reform movement, to distinguish it from inadequate precursors centring on the reigns of Charles I and Anne respectively, started from small beginnings during the War of American Independence, and came to maturity under William IV and Victoria. Before 1832 the process of ridding the Church of England of organizational weaknesses deep-rooted in its history but accentuated by the demagogic and social changes of the period of the Industrial Revolution had taken a conservative form. It depended principally on the energy shown by

[1] Jebb, 67.
[2] A. I. Pearman, *S.P.C.K. Diocesan Histories: Rochester* (1897), 309.
[3] J. H. Overton and F. Relton, *The English Church 1714–1800* (1906), 256.

individual bishops interpreting Acts of Parliament of a permissive kind and by parish clergy whom they advised rather than directed. When the further help of the State was required, it was enlisted through existing agencies, and the aim was to strengthen local enterprise and the power of Ordinaries, not to supersede it. Hence came a string of Acts designed to help incumbents to build parsonages and to empower bishops to compel them to do so (1776, 1781), Acts authorizing bishops to insist on the payment of reasonable stipends to curates (1796, 1813), to enable them to regulate non-residence by annual licence (1803), to restore to Queen Anne's Bounty Board the freedom to spend its resources on parsonages (1803), etc.[4] Ecclesiastics and laymen who planned to reorganize the system existed before the eighteenth century closed, chiefly the Liberal Richard Watson, bishop of Llandaff, who advanced plans to redistribute the revenues of bishops and cathedrals for the improvement of religion at the parochial level as early as 1783,[5] but he was more notorious than influential. When an element of central intervention began to enter, as it did increasingly in the quarter of a century after Horsley's death, the authority was exercised with great caution and respect for the vested interests of clergy and laymen. Herculean efforts were rewarded by mixed success, and while the economically weakest places in the parochial system were slowly eliminated by the operation of parliamentary provision, the principal tasks of church reform were revealed rather than resolved by the bureaucratic activities of the Privy Council's receiver of diocesan returns in the twenty-four years after the Act of 1803 which authorized them. The disclosures, moreover, were neither accurate nor comprehensive, as the latest, strongly quantitative, survey of the subject clearly shows. The author, Dr Peter Virgin, concludes fairly that the case for gradualism in the refurbishment of ecclesiastical institutions, with a slow beginning in the 1780s rather than a sudden onset about 1800, is 'not so much discredited as circumscribed'.[6]

He does not, however, take note of a coherent movement or movements for reform centred on the 1790s and early 1800s, which found an echo in national politics. The Younger Pitt, prompted by Lord Auckland, gave serious consideration to the commutation of the tithe, that contentious prop of clerical incomes which did so much to draw the wrath of farmers to the Church. In 1791 they urged its replacement by a variable corn rent. Pitt took up the suggestion of a corn rent, and put it to the archbishop. Eight years later he

---

[4] See G. F. A. Best, *Temporal Pillars* (Cambridge, 1964), chap. v, *passim*, for a thorough survey of legislation of this kind; also P. Virgin, *The Church in an Age of Negligence; Ecclesiastical Structure and the Problem of Church Reform 1700–1840* (Cambridge, 1989), 64–6.

[5] R. A. Soloway, *Prelates and People: Ecclesiastical Social Thought in England 1783–1852* (1969), 3. For his enterprising proposals to build new churches in the metropolis with public funds and to attract notable preachers to them, in 1800–4, see 286–7.

[6] Virgin, *The Church in an Age of Negligence*, 267.

proposed a scheme for paying tithes into the funds, the proceeds to finance clerical incomes. But except from Richard Watson of Llandaff, episcopal support was not forthcoming.[7]

Bishop Horsley was involved in a conservative Oppositionist venture earlier in the decade. Francis Maseres, a fellow mathematician who had assisted him in the Royal Society controversy, published in 1791 a short treatise, *The Moderate Reformer*, which took the form of an appeal to the archbishop of Canterbury to move in the House of Lords a programme of thirteen points which, if enacted, would render the Establishment 'more useful to the establishment of religion', 'increase the respect and attachment of the people to its clergy', and 'improve the condition of the inferior clergy'. The proposals envisaged increasing the reputation and independence of diocesan bishops by removing the anomalies in the mode of electing them and by annexing substantial preferments to the poorer sees as a permanent arrangement in order to avoid seeking special Government permission to hold them *in commendam*. A modest redistribution of ecclesiastical incomes, by restoring the great tithes of bishoprics, deaneries, and prebends to parishes, was also proposed, as was a ban on pluralities in cathedral prebends and parochial benefices where the bishop possessed no right of institution. Non-residence was to be curbed by requiring clergy suing for their tithes to prove to the court that they had done duty in their churches for forty Sundays in the year in which they claimed the tithe. If they had done less than this, the allocation of tithe arrears might be scaled down accordingly. Finally some of the large, unworkable parishes of the north of England were to be divided. The 'moderation' of these quite biting reforms consisted of safeguarding the rights of present incumbents and patrons and of avoiding suggestions for abolishing the tithe and for tampering with the liturgy and the Thirty-Nine Articles in a manner which his own liberal conscience would have approved.[8] When in the aftermath of the September massacres in Paris, and amidst alarm occasioned by the growth of domestic radicalism, Maseres moved to interest Windham in his plan, he cited the approval of Bishop Horsley. He wrote to the former on 13 October 1792:

I hope you approve of my little tract called *The Moderate Reformer*; and, if you do, I wish you would move the house of Commons to carry some part of it into execution. It would contribute greatly to save the Church establishment from the attacks of those who wish it ill, and when being supported by such just and strong arguments, as are contained in Dr. Priestley's familiar Letter to the people of Birmingham (a most curious and entertaining work,) and Mr. Benjamin Flowers's book on the French Revolution, will one day or other overturn it. Bishop Horsley agrees with me in these opinions, as do Dr. Bole, the prebendary of Westminster, and Dr. Pearce, the Master

[7] E. J. Evans, *The Contentious Tithe* (1976), 79–80.
[8] F. Maseres, *The Moderate Reformer* (1791).

of the Temple. If I were a member of Parliament, it would be my pleasure to bring in such moderate bills for the correction of gross abuses, and I would not wish to be in Parliament for any other purpose.[9]

He suggested meetings in London with Horsley when he returned from Wales for the meeting of Parliament, with Sir Gilbert Elliot, a friend of Edmund Burke, and with Windham himself. Windham was obsessed with the anarchy in France and the military operations on the Continent, but Maseres persisted in his design. By the end of the month he was hoping for an initiative in the House of Lords 'by a committee consisting of the two Archbishops, the bishops of London, Durham, Lincoln, Llandaff and St David's [Horsley], and a few more lay lords that are known to be friends of the Church establishment'.[10] Nothing of consequence emerged immediately, but the exertions of this politically mixed set reveal that the reaction of the conservative side of the nation to French Revolutionary principles was by no means as exclusively negative as is often supposed.

If, as the correspondence seems to indicate, the High Church Bishop Horsley was not averse in principle to a legislative attack on ecclesiastical abuses, it does not follow that he agreed with Maseres in everything he proposed. The extent of his reforming propensities must be judged by his attitude to particular measures when they were raised in Parliament and by his manner of conducting his office as a diocesan bishop and as dean of England's greatest collegiate church, Westminster Abbey. The present chapter will be concerned to explore facets of his role in the reform of the Church at the national level.

TITHE COMMUTATION AND ENCLOSURES

In the minds of the laity the obligation to pay tithes constituted the heaviest grievance against the Established Church. Attacks upon these payments multiplied from about 1770 onwards when, as Professor Evans writes, 'the twin challenges of tithe-free industrial expansion and increased interest in agricultural improvement brought the system under its harshest scrutiny'.[11] Adam Smith and Arthur Young voiced criticisms, which were echoed by lesser men, against a tax which, because it was levied on the gross rather than the net produce, bore with particular severity on poorer land which required heavy expenditure on improvements. Tithing in kind was peculiarly irksome, not only to the farmer, whose routines it interrupted, but to the tithe-owner, who had to agree with the latter the procedure for collecting the crop, and to defray the cost of storage and distribution. By the end of the eighteenth century, therefore, it had been replaced in most places by a monetary com-

[9] BL Add. MSS 37,854, Windham MSS, fos. 15–18, Maseres to Windham, 13 Oct. 1792.
[10] Ibid., fos. 21–2, Maseres to Windham, 30 Oct. 1792.
[11] Evans, *The Contentious Tithe*, 67.

position, which varied a good deal in its fairness to both sides from one area to another, but the earlier crude system of gathering produce survived even in the Midlands and was much more widespread in the north-western and south-eastern extremities of the country. Recent research confirms the charges of contemporaries that tithes, however collected, acted as a real disincentive to agrarian improvement,[12] and soured the relations of clergy and people at the parish level. Even the fishermen, labourers, and industrial workers were occasionally vexed by personal tithes. As a method of securing clerical income the tithe left much to be desired. About a third of it was swallowed by lay impropriators, who might be country squires,[13] while hard-working clergy below the grade of rector or vicar (for example the numerous stipendiary, and even perpetual, curates) had no inherent right to draw it.[14] It is not surprising, therefore, that when the parliamentary enclosure movement gathered force during the last four decades of the eighteenth century, the tithes of the clergy in the parishes affected were by mutual agreement com-muted for additions to the glebe. These were often quite extensive, and increased in proportion to the total acreage of the parish as the years passed. During the period of the French Revolutionary and Napoleonic Wars one-fifth of the arable and one-eighth of the pasture was sometimes allocated.[15]

Among the reasons for the Church's gains was the position of the bishops in the House of Lords, which enabled them to act as 'watchdogs of the clerical interest'. They took more interest in private enclosure bills than did the majority of members of the legislature.[16] The bishop of Bangor, a strict High Churchman of the Horsley kind, was a chairman of committees on private bills in the Lords for most of the 1790s, and other prelates reported occasionally on bills which particularly concerned them.[17] Horsley himself made an unusually forceful intervention in the committee on the contested Weldon Enclosure Bill on 22 May 1792. The Revd William Raye, rector of Weldon, Northamptonshire, dissatisfied with the land allotted to him in lieu of great tithe, had petitioned the Lords against the proposed enclosure of 2,408 acres of common and open fields, meadows, commonable lands, and waste, praying that the tithe might continue to be paid to him in kind and the bill not pass in its present form or that he might be given 'such other relief in the premises' as the House thought fit.[18] Though acting as reporting chairman of the committee, the bishop spoke at great length in favour of the plaintiff and

---

[12] Ibid. 72–6.

[13] Ibid. 8–9.

[14] In practice perpetual curacies had been endowed with tithe since the seventeenth century by grace of the rector. Ibid. 7–8.

[15] W. R. Ward, 'The Tithe Question in England in the Early Nineteenth Century', *Journal of Ecclesiastical History*, 16 (1965), 67–81.

[16] Evans, *The Contentious Tithe*, 96.

[17] e.g. *JHL* 39 (1790–3), 40 (1794–5), 41 (1796–8), 42 (1798–1800).

[18] Ibid. 39 (1790–3), 356, 431; *JHC* 47 (1792), 30 Mar.

entered into the most minute details of the evidence. If he did not convince the House, he certainly talked the bill off the agenda on the 22nd, for having concluded his case he was cut short in mid-sentence, as he resumed with the words, 'Before I sit down', by the entry of the mace to summon the committee to Westminster Hall. When the proceedings recommenced on the following day, after short speeches by the bishops of Bangor and Peterborough, as well as by St Davids, the proposal of a compromise was made by 'a noble viscount' who had been listening to the former debate. This being accepted by the rest of the committee, Horsley was requested to recommend it to the rector's daughter who had been handling her father's case. He did so, seeing little hope of success in further opposition to the bill, although his son Heneage's editorial comment explained that he was and continued to be disappointed that the new terms fell far short of an equivalent for the tithes in kind.[19] H. H. Jebb presented the episode as a bid to 'champion the cause of an oppressed clergyman and to vindicate the truth of a young lady's word'.[20] But the living was a comfortable one. Its unimproved annual value was, on Horsley's own estimate, £558 net in great tithe, plus rent of glebe and tithe of wood, and the compensation eventually offered was acknowledged by him to be 'very liberal in referring to the allotment'. Personal factors may have played some part in explaining the trouble which he took over the case, for the Finch-Hatton family, kinsmen of his patron the earl of Aylesford, were powerful landowners in the Weldon area. But his main concern was for church interests. The arguments which he employed, though not outlandish by the practice of the time, pushed the tithe-owner's claims to their outer limit. The latter's explicit consent to the commutation, he maintained, was essential to the passing of an Enclosure Bill. If this was waived Parliament had the obligation of enforcing justice towards him. Compensation should be a full equivalent to the tithe in kind. Horsley went further than his episcopal colleagues on the committee, one of whom was the rector's own diocesan bishop, in thinking that the accommodation might have been rejected.[21] The truth was that he saw no reason to abandon the ancient system of tithing in produce. Replying to an attack upon it, made by Lord Suffolk in the House of Lords on 6 July 1803, he observed: 'It was well known that no counties were more flourishing than those in which tythes were paid in kind.'[22] The remark showed more prejudice than acquaintance with the agrarian geography of England, but research into Derbyshire livings has lately called into question the financial benefits of commutation to the clergy.[23]

[19] Horsley, *Speeches*, i, 87–163.
[20] Jebb, 103.
[21] Horsley, *Speeches*, i. 87–163.
[22] *Parl. Reg.*, 4th ser. iii (1803), 722.
[23] Virgin, *The Church in an Age of Negligence*, 58–9, citing London Ph.D. thesis by M. R. Austin.

THE CHURCH AND THE LAND-TAX

It would be wrong to regard Bishop Horsley's defence of tithe as symptomatic of a general aversion to change. In some matters he was in advance of his age, and may be counted with Richard Price the Dissenter and his fellow prelate-mathematician Pretyman among those who worked to give public finance a more exact and scientific cast. Calculations relating to the value of annuities formed in the eighteenth century a branch of study in which mathematics and economics were most frequently combined to assist the statesman. Horsley went out of his way to place his proficiency in the former at the disposal of the Government. When the House of Commons was considering Pitt's controversial proposal to introduce a graduated death duty on real estate, he drew the attention of the prime minister's secretary to an ambiguity in the wording of the bill with regard to interests determinable by lives. Pretyman thought the distinction to be without practical importance, but Horsley persisted in setting down his objections in writing for the perusal of ministers. His letter incorporated new rules for calculating the value of a short-term interest in landed property from the tables of annuities for life provided in the bill.[24] Whatever its inherent worth, the exercise was little more than academic, for the entire Estate Duty Bill was shelved in the Commons two days later for reasons of more fundamental objection.[25] The bishop put his mathematical knowledge to more useful effect and to the benefit of the Church of England when he intervened in the process of implementing Pitt's land-tax reforms. In June 1798, as part of a comprehensive overhaul of the fiscal system to meet the strains of the French Revolutionary War, Pitt carried through Parliament an Act[26] making the annual tax on land revenues perpetual and providing for taxpayers to redeem their obligations by transferring to the Commissioners of the National Debt such stock of 3 per cent Consolidated Annuities as would pay a dividend exceeding the amount of land-tax to be extinguished by one-tenth. It was envisaged that landowners would sell or mortgage land to purchase stock which, given to the Government, would free their estates in perpetuity from a certain quantity of tax. The advantages to the landholder seemed great at the time with the price of consols standing at the record low level of 50 in 1798.[27] For the Government, the gain anticipated by Pitt was not just a larger revenue than was produced by the land-tax, but a strengthening of the public credit by absorbing a large quantity of stock and transferring much of the national debt to a landed security.[28]

[24] PRO 30/8/146, Chatham Papers, fos. 137–40, Horsley to unnamed peer, 11 May 1796.

[25] *JHC* 51 (1795–6), 782. For content of bill see ibid. 200–1.

[26] 38 George III, c. lx. cf. W. R. Ward, *The English Land Tax in the Eighteenth Century* (Oxford, 1953), 135–6.

[27] For prices of 3 per cent Consolidated Stock 1758–1800 see table 13 of appendix to T. S. Ashton, *An Economic History of England: The Eighteenth Century* (1953).

[28] *See* Pitt's introductory statement of his purpose to the House of Commons on 2 Apr. 1798. *Parl. Reg.*, 3rd ser., v (1798), 492–3.

Patriotism and the low price of stock ensured that the scheme was launched to a flying start, exceeding the Younger Pitt's most sanguine expectations. According to Dowell nearly a quarter of the debt charge, namely £435,885, was redeemed by landowners in 1798 and 1799.[29] Certain administrative defects stood, nevertheless, in the path of more effective operation.

When the prime minister moved for leave to bring in an amending bill on 6 December 1798, 'another leading object' was 'to make certain regulations respecting ecclesiastical property'.[30] In the form in which it was enacted before the end of the year, this measure contained little to ease the problems of bishops and chapters and incumbents of parochial glebes wishing to redeem their land-tax. It freed them from the restraints of private bills, by-laws, ordinances, or regulations on the sale of land, but also introduced further complications requiring them to give first option of purchase to the beneficial leaseholders and copyholders on their estates. Any subsequent sales of land, rent, and other profits were also made subject to the interest of such holders. At that time bishops and large ecclesiastical corporations often leased their estates for periods of three named lives or twenty-one years, drawing their income not from the annual rent, which was held at a nominal level, but from the entry fines, which might be based, as they were on the lands of the Durham chapter, on one or one and a quarter years' improved value of the property for every seven years of the lease.[31] It is clear that this Act was intended to be supplemented by another during the new year, for it ended with a clause enabling it to be 'altered, varied, or repealed by any Act or Acts to be made in the present Session of Parliament'.

While matters stood thus the bishop of Rochester offered his advice to Pitt. On 17 February he submitted to the prime minister a set of papers relating to the question of how ecclesiastical and collegiate bodies might proceed to the alienation of property for the redemption of land-tax 'without detriment to their own ... corporate interests'. The covering letter, which summarized their contents and has alone survived, explained: 'The investigation is conducted upon strict mathematical principles, to which such enquiries must always be reduced, if we could arrive at safe and certain conclusions. I make no apology, for offering them to you, Sir, in that scientific form which naturally belongs to the subject. It would be an affront to your acknowledged attainments even in the higher mathematics, were they presented to you in any other.'

The précis listed the questions which were treated:

[29] S. Dowell, *History of Taxation and Taxes in England from the Earliest Times to the Year 1885* (1888), iii. 88.

[30] *Parl. Reg.*, 3rd ser., vii (1798–9), 136–7.

[31] R. O'Day and F. Heal (eds.), *Princes and Paupers in the English Church* (Leicester, 1981), 258–9.

1. Upon what principles will lessees expect the Church or College under which they hold, to treat with them, when the body offers the lessees (as they are bound to do by the last act) the refusal of purchase.

2. The principle being ascertained, what will be the price of the Church's disposable interest in her own property, under all the different rates of renewal, which long usage has established in different sees, or chapters. What, I mean, will the price be, according to strict calculations, upon the principle admitted?

3. Would the Church gain or lose, and in what proportion, were she to redeem with the produce of property sold at that price in the present state of the public funds?

4. Finding an apparent gain to the Church in the present state of the public funds, to what point must the funds rise, before that gain will be 0, and the Church redeem, with the produce of property sold at the same calculated price, to her own manifest loss?

Ansr. Consols must rise to $73\frac{7}{11}$ before this can take place.

5. Ought the Church to sell so low as at the calculated price?

Ansr. Certainly not.

6. How then is a minimum price to be settled? Shall it be different for different sees and chapters, according to their different rates of renewal, or a common one for all?

Ansr. I say a common one for all. For altho' this in principle is inequitable, with respect to the Church, it will be more agreeable than the other to the lessees, and for that reason, to the Church herself probably more beneficial.

Horsley then explained his method. This was to deal with the first question on the principle borrowed from 'a very eminent and able land surveyor', namely that 'the perpetuity of the fines is what the Church has to sell'. The second and third questions were approached by calculating the present value of the perpetuity 'by the summation of the infinite series, which the reversionary payments in perpetual succession constituted', using a series which was 'one of the most simple', and by ascertaining the annuity secured upon land which that present value would purchase. Finally this annuity was compared with the annual amount of land-tax which the same sum would redeem to give the gain or loss to the Church.[32]

The mathematical bishop needed to do his sums again. He claimed as an incidental benefit of his computations that they would provide for the first time an accurate assessment of the proportion of church property (exclusive of ancient impropriations) effectively in the hands of laymen. The question was an astute one. Recent research by Dr David Marcombe on the estates of the bishopric and cathedral chapter of Durham have shown that the Church's

---

[32] PRO 30/8/146, Chatham Papers, fos. 137–8, Horsley to Pitt, 17 Feb. 1799.

leaseholders, so far from being oppressed tenants at will, were sometimes substantial yeomen and lesser gentry passing their properties from generation to generation.[33] Unfortunately Horsley's calculations of the Church's genuine share contained two serious omissions. He had the grace (or the prudence) to point these out to Pitt in a letter written three days later, but insisted that they did not invalidate his conclusions on redemption of land-tax.[34]

How far his intervention influenced the sweeping bill which the Chancellor of the Exchequer/premier brought forward in the Commons less than a fortnight later is impossible to establish. The statute, passed on 21 March 1799, not only swept away restraints on the sale of ecclesiastical land which the Act of June 1798 had left intact, but established a central supervisory commission 'for the purposes of regulating, directing, approving, and confirming' all sales and contracts for sale by 'bodies politick or corporate, or companies' for redemption of land-tax. Lord Auckland and Lord Glenbervie were the active Commissioners on whom the work devolved, and a permanent staff evolved at what was to be known as the Church and Corporate Land Tax Office. Equipped by the Act with effective powers to order and control, the Commissioners for the Sale and Redemption of the Land Tax on Church and Corporation Estates approved 3,039 sales of land and contracts for sale, worth about £1,200,000, by 1813, but the heaviest business was done in the first three years of operation. After that progress was much slower, and the Commissioners acted more swiftly to invest in stock than to use this to redeem the tax.[35] Bishops and cathedrals drew greater benefit from the plan than did parish clergy as the following figures for the proceeds of sales down to February 1813 show:[36]

Archbishops and bishops	£254,000
Deans and chapters	£455,600
Rectors and vicars	£213,000
Colleges and prebends	£139,000
Lay corporations	£110,000
Feoffees and trustees for charitable and other public purposes	£9,700
Owners of land with reversion to the Crown	£18,700

The creation of the Commission was nevertheless a furtherance of church bureaucracy which deserves to be set beside the new role cast for the Commissioners of Queen Anne's Bounty from the closing years of the eighteenth century and the establishment of the ecclesiastical department of the Privy

---

[33] David Marcombe, 'Church Leaseholders: The Decline and Fall of a Rural Elite', in O'Day and Heal (eds.), *Princes and Paupers*, 255–75.

[34] PRO 30/8/146, Chatham Papers, fos. 139–40, Horsley to Pitt, 20 Feb. 1799.

[35] *Report of the Commissioners for the Redemption of the Land Tax on Church and Corporation Estates*, 3 May 1810. PP 1810 (325) ix; Ibid. 23 Feb. 1813. PP 1812–13 (71) v.

[36] Ibid. 23 Feb. 1813.

Council Office after 1803. Procedurally, though not in practical importance, it was more advanced than either.

RESIDENCE AND THE PASTORAL MINISTRY

The proof, however, of the effectiveness of the third church reform movement was not the augmentation of the wealth of bishops, colleges, and chapters by improved management but the provision of a more effective ministry at the parochial level. Bishop Horsley was sympathetic towards the attack on non-residence which gathered force as the eighteenth century gave place to the nineteenth. 'My Lords,' he told the Upper Chamber in June 1803, 'the residence of the beneficed clergy upon their benefices, and the abstraction of the clergy from all secular occupations, are two points of principal importance in ecclesiastical discipline.'[37] His concern to enforce them sprang from an ideal of ministry not far behind that of John Keble, in which the duty of the priest was to live among his people, 'to exhibit in his own deportment, and in the good order of his family, the example of a godly and religious life', to relieve the distresses of the poor, to administer to the sick and dying those consolations which 'can only be afforded by the word of reconciliation in the gospel, and by the means of reconciliation offered in the sacraments of the church—to assist the penitent in making his peace with God'.[38] Such purposes, he knew, could not be attained by a non-resident vicar or curate, visiting his church for Sunday 'duty' alone. But in Horsley's view there was a sense of paradox generally lacking in the approach of the Tractarians, and this led him to construe exceptions to the literal application of his principles. Unlike the Ecclesiastical Commissioners of the 1830s who aspired to prune cathedrals for the sake of parish churches, he recognized as legitimate the role of a leisured minority in the clerical body.[39] But it was an intellectual not a social élitism that he sought to uphold. Anxious to distinguish his voice from 'the despicable cant of Puritanism', he assured the Upper Chamber that the pursuit of study, even the study of secular subjects, was a valid use of the clergyman's time, which was not always misspent 'when he is studying the proportions of architecture and the divisions of the monochord'.[40] On the other hand, the practice of the younger clergy of shutting up their books and 'studying men'—by which he meant any form of purposeless behaviour from 'an incessant attendance in scenes of dissipated pleasure' to 'the common polish of good breeding'—was singled out by him for round condemnation.[41] In much of this argument, which he pursued through charges and

---

[37] Horsley, *Speeches*, ii. 119–64.
[38] Ibid.
[39] Horsley, *St. Albans Charge 1783* (1783); cf. O. J. Brose, *Church and Parliament: The Reshaping of the Church of England 1828–1860* (Stanford, 1959), chap. vii.
[40] Horsley, *Speeches*, ii. 119–64.
[41] Horsley, *Rochester Charge 1796* (1796).

parliamentary speeches, the bishop was deceiving himself, and allowing his prejudices to blunt the edge of his reforming urges. Trollope's Vesey Stanhopes, hunting butterflies on the shores of Lake Como, provide a satirical, if generally exaggerated commentary on the use which could be made of the plea of study to cover inexcusable non-residence. Horsley was right to assail the spread of clerical farming as a misuse of the parish priest's time, but he did so for largely the wrong reasons, observing in his speech on the Residence Bill in 1803:

The country curate, if he turns farmer, will take part in the labours of husbandry; he will wield the sithe and the sickle; he will fodder the kine, and help to throw out the dung upon his land, and thus he will be associated with the labouring peasantry: Even the business of the markets, which he will attend to show his own samples and make his own bargains, will mix him too much in familiar habits with the lower farmers; and thus the whole dignity and sanctity of his character will be obliterated.[42]

The view was a commonplace of the age in which it was uttered,[43] but in reality social assimilation could have been deemed a strength.

It was not, moreover, until comparatively late in his career that Bishop Horsley started to campaign actively against non-residence. His earlier published charges, to the St Albans archdeaconry in 1783 and to the diocese of St Davids in 1790, had been concerned with the message of the Church, not its organization. In the charge to the clergy of Rochester in 1796 the purview extended: 'Nothing has so much lessened the general influence of the clergy; nothing so much threatens the stability of the national church', he wrote concerning absenteeism and the resultant neglect of parochial duty. It was partly the broadening effect of experience on a mind which was basically that of the scholar which had wrought the change. But the context in which the arraignment of non-residence was embedded makes clear that the major influence bringing it to the fore was the present threat to the Church from the ideas of the French Revolution. This was not a simple yielding to *force majeure*. His sense of impending danger anteceded the fall of the Bastille and the dissemination of the *Rights of Man* by many years. What was evident was a considered strategy for retaining support, remarkable in an old-fashioned High Churchman in that it anticipated the argument from utility employed by ecclesiastical liberals to urge reform of the Church of England in the greater crisis which befell the Establishment after the passing of the Great Reform Bill.[44]

Following a preference for triads which was taking an increasing hold of social analysis as the eighteenth century progressed,[45] Horsley divided the

---

[42] Horsley, *Speeches*, ii. 119–64.
[43] See Anthony Russell, *The Clerical Profession* (1980), chap. iii, esp. p. 40.
[44] Brose, *Church and Parliament*, 35–6.
[45] P. J. Corfield, 'Class by Name and Number in Eighteenth-Century Britain', *History*, 72 (1987), 38–61.

English laity in his 1796 charge into three groups according to their senti-ments on religion. Firstly, the Christians in conscience and in truth—a very great majority. At the other end of the scale was a very small class which he styled 'the Democratists', void of all religion and avowed enemies to its ministers—loud and active. In between came 'a middle class which may be called the class of the Moralists'. This was not the middle class defined by economic function as conceived by a sequence of writers from John Millar and Adam Smith to Karl Marx and as chiefly understood by the historian. But it had something in common with it: 'respectable serious men; but men who have never set themselves to think seriously about the intrinsic importance of religion, or the evidences of the truth and reality of revelation; and being of a turn of mind not to take things upon trust, have rather perhaps a secret leaning to speculative infidelity'. 'They are friends', he continued, 'to religion for its good services in civil life, but seeing nothing more in it, they would always take up with the religion which they find established'. 'They are our friends', Horsley added, 'because they think the part we act essential to the good of the community; but that being the ground of their friendship, they will be our friends no longer than while we act it well. They consider the emoluments and privileges of the order as a pay that we receive from the public for the performance of the part assigned us; and if they discover in us ... any negligence in the execution, distant as they are in principle from the Democratists, they will be very apt to concur with them, one time or another, in some goodly project for the confiscation of our property and the abolition of our privileges.'

The remedy propounded, however, was curiously inadequate to its likely effects. It was to make non-residence conditional upon the appointment of a curate who would be paid by the incumbent a sufficient stipend to enable him to confine his attention to a single parish. This was more easily said than done. The root cause of absenteeism, he perceived, was in the low value of certain livings which did not permit the employment of a full-time curate. This was not wholly true, for the absence of the rector or vicar also needed to be explained, but the Bishop's appraisal was not lacking in realism. A detailed analysis of the visitation returns for the diocese of London in the second half of the eighteenth century made by Mme Viviane Barrie-Curien shows the importance of curates, serving not as degraded menials but as respected parish priests. Often they were incumbents of nearby benefices.

It is further calculated that by the deployment of incumbents and curates nearly all the parishes had a resident clergyman or one residing in the neighbourhood: 88.6 per cent of the sample in 1766–70, 99 per cent in 1778, and 98.3 per cent in 1790.[46] London, however, was a diocese specially

---

[46] V. Barrie–Curien, 'La Vie des paroisses en Angleterre à la fin du XVIIIᵉ siècle: Encadrement et résidence pastorale', *Histoire, économie, société* (1986), 187–215.

TABLE 1. *Service of London parishes by clergy 1766–1790* (%)

Parishes served by	1766–70	1778	1790
Incumbent alone	52.6	47.9	32.8
Curate alone	26.9	25.4	29.5
Incumbent and curate	20.2	26.7	37
Incumbent and lecturer			0.2
Curate and lecturer			0.6
Lecturer alone	0.2		

favoured with clerical personnel, and it by no means follows that those who lived on or near the spot, whether vicars or curates, gave their whole attention to a single parish. Even in Essex and Hertfordshire country livings were habitually worked in pairs. My analysis of 349 Essex parishes answering the 1815 inquiry reveals that 44 per cent had a resident clergyman to themselves. Of 127 others, sixty-three were involved in arrangements where the vicar of one parish acted also as curate of a neighbouring one. Twenty-nine were served by a pluralist incumbent; thirty-five divided the time of a stipendiary curate.[47] Elsewhere in the country the situation was much worse. Bishop Pretyman's Speculum (*c*.1788) shows that more than a quarter (28 per cent) of 156 parishes in the archdeaconry of Lincoln shared a clergyman with at least two other parishes. Twenty-one of these clergy had each three parishes to serve, seven had four, three had five. It seems probable that the extent of the abuse was affected by the poverty of livings in the region. Of 128 Lincolnshire benefices for which the 1788–92 value is known, two-thirds fell below £100 a year; one-third of them being lower than £50, the qualification for being discharged from first-fruits and tenths.[48]

The only practical solution which Horsley had to offer was recourse to the Curates Act 1796. One of a succession of statutes following a precedent of 1713 which empowered the bishop of the diocese to fix a curate's stipend either on licensing or on subsequent complaint, this Act raised the upper limit of the bishop's discretion from £50 to £75 per annum, and enabled him to assign the parsonage house, its garden, and stable to the curate in cases where the incumbent did not reside for at least four months in the year. Perpetual curacies were subjected to the same obligations as rectories and vicarages with regard to the payment of stipendiary curates, and the bishop was enabled to impose conditions on the curate as for the use of the house. This was the

[47] LPL Fulham Papers, dio. London Visitation Returns 1815 (Essex parishes).
[48] Lincolnshire CRO, Speculum 1788–92, entitled 'Circa 1788: Residence, Value, Curates, Services, Population, Dissenters, Schools'.

Church's own measure, introduced by the archibishop of Canterbury into the House of Lords.[49] Much of Bishop Horsley's Rochester charge was devoted to explaining its provisions. He declared his intention to enforce it, and exhorted his clergy not to evade it by entering into civil contracts between incumbents and their curates. Given the superfluity of clergy competing for employment this was too much to expect. Stipends of £35 to £50 per cure were still being paid to Oxfordshire curates a quarter of a century later.[50] Moreover, the law dealt with only half the problem. It did nothing for rectors and vicars whose stipends were so low that they were obliged to take on a curacy in a neighbouring parish to secure a livelihood.

Within several years Parliament was obliged by external pressure to act more broadly in the matter of non-residence. During the year 1800 a spate of prosecutions for non-residence was brought against beneficed clergymen of London and the provinces, under an Act of the Reformation Parliament, on the allegation of common informers.[51] The 1529 Act was archaic and unfair. It required beneficed clergy to reside on one at least of their livings on pain of a fine of £10 for every month of absence, half the fine going to the informer. Exemptions were granted to bishops' chaplains, peers, and students at the universities, but as residence was understood to mean living in the parsonage house, active and energetic clergy who resided on the spot in their own private houses were vulnerable to attack. The vicar of Norham was convicted at the Durham assize in August 1800 because he took a lodging in the village for the nine months during which his vicarage was being rebuilt.[52] The actions were acknowledged to be vexatious. A contributor to the *Gentleman's Magazine* ascribed them to 'a junto of Jacobins and Atheists' who were 'some time ago expelled from a cellar notorious for sedition in the vicinity of one of our inns of court'. These, he alleged, had circularized 'all the principal Dissenters' for support.[53] Parliament responded to indignant clerical protest, vociferated by bodies such as Sion College,[54] by suspending the operation of the statutes penalizing non-residence, while an amending Act which Sir William Scott, an eminent civilian, had undertaken to frame was being carried. The task proved so difficult and complex that it nearly broke Sir William's health. Delays supervened with the result that the period of suspension had to be enlarged. The first Suspending Bill, which was sought in June 1801, was followed by two more in 1802.

When the House of Lords was approached for a further extension in March

---

[49] *JHL* 40 (1794–6), 648.
[50] Diana McClatchey, *Oxfordshire Clergy 1777–1869* (Oxford, 1960), 75–7.
[51] See *Gent. Mag.* 70/2 (1800), 785, 883, and other evidence noted below.
[52] *The Times*, 16 Aug. 1800.
[53] *Gent. Mag.* 71/1 (1801), 3–4, 223–4.
[54] Sion College Court Register, C, fos. 258–9, 259–61, minutes of general meetings of the London clergy at Sion College, 26 and 30 Apr. 1800.

1803 Bishop Horsley intervened testily and impatiently to curtail its operation from 8 July to 13 May. Inveighing against all bills for suspending existing statutes, he led the attack on 'this temporizing system; which, in attempting to supply deficiency of law, had in fact left us no law at all'. He professed himself 'an advocate for strictly enforcing the residence of the parochial clergy, if it was desirable that religion, morality, and that order so necessary to the stability of government, both in church and state, should be preserved'; and notwithstanding 'all the severity' that belonged to the Act of 21 Henry VIII, he would prefer its continuance to the protracted suspensions. By such arguments he drove the Lord Chancellor, Lord Eldon, who was Sir William Scott's brother, Lord Ellenborough, and Lord Alvanley to promise that this would be the last suspending bill to which they would consent. Eldon had been at first disposed to urge as a ground for caution the risk that non-residents returning to duty might put their curates out of work. Horsley swept the argument aside.[55] More than anyone else he was responsible for ensuring that a replacement for the Henrician statute was brought forward that session. He did not wholly agree with the bill which Scott produced, and made an ostentatious display of his differences, but ultimately he had the wisdom to subordinate his own preferences to the need for action. This was a mercy as advancing years were beginning to erode his memory. On 7 June he started to discuss the details of the measure at its second reading, and when rebuked for this by Lord Rosslyn he admitted that he had 'mistaken the stage of the bill'.[56]

Both then, however, and at the committal proceedings three days later, he affirmed his agreement with its principle. His speech on 10 June is difficult to follow in the *Parliamentary Register*. It stands in marked contrast with the long, lucid, and entertaining discourse reproduced by his son Heneage in the posthumous edition of his speeches.[57] Whether he was misreported or whether the text in the volume represents a plan which he failed to execute, it is to the latter that one must look for an exposition of his aims. One of Sir William Scott's proposals was to replace the inflexible fines of the Act of 1529 by a scale of penalties related to the value of the benefice and the proportion of the year spent away from the living. Horsley approved of this, as also of the disciplinary power to deprive a contumacious incumbent which was to be placed in the bishop's own hands without the interference of his consistory court. The bishop of St Asaph was plainly contemptuous of most of the church courts, and instanced a case from his own experience in St Davids diocese, where an action for absenteeism had foundered because of the inefficiency of the diocesan court in which the judge was himself a non-resident clergyman. Horsley's quarrel was with the clauses of the bill releasing

[55] *Parl. Reg.*, 4th ser., ii (1803), 504–11, 522–31.

[56] Ibid. iii (1803), 552.

[57] Ibid. 558–9; cf. Horsley, *Speeches*, ii. 119–64. Unless otherwise stated the references to the speech on 10 June are taken from the latter.

spiritual persons from the obligation to reside. Absolute exemptions conferred by the bill were too numerous, for example those permitting minor canons of cathedrals and collegiate churches to absent themselves from the livings which they held in plurality. Where bishops were to be empowered to grant temporary licences for non-residence in other cases, such as sickness, the bishop argued that it was wrong to enumerate the sorts of cases as this would put ideas into the heads of would-be applicants for licences. The fictitious illustration which he gave of collusion between a clergyman's wife and the bishop's lady to obtain permission to desert a country charge could have played its part in casting the relationship between Mrs Quiverful and Mrs Proudie.

It was for the proposal to allow appeal to the archbishop against a bishop's refusal of a licence on non-residence that Horsley reserved his fiercest ire. This was 'a most outrageous violation of the ecclesiastical constitution,—not merely the particular constitution of the church of this kingdom, but the constitution of the church catholic, by which every bishop in his own diocese is supreme'. In the version of the speech given in the published edition, Horsley ended with a plan of his own to regulate non-residence. The diocesan bishop should be freed to grant such licences as he thought fit, on condition of reporting annually to the archbishop the duration and cause of each. He was prepared to countenance only such centralization as would have required the archbishop to transmit the report to the king in chancery.

As he did not press his views to a division against it, Sir William Scott's bill passed into committee where the Lords introduced amendments reflecting a wide diversity of interests. It was then returned to the Commons who replaced it by a new bill, which received the royal assent on 7 July 1803.[58] This Act, described by its author as 'merely a provisional or interim measure of church reform', proved to be one of the most important contributions of the un-reformed Parliament to the subject before the creation of the Ecclesiastical Revenues Commission in 1832. Its requirements that the bishops should submit to the Privy Council annual returns of non-residence and other data relating to their dioceses and that the archbishops should likewise report the use of their appellate jurisdiction helped to bring into being a 'miniature Ministry for Ecclesiastical Affairs', the Privy Council Office, and furnished a broad basis of statistical information on which rational decisions could be grounded. In collaboration with the Bounty Board the new department undertook enlightening inquiries stretching beyond residence to the poverty of livings which undermined it.[59] It is worth remarking that Horsley's own proposal, though less elaborate, would have forwarded such purposes.

---

[58] *JHL* 44 (1802–4), 247–8, 255, 275–9, 281–3, 290–1, 303, 314, 319; cf. *JHC* 58 (1802–3), 556–61.
[59] Best, *Temporal Pillars*, 198–203; K. A. Thompson, *Bureaucracy and Church Reform* (Oxford, 1970), 11–13.

PAYMENT OF CURATES ETC.

Horsley gave but a grudging support to one reform proposal: the measure introduced into the House of Lords in 1805 to make the stipends of curates vary with the value and property of the incumbents for whom they did duty. He objected to features of the bill 'derogatory to the dignity of the clerical character' and tending 'to degrade the bishops'.[60] To uphold the status of the whole clerical order and to defend its interests against the encroachments of laymen was more important to him than to assert the rights of poor clergy against rich. Speaking on a bill of 1804 to regulate by law the minimum age of ordination, he was at pains to safeguard the indelibility of holy orders regularly conferred.[61] In the following year he supported the University Advowsons Bill to free the clericalized colleges of Oxford and Cambridge from restrictions on their power to acquire advowsons.[62] The principal achievement of his later years was the carrying of a contentious measure bringing financial relief to the poorly endowed benefices of London. This seems at first sight to exhibit a special bias towards the poor; in fact it was a defence of middle-grade professional interests.

THE LONDON CLERGY AND THE FIRE ACT

Town parishes commanding no tithe, or where the tithe was levied on poorer land or on produce less valuable than corn, were at a disadvantage compared with many situated in the countryside. The only appropriate equivalent of tithe which could be devised for the City of London was a levy on the value of houses and shops, capable of being supplemented by a personal tithe based on the profits of those who lived and worked in them. In medieval times these were first payable on Sundays and occasional festivals, and later regularized into quarterly or yearly remissions. The system never worked well, as the citizens of London continually sought to evade or to reduce their obligations, and the clergy found the incomes from their livings so greatly reduced that in 1634 they petitioned King Charles I for relief. The outbreak of the Scottish War ended Laud's efforts to come to their assistance, and when, after the Restoration, the Great Fire compelled a revision of the parochial system, the new provisions raised as many problems as they solved. The Fire damaged or destroyed eighty-five parish churches.[63] It was decreed by a statute of 1670[64]

---

[60] *Parl. Deb.*, 1st ser., v (1805), 244–5, 383, 704.

[61] Ibid. i (1803–4), 1058–9; ii (1804), 127–8.

[62] Ibid. iv (1805), 449–56.

[63] Sion College Court Register, C, fos. 249–53, 'Case of the London Clergy whose Livings were Regulated by ... the Fire Act'; *Parl. Deb.* ii (1804), 1094. Cf. Christopher Hill, *Economic Problems of the Church from Archbishop Whitgift to the Long Parliament* (1971), chap. xii, *passim*. But Claire Cross's careful study of the assets of the urban clergy of the provinces, many of whom

that thirty-four of these should not be rebuilt, but that their parishes should be united with others. The fifty-one livings thus created were subjected to a later Act of the same session, known as the Fire Act,[65] which allocated fixed yearly stipends raised by rates levied by the lay authorities to the incumbents in place of sundry tithes and obligations. The clergy retained their entitlement to glebes, gifts, and perquisites, but lost their claim to the Easter offering. Only six of the livings were settled at £200 per annum. Thirty-two were assigned less than £150, a quarter of these yielding no more than £100.[66]

Barring the extinction of the Easter offering, these incomes were not exceptionally low for the time, nor did they constitute their recipients' sole source of support. At the close of the seventeenth century forty-three incumbents of City churches had country livings as well,[67] and a diocese book for the archdeaconry of London, compiled about a hundred years later, gives evidence that plurality still cushioned the weaker places in the Church. Among the beneficed clergy of the regulated livings, Dr William Vincent of All Hallows the Great and All Hallows the Less was also headmaster of Westminster School. The occupant of St Ann and St Agnes, Aldersgate with St John, Lothbury was master of Christ's Hospital, and held a living in Essex. A prebendary of Bristol with a parish in Buckinghamshire had St Bartholomew, Exchange. A prebendary of Westminster and domestic chaplain to the Princess Amelia held Christ Church with St Leonard, Foster Lane. A canon of Salisbury with a living in Essex had St Clement, Eastcheap with St Martin, Ongar. Other cases may be found where City clergy, whose incomes were settled by the Fire Act had another benefice in the home counties or even further afield, while the impressive sprinkling of doctors of divinity in their ranks—Dr Douglas, Dr Gaskin, Dr Shackleford—suggests that further research would add to the number of the relatively well-to-do. Even the archdeacon of St Albans, Joseph Holden Pott, occupied a Fire church, St Olave, Jewry with St Martin.[68] Men on the middle rungs of the ecclesiastical ladder, scholars and administrators, took livings in central London for other than economic reasons—to acquire prestige and to rub shoulders with laymen of influence. Horsley misled seriously when he thus compared the lot of the Fire Act clergy in 1804 with what it had been in Charles II's reign: 'If the income was only a competence then, it is very evident that it must be downright beggary now . . . If the clergyman, by his income, was upon a level with

operated in similar conditions to those of the City of London, shows an improvement in their financial position during the first 40 years of the 17th cent., which could, by analogy, modify the unfavourable trend delineated above. 'The Incomes of Provincial Urban Clergy, 1520–1645', in O'Day and Heal (eds.), *Princes and Paupers*, chap. iii.

[64] 22 Charles II, c. xi.

[65] 22 & 23 Charles II, c. xv.

[66] Sion College Court Register, 'Case'.

[67] G. Rudé, *Hanoverian London* (1971), 104.

[68] Guildhall Library MS 9557, London Diocese Book 1770–*c.*1812.

the merchant at the time of the Restoration, he is now with the same income, hardly upon a level with the junior clerk in the merchant's compting house.'[69]

He was right, nevertheless, to suggest that there had been decline. The chief defect of the Fire Act was its lack of provision for the reassessment of the rateable value of properties as economic conditions changed.[70] Fixed incomes were unimprovable incomes, and left their recipients without means of sharing in the expanding wealth of businesses which grew up around them in the second half of the eighteenth century, nor did they provide any cushion against inflation.

Discontent with these faults came to a head in the closing years of the century, as the sharp wartime rise in commodity prices during the 1790s cut back the City incumbents' real incomes. The effect was exacerbated by the vexatious prosecutions for non-residence brought on the testimony of common informers which was reported to a general meeting at Sion College in April 1800.[71] Wounded vanity played as large a part as pecuniary loss in provoking resentment of this, for, as Warden Huntingford wrote to Addington about a proposal for relief: 'Your "Clergy Bill" speaks the sentiments of all with whom I have conversed. Do befriend us against vile informers. Make us amenable to proper authority, but not to knaves and extortioners.'[72]

Defence of the clergy was channelled through Sion College, where the rising stars of the Old High Church firmament, soon to be known as the Hackney Phalanx–Rennell and Van Mildert, Beloe and Gaskin—gathered with lesser known metropolitan clergy in meetings and committees from November 1799 onwards. Their exertions were encouraged by tithe reformers in the House of Commons, keen to divide the urban clergy from their richer country cousins.[73]

At length a private bill to extend the financial provision for the clergy of the City of London whose livings were regulated by the Fire Act was introduced by petition into the House of Commons on 22 February 1804. By established usage such a measure should not have been taken forward into the Lords without obtaining the consent of all whose interests were affected by it. But the promoters failed even to give notice to the parishes which it embraced. The only step which was taken to obtain lay support was to communicate the draft of the bill to the Court of Common Council of the City of London.[74] A more unfortunate moment could scarcely have been chosen for this approach. For, though the Common Council at the outset of the nineteenth century

[69] *Parl. Deb.* ii (1804), 1097.
[70] Sion College Court Register, 'Case', stating that the powers of the assessors terminated in 1681.
[71] Ibid., C, 258–61.
[72] Devon CRO 152M/C, Sidmouth Papers, 1801/OZ 88, Huntingford to Addington, 17 May 1801.
[73] Sion College Court Register, C, 247–54, 258–9.
[74] *JHC* 59 (1803–4), 104; *JHL* 44 (1802–4), 664–5; *Parl. Deb.* ii (1804), 1098, 1104.

was preponderantly loyalist and Pittite, a radical opposition led by Robert Waithman, a prosperous draper, opposed both to the war against France and to the expenditure attending it, was beginning to emerge.[75] The Common Council received the draft of the London Clergy Incumbents Bill on 9 May with sentiments coloured by their resentment of Addington's new income tax imposition. A majority of members agreed to refer the bill to a committee, which negotiated amendments with the promoters. At a subsequent meeting of Council, however, the opposition succeeded in getting the committee's report referred back,[76] and insisted on testing opinion by a public meeting of the inhabitants of the City of London. When the resolutions of the latter had been communicated to the Lord Mayor, aldermen, Common Councillors and others,[77] Waithman rose in the Council on 14 July to state that the Incumbents Bill 'had excited considerable alarm, and, if passed into law, would subject the Citizens of London to a most grievous tax'. On his motion it was resolved unanimously that the Corporation should petition the House of Lords against it, but, in order to avoid the appearance of a purely negative attitude, the Common Council took up the cause of those City clergy who were excluded from its benefits. It was alleged that 'while the incumbents of forty-eight parishes were applying to Parliament for an addition of two-thirds to their present incomes', no relief whatever was proposed for 'fifty-one parishes not included in the Fire Act, which had of late been subjected to exorbitant claims'.[78] The Council's committee was instructed 'to prepare the draft of a Bill or Bills to regulate the whole of the incumbents' and improprietors' [sic] rights in the City of London and report the same to this Court'.[79]

The Clergy's bill was now in serious trouble in the House of Lords. The dissensions in the Common Council were reported at the committee stage on 13 July. Staunch Churchman though he was, Eldon, the Lord Chancellor, made an embarrassing pronouncement. He could not give the measure his concurrence, consistently with the rights of individuals who had purchased property on the faith that no further imposition should be laid upon it.[80] This constitutional point was used by the Whig Duke of Norfolk to oppose the third reading on the 19th, and it was deferred till the following Monday.[81] The bishops of London and St Asaph both spoke for the clergy, but it was Horsley who wrenched victory from defeat. That he, not the diocesan bishop,

[75] J. R. Dinwiddy, '"The Patriotic Linen-Draper": Robert Waithman and the Revival of Radicalism in the City of London, 1795–1818', *Bulletin of the Institute of Historical Research*, 46 (1973), 72–94.

[76] *JHL* 44 (1802–4), 664–5.

[77] *Parl. Deb.* ii (1804), 1105.

[78] *Morning Post*, 16 July 1804; *Morning Herald*, 16 July 1804.

[79] Corporation of London RO, Journal of Common Council, lxxxii (1804–5), fos. 42ʳ–43ʳ.

[80] *Parl. Deb.* ii (1804), 1029; cf. *JHL* 44 (1802–4), 664–5.

[81] *Parl. Deb.* ii (1804), 1069–72.

should have taken the leading part calls for some explanation. Personal connection with the applicants was partly responsible, for George Gaskin, a dean of Sion College, was his old ally in the struggle for relief of the Scottish Episcopalians. A letter of thanks to Horsley from Avery Hatch, the president of the College, could be construed, though not conclusively, to mean that he was a member of the committee which superintended the application.[82] But the cause was in a broad sense a High Church cause, and zeal for the status of the clerical order would have been a sufficient explanation of his activity.

Horsley's speech on 23 July 1804 was lengthy, clever, and packed with information.[83] At close on 72 he had recovered his old fire. He began by disputing Waithman's figures:

It has been said, that the parishes, to which what is called the Fire Act applies, and to which in consequence, this act ... applies, are in number only 48; while the parishes within the City, not affected by the Fire Act, nor by this bill, are 51. My lords, this is a most outrageous falsehood. The parishes which fall under the Fire Act, and under this bill, are not fewer than 86; though the livings, it is true, are no more than 51. For after the Fire of London, it was thought proper to rebuild only 51 of the 86 churches destroyed by that calamity, and by uniting to reduce 69 of the benefices to 34. And thus the 86 parishes made only 51 livings. Still they are 86 parishes. But the parishes which escaped the Fire and are not affected by the Fire Act are 19, and no more.

This was an advocate's presentation, for it was livings that mattered, not parishes. But a portion of the Opposition's case had been shown to be incorrect. Next, he attacked the assertion that the revenues of the nineteen were 'immense, enormous', amounting in one case to £700 per annum in reputed value, in another to £800. The average, he observed, was no more than £290.

At this point one suspects that he was speaking to a brief which others had helped to prepare. But his criticism of the objection that a private bill needed to show the consent of all whose interests might be affected by it showed ingenuity. His answer was to deny that the measure under review, though introduced by private-bill procedures was really a private bill: 'My Lords, it is not a bill for the promotion of private interests; in its object it is a public bill; it is a bill for an object of the greatest national importance that can be brought before parliament. My Lords, a bill for the better maintainance of the London clergy, is a bill for the support of the established religion in the metropolis. And with the condition of religion in the metropolis, its condition in the whole nation is nearly and intimately connected.'

[82] HP 1767, fo. 11, George Avery Hatch to Horsley, 16 Aug. 1804. Hatch acknowledged Horsley's exertions 'from the time that Your Lordship began first in the Committee, to entertain doubts of the validity of that formidable objection, respecting the necessary consent of the various parties concerned in the Bill; to the final success of our application to the legislature'. But the 'Committee' might be the House of Lords Committee.

[83] The following summary and quotations are from *Parl. Deb.* ii (1804), 1089–1106.

The peculiar importance of the London clergy and their maintenance was also invoked by him as ground for dismissing the fear of his fellow prelates and the wealthier country clergy that the bill might furnish a precedent for legislative interference with tithes. He cited the authority of the statute book, 'in which, he alleged, not a single statute from the earliest times to the latest, is to be found relating to tithes in general, in which an express exception is not made of the case of the London clergy'.

Horsley ended his speech with a flourish of disparaging remarks about the opposition to the bill, which was not expressed in petitions alleging detriment to the property of individuals, but generated by unofficial public meetings. When he sat down, leaving the House stunned as much as converted by oratory which occupies seventeen pages of the *Debates*, resistance quickly crumbled. Eldon accepted the argument that the City clergy constituted a special case. The duke of Norfolk, 'after what had fallen from the right rev. prelate', decided not to divide the chamber, and apart from a token expression of dissent from the royal duke of Clarence, the bill was given an unopposed third reading.[84] It became law, in the marginal category of 'local and personal acts to be judicially noted', on 28 July 1804. The Act[85] effected a substantial rise in incomes. Of fifty benefices still controlled by the Fire Act, stipends of more than £200 per annum were allocated to thirty-one, seven of these being over £300, while nineteen of the remainder touched £200. None were below £200. The City Corporation's powers to authorize assessment were renewed, and, in default of their exercise, transferred to two barons of the Exchequer. But the rights of impropriators were protected by law. They were to pay incumbents only so much as they had been accustomed to pay 'before and since the passing of the ... Act of the twenty-second and twenty-third years of the reign of King Charles the Second'. Backed by the reserved powers of Government, the local authorities lost no time in implementing the measure. By the middle of the following month the City churchwardens were making their new assessments.[86]

Horsley's speech at the third reading was duly printed. Dr Gaskin anticipated from its publication benefits over and above those which its delivery had wrought. He expressed the belief that it would 'facilitate the accomplishment of further augmentations to the benefices of the London clergy and discourage future Low Whig assaults on their position', for he added: 'It cannot ... but tend to damp the expectations of those parishes, who meditate an application to the legislature for a repeal of the Act of Hen: 8, which gives 2 sh./9 in the pound to the incumbents of those livings, whose churches were not destroyed by the great fire; & it may be likely to prevent such application. The Church of England will always have reason, on many accounts,

[84] *Parl. Deb.* ii (1804), 1106–9.
[85] 44 George III, *c.*lxxxix.
[86] HP 1767, fos. 4–5, Gaskin to Horsley, 14 Aug. 1804.

to praise God that Your Lordship's name is in the catalogue of her venerable prelates.'[87]

The tribute was not unmerited. Detailed exploration of the bishop's part in the renovation of the Church at the national level establishes his claim to be regarded as a reformer, but one of a moderate and uneven kind. Like earlier High Churchmen in the Laudian mould, he was chiefly interested in reforms which buttressed the temporal pillars of the Church and rescued the clergy from the condescension of laymen. He was less sensitive to the grievances of the laity against the clergy, and stood in with the archbishop of Canterbury and most other bishops against the Younger Pitt's schemes for commutation of tithes. Not all High Churchmen shared his negative attitude to this question. Pretyman, bishop of Lincoln, was an ardent advocate of substituting corn rents, the solution which was adopted in 1836. But Horsley was never complacent about the state of the Church of England. When the French Revolution and the English Republicans arose to challenge the values for which it stood, he developed a concern to refurbish its image in the sight of respectable Englishmen. The remedies which he favoured were piecemeal. He had no vision of an overall reform to be achieved by redistributing revenues, but thought that Parliament should strengthen every bishop to insist on the proper performance of duty in his diocese. One must turn to discover how successful he was in handling his own responsibilities.

[87] Ibid.

9

The Dioceses and the Abbey

IF reform, like charity, should begin at home, few bishops had a wider range of opportunities to practise it. Consecrated bishop of St Davids on 11 May 1788, Horsley was translated to Rochester on 7 December 1793 and to St Asaph on 27 July 1802. That see he held until his death on 4 October 1806. According to a precedent which stretched backwards almost without interruption to 1666 he was allowed to hold the deanery of Westminster *in commendam* with the bishopric of Rochester from 1793 to 1802. His retirement ended the conjunction, which was not organic, and set the Abbey upon its independent course.

THE DIOCESE OF ST DAVIDS

No apology need be made for according to his tenure of St Davids the main share of attention, for it was there that he established his claim to be regarded as a practical reformer. Welsh dioceses in the eighteenth century, under a succession of largely monoglot English prelates, have an invidious reputation for maladministration and neglect. The 'vast and unwieldy' See of St Davids, covering the greater part of southern Wales from Pembrokeshire and Cardiganshire across the northern edge of the coastal bishopric of Llandaff into Brecon and Radnorshire and even across the border into Herefordshire, has been deemed the most unmanageable of all. From the Dovey estuary in the north to the Gower peninsula in the south it was almost as large as the other three Welsh dioceses put together and in the 1830s vastly the most populous. The SPCK diocesan history portrays it as languishing at the beginning of the nineteenth century in the iron age of 'declension and dilapidation', and detects little improvement before 1850.[1] In recent times, however, leading Welsh scholars have presented a less gloomy and more variegated picture of the Principality's eighteenth-century ecclesiastical scene. Bishop Havard has challenged the view that his forerunners of that epoch showed laxity in the conduct of ordinations and confirmations,[2] while Professor E. T. Davies has called attention to a significant literary and educational revival under the auspices of the Church in Wales which began in the 1670s and lasted for about a hundred years. He rightly stresses that the 'real indictment' was not

[1] W. L. Bevan, *St. Davids* (1888), chap. xii.
[2] W. T. Havard, 'The Eighteenth Century Background of Church Life in Wales', *Journal of the Historical Society of the Church in Wales*, 5 (1955), 67–82.

against the 'bishops personally' but against 'the ecclesiastical system', which
inhibited their endeavours.[3] W. Gibson has lately shown that effective reform
of diocesan administration began in the 1760s under Bishop Charles Moss,
but his article reveals unsuccessful attempts to remove the abuse of non-
residence by the members of the cathedral chapter dating back to Bishop
Ottley (1713–23).[4]

Episcopal exertions before Horsley's time encountered nevertheless formidable obstacles, and they failed to remove the characteristic abuses, which,
if not wholly different in kind from those encountered in English dioceses,
were outstandingly greater in degree. Four principal defects may be noted.
There was first a want of continuity at the episcopal level. The average tenure
of a bishop of the insufficiently remunerative See of St Davids between 1705
and 1800 was little more than five years. Horsley's short episcopate set no
new example. When his successor William Stuart gave place to Lord George
Murray in 1801 a clergyman at Aberystwyth wrote to his brother in London
concerning the new diocesan: 'Learn if you can whether he is led by the ears,
the eyes or the nose or taken by the hand—or by what handle to take him—or
if by all the senses united, his own sound judgement and penetration. By the
time his clergy begin to know a little of him by ex[perience] he flies off to
a warmer nest, and leaves many a black [swan] unfledged, like all his predecessors from time immemorial.'[5]

Secondly the chain of command within the diocese was weak, the four
archdeacons (of St Davids, Cardigan, Carmarthen, and Brecon) having been
deprived of their powers over their archdeaconries in consequence of a lawsuit
with the bishop in 1665. The posts continued in the later eighteenth century
as sinecure offices in the cathedral chapter. George Holcombe, a member of a
Pembrokeshire family well endowed with church preferment, was archdeacon
of Carmarthen down to 1789. Charles Moss, son of the bishop of Bath and
Wells, a former bishop of the diocese, was archdeacon of St Davids, appointed by his father at the age of four.[6] The responsibilities of archdeacons
for the behaviour of the clergy and the upkeep of churches were unloaded on
to rural deans who looked after smaller areas. A list compiled about 1800
comprises twenty-one deaneries.[7] It has been authoritatively stated that it was
Bishop Horsley who revived the office of rural dean or at least invested it with
useful functions.[8] This claim cannot be substantiated. Rural deans' visitation

[3] Glanmor Williams (ed.), *Glamorgan County History*, iv. *Early Modern Glamorgan* (Cardiff,
1974), chap. ix.
[4] W. Gibson, 'A Hanoverian Reform of the Chapter of St. Davids', *National Library of Wales
Journal*, 25 (1988), 285–8.
[5] NLW Lewis Evans Letters, fos. 54–5, L. to J. Evans, 27 Jan. 1801.
[6] NLW SD/Misc. B.41, list of benefices, revenues, etc. from *c.*1790.
[7] Ibid., B.39.
[8] D. T. W. Price, *Bishop Burgess and Lampeter College* (Cardiff, 1987), 37; cf. W. T. Morgan,
'The Diocese of St. David's in the Nineteenth Century (2)', *Journal of the Historical Society of the
Church in Wales*, 22 (1972), 12–47.

returns stretching back to 1717 and dealing with residence, fabric, and ornaments of the Church and of the ministers may be inspected in photocopy at
the National Library of Wales, Aberystwyth. The last complete return before
Horsley was appointed is dated 1745, but Bishop Smallwell issued a schedule
of appointment of twenty-one rural deans in 1785, sending to each of them a
letter explaining the several 'matters and things' in respect of which they were
to exercise their office 'in as large and ample a manner as any Rural Dean
hath exercised the same'.[9] The resuscitation of the office of rural dean in the
eighteenth-century Church was an uneven development. It emerges from the
meticulous researches of the Victorian scholar, William Dansey, that, while
in some dioceses rural deans enjoyed a continuous existence from medieval
times onwards, in others they were never appointed. In the diocese of Salisbury
revival probably dated from the tenure of the Restoration bishop, Seth Ward
(1666–8),[10] while at St Asaph a visitatorial and administrative structure of
rural deans reporting to the bishop on the condition of their deaneries existed
more than eighty years before Horsley under Bishop Wynne (1714–27).[11]
These, however, like St Davids, were large dioceses. Not until the half-
century after 1800 did the office become general, being introduced in one see
after another as part of the regular machinery of the English Church.[12]

If Horsley deserves no singular credit for originating it, he made good use
of it to implement his reforms of clergy discipline, as is apparent from the
instructions received by Isaac Williams, rural dean of Ultra Ayron, grand-
father of the Tractarian poet, who had served energetically the bishop's three
immediate predecessors, Yorke, Warren, and Smallwell. Williams was an
important figure in his own right. He not only managed the arrangements for
the rebuilding of churches in his deanery for his successive masters but was
steward of the episcopal lordship of Llanddewi Brefi, responsible for collecting the duty on lead ore raised from the mines at that place. He enjoyed
a confidential relationship with the bishops, and did not neglect the means of
preserving it. Thus Horsley wrote to him in 1792: 'I write in great haste to
thank you in my wife's name as well as my own for your kind remembrance
of us. Perry is a liquor particularly pleasing to her palate—and when it is
good, as I dare say yours is, not hostile to her constitution'.[13]

Remoteness of the bishop from the mass of the clergy and the people was a
third weakness of the system. It was experienced everywhere in the Church in
the eighteenth century. In Wales, however, it was acute, owing to the linguistic

---

[9] NLW SD/Misc. 1174.

[10] W. Dansey, *Horae Decanicae Rurales* (1844), ii, Appendix.

[11] Bill Gibson, 'A Welsh Bishop for a Welsh See: John Wynne of St. Asaph 1714–27', *Journal of Welsh Ecclesiastical History*, 1 (1984), 28–43.

[12] Dansey, *Horae Decanicae Rurales*, Appendix, esp. 457 stating that the 'ancient ecclesiastical office of Rural Dean has been revived in 18 English dioceses since the year 1800'.

[13] NLW 6203.E/41, Horsley to Williams, 11 Oct. 1792.

barrier which prevented the Welsh-speaking laity of the countryside from understanding what their father in God had to say to them on the few occasions when he visited them, notably at confirmations. Horsley did not break completely from the old style, but he made determined efforts to improve upon it. He was enthroned by proxy on 5 June 1788, one of the cathedral canons, William Holcombe, taking his place for the solemnities.[14] His only recorded visitation during an episcopate of more than five and a half years was his primary in 1790. This was below the norm of once in three years, when the opportunity was also taken to confirm the laity. According to usual eighteenth-century practice in the diocese the clergy and the confirmands were assembled in the principal or county towns, and though the bishop made valiant efforts to cope with the wretched communications of the area, the schedule was too tight to permit much intercourse with either. 'As I find that I have no carriage road from Cardigan to Fishguard', he replied to the rural dean of Ultra Ayron, 'but by way of Haverfordwest, it will be necessary that I should leave Cardigan as early as possible in the afternoon of Tuesday the 20th. And for this reason the days of visitation and confirmation at that place cannot be interchanged. The visitation therefore must stand for Monday 19th. I should hope that by going late to church on that day, the inconvenience to the clergy will be obviated.'[15]

Visitation, however, was far from being the only means by which Samuel Horsley came to know his diocese. He was in residence in the palace at Abergwili near Carmarthen within three months of his consecration, and lost no time in going to inspect the decaying cathedral at St Davids and dispatching circulars to bring the unsatisfactory ministry of stipendiary curates in his straggling dominion under strict surveillance and control.[16] There is evidence of one kind or another to prove that he resided within its confines every summer from 1788 to 1793 (inclusive) and that he usually went there soon after the close of the parliamentary session in June. A letter from his sister Sarah disclosed his subsequent itinerary. She told how she returned from Wales with him in October 1788 and how the bishop took in Gloucester on the way back 'where he keeps two months residence on his prebendal stall'. From thence she returned with the family to London in December.[17] Hence it seems that he devoted about half the year to the Church's business away from the House of Lords. In his diocese there was not much that escaped his attention. Soon after his appointment he opened a new diocese book or gazetteer. Entries over his own signature revealed impressive command of detail rapidly acquired. For the parish of Llanunus in Ultra Ayron deanery he

---

[14] NLW SD/Ch.B.8., 157.
[15] NLW 6203.E/33, Horsley to Williams, 10 July 1790.
[16] NLW SD/Ch.B.8, Horsley to precentor and chapter, 23 July 1789; NLW 6203.E/6, Horsley to Willams, 18 Aug. 1788.
[17] HP 1769, fos. 24–31, Sarah Horsley to F. Horsley, 24 Jan. 1790.

added on 10 October 1788: 'Llanunus. The true name of this place, as I am informed by the Rural Dean and others, is Gwnnus, Gwnuws, or Llannwnus, appears to have been originally a chapel annexed to Lledrod and to have been separated from the mother church by augmentation. See Lledrod.' The firmness of his control over appointments to individual parishes stands out from the following insertion for Llangolman and Llandilo in Pembrokeshire which had been united with Maenclochog until the decease of the incumbent Morgan Rice:

Upon the death of Mr. Morgan Rice, which happened on the 28th day of June 1790 William Edwards Clark tendered a presentation of himself under the hand and seal of William Wheeler Bowen of Lambston in the County of Pembroke to the vicarages of Maencloghog, Llangolman and Llandilo as united. Thereupon I caus'd the register of the diocese to be search'd and not finding any entry of a union of Maencloghog with Llangolman and Llandilo, I refused to grant institution to Maencloghog with the other under one presentation. The patron acquiesced and in a few days the same William Edwards came again with a presentation under the name and seal of the same William Wheeler Bowen to Llangolman and Llandilo singly, upon which institution was granted (August 3rd 1790), and sequestration was issued at the same time of the remaining vacant living of Maencloghog to the Rev. John Foley Curate and the Churchwardens of the Parish. S. St. Dds.

The same care was taken to regulate the number of services after the 1790 visitation articles had been received and studied. The bishops's practice seemed to be to issue instructions to Crown livings in order that these might serve as a model to the rest. Hence Rudbaxton in Pembrokeshire, which had previously held services once a Sunday, on Christmas Day, and Good Friday, received the following order:

Sept 22nd 1790. Ordered that henceforward divine service be performed in the parish church of Rudbaxton both morning and afternoon every Lords Day throughout the year. And that these festivals be observed: Namely. The feast of Our Lord's Nativity. Ash Wednesday. Good Friday. The Monday and Tuesday after Easter. The Feast of Our Lord's Ascension. The Monday and Tuesday after Whitsunday and the Anniversary of his Majesty's Accession. S. St. Dds.

Similar mandates were despatched to Llangoedmor and to Llanllwchaiarn in Cardiganshire, to Killrheddin and to Manerdivy in Pembrokeshire, adding in some cases Easter Eve and Whitsun-eve to the feasts to be celebrated, while the united churches of Narberth and Robeston were required to keep Wednesdays and Fridays in Lent and every day in Passion Week and to celebrate the Sacrament of the Lord's Supper monthly.[18]

Bishop Horsley held ordinations once a year, and in the best traditions of the eighteenth-century episcopate, examined candidates personally, looking

[18] NLW SD/Misc. B.41.

carefully into their titles. According to his earlier biographer he endeavoured to make himself likewise known to the laity by preaching frequently in parish churches, especially on the days when the Sacrament was administered. He was not a popular bishop in the democratic sense, and lacked the ability of his nineteenth-century successor Bishop Thomas Burgess to come to terms with the rising linguistic movement among the Welsh. A particular disadvantage was his vendetta against the Unitarians, who, though still few in number, held within their ranks the most distinguished of the bards, Iolo Morganwg (Edward Williams). A letter to a later bishop of St Davids, credibly ascribed to Iolo, accused the 'cursing and swearing Horseley' of hunting down a handful of supposed Unitarians with the 'cry of mad dog', of collecting 'a huge host of unitarian hunters' and of starting 'a few suspected individuals' as 'fair game'.[19] This was contrary to his public profession,[20] but he was under constant attack by another Unitarian apologist, David Jones, who published a series of skilfully penned 'letters' against him during the four years after his 1790 visitation charge under the pseudonym of 'Welsh Freeholder'. But until the 'Horsleyan tally ho' united them, his enemies were, on Iolo's confession, few in number. When 'Welsh Freeholder' sent his first effusion to a country newspaper of considerable circulation in the diocese, the editor refused to print it on the ground: 'The Bishop must have many friends in his diocese, and perhaps of some consequence. Anything like an attack upon him will therefore certainly occasion more than his resentment alone.'[21] His sister even learned of 'universal lamentation throughout his diocese from all ranks of people upon his quitting it'. She was told by a gentleman in the country at the time that the clergy went into 'general mourning', and one and all agreed 'that there had not been a Bishop in the memory of the oldest man amongst them, that had done the good, or was so universally beloved as our brother'.[22]

When allowance is made for Horsley's perpetually sharp manner it is easier to believe that he was respected than that he was beloved. It was as an organizer more than as a pastor that his talents shone, and these were most successfully brought to bear upon the weaknesses of the fourth category: those which impeded the execution of a satisfactory ministry at the parochial level. Non-residence and pluralities were widespread in the Church at the end of the eighteenth century, but in South Wales and especially in the diocese of St Davids they were present to an exceptional extent. The rural deans' visitation returns for 1809 disclose that 308 of the 424 benefices listed (that is 72 per cent of the whole) lacked a resident incumbent.[23] As residence was somewhat

---

[19] NLW 13145.A. fos. 343–5.
[20] See above, pp. 83–4.
[21] 'Welsh Freeholder', *A Letter to the Rt. Rev. Samuel, Lord Bishop of St. Davids on the Charge He Lately Delivered to the Clergy of his Diocese 1790*, 'Advertisement' 5.
[22] HP 1768, fos. 192–9, E. to F. Horsley, 20 Dec. 1793.
[23] NLW 9145.F.

arbitrarily defined at that time it cannot be assumed that the defaulters were not doing duty in their churches. Even so, the 28 per cent residence level for St Davids compares very unfavourably with other dioceses and areas about that time, for example 39.4 per cent for the diocese of Oxford in 1778, 59.3 per cent for Exeter in 1779, 38.6 per cent for Worcester in 1782, 41.9 per cent for London in 1790, 38 per cent for Oxford in 1808. Only the district of South Lindsey in Lincolnshire, with 25.1 per cent in 1830, showed anything like the St Davids figure.[24] The poverty of the Church in the diocese underlay the discrepancy. This extended downwards from the See itself, valued at £900 per annum in 1762, though yielding in practice £1,200 by 1804,[25] to the multitudinous parishes and chapelries. In the early years of the eighteenth century, well over two-thirds of livings were classified as impoverished (that is under about £50 per annum) when the national average was approximately 52 per cent.[26] Since then a large quantity of Bounty money had been poured into the diocese, mostly to increase poor benefices by lot, but even this was not enough to change the situation fundamentally. Sometimes the augmentations were used to set inadequately endowed chapelries on a separate course from the livings with which they had previously been combined, thus adding to the number of wretched provisions.

Impoverishment has been principally ascribed both by observers and by historians to the impropriation of ecclesiastical property by wealthy laymen. This prevailed to a more than usual extent in the diocese because the monastic interest from which these impropriators inherited their claim to tithes and other rights in parish churches had been very large there and had included English abbeys such as Tewkesbury and Keynsham, which had been given a large number of parishes in South Wales.[27] Bishop George Bull claimed that when he became bishop in 1705 he found half the livings of St Davids in private hands; Bishop Havard has stated that well nigh two-thirds of the 300 parishes in the eighteenth-century diocese were in the hands of impropriators.[28] Impropriation varied in degree from parish to parish, and it is better to view it as a fraction of the total revenue of the churches of the diocese. The distribution of the rent-charge granted in lieu of title at the general commutation of 1836 furnishes the closest approximation to that figure. The allocation of rent-charge made to laymen at the general commutation of 1836 suggests that they may have previously enjoyed slightly less

[24] V. Barrie-Curien, 'La Vie des paroisses en Angleterre à la fin du XVIIIᵉ siècle: Encadrement et résidence pastorale', *Histoire, économie, société*, 2 (1986), 187–215.

[25] J. Fortescue (ed.), *The Correspondence of George the Third, 1760 to 1783* (1927), 33–44; cf. Morgan, 'The Diocese of St. David's in the Nineteenth Century (1)', *Journal of the Historical Society of the Church in Wales*, 21 (1971), 5–49, quoting an average figure for 1804.

[26] In R. O'Day and F. Heal (eds.), *Princes and Paupers in the English Church 1500–1800* (Leicester, 1981), 247 (by Ian Green).

[27] In D. Walker (ed.), *A History of the Church in Wales* (Penarth, 1976), 103 (by O. W. Jones).

[28] Havard, 'Church Life in Wales'.

than one-third (that is 32 per cent) of the aggregate of parochial tithes. But when to this sum is added the appropriations of semi-sinecurist ecclesiastical bodies like the cathedral chapter and Christ's College, Brecon, it appears that nearly 58 per cent of the revenues of St Davids parishes was alienated from its proper and original use. Through a careless and unenterprising method of leasing, the tithes taken by the church corporations were also virtually played into the coffers of laymen, while the twelve prebends of Llanddewi Brefi in Cardiganshire were all lay fees by the end of the eighteenth century.[29]

While English and Anglo-Welsh families like the Chichesters of Devon, the Copes, the Harleys, the Mansels of Carmarthenshire, and the Mainwarings of County Hereford disposed of the modest wealth of the Church, the units of pastoral care fell drastically short of funds. Forty years after the Horsley era there were only one or two really affluent livings tenable in the diocese, such as the rectory of Llangattock in Breconshire worth, with its annexed chapelries, £1,123 per annum.[30] Some vicarages, notably in Brecon archdeaconry, were allowed to retain no more than one-third or one-half of the tithe, while between a quarter and a third of the livings in the diocese (that is 28.6 per cent) were merely curacies in the charge of a licensed curate whose stipend was paid by the impropriator or appropriator.[31] Moreover, the Welsh gentry resorted to fraud to evade their obligations in the matter. Curates were made to serve on sham or fictitious titles which gave no guarantee of an adequate stipend. A letter from the bishop's financial agent, Canon William Holcombe, to a Cardiganshire gentleman shows the extent of the abuse and the steps which were being taken to curb it when Horsley came to St Davids:

So your countrymen are at their old tricks again; Half our titles of deacons from Cardiganshire! I could wish from my soul the gentlemen of your country, were less given to smuggling and divinity, or at least that you would deal in better goods. To be serious, we have no doubts of you and your brother in law, but who will answer for Vavasor Davies, and Mr Thomas of Bangor, who have each had the modesty to send titles? The first to a Mr Timothy Evans, and the 2nd to a Mr William Pritchard, both which titles will infallibly be rejected, except you will take upon to assure his Lordship, that they are real, and that you believe the stipends will be paid. Mr David Williams of Caron hath granted a title to a Mr Richard Davies, of Caron; Can you answer for this? For my own part I can't help thinking very moderately of the said Mr David Williams, as he granted a sham title some time ago on Sputty Hourin, and the man afterwards came to the Bishop and declared he was starving, and his time was out. Mr. Thomas Davies, Curate of Llanavan, has again started *that title*, though it was rejected last year: Have you anything to say, in behalf of it?[32]

---

[29] Morgan, 'St. David's (1)'; NLW SD/Misc. B.39, fo. 105, for the Llanddewi prebends.

[30] Morgan, 'St. David's (1)'.

[31] Calculated from parochial data in NLW SD/Misc. B.41 with occasional additions from B.39.

[32] NLW 6203.E/47, letter from W. Holcombe (Abergwili) 6 Sept. 1788.

In this climate of uncertainty of tenure and slender remuneration, curates of the same peasant stock as their parishioners resorted to pluralism to make ends meet, and chapels languished in ruins. Sarah Horsley, the bishop's half-sister, referred in 1790 to 'numbers' of these 'patient poor, plodding labourers of the vineyard' who 'were supporting a wife and large families upon a miserable pittance of 10, 12 or 15 pds a year with the care many of them of 6 churches'.[33] Erasmus Saunders had written nearly seventy years earlier of curates 'being forced to a perpetual motion', having to serve three or more churches every Sunday to earn as little as £12 per annum.[34] This Anglican version of the itinerant ministry cannot but have been destructive of pastoral work during the week.

At the other end of the scale the ancient cathedral of St Davids needed a heavy expenditure to prevent a total collapse of the west front. This was being slowly pushed from the vertical by the tilting Norman columns of the nave which must eventually follow it to the ground.[35] Prompted by the bishop's early interest, the chapter made a start in July 1788 by ordering a repair of the organ and the roofing of one of the chapels. Twelve months later Horsley, who was *quasi-decanus* as well as bishop, intervened forcefully to propose a complete repair, which would 'restore to its original beauty and grandeur . . . one of the noblest monuments that our island has to boast'. He suggested an appeal to the public for funds, which members of the capitular body might encourage by their own liberality. In response to his exhortation the chapter commissioned John Nash, then a relatively inexperienced local architect, to survey the whole building for alterations and additions which were to be superintended by Wyatt. In the event Nash superintended the reconstruction. Work was begun on the audit house and the chapter house, and in 1791 contracts were signed for the new west front, built in a hybrid Gothic and Norman style which the Victorians replaced. By July 1794, £2,015 had been expended on the renovations, £1,931 of which was raised by subscription. Horsley himself pledged £100. His zeal in promoting the enterprise sprang from its connection with the larger purpose of church reform. He wrote to the precentor and chapter:

The condition and external appearance of these sacred fabrics, is a matter, as you cannot but be sensible, which lies exposed to the public eye, and by the impression it will naturally make on the minds of the people must nearly affect the interests of religion, and still more immediately the credit of capitular bodys.[36]

At St Davids the last need was especially urgent, as, until quite recently, the canons had operated a system of rotating residence which enabled them to

---

[33] HP 1769, fos. 24–31, Sarah to F. Horsley, 24 Jan. 1790.
[34] Morgan, 'St. David's (2)'.
[35] John Summerson, *The Life and Work of John Nash Architect* (1980), 16; T. Davis, *John Nash: The Prince Regent's Architect* (1966), 20.
[36] NLW SD/Ch.B.8, 167–8; Ch. Accts., 28–31, 41; Ch. Misc. 211–12, 220–5.

spend ten months a year away from 'the crumbling city of St. Davids', where the dignitaries' houses had long been demolished.[37]

Fittingly, however, it was to the problem of the parochial ministry that Horsley turned his earliest attention, and it was upon this that he made the most enduring impression. The first necessity was to assess the deficiency. On 24 July 1788 he addressed to the rural deans a letter remarkable for its blend of bureaucratic particularity and affection:

Wishing to obtain exact information of the state of my diocese with respect to the residence and non-residence of the clergy, in order to apply the most summary and effectual remedies to an evil which I have too much reason to think prevails in a degree which it were criminal to tolerate, I mean the neglect of parochial duty; I desire you to transmit to me, *by the 14th of August*, a correct list of all the parishes in your deanery, with the names of the incumbents, curates, the places of their residence, and the distance of those places from the churches which they serve. For this purpose I send you herewith a sheet of paper properly ruled & titled. The whole sheet is divided into nine vertical columns. In the third column on the left entitled *parish* enter the name of each parish. On the same horizontal line with the name of the parish, in the next column entitled *Incumbent*, enter the name of the present incumbent. Again in the next column entitled *Place of Residence*, on the same horizontal line, enter the name of the place where the incumbent usually resides, and in the next column entitled *Distance*, enter the distance of that place from his parish church in miles. In the seventh column entitled *Curate*, still on the same horizontal line enter the name of the Curate: and in the eighth column, entitled place of residence, enter the name of the place where the curate resides: and in the ninth column, entitled *Distance*, the distance of that place from the parish church. The two first columns on the left have no titles. In the first of these be pleased to number the parishes 1.2.3. etc regularly from the top downwards, and in the second column distinguish the rectories, vicarages and curacies by the letters R. V. or C. as the case may be. By a return of the sheet thus filled, at the time above specified, by the post, you will much oblige,

Revd. Sir,

Abergwilly   Your loving Brother

July 24th 1788   Samuel St. Davids[38]

From the data which reached him he quickly concluded that the service of curates 'unlicenced, and insufficiently paid' was the principal abuse which, 'with God's assistance', he had to correct, and took prompt steps to bring the system under regulation. Within days of the date fixed for the receipts of the rural deans' returns, he supplied those officers with bundles of printed circulars to distribute through their apparitors to the minister of every church and chapel of their deaneries. These required curates to exhibit their licences to the rural dean on or before 14 September 1788. Those unable to produce a licence were commanded to appear before the bishop between 10 and 27

---

[37] Gibson, 'Hanoverian Reform'.
[38] NLW 6203/39, Horsley to Williams etc., 24 July 1788.

September at his palace at Abergwili fortified by a nomination from the incumbent of each of the parishes which they served, a testimonial of their life and character signed by three clergymen, and their letters of orders. With the same meticulousness which characterized their earlier instructions, the rural deans were directed how to receive a curate who came to them to exhibit his licence. They were to be 'pleased to enter the name of the parish or chapelry to which he is licensed, the curate's name, the date of the licence by the year, month & day (as thus 1787 March 2) the stipend assign'd in the licence, the reputed value of the benefice and the names of any other churches which the same curate serves, in the columns of the ruled sheet successively according to their titles'. The last columns were for observations on 'the duty to be done in the several churches'.[39] The ruled sheet provided for these details was to be returned to the bishop by the first post after 14 September, thus enabling him to check whether the response of the clergy to his command to apply to him for licences was adequate. His object was to implement a new rule 'under which no curate in the diocese was to have charge of more than two churches, nor for the care of each less than fifteen pounds per annum'.[40] The extent of the operation is attested by the diocese books. In a See containing about 470 ancient parishes and fewer benefices, nearly 100 licensings were effected in the year 1788 with stipends fixed principally at £15 but some at £20 or £30 and one even of £50. It seems certain that this figure, greatly in excess of the customary annual number, was largely composed of curates already serving under irregular arrangements who trekked to Abergwili to take out proper licences. Thirty-nine of these changes were in the arch-deaconry of Brecon which embraced some of the most remote areas of the diocese, but included some where the new mining and metallurgical industries were to grow. Horsley's reforms set in course a sustained levelling-up of curates' incomes. By the time of his successor William Stuart, who was bishop from 1794 to 1800, a minimum of £15 per chapel had been turned into a norm of £20, and from 1797 onwards, after the passing of the Curates Act, entries of £40 and even one of £52. 10s. figured prominently in the specula.[41] There was no return to the standards of mid-century, when stipends of £6, £7, or £8 were entered and when, in the vast majority of cases, no record of the amount seems to have been preserved by the diocesan.[42] It seems prob-able that tighter control and higher remuneration curbed the excesses of pluralism among curates, but the records are not specific enough to allow such progress to be measured, especially in view of the similarity of Welsh

---

[39] NLW 6203/6, Horsley to Williams etc., 16 Aug. 1788. For the printed circular to clergy dated 15 Aug. see NLW 6203/16.

[40] HP 1769, fos. 24–31, Sarah to F. Horsley, 24 Jan. 1790.

[41] The above information is based on an analysis of two diocese books, NLW SD/Misc. B.39 and 41.

[42] Ibid., B.42.

names. For many years after the overhaul the regulations imposed through the licensing system were frequently evaded by recourse to sham titles and private agreements. As the manuscript letters of Lewis Evans, one curate of west Wales, testify, these still abounded.[43] The need to increase payments to their curates may have led some incumbents to adopt the alternative of residing themselves, but there is no evidence of a consistent trend in that direction in the diocese books. The problem of clerical non-residence remained unsolved in the third decade of the nineteenth century.[44]

Even with the higher scales introduced by Horsley, remuneration in the diocese was insufficient to attract a graduate ministry such as had become common in the Established Church by the eighteenth century. Prominent among the bishop's achievements, therefore, was his endeavour to provide an alternative training for the peasant clergy who filled the meaner posts. The need was of long standing. While 61 per cent of the clergymen of the diocese of St Asaph were graduates in 1710 and 63 per cent of those of Llandaff in 1726 were of like status, the corresponding figure for the See of St Davids in 1714 was 87 out of 265, that is 32 per cent.[45] No improvement can be discerned for the second half of the century. Diocese books for that period record the letters of a degree against the names of the clergy of only about a quarter of the livings in the large archdeaconries of Brecon and Carmarthen, principally rectors or substantial vicars.[46] As Bishop Havard has pointed out, University reform ultimately closed the doors of Oxford and Cambridge to poor men's sons by putting an end to servitorships by which they had previously worked their way through college.[47] Only occasionally were curacies in the diocese filled by graduates, and these were usually perpetual curacies. Thomas Luntley LL D was licensed to the two Herefordshire benefices of Rowlston and Llansillo in 1772. John Williams LL B was perpetual curate of Llanelweth in 1784.[48] Most curates, however, who were the sons of small farmers, tradesmen, or craftsmen, or came themselves from impoverished clerical families, were obliged by financial restraints to make do with a local education in the diocesan grammar schools or private venture schools. Some went to Nonconformist academies, such as the Presbyterian College at Carmarthen and the school of David Davis, Castell Hywel.[49] The provision made by these was by no means contemptible. The Carmarthen Dissenting Academy taught Greek Testament, Hebrew Psalmody, and Pietetus (*sic*), as well as Astronomy, Trigonometry, and Lampe's Ecclesiastical History, to

[43] NLW 22,131.C, esp. fos. 40–1, 50–1.
[44] Morgan, 'St. David's (2)'.
[45] G. H. Jenkins, *Literature, Religion and Society in Wales, 1660–1730* (Cardiff, 1978), 213–14.
[46] NLW SD/Misc. B.39 and 41.
[47] Havard, 'Church life in Wales'.
[48] NLW SD/Misc. B.41.
[49] Morgan, 'The Diocese of St. David's (3)', *Journal of the Historical Society of the Church in Wales*, 23 (1973) 18–55.

students from all over Wales and one from London in the 1740s. It was never, however, fully acceptable to Anglicans, for at that time one of its products was reported to have tried unsuccessfully 'to be ordained in the Church'.[50] More suitable were the endowed grammar schools founded in the several towns and villages of the diocese, licensed by the bishop and often staffed by clergy. From the later years of the eighteenth century onwards three such schools, under a succession of distinguished headmasters, started to acquire so high a reputation for the teaching of the classics that they attracted pupils from great distances who took up their abode in lodgings and inns, where they could live more cheaply than at boarding-schools and universities. Ystrad Meurig in Cardiganshire, founded by the Welsh poet Edward Richard, was outstanding before 1757. It was followed by the grammar schools at Lampeter and Carmarthen which reached their apogee after 1815.[51]

It was to the reputable Welsh public schools that Bishop Horsley turned to assist him in the reform of the training of candidates for ordination. Most of the credit for improving the system has been accorded to Bishop Thomas Burgess, who took the steps which led to the opening of St Davids College, Lampeter in 1827.[52] Nearly forty years earlier Horsley propounded a solution on different lines. It was a corollary of the raising of clerical stipends. A long letter to the schoolmasters addressed by the bishop on 17 October 1788 began:

That the labourer should be worthy of his hire, is a maxim of such wisdom and authority, that I should have felt but little satisfaction in my late regulations for augmenting the stipends of the curates, throughout my diocese, had I not a further view to the encouragement it would afford to their better education, indeed, I must have considered it in a great measure, as an unjust demand on the incomes of the several incumbents, had it not in its consequences led it to an object of the first importance to them and the public, the having their churches supplied by abler assistants, and in a much more regular manner.

He proposed to follow the example of his 'honoured' predecessor, Bishop Edward Smallwell (1783–8) in requiring that all candidates for deacon's orders who brought no testimonial from either of the Universities should produce certificates that they had spent the last three years without inter-mission 'at some reputable public school', of which there were many in the diocese. He announced his intention to designate those peculiarly suited to the purpose.

Horsley's plan, however, far exceeded the precedent. He proposed to enlist the help of the schoolmasters in a purposeful scheme of training for ordina-

[50] NLW 5456, Thomas Morgan's Diary, 19 Oct. 1743; Ibid 5457, notebook, lists of students at Carmarthen with Morgan 1743, with comments on their subsequent careers.

[51] Morgan, 'St. David's (3)'; Price, *Bishop Burgess*, 51.

[52] Cf. Ibid., *passim*; Morgan, 'St. David's (3)'.

tion which would take the place of both the Universities and of the later theological colleges for those who could go no higher. They were to keep a separate register of divinity students and to select them by special criteria. The course was designed for youths who had already received a grammar school education, for the masters were instructed 'to admit no students in divinity, who have not made such a proficiency in school learning as to be able to construe the Greek testament, and the common Latin authors with tolerable facility'. Not only persons of bad character were to be excluded but those who had been 'engaged in any low or menial occupation, those with speech defects or with other remarkable deformities of person'.

From these instructions the bishop went on to prescribe the essentials of the syllabus which was to be taught to those who were selected. Rightly he insisted that the Greek Testament should be the chief object of study, which was to be aided by the use of Whitley's Paraphrase for the annotations and of Michaelis's Lectures on the New Testament, 'the best perhaps on the subject'. In a crash course for makeshift ordinands it was perhaps pedantic to insist that the 'Greek should always be construed into Latin', and even more that the proper pronunciation of Latin should be cultivated by reading the poets Virgil and Juvenal. But there were some wise and sensible provisions. The books marked with an asterisk, on which the bishop would examine the candidates before ordination, were Burnet on the Attributes, Pearson on the Creed, Wheatly on the Common Prayer, Secker on the Catechism, and Grotius' *De Veritate*, which was to be studied with Jenkins's *Reasonableness of Christianity* as a commentary. Butler's *Analogy* and Ditton on the Resurrection were listed among books to be 'carefully construed over, and studied'. These would equip the priest both to teach his flock and to defend the faith against encroaching rationalism. Moreover, the training was to be practical. In teaching their pupils masters were to be 'very attentive to their reading clearly and distinctly and to exercise them often in reading the Common Prayer aloud, with proper stops and emphasis; in which you may be much assisted by Sheridan's Lectures, the only book professedly written on the subject'. The bishop added that reading select sermons in the same manner would be attended with advantage, and the students were to attend sermons constantly and to make abstracts of what they had heard. These were to be handed to their teachers on the following morning, which would 'insensibly habituate them to composition'. Regrettably the art of sermon construction was not to be more 'sensibly' inculcated. But in view of the charge of arid moralizing which is so often brought against the Hanoverian Church of England it is important to note that Bishop Horsley especially stressed the cultivation of a 'good disposition' by reading which embraced Chrysostom's *De Sacerdotis* [sic] and by looking to God in prayer.[53]

---

[53] NLW 6203.E/48, Horsley's instructions to schoolmasters, 17 Oct. 1788.

The most serious omission from this balanced programme of study was any mention of the need for proficiency in the Welsh language. Horsley, who collated an English clergyman unable to speak the tongue to the 'Welch' living of Llanboidy in the archdeaconry of Carmarthen,[54] was little more sensitive than most English bishops to the linguistic needs of his diocese. Burgess, who later befriended the Dyfed Cambrian Society, was much the exception to the rule, and this fact has won him inordinate praise from Welsh historians.[55] Horsley, however, at least published a Welsh translation of his visitation charge, and his library at St Asaph included a Welsh grammar.[56] His plan for the general education of ordinands was in some respects more practical, because less expensive to parents, than Burgess's collegiate schemes. The course would last three years instead of four, and residence was not prescribed. But both suffered from the same underlying defect, for anyone who could pass through so selective a social and academic net would be able to attain 'a more prestigious and less arduous course at Oxford or Cambridge'.[57] In his letter to the schoolmasters Horsley viewed with equanimity the fact that his rules might cause some to give up all thought of ordination, for he preferred quality to quantity. But quality would not in practice be attained while a maldistribution of the Church's patronage and benefices necessitated cheap and shoddy labour to keep the system working. There was much of it about after Horsley's time. It was perhaps with some exaggeration that Bishop Burgess's biographer wrote of ploughboys being ordained after a year's schooling,[58] and the fact that 'fat-headed dulness' was attributed by Bishop Stuart's chaplain to Lewis Evans early in 1797 did not impede his ordination to the priesthood eight months later.[59]

THE SEE OF ROCHESTER

Translation to Rochester in 1793 was financially a modest promotion. The See itself was worth less than St Davids—a mere £600 per annum in 1762, compared with St Davids' £900. But the handsome commendam which accompanied it, the deanery of Westminster, valued at £900 at the same date,[60] tipped the exchange in Horsley's favour by about two-thirds of his former income, a gain which was partly offset by the surrender of lesser preferment.[61] These figures, which are the nearest available, probably err on the low side for the end of the century. Westminster Abbey, with estates in

[54] NLW SD/Misc. B.39 and 41.
[55] Price, *Bishop Burgess*, 61, samples assessments of him.
[56] LPL 2810, 279–91, W. J. Palmer, 'An Account of Horsley's Manuscripts'.
[57] Price, *Bishop Burgess*, 53.
[58] Morgan, 'St. David's (3)', citing C. J. Harford.
[59] NLW 22,131.C, fos. 40–2, L. to J. Evans, 1 Feb. and 31 Oct. 1797.
[60] Fortescue (ed.), *George the Third*, i. 33–44.
[61] He gave up the rectory of Newington Butts. *DNB* xxvii. 383–6.

not fewer than eighteen counties, mostly situated in the prosperous agrarian south-east of England, was a waxing asset at that time. The dean's third of the corn rents alone rose from £138. 11s. 9½d. in 1793 to £378. 15s. 5½d. in 1800, though the latter was a somewhat exceptional year.[62] A benefit which he especially welcomed was the reduction of his living costs. With no private fortune he had found the expense of removing a large family, consisting of unmarried sisters as well as an ailing wife and a son, twice a year upwards of 200 miles between London and Abergwili, together with the other incidents of office, far more than the income from his preferments would bear, especially as he had been unable to obtain possession of one of the commendams previously granted to him, Marylebone. He confessed to pecuniary embarrassment in May 1791 when he wrote explicitly to Pitt on the day after the death of Bishop Thurlow, asking to be remembered in the 'removals which may be occasion'd by the vacancy of the see of Durham'.[63] For the relief he desired he had to wait for the gratitude which followed his loyalist sermon in the Abbey after the execution of the king of France. When it came, it brought him the remission of £220 per annum house rent in London by having the use of the deanery. Bromley Palace in Kent, seat of the bishops of Rochester, provided a second official residence not far from the capital. The house and grounds had been much improved by the previous bishop. Moreover, the advantages of being dean of Westminster were not purely economic. Inaccessible and detached though it was by modern cathedral standards, the Abbey never ceased to be a national shrine, a house of kings, and so distinguished a Westminster address as the deanery brought its occupant into free and continuous contact with the leading noblemen, politicians and statesmen, thinkers and writers active at the time. In short it gave him the opportunity to become a national figure. Though unspoken, this was undoubtedly an assumption underlying Bishop Horsley's pleasure at his new preferment. When he came out of Wales at the end of 1793 his sister observed that 'he never looked better in his life or appeared in better spirits'.[64]

After the tangle of St Davids, the bishopric of Rochester was a light burden to carry. Situate in the north-west corner of Kent, from Deptford to the Medway towns of Chatham and Rochester, it stretched southwards in the shape of a square through chalky downland to a little beyond Tunbridge Wells. Deducting those of the large peculiar of the archbishop of Canterbury embedded within it in the deanery of Shoreham, the benefices under the bishop of Rochester's direct jurisdiction numbered in 1835 only ninety-four.[65] The diocese was by far the smallest in England, though it was also one of the

---

[62] Westminster Abbey Muniments, 33,553, Receiver General's Accounts 1794; 33,824–32, Treasurer's Accounts 1793–1801; 34,093–101, Steward's Accounts 1793–1801.

[63] PRO Chatham MSS 30/8/146, Horsley to Pitt, 28 May 1791.

[64] HP 1768, fos. 53–6, A. to F. Horsley, 15 Dec. 1793.

[65] PP 1835 [67] xxii, tables.

oldest. In Victorian times it was to be pulled about to serve the needs of the Church of the metropolis, by being first transferred across the Thames to Essex and Hertfordshire and afterwards converted into a Thames-side straggle through south London, preparing the way for the creation of the diocese of Southwark. At the close of the eighteenth century, however, it was a Kentish rural diocese with some thriving sea-ports on its northern shores.

Not only was the bishopric smaller, but the livings were for the most part comfortably endowed. The Ecclesiastical Duties and Revenues Commissioners in their second report published a list of dioceses showing for each the number of benefices with a population of 500 and upwards but falling below the annual value of £150, the minimum level to which it was proposed to raise them. Rochester, with only two, appeared to have the best record in the country, for which the total (for twenty-six bishoprics) was 1,440. An accompanying policy statement was less favourable. In this thirteen livings in the diocese (14 per cent) were noted to be poor enough to be eligible for augmentation by a scale which varied in accordance with their populousness. But this at least was in shining contrast with Chester's 348 (63 per cent), St Davids' 219 (54 per cent) or even St Asaph's forty-eight (37 per cent).[66] Pluralities and non-residence could not therefore be justified by impoverishment with the same conviction as in St Davids. These abuses were nevertheless present to about the average extent. Sixty cases of non-residence by the incumbent were cited in the parliamentary returns for 1805, that is 63.8 per cent as compared with 65.7 per cent for the country as a whole four years later.[67] Research into other dioceses warns against equating these percentages with clerical absenteeism, for non-resident clergy often lived near enough to their parishes to take regular duty, came to some arrangements with their neighbours, or paid a stipendiary curate to reside.[68] Bishop Horsley, who directed his primary visitation charge in 1796 mainly against neglect of parochial duty, was, as we have seen, indulgent towards the absence of scholar priests and those serving the Church in a distinguished capacity elsewhere, provided that a resident curate was installed in the living. His policy was reflected in the parliamentary residence return for Rochester for 1805, relating to only the second full year after his departure. In it the chief causes for non-residence were given as:

Residence on other livings	21
Literary or ecclesiastical appointment elsewhere	13
Offices in cathedrals	6
Want or unfitness of the parsonage house	6

[66] PP 1836 (86) xxxvi. 22–4; 1835 (54) xxii. 12, tables.

[67] PP 1809 (234) ix. 25; cf. Barrie-Curien, 'La Vie des Paroisses', 188.

[68] Diana McClatchey, *Oxfordshire Clergy 1777–1869* (Oxford, 1960), 31; Barrie-Curien, 'La Vie des Paroisses'.

At Rochester Horsley gave less to diocesan administration than he had been wont to do at St Davids. As his importance increased, he could no longer cope with the detail as efficiently as before, and was more inclined to leave matters to underlings. After seventeen months in the diocese he suddenly postponed his first visitation to another year, causing annoyance to his arch-deacon, who was obliged hastily to substitute a visitation of his own.[69] Control of ordinations began to falter. He omitted to take note of the address of a clergyman in the diocese whose brother he had promised to ordain, so that when the opportunity arose his chaplain William Crawford was obliged to seek him out by writing to a neighbour.[70] Such faults were aberrations from his fixed habits of mind. It is conceivable that in 1795–6 he was already begin-ning to suffer early warnings of the 'severe fit of illness' which for some time disqualified him from writing on any subject in 1799.[71] The sunken eyes and sallow complexion of a portrait of the Rochester period[72] bespeak a condition conducive to intermittent health failure.

He remained, however, an unbending disciplinarian. A prebendary in the cathedral convicted in the Court of King's Bench at Westminster of criminal conversation with the wife of the earl of Cardigan was inhibited by the bishop from officiating there pending proceedings for his deprivation and degradation from the priesthood. It was further ordered that the inhibitory letters patent should be read publicly at divine service in the cathedral church on Sunday 16 November 1794. These proceedings were taken to avoid scandal![73] In matters of church law he pronounced authoritatively and in a broadly conservative sense. Advising his nephew William Jocelyn Palmer on how to handle a tithe dispute arising from an enclosure in his own parish—Mixbury, an Oxfordshire living in the gift of the bishop of Rochester—he wrote learnedly:

My Dear William

I have been so much taken up in the parliamentary business that I have not had a moment's leisure to reply sooner to your letter of the 25th. I now write to answer your question about the proffits of the vacancy. By the 28 H.8 Chap. II s. 3 it is enacted that the 'tithes, fruits, oblations, obventions, emoluments, commodities, advantages, rents and all other whatsoever reserves, casualties or profits, certain and uncertain, affering or belonging to any archdeaconry, deanery, prebend, parsonage, vicarage ... or other spiritual promotion, benefice, dignity or office, within this realm ... growing, rising or coming during the *time of vacation* of the same promotion spiritual shall belong and affer to such person *as shall be thereunto next presented*, promoted, instituted, inducted, or admitted.

---

[69] Bodl. Eng. Misc. d.156, fo. 64, Law to Noble, 6 May 1795.
[70] Ibid. fos. 83, 91, Crawford to Noble, 7 and 16 Apr. 1796. Crawford, who resided at Newington, Surrey, was a former curate to Horsley, and had been one of his chaplains since 1788. HP 1768, fos. 27–30, A. to F. Horsley, 18 Aug. 1788.
[71] NLS Acc. 4796, Box 122, Horsley to Bp. Abernethy Drummond, 16 Oct. 1799.
[72] See Engraving by S. W. Reynolds at the British Museum.
[73] Dio. Rochester, Bishop's Court Muniments 1790–1814, fos. 62–4.

By the next clause any person who shall receive the proffits coming during vacancy, and refuse to restore them to the next incumbent shall forfeit the treble value, one half of which forfeiture shall go to the King, the other half to the incumbent.

By the 9th clause of the same Act, if an incumbent leases his benefice for a year and dies, the lessee shall hold and enjoy his lease to the end of the year, 'paying *to the successor* all such rent and services as for the remnant of the said year shall upon such lease be due'.

You may depend upon it, that it is in general clear and settled law that all proffits becoming due during vacation belong to the successor, without any claim of the predecessor's heirs or executors for the portion of the year, half year, or quarter which he survived. Burn indeed in his Ecclesiastical Law, has advanced an opinion that the case of a leased benefice is alterd by a statute of Geo.2. But he is mistaken in that, as in many instances [I] mean. The statute of Geo.2 which he alleges has no sort of bearing upon ecclesiastical property, but relates only to persons holding *by lease* determinable on their own lives. Clergymen hold the temporalities of their preferments by no such tenure, and the statute has no relation to them.

Palmer was warned to check the provisions of the Mixbury Bill, as it was very common in recent Enclosure Bills commuting tithes to divide the kind of the broken year between predecessor and successor 'in direct contradiction to the antient, better law', and the letter ended with a further caution against Burn's book which was 'much in use among the clergy' but 'full of errors', The bishop recommended instead Watson's *Clergyman's Law*.[74]

During the Rochester period Horsley's High Churchmanship was evident not only in using his legal training to combat the encroachments of statute and the law books upon ancient ecclesiastical law but in strengthening traditional devotion. In particular he strove to rescue the rite of confirmation from the loss of solemnity which it had sustained. Owing to the large numbers of young people confirmed together in one place at the infrequent episcopal visitations, it had degenerated into an idle ceremony attended by much rowdyism in the locality. At the time of his second visitation in 1800 Horsley issued a printed circular to the parish clergy instructing them how to prepare their candidates for the occasion. Each was to come to the area centre where confirmation would be administered armed with a ticket of recommendation from the minister of his or her parish without which none would be admitted to the service. Except in extraordinary circumstances, confirmands were to be at least 14 years of age. Not only were they to be taught to say the Lord's Prayer, the Apostles' Creed, and the Ten Commandments, and further instructed in the Catechism; they were also to receive teaching on the nature and import- ance of the 'apostolical rite' which they were undergoing 'in private con- ferences as well as in public discourses from the pulpit'. It is curious that at a visitation chiefly remembered for his attack on the Sunday Schools Bishop

---

[74] Bodl. Eng. Misc. c.690, fos. 22–3, Horsley to W. J. Palmer, 5 Apr. 1802.

Horsley should have emerged as an early advocate of the confirmation class.[75]

While he was bishop of Rochester he found much of his time consumed by State business. The war and the accompanying food crises refurbished in practice the partnership of Church and State which Horsley defended in theory. When, in the interests of regulating the food supply, the Lords Spiritual and Temporal in Parliament entered into an engagement in December 1795 to reduce the consumption of wheat in their families by at least one-third, and the Privy Council recommended to the magistrates to enjoin a similar restraint on schools, houses of industry, and places of confinement, Home Secretary Portland drew in the bishops to publish the measures, and Horsley was quick to respond. On 7 January 1796 he dispatched a circular letter to the clergy of his diocese, urging them 'to be among the foremost to promote, by your advice and your example, this godly plan of charitable self-denial in the higher ranks, for the more effectual relief and comfort of the poor'. The letter entered fully into the reasons for the alarming scarcity of wheat and the enormous increase in the price of bread, explaining that the calamity was due not, as some believed, to combinations among dealers in corn and flour but to the shortfall of the last harvest, which because it was general in Europe and America could not be made good by importation. It was ordered to be read in churches, together with the parliamentary resolutions.[76]

As teachers of morality clergymen were uniquely placed to influence the conduct of their neighbours, while as schoolmasters and magistrates they enjoyed a direct control over foundations. As tithe-owners they were also well placed to supply Government with information about the state of the crops. In November 1800, faced by another rise in the price of grain, Portland called upon the bishops to circulate queries 'among such of the clergy as by their residence in market towns, or being in the habit of taking their tithes in kind, are thought most capable of furnishing the most authentic information', in order to be 'prepared against the meeting of Parliament'. The bishop of Oxford demurred at using the clergy as inquisitors, and engaged a few private investigators. But Horsley had no such scruples. He sent out the questionnaire on 5 November with instructions how to fill it in.[77] In the following year he collaborated in a survey of the last year's crops, designed to assist 'H. M.'s confidential servants' to estimate the 'effects of inclosures and other parliamentary provisions in the agriculture of the country'.[78] Evidence obtained from the clergy was sometimes informative, but it also embodied 'guesstimates'

---

[75] Ibid. d.157, fo. 40, circular, 1 Sept. 1800; cf. Anthony Russell, *The Clerical Profession* (1980), 133–4, 139–40.
[76] Bodl. Eng. Misc. d.156, fos. 71–2, circular, 7 Jan. 1796.
[77] Ibid., d.157, fo. 65, circular, 5 Nov. 1800; cf. Bodl. Top. Oxon. d.355, fos. 19–20, Randolph to Lambard, 20 Nov. 1800.
[78] Bodl. Eng. Misc. d.157, fos. 105, 109, circulars, 20 Sept. and 4 Oct. 1801.

and presented contradictions such as most bishops were ill-equipped to resolve.[79]

As bishop of Rochester Horsley was distinctively involved in State service of another kind, the organization of home defence. His role in this nationally will be discussed in Chapter 12. Here it will be sufficient to note that his interest was especially relevant to the needs of the area where he exercised episcopal charge. During the critical months of 1797, when the threat of invasion came across the North Sea, Rochester diocese was not far from the front line. The hazard derived less from De Winter's fleet and landing force at the Texel than from the hostile operations of the Nore mutineers upon shipping in the Thames. Loyal sailors constructed booms across the Medway to protect Chatham, Rochester, and Sheerness, and a mortar battery was set up over the river.[80] Though Duncan's triumph at Camperdown ended the local menace, excitement persisted in northern Kent when, shortly afterwards, the Secretary of State for War called for widespread arming of the people to meet invasion wheresoever it might descend.[81] None were more ardent to serve in the volunteer corps than the clergy of that region. A vicar of Wilmington wrote to his friend on 10 May 1798, commenting that 'it was high time for our ecclesiastical rulers to check the arming influenza of their inferior brethren; for in the vicinity of Maidstone there were four, who were to be recruited captains, with cockades instead of roses in their beavers'.[82]

WESTMINSTER ABBEY

To eighteenth-century visitors the Collegiate Church of St Peter in Westminster was one of the least inspiring of the sights of London. The German pastor Carl Moritz wrote down his arrival impressions in 1782: 'In contrast with the round, modern, majestic cathedral of St Paul's on the right there rises on the left the long medieval pile of Westminster Abbey, with its enormous pointed roof.' Inspection of the interior convinced him that it was a gloomy place, its side walls already devoted almost entirely to monuments of great admirals carved in marble, which made 'but a pointless impression with all their pomp and embellishment'.[83] Poets' Corner was a place of veneration, especially to the men of letters who aspired to be commemorated there, but there was a growing feeling as the century reached its close that the Abbey

---

[79] As in the diocese of Oxford. See Bodl. Top. Oxon. d.355, fos. 19–20, Randolph to Lambard, 20 Nov. 1800. Mark Noble, a plantation farmer who did not take tithe in kind, answered the 1800 queries transmitted by Horsley 'as well as my limited information permitted'. Bodl. Eng. Misc. d.157, fos. 66–7, Noble to Horsley, 9 Nov. 1800.

[80] James Dugan, *The Great Mutiny* (1970), 248.

[81] Ian R. Christie, *Wars and Revolutions: Britain 1760–1815* (1982), 241–2.

[82] Quoted from Jebb, 117–19.

[83] C. P. Moritz, *Journeys of a German in England in 1782*, ed. R. Nettel (1965), 26, 77–9.

was over-packed with tombs, and that it was time to erect memorials, as in the case of Dr Johnson, in the almost empty St Paul's.

Visitors' descriptions could mislead, especially when applied to a building closed to the public except at service-time, and viewed, on entry through a small door which led straight into Poets' Corner, by the payment of a fee of 6*d.* a time (raised in 1799 to 9*d.*) which did not yet cover admission to the whole building. Even during the eighteenth century the Abbey was not just a 'pile'. It was a corporate body with a continuous life of its own, serving regularly the needs of select groups of people and more occasionally attracting to itself far larger numbers. The Elizabethan statutes of the college prescribed that two choral services should be held each day, on weekdays as well as on Sundays at 8 or 9 in the morning and at 4 in the afternoon. They were still being performed at the beginning of the nineteenth century.[84]

For those who preferred their music in a less stylized form the Abbey hosted festivals in 1784, 1785, 1786, 1787, and 1791 with orchestra and massed choir, and Handel the favourite composer. Colourful ceremonial declined as the occasion for it passed after the coronation of the long-lived George III in 1761, but it was kept alive on a smaller scale by the successive installations of the Order of the Bath. In 1803 Joseph Farington acquired his ticket for the main aisle of the great church so that he might see the procession of the knights from the House of Lords over a platform across Old Palace Yard and through the Abbey into Henry VII's chapel.[85] Funerals not only of royalty but of other distinguished persons sustained for most of the eighteenth century a popular interest in Westminster Abbey in line with what Mr E. P. Thompson has discerned as 'the "underground" of the ballad singer and the fair-ground'. They did so partly by providing a spectacle which attracted a crowd. Burials at night-time, attended by torchlight processions and river caravanserai, conduced to an excitement which could end in disorder within the sacred edifice as at the funerals of the earl of Bath in 1765 and of the duchess of Northumberland in 1776.[86] Before Samuel Horsley became dean, growing fear of the mob brought discouragement of these rumbustious proceedings. Except for royalty, the last of the funerals by torchlight, that of Lady Charlotte Percy, was in 1781, the year after the Gordon riots.[87] But interments of the great popularized the Abbey in a further way, by providing the occasions for bringing thither the waxen images of the deceased, which were in some cases allowed to remain in the building for many years to come, as an attraction for visitors of a certain brand of curiosity.

---

[84] Jocelyn Perkins, *Westminster Abbey: Its Worship and Ornaments* (Alcuin Club Collection, 38; 1952), i. 152, quoting contemporary evidence for 1803; iii. 143, 154.

[85] James Greig (ed.), *The Farington Diary* (1923–8), ii. 100.

[86] E. P. Thompson, *The Making of the English Working Class* (1963), 59; Edward Carpenter (ed.), *A House of Kings* (1966), 243–5.

[87] A. P. Stanley, *Historical Memorials of Westminster Abbey* (1868), 341.

William and Mary and Queen Anne were still in good condition in 1754, but a major 'draw' must undoubtedly have been the Duchess of Richmond of Charles II's reign bedecked in coronation robes and standing 'at the corner of the great East window' under clear crown glass with her favourite parrot in the set. As a burial custom, developing originally from the exhibition of the corpse, the practice of depositing an image in wax was already declining before the century ended. Necessitous canons, who had supplemented their incomes by displaying these exhibits, strove to counter the change by encouraging the making of images purely for display. This was done at Westminster for Nelson after his body had been taken to St Paul's. But the spread of Victorian values in the half-century before Victoria told against such stratagems which Dean Stanley compared with 'the counter-display of relics by the rival monasteries of the Middle Ages'.[88] It would have been more facetious but might not have been less exact to say that the Abbey had been overtaken by Madame Tussaud's.

The transition to more serious usages had already begun when Horsley was dean. At that time the affairs of the Abbey were conducted by two different sets of clergy. The upper echelon was occupied by the prebendaries, twelve in number, required by the unconfirmed statutes each to reside for four months in the year. They shared with the dean the obligation to form a chapter which would conclude agreements with the tenants of the Abbey lands, regulate the stipends of the staff, and generally administer discipline among them. Theirs, however, being Crown appointments falling within the scope of the eighteenth-century patronage system, they included in their ranks a number of scholarly pluralists unable to comply with the residence requirements. Among the prebendaries of 1795 were the bishop of Chester, William Cleaver, Dr Nathan Wetherell, master of University College, Oxford since 1764, and Dr William Bell, who was also treasurer of St Paul's cathedral for half a century from 1766.[89] In consequence they took to residing singly for one month each, and it became difficult to muster more than four prebendaries except at the height of the London season to transact capitular business or do duty in the Abbey. Horsley wrote to the Home Secretary in June 1799 as was requisite in the case of a royal foundation: 'As the season of the year is now fast approaching when the prebendaries will be leaving town to reside upon their livings, and our bargains with many of our tenants are yet to be concluded, it will greatly expedite the redemption of our land tax if the Dean with four prebendaries without proxies be allowed to make a chapter.' The answer, framed by the Advocate-General, implied that the dean already had the power which he requested.[90]

---

[88] Ibid. 341–4.
[89] *Court and City Register for the Year 1795* (1795), 203–4.
[90] Westminster Abbey CAB xiii, fos. 179–81, 8 Aug. 1799.

Below the prebendaries stood the 'Inferior Officers and Ministers'. Six minor canons, including the 'chanter' or precentor, headed the musical foundation provided by Elizabeth I's charter. Though in holy orders, they were mainly recruited from the lay vicars, and had specialist interests in music. Their principal task was to chant the daily offices with the choir, for which purpose they took turns in months of waiting. They were also paid a small additional allowance for reading early prayers in the Abbey. At the junior end of the scale they shaded into the twelve lay vicars or singing men, reduced to eleven in 1797–9, while ten boy choristers made up the rest of the Elizabethan musical establishment, outside which there was an organist.[91]

Occupants of no fewer than nineteen other posts, mainly lay, were listed among the principal officers of the collegiate establishment at Westminster in 1823. They included the headmaster and second master of Westminster School, the High Steward and High Bailiff of Westminster, City officers appointed by the Dean and Chapter, the Receiver-General and Coroner, the Registrar of the Consistory Court, the Surveyor of the Abbey Church, the Clerk of the Works, the Beadle of the Great Cloisters, down to the humble vergers, of whom there were eight in 1769, enjoying the perquisite of used candles from evening prayers.[92]

Samuel Horsley proved to be a strong dean, attentive to the business of the Abbey. Unlike his predecessor—Thomas, a semi-invalid unable to attend the meetings of the chapter—he set a pattern of rigid insistence on obedience to the statutes, which gave the dean alone control over appointments.[93] He was nearly always present at chapter meetings which were held eight, ten, fourteen, and once nineteen times a year during his period of office, even though the king's letter obtained just before his coming would have allowed him to absent himself whenever he wished.[94]

Though the Abbey church was thoroughly restored during the eighteenth century to save it from the collapse which threatened it at the end of the seventeenth, most of the work had been done by the time of Horsley's decanate.[95] But the south cloister, the deanery, and, most important of all, Henry VII's chapel demanded and received urgent attention. A chapter act of 23 May 1794 read:

Ordered that a contract be executed with Mr John Armstrong for putting on a new roof to King Henry the Seventh's Chapel to be made of oak and fir timber and

[91] Carpenter, *A House of Kings*, 416–31. Westm. Abbey Mun. 33,824–32, Treasurer's Accounts 1793–1801; CAB, fo. 60, 12 Mar. 1794.

[92] E. W. Brayley, *The History and Antiquities of the Abbey Church of St. Peter Westminster* (1818), i, Preface; cf. Perkins, *Westminster Abbey*, iii. 143.

[93] Carpenter, *A House of Kings*, 215, 459–60.

[94] CAB xiii.

[95] Carpenter, *A House of Kings*, chap. xiii, *passim*.

covered with lead in the manner recommended by Mr Wyatt for the sum of seven hundred and eighty pounds.

Ordered that a contract be executed with Mr John Armstrong for a new roof on the South Cloyster for the sum of eighty nine pounds ten shillings and the old lead now thereon to be finished in six months.

Bills for these two items were discharged six months later,[96] but it was not until 1808–22, when Horsley had ceased to be dean, that the main work of restoring the chapel was effected with the aid of a large parliamentary grant.[97]

He was remembered not as a builder but for his encouragement of the Abbey's regular music and for the improvement of its liturgical performance. A close connection had formerly existed between Westminster's musical establishment and that of the Chapel Royal in Whitehall, the two foundations enjoying the same organists while gentlemen of the Chapel Royal often served as lay vicars of Westminster Abbey and sometimes as vicars choral at St Paul's cathedral as well. This brought to the Abbey the benefit of being able to draw on the traditions of the Chapel Royal which for centuries was 'the main driving force of English music'. But it also meant that the singing men were in such demand that they were tempted to skimp their duties at the Abbey, while lay vicars secure in their freehold tenures appointed substitutes to represent them on a permanent basis. Horsley's arrival as dean coincided approximately with a reforging of the link with the Chapel Royal, for after an interval of sixty-six years the organist's stool in the two churches was again occupied in 1793 by the same tenant, Samuel Arnold, a prolific composer and an editor both of the works of Handel and of cathedral music.[98] The new dean made it his business to encourage his work. An act of chapter passed only a week after Horsley's installation ordered 'that the Treasurer do purchase six setts of Dr Samuel Arnold's Cathedral Music in three volumes for the use of the Choir'.[99] In the following year the dean and chapter subscribed for eight copies of the Rev. William Jones's 'Church Services'.[100] It was, however, by tightening discipline among the lesser clergy and lay singers that his distinctive impact was assured. The strictness of the new regime was obscured by the augmentation of the comforts of men of this class which was gratefully acknowledged in a letter sent to him by 'the Precentor, Minor Canons and Lay Clerks of the Collegiate Church' on 7 July 1802, when he was translated to St Asaph.[101] But the chapter records show that the benefits were usually conferred in response to an application and that they

---

[96] CAB xiii, fos. 68, 74, 23 May and 28 Nov. 1794.
[97] Brayley, *St. Peter Westminster*, i. 22–5.
[98] Carpenter, *A House of Kings*, 421–5, 428.
[99] CAB xiii, fo. 55, 13 Dec. 1793.
[100] Ibid., fo. 91, 4 May 1795.
[101] Westm. Abbey Mun. 66,461, letter signed Weldon Champneys, Precentor, 7 July 1802.

were made conditional upon a better performance of duty. Thus the act of chapter for 12 March 1794 ran:

A Memorial of the Chanter and Minor Canons praying for an augmentation of their stipends being this day taken into consideration, it is agreed and ordered.

That the yearly sum of one hundred and twenty pounds in addition to salary be paid to each minor canon by the treasurer at four equal quarterly payments.

That this payment do commence from Lady Day 1794. That of the three minor canons who are in waiting every month two shall attend divine service in the choir every Lords Day throughout the year, Christmas Day, the thirtieth of January, Good Friday, the Monday and Tuesday in Easter week, Ascension day, the Monday and Tuesday in Whitsun week, the King's accession and days of general fast and thanksgiving appointed by public authority and on all other days at morning prayer, and two being present the third shall not incur any penalty by absence. But if it shall happen that one only shall attend at any of the aforesaid times, the two absentees shall forfeit five shillings each or if the neglect happen on a Sunday ten shillings each, and if it shall happen four times within any one month that divine service in the Choir at morning prayer shall have been without the attendance of more than one minor canon in that case these two of the three minor canons in waiting for that month who shall have been three times absent shall forfeit two pounds each. These forfeits to be stopped every quarter out of this augmentation.

That one Minor Canon may attend for another but a Minor Canon shall upon no occasion employ a substitute who is not a member of the Choir without the approbation of the Dean.

That the prayer for the Church Militant shall always be used and read by one of the Minor Canons in waiting except on Sacrament days.

That one of the Minor Canons in waiting shall always assist at the Sacrament. And if it happens that one of the Minor Canons in waiting preach, the other shall read the prayer for the Church Militant.

That a copy of these orders be sent to every one of the Minor Canons by the Chapter Clerk.[102]

In the two penultimate provisions one may discern a growing emphasis on the distinctively clerical character of the canons minor, which was also seen in the regular assumption of the title of precentor by the cantor after 1794.[103] Nevertheless, the organist and the choirmen were not left out of the improvement. On 24 February 1796 the organist and lay clerks made application for an augmentation of their stipends. In response, the chapter ordered an addition of £12 a year to both, but imposed conditions. Failure to attend choir duty fifty times in the month of waiting brought a month's forfeiture of the augmentation. If three lay clerks were absent the absentees were to be fined

---

[102] CAB xiii, fo. 60, 12, Mar. 1794. The value of the augmentation is given in the Treasurer's Accounts as £60 for the half-year ending Michaelmas 1794, £120 for the year ending Mich. 1795, £120 at Mich. 1796, £115 at Mich. 1797, £116 at Mich. 1798, £116 at Mich. 1799, £119 at Mich. 1800, and £119. 10s. at Mich. 1801. Westm. Abbey Mun. 33,825–32.

[103] Carpenter, *A House of Kings*, 417.

five shillings each, and substitutes were to be drawn only from the lay clerks not then in waiting.[104]

It is unlikely that the system of provisional rewards did not induce a substantial betterment of performance. Complaints of slackness in the conduct of Abbey services continued to be heard well into the nineteenth century, notably from John Jebb writing in 1843,[105] but it is probable that these were exaggerated under the growing influence of heightened ecclesiological standards at that time. Dean Horsley's methods of reform reflect the principle on which he acted as a bishop of the Church at large, which was to strengthen ministry at the humbler levels without much abating parasitic encroachment at the top. Thus non-resident prebendaries like the bishop of Chester were left to atone for their absence by paying small pecuniary mulcts which were divided among the resident prebendaries or given to the poor.[106]

Less apparent to historians was the contribution which he made to the finance of the collegiate church. The revenues of the establishment, amounting in 1794 to £5,456. 15s. 6d., were principally derived from lands and appropriated rectories situated in eighteen counties of south-eastern England and the southern Midlands, and let out on farm to lay landlords who sometimes sublet their holdings. Of the aggregate, £1,107. 6s. 10d. was yielded by Westminster itself, where it mainly took the form of rents of tenements, and £358. 15s. 0d. by other parts of London, but the largest single item, constituting nearly one-third of the whole, comprised the essentially rural fines levied on the grant of copyhold lands.[107] In the early years after the dissolution, as indeed before it, Abbey leases had been for long periods—fifty or even eighty and ninety years—but from a comparatively early date the practice of renewing these leases after short spells of four to six years had arisen.[108] David Marcombe has characterized as 'the classic form of chapter leasehold' at the end of the seventeenth century that which existed in Durham: 'a nominal reserved rent to the church every year, and an adjustable fine of one year's value every seven years'.[109] Horsley began his deanship at Westminster by bringing a businesslike approach to fining. On 18 December 1793 the dean and chapter ordered:

that from henceforth every lessee of the College applying for a renewal of his lease do deliver to the Chapter Clerk three months before such renewal a true and exact terrier of the premises by the lease demised and the names of the several under tenants and the rents actually paid by them. And in case any lessee neglect to exhibit such terrier or the Dean and Chapter shall suspect any fraud or concealment in the terrier delivered,

---

[104] CAB xiii, fo. 106, 24 Feb. 1796.
[105] Quoted from Perkins, *Westminster Abbey*, iii. 149–50.
[106] CAB xiii, fos. 8, 83.
[107] Westm. Abbey Mun. 33,553, Receiver General's Accounts 1794.
[108] In O'Day and Heal (eds.), *Princes and Paupers*, 53–4, 60.
[109] Ibid. 259.

the premises, previous to any agreement for renewal, shall be surveyed by such person as the Dean and Chapter shall appoint, and the expense of the survey shall be added to the fine and paid by the lessee.[110]

Correct information was followed by pressure to tighten the Abbey's terms. As we have seen, bargaining with tenants, which was by then related to land-tax redemption, had by 1799 become a reason for the dean's wishing to rid himself of impediments to the transaction of chapter business. Two years later in January 1802, when Lord Willoughby de Broke tried to shift the burden of increasing the stipend of the curate of one of the rectories which formed part of the estate which he leased from the collegiate church on to that institution, Horsley resisted strenuously. His letter to the college treasurer shows both that fines were being increased and would be increased further. Admitting that if the lessee consented to raise the curate's salary, an abatement should be made from his renewal fine, he explained:

But by an abatement to that amount upon the fine I mean not that so much less is to be taken now than was taken at the last renewal but that so much is to be deducted from the fine we should otherwise insist upon now according to our estimate of the present improv'd rent of the estate. Indeed if our rate of fining was rais'd to what it ought to be, I think it would be but equitable that upon every renewal the stipend, paid by the lessee to the curate should be considered as reserved rent. For it is an annual payment on behalf of the Chapter, which I know not how to distinguish from a payment to them. This however will not increase the abatement at the present time, but is a matter to be consider'd at future renewals.[111]

The undergoing calculations of the annual income of Westminster Abbey, based upon the Receiver General's Accounts show that the benefits of Horsley's careful shepherding of resources did not begin to accrue to the Abbey until the closing years of his deanship but continued afterwards. The short-lived rise of input in 1797 represents only a 'compensation' £2,000 paid by a gentleman for his appointment to the office of High Bailiff of Westminster and carried to the fabric fund.[112] 'Rents', as Professor F. M. L. Thompson has put it, 'moved stickily and jerkily', constrained both by reluctance to put up rents on sitting tenants 'unless there was a glaring alteration in prices and farm profits' and by the exigencies of leases.[113] The most dramatic and sustained rise in wheat prices of the wartime period dates from 1800. It is reflected in the Abbey's receipts:[114]

---

[110] CAB xiii, fo. 58, 18 Dec. 1793.

[111] Westm. Abbey Mun. 65,568, Horsley to Smith, 23 Jan. 1802.

[112] Ibid. 33,556, Receiver General's Accounts 1797.

[113] F. M. L. Thompson, *English Landed Society in the Nineteenth Century* (1963), 217.

[114] Calculated by subtracting from the total charge for the year the sum of the cash in hand and the arrears at the foot of the previous year's account, as these two items were carried forward. Westm. Abbey Mun. 33,550–63, Receiver General's Accounts 1792–1804.

1793	£5,139. 13s.	2d.	1799	£4,110. 6s. 10¼d.
1794	£5,456. 13s.	9d.	1800	£5,705. 9s. 5¾d.
1795	£5,099. 2s.	6¾d.	1801	£5,504. 9s. 4½d.
1796	£4,172. 11s.	7d.	1802	£6,296. 6s. 6d.
1797	£7,317. 15s.	10d.	1803	£8,213. 17s. 1½d.
1798	£4,238. 8s.	0¼d.	1804	£9,380. 10s. 10d.

BACK INTO WALES: DIOCESE OF ST ASAPH

It is not obvious why Samuel Horsley left Rochester with its stately Westminster commendam for a Welsh diocese even more remote than that which he had quitted nine years earlier. Because of his talents and his intense patriotism he might have expected something higher. His name had been mentioned in connection with the vacancy in the Irish primacy which occurred on the death of Archbishop Newcome in 1800, but George III had procured it for the Hon. William Stuart.[115] His sympathies with the English Catholics cannot have commended him for such a post when ministers were about to thrust Catholic emancipation upon the unwilling monarch. A more serious disability rested in his middle-class origins, for episcopal appointments in the early nineteenth century were rising to the acme of preference for noble families. Horsley was respected at court but in a somewhat patronizing way. The king spoke highly of his 'learning and piety', and allowed him to dedicate his translation of Hosea to the royal person, but Queen Charlotte thought it necessary when referring to his ungainly wife to notice 'her ladylike bearing'.[116]

The bishop's reasons for accepting St Asaph were chiefly personal. The pecuniary difficulties which had caused him to write to Pitt in 1791 had not grown less during his sojourn in Westminster, where the temptation to indulge his taste for good living must have been maximized. When he returned to Wales, it was reported from London in confidence to one of his new neighbours that 'he is sd to be in very necessitous circumstances ... so that, as St Asaph is sd now to be a very valuable Bp^k in that respect it will suit him very well'.[117] Its value cannot be confidently stated. H. H. Jebb's figure of about £7,000 per annum is almost certainly far too high, for £7,500 was the gross yearly income returned by the Ecclesiastical Revenues Commissioners in 1835.[118] But allowing likewise for the effect of the intervening growth of industry and economy on rents and tithes, the yield at the close of the eighteenth century must have been in considerable excess of the £1,400 a year

[115] Bodl. Top. Oxon. d.355, fos. 17–18, Randolph to Lambard, 22 Sept. 1800.
[116] HP 1767, fos. 23–4, Portland to Horsley, 15 and 18 May 1801. DNB xxvii. 383–6.
[117] NLW 12,422.D/48, Wynne to Lloyd, 9 Dec. 1802.
[118] Jebb, 171; cf. PP 1835 [67] xxii, table 1.

cited in the correspondence of George III for 1762.[119] The bishop's income
was derived, as had been that of his predecessors for at least sixty years, not
only from the property and entitlements of the see itself but from those of
attached offices and sinecure rectories. Thus Horsley on his appointment was
authorized by royal warrant to hold with the bishopric the archdeaconry of St
Asaph cathedral, the rectory of Llandrinio in Montgomeryshire, and any other
two sinecure livings in his gift, one of which would be Llandrillo-yn-Rhos.[120]
It is uncertain whether the commendams were included in the amount quoted
for 1762 as they were in that for 1835, but if the difference between the two
figures is distributed evenly over the intervening seventy-three years, an
approximate £4,700 is reached by 1802. This may be compared with a
possibly incomplete account of rents, tithes, etc. for 1790–3 in the St Asaph
diocesan records, totalling £3,647. 14s. 6½d.,[121] to render feasible the suggestion that Bishop Horsley received in his new diocese something in the
region of £4,000 to £4,500 per annum.

In the view of his sister Elizabeth the 'vastly superior' patronage of the see
enhanced its attractiveness 'to himself and those he has to provide for'.[122] An
unusually high proportion of livings in the diocese of St Asaph, including a
number of sinecure rectories, reposed in the gift of the bishop.[123] Previous
holders of the office had been in the habit of appointing members of their own
families to the choicest of these,[124] and Horsley made no break with the
tradition or with the use of church preferment to serve friends. He was
subject, moreover, to strong family pressures which ultimately exhausted his
patience. Half-brother John was especially importunate, and when his son's
army career ended in disgrace, a sister had to warn that, if the bishop were
asked to help a ruined relative into a career in the Church, 'it would reduce
him to a very painful and difficult alternative'.[125] But the most pressing need
which the translation to St Asaph met was to establish a patrimony for his son
Heneage. Married in June 1801 to Frances Emma Bourke, a half-cousin of
Edmund Burke, and already launched in the clerical profession as rector
of Woolwich, Heneage Horsley was rapidly promoted in his father's new
diocese. He obtained the vicarage of Chirk (£500 to £600 per annum) with
one of the two prebends of Llanfair in St Asaph cathedral in October 1803,
the vicarage of Gresford (£840 per annum) in the following October, and the
rectory of Castle Caereinion in Montgomeryshire (£600 per annum) in June
1804, yielding in the aggregate an income which must have been well in

[119] Fortescue (ed.), *George the Third*, i. 3–44.
[120] LPL VB1/13, fo. 126; NLW SA/Misc. 1747 and 1260.
[121] NLW Welsh Church Commission, 3/79 and 82.
[122] HP 1768, fos. 224–33, E. to F. Horsley, 5 Dec. 1802.
[123] NLW SA/MB/20, list for 1807 suggests above two-thirds.
[124] D. R. Thomas, *SPCK Diocesam History of St. Asaph* (1888), 101–2.
[125] HP 1768. fos. 112–15, A. to F. Horsley, 13 Mar. 1806, cf. fos. 97–100, 9 Mar. 1803.

excess of £2,000 a year.[126] Meanwhile the substantial benefice of St Martin's in the rural deanery of Llangollen was conferred by the bishop on John William Bourke, presumably a kinsman of his daughter-in-law, to whom and to whose children he was passionately devoted. It is fair to say, however, that the living was not given to Bourke until it had been strongly pressed upon a poor scholar from Oxfordshire, who not only twice refused it, but burned his letters of orders to prevent himself from yielding to the temptation to comply.[127] Horsley's nepotism was not on the scale of that of his notorious contemporaries, Bishops Brownlow North and Pretyman, but he did practise it, as did also some reforming bishops, like Charles Sumner and Samuel Wilberforce, down to the middle to the Victorian era.

The aggrandizement of Heneage was part, moreover, of a larger plan affecting Samuel Horsley's own future which was fundamental to the move to St Asaph. He had resolved gradually to retire, and laden with an ailing wife, needed both a retirement home and someone to minister to his comforts. He explained to his son in 1804:

When I was translated to St. Asaph, in the hope, which I thank God has not been disappointed, that I should settle you comfortably in that country, I laid my plans for making it the nest of my own old age. I remov'd my Library to St. Asaph, considering the palace from the moment I became the owner of it, as my own. I tho't that while my ability of public business remain'd I might pass a few months of the year, and a few months only, in London, and that the far greater part of the year, and in a short time the whole of it, would be spent at home in your society, and in the playful circle of my grandchildren.[128]

Though this was scarcely an ideal approach of a new bishop to his duties, Horsley is not personally to be blamed for the want of facilities for retirement in the eighteenth-century Church. Indeed, for a limited period, the rearrangement of his year might have benefited his diocese. Unfortunately things did not turn out as planned. On the first of their annual sojourns in Wales in 1803, the dropsical Mrs Horsley became so ill that, in sister Anne's view, no one ever thought she would have arrived back in London alive.[129] After that experience she developed a resistance to the bishop's schemes for settling in St Asaph. His own illness blunted his hopes of returning thither in the summer of 1804,[130] but after his wife's death on 2 April 1805 he could scarcely wait for the business of the session to release him. His servants were

---

[126] For particulars of Heneage Horsley, his marriage and preferments, see Jebb, 167–8; HP 1768, fos. 90–3. D. R. Thomas, *The History of the Diocese of St. Asaph* (Oswestry, 1908), i. 166. Values (for 1807) from NLW SA/MB/20.

[127] NLW SA/MB/20; NLW 12,419.D, fo. 32, Horsley to Lloyd, 9 Feb. 1803; 12,422.D, no. 29, Tisdall to Lloyd, 9 Feb. 1803.

[128] HP 1767, fos. 145–6, Horsley to H. Horsley, 16 June 1804.

[129] Ibid. 1768, fos. 117–21, A. to F. Horsley, 7 Mar. 1804.

[130] Ibid. 1767, fos. 145–6. Horsley to H. Horsley, 16 June 1804.

dispatched to Wales by stage-coach on the Tuesday before 12 July.[131] It must be admitted that his eagerness to be there stemmed more from anxiety to enjoy the society of Heneage's wife and the children at the episcopal palace than from concern for the affairs of the diocese, but although St Asaph claimed less of his attention than either of his previous bishoprics he remained capable, notwithstanding his failing health and personal grief, of outstanding bursts of energy and decisiveness. His official visitation in March 1806 was a rushed exercise, but he performed it despite fears for his health. He wrote to his daughter-in-law Fanny:

I shall be glad when my business is over. I reached Machynlleth the first night , rather late, but found there a very excellent Welsh inn, where I had a good bed, and they crammed me with all the produce of the country, almost gratis. The confirmation at Machynlleth on Tuesday was nothing at all, the number being very small. The journey across Montgomeryshire from Machynlleth to Newtown lies through the most beautiful part of North Wales that I have seen, except it be the Vale of Llangollen . . . At Newtown again I had good accommodation. Mrs. Lewis, the clergyman's lady, set out a very elegant breakfast, and shew'd me two very agreeable children, a boy and a girl. She had a third but she would not shew it. She said it was too young to exhibit. Therefore I confirm'd about 700. Yesterday at Pool I confirm'd 1400, and this day they give me reason to expect more than 2000 here [Oswestry]. Tomorrow I go to Llanfyllin which is the last place of confirmation. I shall stay at Llanfyllin till Sunday, when if it please God, I shall return to this place, in order to visit here on Monday. Mr. Palmer is in good health, bears his fatigue wonderfully, and if he knew I were writing would desire to be most affectionately remembered. I hope I shall find my favourite Ann Maria Holford at St. Asaph upon my return. I hope to dine at home on Thursday. But you must have dinner earlier than 5.[132]

A bishop's influence was exerted, however, not by visitation alone but by correspondence and sometimes by interviews at the palace. While at St Asaph, Horsley used both methods to continue his work of reform. The problems which he faced, and which he discussed in his primary visitation charge, were of two kinds. The first, the ubiquitous need to ensure clerical residence, was less pressing in the diocese of St Asaph than elsewhere. He affirmed in the charge that the see afforded but few instances of culpable non-residence.[133] Culpable non-residence, however, might mean little more than non-residence 'without exemption, notification or licence', avoidance of which might yet cover a multitude of neglects. The clergy returns at the 1806 visitation furnish a more exact indication of the position. Of ninety-eight benefices for which meaningful information exists—well over one-half—fifty-four (that is 55 per cent) had incumbents who resided upon them or lived in the neighbourhood

---

[131] Ibid., fos. 49, 54, Horsley to F. E. Horsley, 10 Apr. and 12 July 1805.
[132] Ibid., fo. 42, Horsley to F. E. Horsley, 8 Mar. 1806.
[133] Jebb, 174–5.

or did duty.[134] The percentage was marginally lower than in 1799 (60 per cent).[135] This was not necessarily inconsistent with the beginnings of reform, for abuses had to be discovered before they could be set right. There are signs, however, in the cruder but more comprehensive parliamentary returns that in an already relatively well-organized diocese improvements were being effected. Total non-residents were down by fourteen in the year ending 25 March 1806 as compared with 25 March 1805, the most marked reduction being in cases exonerated by infirmity of body.[136] Bishop Horsley, who was particularly suspicious of excuses offered on this account, nevertheless had to proceed slowly and tactfully in putting the law into effect, for evasion was practised by some of the most powerful clergymen in the diocese. H. W. Eyton of Leeswood Hall, a country gentleman in orders, who had been rural dean of Bromfield and Yale and an active adviser of Horsley's predecessor, Bishop Bagot, deserted his vicarage of Mold for the waters of Bath, pleading the exigencies of his wife's and daughter's health. In August 1803 Bishop Horsley wrote to him to remind him of the penalties which he would incur under Sir William Scott's Non-Residence Act, and asked him to provide a medical certificate as a condition of granting him a licence to protect him from civil action. Eyton's reply was unsatisfactory as to the necessity of the treatment, and when the bishop refused to accept his offer of the testimony of an 'obscure apothecary', he riposted angrily, and broke off the negotiations with his Ordinary. At the beginning of the following year (1805) he renewed his application for a licence to reside in Bath in a civil tone, supplying firmer proof of his daughter's condition, and offering to supplement his apothecary's affidavit with the opinion of an eminent physician which the bishop had demanded. Horsley seized the olive branch. The licence was granted, and Eyton received from His Lordship a polite letter of condolence on the continuance of his daughter's ill health. Six months later he returned to Mold, and received licence to live in his own house on no other evidence than his own assurance that the parsonage was 'much too small' for his family and with no further stipulation than that his curate must be licensed, and receive the bishop's regular assignment to continue to live in the vicarage house 'pursuant to the 36 of the King'. Horsley commented slyly on the reason for his return which was not stated, namely that the health of the Eyton family was so far established as to permit it.[137]

Fashionable non-residence needed to be lightly handled because Samuel Horsley at the time of his appointment was not without enemies in high quarters. J. Wynne tried to poison the mind of the influential John Lloyd of Wickwar against him by representing him as eccentric and violent against

[134] NLW SA/QA 14.
[135] 48 out of 80 benefices. NLW SA/QA 11–12.
[136] Reduced from nine to four. PP 1809 (234) ix.
[137] NLW Leeswood Hall MSS, esp. 1448–52, 1469, 1483, 1499, 1522, 1707, 1806.

Dissenters, and likely to quarrel with his dean, a son of the Latitudinarian Bishop Shipley.[138]

Other irregularities presented a more serious problem, and sometimes called for sterner treatment. In his primary visitation charge the bishop showed a particular concern for flaws in the publication of banns of marriage and failure to ensure that marriage was solemnized in one of the churches where the banns were called; also about the large number of clergymen officiating as curates without licence.[139] This was an abuse which his predecessors had failed to curb. More than a half of the fifty-two curates returned at the 1806 visitation (56.5 per cent) were unlicensed.[140] Horsley's skilfully worded questionnaire, disentangling the issue of licensing from other questions asked about curates, helped to bring the facts to light and to make it possible to apply a remedy. Bagot had asked in 1799:

Have you a licensed curate residing in your parish? Or what distance from it? What is his name? What salary do you allow him? Doth he serve any other, and what, cure? If you employ a curate who is not yet licensed, hath the Bishop been informed of it by you, with particulars of his character and education? And how long have you employed him?

He received much less unambiguous information than did the mathematical Horsley with his two separate and direct questions: 'II. Have you a Curate? III. Is he licensed?'[141]

Licensing was important because it gave the bishop control of selection. He used it to free the Church from the influence of Methodism, which in northern and central Wales presented the principal challenge to its authority, there being little Dissent of the older kind in the region. Methodists were not, as Horsley recognized, 'Dissenters in doctrine from the Established Church', nor even a single denomination. Churchmen, Dissenters, and Anabaptists were found in their ranks.[142] But in parts of Montgomeryshire especially, the main body, known as Calvinistic Methodists, were using their Sunday Schools to take catechizing out of the hands of the clergy with the aid of a printed catechism of their own, enlarged upon the Prayer Book version. Zealots among them were withdrawing from Communion in the parish churches, and associating with the Independents.[143]

A manuscript in the National Library of Wales[144] shows how Horsley reasserted his licensing powers to check the erosion of church discipline.

---

[138] NLW 12,422.D/48, Wynne to Lloyd, 9 Dec. 1802.
[139] Jebb, 174–5.
[140] NLW SA/QA 14.
[141] Ibid. 11–12, 14.
[142] Jebb, 175–6.
[143] NLW SA/QA 14, esp. Llanllugan (no. 60), Llanwyddelan (no. 75), and Castle Caereinion; Jebb, 175–8.
[144] NLW 10,854, Frondirion MS 41.

Simon Lloyd, curate of Llanuwchllyn, an extensive parish adjacent to Bala Lake, had been serving unlicensed since the death of his predecessor in May 1800. No parsonage was attached to the church, and the curate, a man of local family, appears to have lived in his own mansion in or near the town of Bala. The stipend was £20 per annum. He had taken up his appointment at the invitation of the agent of the impropriator, Sir Watkin Williams Wynne, acting with the churchwardens and some of the parishioners. Sir Watkin, however, subsequently held up the nomination, having heard that Lloyd, originally ordained on a title in the diocese of Bristol, had been in the habit of attending Welsh Methodist meetings. He was at length summoned by Lewis Hughes, Bishop Horsley's secretary, to attend for interview at the palace in St Asaph, where the question of licensing him would be decided in the presence of assessors. By the curate's account Horsley conducted the inquiry in a manner which was searching, sarcastic, and severe. Examining him on the churches he had previously served during his twenty years in the diocese, the bishop snapped him up sharply when he volunteered one which had not been mentioned, and picked at a minor alteration of the nomination form, which told rather for than against the candidate's honesty. It was over attendances at the Methodist services of Thomas Charles of Bala, however, that the greatest acrimony arose:

Q. By the Bishop. How long is it since you attended a Conventicle? As nearly as I can recollect, I answered, that I had not for about two years. I was then asked, since I had been in the habit of attending conventicles, what was the reason of my discontinuing my attendance at them? I replied that I might not give offence to my Brethren the Clergy and a wish to continue in the Church. Q. Does Mrs. Lloyd and your family attend the conventicle at Bala? Yes, my Lord. The Bishop said, I say nothing with respect to Mrs. Lloyd attending there but, Do you think it right to suffer your children to go there? A. Yes, my Lord I do. His Lordship repeated the question . . . I answered as before. The bishop then broke out into an indecent ebullition of temper exclaiming in a loud tone of voice, 'Now I perceive that you have been attending upon fanatical preachers and that you are a fanatic yourself'. To this I made no reply.

As the examination proceeded, Lloyd explained that his children went frequently to church when the weather permitted, but the bishop gave it as his opinion that it would be better for them to read the prayers of the Church at home than to attend on the ministrations of Thomas Charles of Bala, a Methodist pioneer of Sunday Schools. Having further elicited from Lloyd that about twelve years earlier he had received the Sacrament in the Bala chapel, he refused to accept his 'presumption' that Charles was a regularly ordained deacon and priest, and exclaimed, 'I will have that Mr. Charles into my court.' The accused was then questioned by another interrogator about his use of extempore preaching, but emerged confident that the only charge which carried weight was that he had omitted to catechize the children of the parish, none of them having responded to his notice, because Dissenters formed the majority of the parishioners. He was then asked to withdraw to another room while the assessors considered his answers. When he was recalled after about ten minutes, the bishop, whose frown had turned into 'a soft, sarcastic smile', questioned him about his opinions on episcopal ordination and whence it originated. Lloyd recounted:

I replied, The Apostles received their authority to preach the Gospel from God—from Christ you mean said the Bishop. I have no objection said I to say Christ for Christ was God. 'And how afterwards' said the Bishop. I proceeded. The power which the Apostles received from Christ, they delegated to faithful men and so on to the present time. 'Here' said the Bishop with a sneer 'You and I agree wonderfully well' but it immediately occurred to my mind that an argument might be borrowed against me from this my testimony for episcopal ordination and that I might be charged with inconsistency if upon my exclusion from the Church I joined the Methodists. I therefore added in substance as follows. 'Notwithstanding my predilection for episcopal ordination and the Church of England yet from what I had read I had learnt to think favourably in the judgement of charity of the Reformed Churches on the Continent'. B. The judgement of Charity is quite another thing. We have had Bishops who were doctrinal Calvinists and perhaps they were the best bishops that we have had, but for a presbyter to ordain a presbyter is monstrous.

Lloyd then endeavoured to defend himself. He thought the Church of England the best constituted national Church in the world and had deliberately chosen to serve in its ministry, though he had private means, and frequently travelled nearly ten miles from home to the extremity of his present parish on parochial duty. After listening attentively to this short defence, the bishop remarked, 'I certainly shall not license you to the perpetual curacy of Llanuwchllyn.' As he and his assessors were retiring from the room, Lloyd, with an execrable sense of timing, asked whether he was discharged from his cure. The bishop, turning back a little, answered in the affirmative, and ordered his secretary to arrange for a supply to be sent and for the living to be sequestered. The nomination made by the impropriator was mistakenly handed to Lloyd with his letters of orders, and he had to be requested to return it.

The above account sets Horsley in a bad light, but the source was scarcely impartial, and part of the document has been lost. The bishop's overbearing conduct can scarcely be doubted. The same note was struck in his correspondence towards the end of his life. Hearing that the widow of a former incumbent had appealed against his decision in the allocation of a tithe of lambs he wrote to her husband's successor: 'I really am not at leisure to argue the point with Mrs Roberts, but the opinion I gave in my letter to Mr Anwy C of the 30th December, is right, and I care very little whether Mrs Roberts is satisfied with it or no.'[145] His patience had not improved with age. In the

[145] NLS 589/1431, from Horsley, 21 Feb. 1804.

Llanuwchllyn case, however, he had at least given the curate the benefit of trial by jury before refusing him a licence. On his own showing Lloyd's irregularities had been slight, but so had been his efforts to uphold the teaching ministry of the Church in his parish. He omitted to say, however, that he and Thomas Charles had been bosom friends since their years together at Jesus College, Oxford, or that he had been ejected from a Denbighshire parish for consorting with the Methodists.[146] In the view he took of these contacts the bishop may be said to have acted in a narrow spirit. He is to be judged, however, not by the standards of modern ecumenism but by the sense of the importance of church order which he shared with other eighteenth-century High Churchmen and by the revolutionary challenge to his values presented by the imminent lurch of a swelling Welsh Methodism towards separation. Perhaps he reacted to the crisis in the wrong way, making the breach more not less certain. But it is easy to be wise after the event.

In the overall trend Samuel Horsley's activities in his dioceses and at Westminster Abbey confirm the judgement of his national career, that he was a genuine proponent of Church reform. Indeed his exertions began at the local level for pragmatic reasons. He was obliged to cut his teeth on one of the most ineffectively organized bishoprics in the Anglican Church. His early experiences at St Davids left him with an awareness of the importance of the role of curates in securing an adequacy of clerical residence, and whether in the parishes or in the Abbey, he was particularly attentive to the financial needs of the working clergy, being unable, and to a certain extent unwilling, to exert too much pressure on those whose duties they performed. His reforms ranged over a wide area of Church life, including training for the ministry and cathedral services, but he was practical in his interests and did not neglect the fundamentals of ecclesiastical finance. In his closing years, when promoted to a bishopric which was in better order, he became more demanding but also less effective and sure-footed.

[146] *Dictionary of Welsh Biography* ed. J. E. Lloyd and R. T. Jenkins (1959), 588–9.

High Church Champion

SAMUEL HORSLEY was a High Churchman in the English Catholic tradition, which stretched from the Laudians and before to the Tractarians and beyond. He accepted the label in his *Remarks on Dr Priestley's Second Letter* published in spring 1786: 'As for the outcry about my intolerance, and my bigotry to what he calls high-church principles, it gives me rather pleasure than uneasiness ... I glory in my principles; I am proud of the abuse, which they may draw upon me.'[1] Four years later, in the more familiar context of the St Davids charge he gave it a meaning:

in the language of our modern sectaries, every one is a high churchman, who is not unwilling to recognize so much as the spiritual authority of the priesthood,—every one who, denying what we ourselves disclaim, anything of a divine right to temporalities, acknowledges, however, in the sacred character, somewhat more divine than may belong to the meer [*sic*] hired servants of the state or of the laity; and regards the service which we are thought to perform for our pay as something more than a part to be gravely played in the drama of human politics. My reverend brethren we must be content to be High Churchmen according to this usage of the word, or we cannot at all be churchmen.[2]

His High Churchmanship has puzzled the historians, who have seen him mainly as a champion of general Christian orthodoxy in the Trinitarian controversy as did Overton and Relton many years ago,[3] or have set him in the context of another pan-Anglican concern, the politico-theological defence of establishment against the attacks of radicalism and radical Whiggery, as Dr J. C. D. Clark has recently done.[4] Both perspectives are legitimate, but they are not sufficient to categorize the man. Thus, as Dr Clark observes, Horne, Hallifax, and Horsley were regarded by radicals as 'three reactionary intellectuals' preferred by Pitt in the Established Church,[5] but of these Horne and Horsley were positively Catholic in theology, while Hallifax's Warburton lectures for 1776 were strongly Protestant.[6] The difficulty in giving recognition to Horsley's principles stems from two assumptions rooted in the minds of

---

[1] Quoted from Horsley, *Tracts in Controversy with Dr. Priestley* (Gloucester, 1789), 341.
[2] Horsley, *St. David's Charge 1790* (1790).
[3] J. M. Overton and F. Relton, *The English Church 1714–1800* (1906), 254–7.
[4] Clark, *English Society*, chap. IV, esp. 230–4.
[5] Ibid. 230.
[6] Hallifax was classified by Kilvert with other practitioners of free speculation at Cambridge such as Balguy, Powell, and Ogden. F. Kilvert (ed.), *Memoirs of the Life and Writings of Richard Hurd* (1860), 203.

church historians, both of which require modification. The first of these, that authentic High Churchmanship ceased to count after the middle of the eighteenth century, being replaced by an undefined 'mere barren orthodoxy' which F. D. Maurice found characteristic of Oxford in 1829,[7] is quite inconsistent with Horsley's acknowledged importance in the thought and activity of the time, or with the reinforcing influence of others.

Equally irreconcilable is the related belief that the genuine High Church tradition embodied an inflexible anti-Erastianism which could not coexist with the subordination of the ecclesiastical to the temporal authority that developed under the Hanoverians. Thus, Dr Mark Goldie has affirmed that the 'doctrine of the Two Societies was the bedrock of High Church ideology'.[8] He is more successful in showing it to be a tenet of the Nonjurors and of High Churchmen of the Revolution era than in proving that it was an intrinsic and permanent High Church conviction. G. V. Bennett, who took a different view of the High Churchmanship of Atterbury, nevertheless saw the wreck of that prelate's vision of a protective alliance of the Church of England with the English monarchical State in the management of the Church by Walpole and the Pelhams after 1730.[9] He overlooked, however, the fact that an alliance of Church and State was taught much later by Churchmen of quite moderate views while those of a decided High Church cast continued to use the mystical language of union under God. What was perceived was a shift in the balance between the two powers, not an abrupt change of system.

In order to appreciate Horsley's position it is necessary to enquire first into what his High Churchmanship comprised, then to establish where he stood in relation to other church leaders who were sometimes bracketed with him, and how important these were in the composition of the later Georgian Church.

His outlook embraced four distinctively High Church features. Firstly, he believed strongly in the divine origin of the ministerial commission and that episcopacy was the means chosen by the apostles for transmitting spiritual authority to the clergy down the ages to his own time. As it has been shown, he bore witness to this conviction as early as 1784, in the debate with Priestley. He expressed publicly in the House of Lords his sympathy with the Scottish Episcopal ideal of a 'pure spiritual episcopacy' present in the Church in the earliest ages when struggling to free that Church from the penal laws in 1790–2. The same belief underlay the fierce denunciation in his St Davids charge of those who held the clergy to be 'meer [*sic*] hired servants of the state'; they were 'out of the Church—severed from it by a kind of self-excommunication'.[10] But it was in his parliamentary speech on the Non

---

[7] Quoted from R. W. Church, *The Oxford Movement: Twelve Years, 1833–45* (1891), 11 n.
[8] Mark Goldie, 'The Nonjurors, Episcopacy, and the Origins of the Convocation Controversy', in Cruickshanks (ed.), *Ideology and Conspiracy*, 15–35.
[9] *Tory Crisis*, chap. xvi.
[10] *St. David's Charge 1790*.

Residence Bill in 1803 that he stated it in its simplest and most explicit form. Speaking of the archbishop of Canterbury's authority over diocesan bishops, he declaimed:

We derive only from him the power of order; which is given by consecration, and can be given in no other way...And this power of order is always described by the canonists as a distinct thing from the diocesan authority: And it is distinct, and indeed in its nature is a higher thing: Christ first gave it to the apostles; the apostles conveyed it to others; and those only who have derived it from the apostles in perpetual succession have power still to convey it.[11]

It was questioned by contemporaries, and has been doubted by historians whether a belief in apostolical succession survived in the Church during the half-century or more before Newman revived it in the *Tracts for the Times*. Bishop Charles Blomfield is said to have remarked to Joshua Watson, a leader of the Hackney Phalanx, that he could count on the fingers of one hand the number of those who still held to it, to which Watson replied: 'My Lord, there are a good seven thousand.'[12] Norman Sykes allowed for its continuance in the post-Reformation Church of England only in diluted form. He argued in the Gunning Lectures 1953–4 and the Cadbury Lectures of the following year that while the Anglican divines of the mid seventeenth century sustained a continuing apologetic for episcopacy, they held it to be *divino jure* only in the sense that it was of apostolical not of dominical appointment; and that its absence did not invalidate the ministries of churches like the Continental Protestant communions which had been forced to abandon it by historical necessity. Even 'the traditional pre-Tractarian high-church position' regarded bishops as being 'of the *bene* or *melius esse* of the church rather than of the *esse*', he affirmed.[13] His case was answered by A. L. Peck, who went carefully through Sykes's sources and demonstrated that most of them were patient of a different interpretation. He showed that Sykes considerably underplayed the importance of 'necessity' as the 'only ground on which the seventeenth century Anglican writers admitted the "validity" of non-episcopal orders and sacraments', that is they believed that God had himself intervened to waive the 'divinely appointed requirement of episcopacy' in circumstances where its retention had become impossible. For the eighteenth and early nineteenth centuries he was able to shift less of Sykes's ground, but a re-examination of the latter's evidence even for that period revealed in Smalridge, Wake, and Heber a stronger insistence on the requirement of episcopal ordination than had been suggested, while the propriety of employing German Lutheran missionaries in India was shown to have been repeatedly challenged in the

---

[11] Horsley, *Speeches*, ii. 157.
[12] A. B. Webster, *Joshua Watson: The Story of a Layman, 1771–1855* (1954), 19.
[13] Published as N. Sykes, *Old Priest and New Presbyter* (Cambridge, 1956). See esp. 81, 166.

SPCK from 1713 onwards.[14] Martin Routh was untypical, it seems, in opposing the idea of using Danish bishops, who could claim no unbroken succession, to consecrate Seabury in 1784, but the lack of a more broadly based resistance was probably indicative of ignorance of Danish church history rather than of indifference to the necessity of succession.[15]

Horsley's insistence upon the need was theologically unqualified. He told Simon Lloyd of Bala that 'for a presbyter to ordain a presbyter is monstrous'. The belief was tailored, however, in a characteristically eighteenth-century way, to the needs of establishment. Thus the principal object of the section of his speech on the Non Residence Bill from which the remark about apostolical succession was taken, was to assert that a 'bishop derives the whole of his diocesan authority . . . from the King; not an atom from the archbishop'. This was a necessary part of his case against granting right of appeal to the metropolitan in residence cases. He, nevertheless, found it requisite to draw a theoretical distinction between this *potestas jurisdictionis*, which belonged to civil establishment, and *potestas ordinis*, which came by consecration. The former embraced 'our temporalities, and all our secular authorities and prerogatives'—Horsley equated it with 'the whole of [a bishop's] diocesan authority'. The latter was 'the spiritual capacity of exercising those sacred functions which none without that power can perform'. The last seven words of this definition stood between his teaching and a practical Erastianism,[16] for he had told the Scottish Episcopalians that even the authority of bishops to consecrate and ordain could not be allowed to operate in an Established Church without the king's consent.

Apostolical succession was not used by Horsley to fight the State for clerical privileges and immunities, as Atterbury had employed it a hundred years earlier in the battle for a sitting Convocation. It was valued, nevertheless, as an aid to devotion and a claim to respect for the clergy over what was accorded to Nonconformist ministers; more occasionally as a qualification of parliamentary encroachments on the remaining spiritual independence of the Church. When a bill to regulate the age of admission to holy orders came before Parliament in 1804, Horsley accepted a clause voiding at law the ordinations of those admitted at an earlier age, on the analogy of a nullity declared when a marriage had been improperly solemnized, but he was careful to explain to the House that 'ordination could not be done away with when regularly conferred'. The *sacerdotium catholicum* was 'that which no secular power could either give or take away'.[17]

The bishop admitted that in the view he took of the authority annexed to

[14] A. L. Peck, *Anglicanism and Episcopacy* (1958), esp. 27, 41, 44–9.
[15] J. E. Pinnington, 'Anglican–Danish Relations: From the American to the Icelandic Consecration Proposals, 1784–1866', *Journal of Ecclesiastical History*, 21 (1970), 341–55.
[16] Horsley, *Speeches*, ii. 156–9.
[17] *Parl. Deb.*, 1st ser., i (1803–4), 1058–9; ii (1804), 127–8.

apostolic ministry he was retreating from traditional High Church pretensions. In his St Davids charge (1790) he affirmed that a High Churchman 'in the true [and historic] sense of the word' was 'one who claims for the hierarchy, upon pretence of a right inherent in the sacred office, all those powers, honours and emoluments, which they enjoy under an establishment'. His own claim was to 'spiritual authority', to which the will of the prince must give civil effect, that is not only temporal possessions and the 'rank and dignity annexed to the superior order of the clergy', but even the jurisdiction exercised in the church courts. By disentangling apostolical succession at the theoretical level from the factors creating prelatical power Horsley made an important advance towards purifying it. While remaining himself a thoroughgoing exponent of the union of Church and State, he helped to fashion the instrument which the Tractarians used half a century later to create an alternative foundation for the Church of England, uniquely spiritual in character.

Samuel Horsley's High Churchmanship was signalized in the second place by a leaning to the Catholic view of the Eucharist. Like other churchmen of the eighteenth century he admitted to a preference for the Communion service in the first Prayer Book of King Edward VI entitled 'The Supper of the Lorde and the Holy Communion, commonly called the Masse', over the amended version of 1552, which divided the central Eucharistic prayer, and removed those features of the ancient order most strongly suggestive of the sacrifice of the Mass and the real presence of Christ in the Sacrament. This emerged from his remarks on the Communion Office of the Scottish Episcopalians published in 1764, which, while using language similar to that of the English 1549 Book, added features of its own, derived from primitive Eastern liturgies, later recovered, emphasizing even more strongly the sacrificial character of the Eucharist and the objectivity of the change in the elements at consecration. The words 'which we now offer to thee' were added to 'with these thy gifts' at the oblation. In the *epiklesis* or invocation of the Holy Spirit the 1549 prayer that the bread and wine 'maie be unto us the bodye and bloude of thy moste derely beloued sonne Jesus Christe' was converted into 'may *become* the body' etc.[18] Horsley gave his approval to the Scottish service in a letter to the bishop of Edinburgh in October 1799, and again to John Skinner in 1806. This does not necessarily mean that he subscribed to the extreme High Church doctrines of Johnson of Cranbrook that Christ was offered at every Eucharist in a 'proper' and propitiatory sacrifice under the forms of the bread and the wine. But he was in advance of most eighteenth-century Anglicans in accepting a change in the elements brought about by consecration and a subsequent presence of Christ, which sensibly he refused to define. Thus he wrote to Skinner:

---

[18] W. K. Lowther Clarke and Charles Harris, *Liturgy and Worship* (1954), 345; cf. *The First and Second Prayer Books of King Edward the Sixth* (Everyman edn.), 212–30, 377–93.

With respect to the comparative merit of the two Offices for England and Scotland, I have no scruple in declaring to you, what some years since I declared to Bishop Abernethy Drummond, that I think the Scotch Office more conformable to the primitive models, and in my private judgment more edifying that that which we now use; insomuch that were I at liberty to follow my own private judgment I would myself use the Scotch Office in preference. The alterations which were made in the Communion Service as it stood in the First Book of Edward VI to humour the Calvinists, were, in my opinion, much for the worse; nevertheless I think our present Office is very good, our form of consecration of the elements is sufficient; I mean that the elements *are consecrated* by it, and made the body and blood of Christ in the sense in which our Lord himself said the bread and wine were his Body and Blood.[19]

His language may be contrasted with that of the central Anglican Daniel Waterland which appeared to deny consecrating effect to any formula and to derive it from the universal operation of the law of Christ:

we are to consider what effect the words of our Lord, 'This is my body,' are conceived now to have in the Eucharistical consecration. It is not meant (as the Romanists are pleased to interpret) that the pronouncing these words makes the consecration: but the words then spoken by our blessed Lord are conceived to operate now as virtually carrying in them a rule, or a promise, for all succeeding ages of the Church that what was then done when our Lord himself administered, or consecrated, will be always done in the celebration of the Eucharist, pursuant to that original.[20]

Reverence for the older liturgies was consonant with a third characteristic of his High Church outlook: an emphasis upon the mysterious quality of the Christian religion. This was the antithesis of the cult of plainness spread at mid-century by Latitudinarian divines like Archbishop Herring and Bishop Hoadly, and reflected in dull, moralistic sermons preached from pulpits up and down the country. Hoadly had condemned Bishop Berkeley as a mystery-monger who produced 'a sort of sublime fog that looks bright and makes one giddy'.[21] As Bishop Woodford recognized, in a patronizing Victorian assessment of his preaching, Horsley's sermons were marked by 'extreme clearness'. He was right in this but in little else about him. By dwelling only on his solid learning and logical precision, his clearness of thought and simplicity of belief, he reduced him to a scholar-preacher, fitted, though not to be relegated 'to the undisturbed repose of quiet libraries', at most to be resuscitated for the purpose of allaying the fears of polite Victorian doubters.[22] The real Horsley was of warmer blood. He dwelt upon the wonder rather than the orderliness

---

[19] J. Dowden (ed.), *The Scottish Communion Office 1764* (Oxford, 1922), 84–5.

[20] Daniel Waterland, *A Review of the Doctrine of the Eucharist* (orig. pub. 1737; Oxford, 1896), 97–8.

[21] R. W. Greaves, *On the Religious Climate of Hanoverian England* (Inaugural Lecture, Bedford College, London; 1963).

[22] J. R. Woodford, 'Horsley the Scholarly Preacher', in J. E. Kempe (ed.), *The Classic Preachers of the English Church*, 2nd ser. (1877), 36–53.

of the divine dispensation. Death, the after-life, the virgin birth of Jesus, the fulfilment of prophecy, these were the themes of his discourses, which, as Woodford had been informed, drew crowds to parish churches such as St James, Piccadilly. Woodford ascribed to him a 'simple and childlike accept-ance of Holy Scripture', deeming him content, once he had traced a doctrine to the Bible, to probe no further. In fact, he was a master of complex allegory. In the four sermons on Psalm 45, undated but probably delivered between 1793 and 1801, he criticized the Reformed churches for interpreting it literally as referring to Solomon's marriage to Pharaoh's daughter when it should have been treated as the type—he did not use the word—of the 'great mystical wedding' where 'Christ is the bridegroom and the spouse his church'. The queen consort was 'the church of the natural Israel, reunited by her [foretold] conversion, to her husband, and advanced to the high prerogative of the mother Church of Christendom'. The king's daughters were the churches gathered out of the Gentiles between the expulsion of the wife and her return. The sermons attacked Calvin's influence on the study of prophecy in terms which speak eloquently of the spirit of the preacher:

Calvin was undoubtedly a good man, and a great divine; but with all his great talents and his great learning, he was, by his want of taste, and by the poverty of his imagination, a most wretched expositor of the prophecies, just as he would have been a wretched expositor of any secular poet. He had no sense of the beauties, and no understanding of the imagery of poetry; and the far greater part of the prophetical writings, and all the psalms without exception, are poetical.[23]

Horsley was himself a student of both. His first major contribution to biblical scholarship was a translation with notes of Hosea, perhaps the most intimate of the prophetical books, which appeared in 1801. He published no later studies in the field, being evidently a perfectionist, for he bequeathed in manuscript a mass of important critical and research material on the Old Testament which kept his son Heneage busy preparing it for the press over a period of nearly thirty years. The first item to be selected was a translation of the Psalms with notes critical and explanatory.[24] It came out in 1815, to be followed in due course by critical treatises on the prophets and the historical books.

The bishop believed that 'there is nothing in the great mystery of godliness, which the vulgar, more than the learned, want capacity to apprehend'. He therefore exhorted his clergy in the primary charge at St Davids (1790) to be careful not to propagate 'that delusive dangerous maxim "that morality is the sum of practical religion", lest you place the totality and perfection of the thing in a very inconsiderable part'. They were to preach justification by grace through faith, 'For that we are justified by faith, is not on account of any merit

[23] Horsley, *Sermons*, i (1810), 61–77.
[24] Ibid., i–ix.

in our faith, but because faith is the first principle of that communion between the believer's soul and the divine spirit, on which the whole of our spiritual life depends.'

For him, as for St John, the Incarnation was 'the cardinal doctrine of Christianity'.[25] His Christmas sermon on the text 'Hail, thou that art highly favoured!' began thus: 'That she who in these terms was saluted by an angel should in after years become an object of superstitious adoration, is a thing far less to be wondered at than that men professing to build their whole hopes of immortality on the promises delivered in the sacred book . . . should question the truth of the message which the angel brought.'[26] But incarnation was valued for its necessary connection with redemption. It was essential to 'the effectual atonement of man's guilt by the shedding of his blood'. In a 'wonderful scheme' it was effected that 'the same God who in one person exacts the punishment, in another himself sustains it; and thus makes his own mercy pay satisfaction to his own justice'.[27] The common ground between this teaching and that on which Evangelicals of all types based their emotional conversion experiences is sufficiently apparent. But Horsley found no place in his scheme for antinomianism and fanaticism. The historic controversy about faith and works was 'a meer [*sic*] contest about words', for no one would impute to the Reformers 'the absurd opinion, that any man, leading an impenitent wicked life, will finally upon the meer [*sic*] pretence of faith (and faith connected with an impenitent life must always be a meer pretence) obtain admission into heaven'. The Methodists he could not acquit of antino-mian tendency, though he hoped charitably 'that it is to be found only in the language of the more illiterate of their teachers'.[28]

The fourth component of the bishop's opinions that placed him squarely in the High Church camp was the importance he assigned to tradition as a mentor of church doctrine and practice. Like most Protestant theologians he acknowledged a special inspiration in the first preachers of Christianity, which gave to Holy Scripture a peculiar authority. It was, nevertheless, to antiquity, the whole history of the Church in the first three centuries AD, that he looked to vindicate the scriptural faith. In the controversy with Priestley about the Christological doctrines of the original Christians his emphasis was not on the testimony of the Bible alone but on the continuity of belief throughout the early Christian era. The faith of the Church of England was proved to be the original faith 'by a tradition traced with certainty to the apostolic age'. Moreover, the patristic writers had a distinctive role to play in proving that revealed truth was reasonable. The case as stated in the charge to the clergy of the St Albans archdeaconry ran thus:

[25] Ibid. 163–92.
[26] Horsley, *Sermons*, iii (1816), 66–89.
[27] Horsley, *Sermons*, i. 163–92.
[28] Horsley, *St. David's Charge 1790*.

The importance of the argument from tradition rests upon the supposed infallibility of the first preachers. The opinion of their infallibility rests upon the belief of their divine illumination. The consequence of a divine illumination, is that their whole doctrine must have been, not indeed obvious to the human understanding . . . but consonant to the highest reason . . . and though not free from paradoxes, certainly not encumbered with contradictions . . . The reasonableness of our faith will be best understood from the writings of the fathers of the first three centuries.[29]

In his use of antiquity to confirm the Scriptures Horsley drew very close to the Oxford Movement half a century later. Newman in the *Lectures on the Prophetical Office* wrote: 'Whatever doctrine the primitive ages unanimously attest, whether by consent of the Fathers, or by Councils, or by the events of history, or by controversies, or in whatsoever way, whatever may fairly and reasonably be considered to be the universal belief of those ages is to be received as coming from the Apostles.'[30] Horsley's approach was determined partly by the ground on which his opponent had chosen to fight, but it was also the consequence of his own intense interest in history.

Respect for tradition did not leave him uncritical of contemporary Roman Catholicism, its beliefs, and devotional practices. He recognized that the Blessed Virgin Mary had become 'an object of superstitious adoration', and there was no doubt in his mind that the Church of England was purer. Nevertheless he did not scruple to invoke the teaching authority of the historic Catholic Church both before and after the religious changes of the sixteenth century to support his preaching, for of this Church he held Anglicanism to be part. In a well-known sermon published two years before his death he treated the descent of Christ into hell as a 'catholic belief' advisedly retained by the Church of England at the Reformation. On it he built a conception of the intermediate state of the soul between death and the general resurrection at the last day, which differed both from the Roman Catholic doctrine of purgatory, a place of temporary and expiatory punishment, and various Protestant opinions which, in order to assert the immediacy of final judgement, assumed either that the whole person was extinguished or that the soul slept until the dreadful trumpet sounded to arise. Seventeenth-century expositors had differed in their explanations of the meaning of Christ's descent into hell, some thinking it to be a binding of Satan in his own domain, others a reclaiming of his body from the grave, but had not habitually seen any redemptive process at work in it for those in the realm of departed souls. Neither did Horsley. Preaching from the text 1 Peter 3: 18–20, which spoke of Christ's preaching 'unto the spirits in prison', he took it to refer to souls which had found forgiveness before death and were waiting 'in joyful hope of the consummation of their bliss'. But he claimed from the fact of Christ's

---

[29] Horsley, *St. Albans Charge 1783*.
[30] Quoted from Owen Chadwick, *The Mind of the Oxford Movement* (1963), 123–4.

having preached to these spirits that theirs must have been an active and responsive state, though he did not also draw the deduction that they might profit by the prayers of the living.[31]

Seen in relation to Bishop Horsley's ideals the religious climate of the age in which he wielded influence in the Church, broadly the years 1783–1806, presents us with a paradox. On the one hand, the inexorable advance of English society, and with it the national Church, in a direction opposed to High Church principles assumed accelerated pace. No assessment of the general scene would be even faintly realistic which did not stress the progress towards an ecclesiastically plural society apparent in the unprecedented growth of Nonconformity from the 1770s onwards.[32] Nor could it fail to take account of the alienation from all organized religion which was taking place in the still comparatively few larger cities and in parts of the countryside where agricultural improvement enriched the clergy but nourished anti-clericalism.[33] Doctrinaire infidelity was comparatively rare. More widespread was a secularization of life encouraged by the new work rhythms which the Industrial Revolution brought in its train. The curate of Ashton-under-Lyne answered the visitation questionnaire of 1804:

It cannot but affect with deep concern every serious person, who hath the welfare of Christianity at heart, to observe the infidelity of some and the indifference and carelessness of others, with respect to religion . . . there are many families, especially in the hamlets of Audenshaw and Charlestown, who totally absent themselves from all public worship. The heads of many families among the lower ranks of the community even permit and encourage their children to wander up and down during the time of divine service; what is still more lamentable, the constables inflict no punishment upon them for fear as they say of incurring the odium and malevolence of their neighbours. The parents themselves allege that as their children are confined in the factories during the week, they think it necessary that they should have some relaxation on the Sunday. It is not uncommon, too, during the summer, to see many guilty of a flagrant violation of the Sabbath by making hay on that sacred day . . . I have also to add that the cotton manufacturers make a constant and common practice of employing engineers and wheelwrights to repair their engines and machines on the Lord's Day. O' tempora. O' mores.[34]

Good clergymen as well as bad were conscious of a repudiation of their authority in a subversive ferment brought partly by the spread of democratic

---

[31] Horsley, *On Christ's Descent into Hell and the Intermediate State: A Sermon on I Peter III, 18, 19, 20* (1804). For earlier Anglican writings on this theme see P. E. More and F. L. Cross, *Anglicanism* (1962), 266–9.

[32] A. D. Gilbert, *Religion and Society in Industrial England* (1976), 34–5.

[33] W. R. Ward, 'The Tithe Question in England in the Early Nineteenth Century', *Journal of Ecclesiastical History*, 16 (1965), 67–81; E. J. Evans, 'Some Reasons for the Growth of English Rural Anti-Clericalism, *c*.1750–*c*.1850', *Past and Present*, 66 (1975), 84–109.

[34] Chester CRO EDV 7/3/19, dio. Chester Visitation Articles 1804, return of John Hutchinson.

ideas and partly by economic change. Nor was the revolt against church discipline confined to the poor. Divorce by Act of Parliament, a luxury mainly confined to the rich, lurched forward in the 1790s encouraged by the example of the French Constituent Assembly, which introduced civil divorce in 1792.

Doctrinally the period was characterized by little innovation. A continued progression of Latitudinarian opinions already formulated before the middle of the eighteenth century was discernible in its closing years. Richard Watson, bishop of Llandaff from 1782 to 1816, claimed in his *Anecdotes* to have reduced the study of divinity to the compass of the Bible, 'being much unconcerned about the opinions of councils, fathers, churches, bishops and other men, as little inspired as myself'.[35] But his contempt of patristics scarcely exceeded that of Conyers Middleton writing in 1748/9.

Change might have been swifter had it not been for a countering reaction in favour of older values which had been proceeding side by side with it, since the 1750s at the latest, and was entering upon a new burst of energy in the 1780s. Seven or eight of the thirty-five English and Welsh bishops holding their sees while Samuel Horsley was bishop of St. Davids, can be identified as High Churchmen in a more positive sense than the colourless term 'orthodox', which was commonly applied to them, conveys. They were not mere 'Church and King' Tories and their divinity, while less intense than that of their predecessors a hundred years earlier, had much in common with it. With Horsley, George Horne, the Hutchinsonian bishop of Norwich, and John Douglas, bishop of Carlisle and Salisbury, were singled out by the future Judge Park as men who believed that in spiritual concerns the episcopal character could neither be given nor taken away by the secular power.[36] Douglas corresponded with a Nonjuring bishop, William Cartwright of Shrewsbury, about the Eucharistic practices of his communion which he had studied in his youth. He recognized the antiquity of the usages, but did not consider them to be essential.[37] Horne, preaching in Oxford in 1772, viewed 'the holy eucharist' as a commemorative sacrifice, to be interpreted in the light of the tree of life, the 'prefigurative sacrifices' of the Old Testament, the paschal lamb, and the manna in the wilderness.[38] William Cleaver, bishop of Chester, held forth in similar language from the same pulpit in 1787.[39] It was said of William Markham, archbishop of York in 1784, that his 'nonjuring principles' were his 'brightest jewel',[40] while John Warren, bishop of Bangor 1783–1800, was commended to the highly particular Scottish bishops as

[35] Quoted from C. Smyth, *Simeon and Church Order* (Cambridge, 1940), 103.

[36] F. C. Mather, 'Church, Parliament and Penal Laws: Some Anglo-Scottish Interactions in the Eighteenth Century', *English Historical Review*, 92 (1977), 540–72.

[37] Bodl. Add. MSS D.30, fos. 92–3, 94, Carliol to Cartwright, 16 June and 14 July 1789.

[38] Jones, *Horne*, iv. 58–9.

[39] Cleaver, *Sermon on the Lord's Supper* (Oxford, 1790).

[40] Richard Sharp, 'New Perspectives on the High Church Tradition: Historical Background', in G. Rowell (ed.), *Tradition Renewed* (1986), 6.

being likely from 'his excellent Church principles' to befriend their cause.[41] Pitt's tutor, the bishop of Lincoln, George Pretyman, had High Church leanings. In his *Elements of Christian Theology*, published in 1799 as a manual for ordination candidates, he taught that an uninterrupted succession of bishops was essential to the power of consecrating and ordaining in 'every church, in which episcopacy prevails', but that although that regimen was of apostolical institution, there was no precept in the New Testament which commanded that all churches should be so governed. His sacramental doctrine was akin to that of Waterland. Baptism and the Lord's Supper were federal rites, in which men and women made professions, and God promised in return his secret assistance in performing the work of their salvation. The Communion was in essence commemorative of the sacrifice on the cross, and there was no partaking of Christ in it except by faith.

Lewis Bagot, bishop successively of Bristol, Norwich, and St Asaph, was as strongly opposed to Hoadly's Eucharistic doctrine as to Socinianism. Taking his stand on the teachings of the great Anglican divines of the seventeenth century, notably Isaac Barrow, whose *Doctrine of the Sacraments* he reprinted in 1781, he insisted, against a prebendary of Westminster, that these ordinances were appointed means of conveying 'certain and substantial' benefits[42] in the use of them. Meanwhile, Charles Agar, archbishop of Cashel, one of the most energetic and agile leaders of the Protestant Church of Ireland in the last two decades of the eighteenth century, showed an unusual zeal for Catholic ceremonial when he attended a funeral in Tipperary 'dressed in his full pontificals, with his mitre on his head'.[43]

Other bishops were at least practical High Churchmen. They were distinguished not by their known doctrines but by their attitudes: their earnestness, their special concern for church defence, and their strong opposition to both Latitudinarian heterodoxy and the fanaticism of Methodists and Evangelicals. Into this class fell Horsley's friend, Samuel Hallifax, bishop of Gloucester, who on King Charles's Day 1788 denounced 'the unruly workings of that spirit, (improperly called the Spirit of Reformation) which, under the pretence of preventing or correcting abuses in our religious polity... would too probably... be followed by the most ruinous effects'.[44] John Moore, archbishop of Canterbury; Shute Barrington, bishop of Durham, an ardent opponent of a relaxation of the Thirty-Nine Articles test, ultimately looking forward to reunion with the Roman Catholics against the enemies of Christianity; Richard Hurd of Worcester, a stickler for the external dignities

---

[41] Mather, 'Church, Parliament and Penal Laws'.

[42] Lewis Bagot, *A Letter to the Rev. William Bell* (Oxford, 1781). Barrow's treatise taught that in the Eucharist we 'behold Our Lord in tenderest love, offering up himself a Sacrifice to God.'

[43] F. C. Mather, 'Georgian Churchmanship Reconsidered', *Journal of Ecclesiastical History*, 36 (1985), 255–83.

[44] S. Hallifax, *Sermon before the House of Commons, January 30 1769* (Cambridge, 1769); *Sermon before the Lords Spiritual and Temporal, January 30 1788* (1788).

of his office; Charles Moss, bishop of Bath and Wells, a lingering protégé of the Tory High Churchman Thomas Sherlock, belonged in their several ways to the same category.[45] The learned John Randolph, consecrated bishop of Oxford in 1799 after holding professorships in poetry, Greek, moral philosophy, and divinity, was a firm rationalist in sacramental doctrine but 'high' in his opposition to the antinomianism of the twice-born and in being, in a pragmatic and non-theoretical way, a strenuous champion of clerical immunity from State interference during the third church reform movement. In 1805 he introduced a bill to free Oxford and Cambridge colleges from restrictions on the acquisition of livings.[46] High Churchmen of these two kinds made up about a half of the bench of bishops at the turn of the century. After the death of Hinchcliffe in 1794, Richard Watson was the sole surviving Latitudinarian.[47] Evangelicals had not yet appeared as bishops.

Beneath the episcopate, strict High Churchmen were to be found in cathedral preferments, headships of houses in the University of Oxford, and rich or influential parish livings. Horne, before he became a bishop, was dean of Canterbury, where his friend, George Berkeley, a man of similar Churchmanship, held a prebend. Horsley held the Abbey *in commendam*, Pretyman St Paul's. Nathaniel Wetherell, a relic of Oxford Toryism of the first half of the eighteenth century, reared on a diet of passive obedience, loyalty to Church and University, and mystical Hutchinsonian theology, lingered in the deanery of Hereford from 1771 until his death in 1807. He was also master of University College, Oxford for the whole of that period, and the father of Sir Charles Wetherell, the Ultra-Tory politician.[48] Thomas Rennell, master of the Temple, and from 1805 dean of Winchester, was of a younger generation. He lived to talk 'a little High-Churchery' with the eminent Victorian, Dean Hook.[49] On that side of the Church, Martin Routh was the chief luminary in Oxford. A patristic scholar of distinction respected by the Tractarians, he issued a prospectus of his *Reliquae Sacrae*, an edition of the pre-Nicene fathers, in 1788, and was president of Magdalen College for sixty years from 1791.[50] Whether clerical or lay, High Churchmen managed to occupy key positions in the eighteenth- and early nineteenth-century Church of England which enabled them to exert an influence quite out of proportion to their numbers. The Canterbury cathedral set had ready access to the primate.

[45] Particulars of these four bishops have been drawn from C. J. Abbey, *The English Church and its Bishops 1700–1800* (1887) and *ODCC*.

[46] *Concise DNB* i. 1086; Bodl. Top. Oxon. d.353–6, letters from Randolph to Lambard.

[47] J. Gascoigne, 'Anglican Latitudinarianism', *History*, 71 (1986), 22–38. Except perhaps for the marginal John Butler (Hereford) who died in 1802.

[48] For Wetherell's early views and career see Ward, *Georgian Oxford*, esp. 205–6, 256–7. The date of his appointment as dean of Hereford, wrongly stated in J. Foster's *Alumni Oxonienses*, 2nd ser., i (Liechtenstein, 1968) is confirmed as 1771 by *Gent. Mag.* 41 (1771), 523.

[49] W. R. W. Stephens, *Life and Letters of Walter Farquhar Hook* (1881), 73.

[50] *ODCC* 1207.

George Gaskin, rector of Stoke Newington and of St Benet, Gracechurch Street, was secretary of the SPCK from 1785 to 1823, and powerfully influenced the policies of that important opinion-forming body.[51] Samuel Glasse, one of the Hutchinsonian brotherhood, was chaplain in ordinary to the king from 1772, able to talk to 'a *very great* man' about the disposition of the deanery of Worcester, though not on that occasion to prevail.[52] It was a mark of his type that in his parish of Wanstead, he gathered above 200 people for an Ascension Day service and that builders' labourers erecting an adjacent church laid down their tools and attended.[53]

Prominent among High Church laymen were William Stevens, treasurer of Queen Anne's Bounty 1782–1807[54] and Alexander Knox, private secretary to Lord Castlereagh during the struggle for the Act of Union. Both were lay theologians as well as organizers. Knox's letter to his old friend, the future Bishop Jebb of Limerick, written at the close of the eighteenth century, fired the enthusiasm of the latter for his Churchmanship, which was that of 'the great Caroline divines'.[55] Other names could be added to the list.

True High Church theology is thought to have had an almost negligible following at grass roots level by the 1790s—'no more than one hundred in all', according to a recent estimate.[56] It might seem preferable to regard that support as uneven, varying with the depth of the opinions held. Advanced doctrines of Eucharistic sacrifice and presence and esoteric interests in ecclesiology were, indeed, confined to the few. But the mild High Churchmanship of the *British Critic*, which at that time consisted of little more than an opposition both to Calvinistic excesses and 'that human invention falsely called Rational Christianity',[57] and a positive conviction that the Church of England was apostolical in her government, doctrine, and worship, enabled that review to build up a circulation of 3,000 by the end of the eighteenth century.[58] These figures make credible the claim advanced later by Joshua Watson that believers in the doctrine of apostolical succession, which the *Critic* strenuously advertised from about 1806 onwards, counted for thousands rather than for hundreds,[59] though similar conclusions should not be drawn for all the theology of the Old High Church.

The impulse to direct and consolidate what support there was came not

---

[51] H. Cnattingius, *Bishops and Societies* (1952), 52–3; cf. A. Clissold, '*The Resurrection and the Life*': *Sermon on the Decease of the Rev. George Gaskin* (1829).

[52] Poyntz Letters, S. Glasse to C. Poyntz, 26 Feb. 1783; cf. *Concise DNB* i. 501.

[53] Poyntz Letters, S. Glasse to C. Poyntz, 1788.

[54] G. F. A. Best, *Temporal Pillars* (Cambridge, 1964), 539.

[55] R. B. McDowell, *Ireland in the Age of Imperialism and Revolution 1760–1801* (Oxford, 1979), 205.

[56] Nancy U. Murray, 'The Influence of the French Revolution on the Church of England and its Rivals, 1789–1802', D.Phil. thesis (Oxford, 1975).

[57] *British Critic*, 1 (1793), Prospectus.

[58] S. Rivington, *The Publishing Family of Rivington* (1919), 100.

[59] See above, p. 202.

from Horsley nor from any other traditionalist bishop, but from men of humbler rank, the parish priests and laity of the Hutchinsonian fraternity, who had already experience of some degree of union. The Society for the Reformation of Principles was launched early in 1792 by the veteran William Jones of Nayland to wage literary war against 'sectaries, republicans, Socinians and infidels'.[60] It is chiefly remembered as the founder of the *British Critic*, but the connection is more tenuous than is commonly believed.

Though some 'mighty' plan had been germinating in the old campaigner's mind since August 1789,[61] when it caught the elation generated by Horsley's championship of the orthodox cause, the immediate stimulus to the formation of the Society most probably came from the application of the English Unitarians for a Relief Bill.[62] A few disciples of Jones—Thomas Calverley of Ewell, Nathan Wetherell, Samuel Glasse, and John Parkhurst—gathered round him at Nayland parsonage, as did several younger associates.[63] The results were at first disappointing. By the end of September he was bewailing the failure of his scheme in a Latin ode.[64] His humble status as a Suffolk country clergyman and the eccentricity of his opinions stood in the way of success. But a letter in the Boucher Papers, written two months later, shows the importance of William Stevens's business acumen in snatching victory from defeat. Stevens worked hard to drum up press support through George Robinson, a London bookseller and reviewer, who had been trained by Rivington's, the main 'Church' publishers. Robinson offered to find space in the *Critical Review*, a journal circulating at 2,500, for theological reviews contributed by 'any divines sound in the faith who will engage in the work'. He hinted that he might 'set up a review himself in opposition to the [Unitarian] *Monthly* which he would engage to write down'. Jones helped the recovery by turning his hand to writing loyalist tracts of a popular genre at a time when the Reevesite Association for the Preservation of Liberty and Property was massaging the market for such works. Robinson was 'much pleased with Tom Bull', and sent it to his friend Archibald Hamilton, proprietor of the *Critical Review*. Robinson wanted to print 50,000 copies, but Stevens wondered at the cost.[65] Some sort of deal was done. Jones wrote the tracts, and Rivington's brought out the *British Critic* under the editorship not of Jones but of two scholarly High Churchmen: the philologist Robert Nares and the bibliophile William Beloe, both afterwards librarians of the British Museum.[66]

[60] W. Stevens (attrib.) *A Short Account of the Life and Writings of the Rev. William Jones* (1801), pp. xxxv–xxxvi.

[61] Locker Lampson MSS B.3/37, Stevens to Boucher, 19 Aug. 1789.

[62] See above, p. 86.

[63] E. Churton, *Memoir of Joshua Watson* (Oxford, 1861), i. 27–9.

[64] Stevens, *A Short Account*, Appendix, pp. lvi–lix.

[65] Locker Lampson MSS B.3/65, Stevens to Boucher, 21 Nov. 1792.

[66] Rivington, *Publishing Family*, 100.

Though not involved in the venture, Bishop Horsley contributed to it occasionally. He wrote a learned dissertation on the sacred names of God in the Hebrew language, in answer to Dr Geddes, in the number for February 1802,[67] and on his death his library was found to contain annotated copies of Newcome's *Minor Prophets* and Stock's Isaiah 'as if for a review which the Bp. had promised the *British Critic*'. There were also letters to the editor.[68]

Strict High Churchmen who found the polite literary format of the *Critic* too weak an instrument to express their ardour, looked first to the Tory *Anti-Jacobin Review* as an outlet. William Stevens endeavoured to persuade the proprietor John Gifford and his colleagues to take on board a series of biographical sketches of Jones of Nayland.[69] The connection foundered on the extremism of some of the High Churchmen and their breach with the Evangelicals, proclaimed to the world by the collision between the exclusive Calvinism of John Overton's *True Churchman Ascertained* (1801) and the Laudian zealotry of Archdeacon Daubeny's *Guide to the Church* and *Vindicia Ecclesiae Anglicanae*. Association with such intellectual dinosaurs as Jones and Daubeny proved in the long run to be more than political adventurers like Gifford could swallow. Daubeny was bursting with indignation against the 'hop, stop and jump' divinity of the mildest Evangelicals like Jonas Dennis, trained, as he believed, in Hannah More's school for the younger clergy, 'in which they gain as much knowledge in a few lectures as old divines have been able to draw from a whole row of bulky folios turn'd over *nocturna et diurna manu*'.[70] It was left to High Churchmen of broader outlook to found a new periodical of their own which papered over the cracks with the Evangelicals. When the *Orthodox Churchman's Magazine* was launched in March 1801, the introductory thrust was against Catholic emancipation, atheists, Deists, and Dissenters rather than against Methodists,[71] and 'moderation and christian charity' was promised towards 'all consistent and moderate Dissenters'.[72] The chief mark upon it was that of William Stevens. The address in the first number proclaimed the old shibboleth 'that the church is in danger'. It cited Stevens's *Treatise on the Nature and Constitution of the Christian Church*, and was followed by the first instalment of the biography of Jones of Nayland which Stevens had been trying to place in the *Anti-Jacobin Review*.[73]

One thing which the *OCM* demonstrated was that High Churchmen could enter the expanding field of popular journalism. Well-written articles and managed correspondence were used to give practical teaching on a variety of church matters ranging from the revival of Convocation to praying for the

---

[67] *British Critic* 1st ser., 37 (1811), 55.
[68] LPL 2810, Palmer Papers, 279–91, W. J. Palmer, 'An Account of Horsley's Manuscripts'.
[69] Locker Lampson MSS B.3/84, Stevens to Boucher, 4 June 1800.
[70] Locker Lampson MSS B.5/15, Daubeny to Boucher, 16 Apr. 1800.
[71] *OCM* 1 (1801), 1–3, address 'To the Public'.
[72] Ibid., p. v, Preface.
[73] Ibid. 1–11.

dead, from ancient fonts and baptisteries to ministerial scarves and the correct positioning of altars.[74]

Interest in such matters was small at first, and to improve the halting circulation distribution was transferred in 1804 from Spragg's of Covent Garden to Rivington's, with the intention of extending from ecclesiastical antiquities to science, *belles-lettres*, and poetry.[75] But the original design was not abandoned. In 1803 Rivington's, the *Anti-Jacobin Review*, and Spragg's collaborated in promoting a *Churchman's Remembrancer* to reprint earlier church defence writings.[76] In the following year the *OCM* was commending two papers by a body known as the Endeavour Society on the observance of Lent and the Sacrament of the Lord's Supper respectively.[77]

High Church revival was thus guided through its early stages not by associations but by periodicals and publications. Cohesion was, therefore, weak, though the need to achieve it was being urged during the opening years of the new century. In 1802–3 the cry was raised in the *OCM* that neighbouring clergy should confer respecting the best mode of promoting religion in their parishes and to form book societies. A correspondent wrote:

at present the clergy have no point of union. Like insulated bodies, which have lost their attraction, they stand aloof from each other. If their forces, however, were consolidated, and they made the opposition of their enemies a common cause we should not, as we so often do, see a sort of dastardly temporising spirit amongst our order, some favouring one sect, some another, nay some so inconsiderate as to oppose the well meant exertions of their brethren to stem the tide of heterodox opinions. I allude to a late controversy in this county [Cornwall], in which the friends of the church, besides being splashed very plentifully with abuse by their opponents, encountered enemies where they should have found friends. Frequent meetings would prevent this, and engage us to cooperate.[78]

His appraisal was a just one. Aside from their quarrels with 'Church' Evangelicals, the High Church leadership was itself split by disputes in the SPCK Board over the content of the annual charity schools sermons and the form of the anniversary service for the schools in St Paul's cathedral. Bishop Horsley was heavily involved in both. The first was provoked by the successive attacks of the preachers, whose addresses were printed and circulated, on the classical curriculum of the public schools, associated by some with the atheism of the French Revolution. It surfaced at the Society's general meeting in December 1801, when a request by William Vincent, headmaster of Westminster School, to circulate a protest against the printed version of the sermon of Bishop O'Beirne was rejected. Jones of Nayland and Thomas

[74] Ibid. 1 (1801), 241–4; 6 (1804), 92–4, 242–3, 294–7.
[75] Ibid. 6 (1804), 1–4, 168–74.
[76] Ibid. 4 (1803), 243–4.
[77] Ibid. 6 (1804), 163–8.
[78] Ibid. 4 (1803), 171–2.

Rennell had led the attack on the public schools, which was firmly backed by the secretary of the Society, George Gaskin. Other High Churchmen with strong academic interests, such as Charles Daubeny, the Wykehamist, Samuel Horsley, the natural protector of Westminster School, together with the spokesmen of the *OCM*, raised their voices with the bishop of Oxford's in defence of Vincent and the schools.[79] Bishop Randolph, however, found his 'brother of Rochester' an embarrassing ally, when he put down a cooling motion at a general meeting which Horsley chaired: 'I could not repress him & he would enter into the subject at large with all his violence. He was very entertaining but did us great harm, particularly when he would enter into the proceedings of the Board.'[80]

Before Randolph won his point an even sharper quarrel erupted between the Society and the patrons of the Anniversary Meeting of the Charity Schools, when the latter decided that an anthem, to be sung by 100 girls from the various schools, should be substituted for the plain Psalm 113 at the anniversary service in St Paul's on 20 May 1802. In a meeting heavily attended by friends of William Stevens, it was agreed to sweep aside a compromise solution proposed by the dean of St Paul's (Pretyman) that the anthem should be presented that year, and the old-fashioned psalmody restored in the following year. Feeling ran so high that the meeting resolved to transfer the festival to another church unless the Society was permitted to control the order of service.[81] The chairman of the meeting (Horsley) doubtless had the Abbey in mind, for as dean he had been perfecting his choir in the older forms.

There were degrees of High Churchmanship then as now. Pretyman was a moderate, commended for his temperateness by Porteus, bishop of London, a serious Low Churchman. There were also acute personal rivalries in the camp. Bishop John Randolph could not conceal his dislike of Horsley—'your strange bishop'[82] as he described him to a clergyman friend of Sevenoaks— while Daubeny, when writing to Jonathan Boucher, could scarcely mention Stevens without calling him 'your friend (tho' I am sorry to say not my friend)'.[83] Based on Bath and Salisbury, the author of the *Guide to the Church* had only tenuous links with the London group through Boucher and through Joshua Watson, who had married his niece. His extreme and uncompromising opinions in both politics and religion made him intensely critical of most other High Churchmen, whom he dismissed too readily as hedgers, and his cynical assessment of personalities made him a difficult person to work with. He

[79] SPCK Minutes, xxxiii (1800–3), fos. 184–6, 217, 239; cf. C. Smyth, *Simeon and Church Order*, 56–70.

[80] Bodl. Top. Oxon. d.355, fos. 56–7, Randolph to Lambard, 8 Apr. 1802.

[81] SPCK Minutes, xxxiii (1800–3), fos. 226–8, 237–9.

[82] Bodl. Top. Oxon. d.355, fos. 17–18, Randolph to Lambard, 22 Sept. 1800.

[83] Locker Lampson MSS B.5/3, Daubeny to Boucher, 28 Dec. 1798; cf. B.5/22, do. to do., 29 May 1801.

believed Stevens to be himself 'fundamentally an honest man', but not dis-criminating enough in his judgement of others, that is too broad-minded a High Churchman.

Except as a loose bond of sentiment no High Church party was to be found when Horsley died in 1806, not even a Hackney Phalanx, for William Stevens had led his 'friends' from Broad Street, London. Even so, a loosely com-pacted High Church movement had established a momentum. This was evident in an increase of publishing activity in the SPCK from the later 1790s, as a new set of activists connected with Stevens penetrated its meetings. The output of New Testaments, Prayer Books, and other books and tracts rose steadily year by year in the decade after 1797 and dramatically from 1811, if not a little earlier.[84] Lay involvement of a political kind occurred at the local level. In Shoreditch and Clerkenwell Church parties formed to resist the combined efforts of the Methodists and the Calvinists to command the elections to parochial office. Their opponents at first made most of the running. In March 1805, however, the respectable inhabitants of Clerkenwell rallied to a public meeting at the Crown Tavern on the Green, and resolved to form an association which would support the nomination of persons 'thoroughly well affected to the constitution in church and state' to offices in the parish.[85]

From about the end of the first decade of the nineteenth century renewal entered a more advanced phase, as Norris and Joshua Watson consolidated their base in Hackney, and exerted an influence which pulled together the High Church movement in the country into a more coherent whole. Their grip on the journalism of the movement was much extended by the purchase of the *British Critic* in the winter of 1811–12 and by subsequent ventures, but the most noticeable change was in organization. The coming of the great associations, such as the National Society for Promoting the Education of the Poor (1811), the Westminster Association for German War Relief (1814), and the Church Building Society (1817) brought a new unity and a new con-fidence. When Britain emerged from the strain of the Napoleonic Wars in 1815, an awareness was dawning of a development in the national life which had gathered force during the preceding quarter of a century and which later historians have been slow to notice:

However various have been the attacks to which the Church of England has been of late exposed . . . one good effect at least has resulted from the very dangers with which she has been threatened, that a host of her faithful sons among the laity as well as the clergy have rallied under her banners and presented a phalanx of defenders, which would have done honour even to her best ages.[86]

---

[84] See below, Appendix A.
[85] *OCM*. 7 (1804), esp. 46–8, 107–13, 187–92, 275–84, 348–50, 414–26; Ibid. 8 (1805), 118–22, 199–200, 247–50.
[86] *British Critic*, 2nd ser., 3 (1815), 645–9.

The achievements of the later years fall outside the scope of this study, for Horsley did not live to see them. His contribution was to shaping and sustaining the High Church revival in an earlier heroic era when enmity was at a height. His role had been individual and detached, that of a champion rather than a leader. But his stalwart and often talented conduct of public business had put stiffening into church defence, and had helped to carry the Hanoverian ecclesiastical establishment through the most severe crisis in its existence before the time of the Reform Bill.

CHURCH HOUSE LIBRARY
ECTON HOUSE
NORTHAMPTON NN6 0QE

BOOK No _ _ _ _ _ _ _ _ _

CLASS No _ _ _ _ _ _ _ _ _

DATE added _ _ _ _ _ _ _ _

II

A Presence in Politics

THE House of Lords in which the bishop sat was a quiet and relatively undemanding place. Attendances were low. For five of the six sessions 1785–96 the median frequency of participation by those peers who attended at all was less than fifteen times a session.[1] The acknowledged duty of the Upper House was, as Charles James Fox defined it, to preserve the balance of the constitution by equalizing and meliorating the powers of the other two branches, the Crown and the House of Commons.[2] Though there were exceptional times, as in April 1804 when the House was obliged to join the Commons in ousting incompetent ministers sustained by the Crown, this usually meant providing the king's chosen ministries with the support they needed to survive. This function was accomplished without great effort, for at most times the balancing weight of the House of Lords was latent. After 1783–4 overt trials of strength between the two chambers were avoided until the decade of the Reform Bill. Moreover, within the House friction was minimized because the massive peerage creations undertaken by the Younger Pitt in the closing decades of the eighteenth century had done nothing to shake the aristocratic cohesion there.[3] Even the rebel minorities which fenced with the Government over the suspension of habeas corpus and the conduct of the war against the French Republic comprised the blue blood of the land: the dukes of Norfolk, Bedford, and Grafton, the earls of Derby, Lauderdale, and Albemarle, as well as others of equal lustre but more recent title.[4] Radical whig peers like Stormont and Richmond subscribed to the same underlying constitutional assumptions as the rest of their order,[5] and even on the specific issues where real differences existed, the Opposition was seldom able to raise minorities of more than a dozen, especially after the Portland Whigs had gone over to the Government.

The Upper House nevertheless played an important part in governing Britain. The greatest national issues were debated at length and with eloquence within its walls. Though most legislation originated in the Commons, the Lords felt a special mission to interfere with certain kinds of it: that which

---

[1] M. W. McCahill, *Order and Equipoise: The Peerage and the House of Lords, 1783–1806* (1978), 14–15.

[2] Ibid. 1.

[3] A. S. Turberville, 'The Younger Pitt and the House of Lords', *History*, NS, 21 (1937), 350–8; id., *The House of Lords in the Age of Reform 1784–1837* (1958), chap. iii.

[4] *Parl. Reg.* xxxix (1794), 335, 384.

[5] McCahill, *Order and Equipoise*, 12.

raised questions of oaths and conscience, where the Lord Chancellor would want his say, alterations to the legal code and judicial procedures, laws affecting the privileges of the Established Church, where the bishops had some claim to be consulted, and more curiously measures to reform election procedures, to develop trade, and to regulate agriculture and poor relief. Bills in these categories were notoriously prone to be dropped or rejected in that House. A limited revising function was performed in relation to some carelessly drafted public bills, but much of the time of the House was consumed by private bills—Canal Bills, Enclosure Bills, Estate Bills—large numbers of which came before it in the later eighteenth and early nineteenth centuries. These were dealt with in committees, and though the task of reconciling conflicting interests was at first feebly performed, a redefinition of procedures from 1792 onwards enabled a firmer grip to be exerted by the end of the eighteenth century.[6]

Bishops played an important part in most branches of the Lords' activities. The nature of their role has been lately reassessed in a broader revision of the relationship of the House to the king and his ministers.[7] It used to be believed that the twenty-four English bishops and two archbishops, and the four representatives of the Irish bench chosen after the Union, formed, with the Scottish representative peers, household officers, and the peers recently promoted or honoured by the Government, 'a party of the crown', so firmly attached by patronage to the king's ministers as to play a considerable part in ensuring the Lords' permanent 'subservience to the executive', at least on major issues.[8] It was through gratitude for their existing appointments or through hope of preferment to a richer see that the prelates were held. As the *Rolliad* gibed:

> You rev'rend Prelates, rob'd in sleeves of lawn,
> Too meek to murmur, and too proud to fawn,
> Who still submissive to their Maker's nod,
> Adore their sov'reign and respect their God;
> And wait, good men, all worldly things forgot,
> The humble hope of Enoch's happy lot.[9]

It has long been recognized that such an explanation is too mechanical to embrace all episcopal behaviour, but Dr Michael McCahill has cast the emphasis in a different way, laying it upon their independence, their detachment from politics, their concentration on ecclesiastical questions. There is truth in this revision, but it goes too far.

---

[6] Ibid. 41–8, 59–60, 62, 105–12 for evidence supporting these generalizations.

[7] Ibid.

[8] D. Large, 'The Decline of "the Party of the Crown" and the Rise of Parties in the House of Lords, 1783–1837', *English Historical Review*, 78 (1963), 669–95.

[9] Turberville, *House of Lords*, 301: 'Enoch was translated that he should not see death' (Hebrews 11: 5).

McCahill divides the forty-four late eighteenth-century bishops whose allegiance is known to him into the following categories: 'twenty-seven were undoubtedly the king's friends: six were former royal tutors or chaplains who owed their elevations to the king; nine others followed the lead of lay patrons who were themselves loyal partisans of the crown. Six, however, were genuinely independent, and ten followed lay patrons at least briefly into opposition. In fact the most remarkable political feature of these men was their loyalty to their various patrons.'[10] The separation of the submissive from the non-submissive appears too sharp. Samuel Horsley is placed among the independents, alongside Richard Watson, bishop of Llandaff, and Jonathan Shipley, both basically Opposition Whigs.[11] Horsley, though he owed little directly to George III, owed much to Bishop Hurd and Lord Chancellor Thurlow, friends of the monarch. He did not hesitate to ask favours of the Younger Pitt, and as late as 1801 sought and obtained permission to dedicate his translation of Hosea to the king.[12] The most accurate test of his attachment is to be found in the division lists of the House of Lords. As Dr Large has explained, few of these survive for the period before 1830, though the names of peers in the anti-Governmental minorities are more frequently given in the *Parliamentary Register* or in Cobbett's *Parliamentary History and Debates*. Table 2, showing episcopal alignments in twelve divisions, chosen because they reflect the main political struggle between Government and Opposition, has been compiled in most cases by deducing the identity of the pro-Government majority by subtracting the known minority from the bishops listed as present on the day in the Lords Journals. This is an inexact method because it makes no allowance for comings and goings, and because it conflates abstainers and voters for the ministry.

It is clear from the table that few bishops voted against the Government, though more of them did so when the respectable and patriotic Grenvillite opposition had been added to the Foxites. Staying away from divisions after the fashion of Bishop Watson was a more usual way of registering dissent. It also seems evident that a sizeable proportion of the bench, changing slowly in composition as the years progressed, furnished much of the Government's majority at crucial times. After the primate, Samuel Horsley was the most stalwart member of this group, which also included Shute Barrington, bishop of Durham, James Cornwallis, bishop of Lichfield, and curiously Brownlow North of Winchester, but the pattern of his behaviour changed from 1798. He became far less reliable, missing divisions, and even voting with the Opposition against the preliminaries of the Peace of Amiens.

More instructive than his lurch towards Opposition was the way he went about it. Horsley was connected with the Grenvillites in their assaults upon

---

[10] McCahill, *Order and Equipoise*, 162; cf. pp. 146–7.

[11] Ibid. 162 n. 5.

[12] HP 1767, fo. 24, Portland to Horsley, 18 May 1801; cf. above, pp. 62–3, 178, and 191.

TABLE 2. *Voting by bishops in House of Lords divisions*

Year	Issue	Overall majority (all peers excluding proxies)	Bishops in Opposition	Bishops with Government
1788	Regency proposals	99–66	North, Watson, Wilson	*Horsley**, Porteus, Thurlow, Moss, Douglas, Barrington, Hinchcliffe, Hurd, W. Cleaver, Pretyman, Warren, Hallifax, Abp. Moore
1794	Suspension of habeas corpus	95–97	None	*Horsley*, Moss, Douglas, Barrington, Warren, Cornwallis, Manners-Sutton, Vernon, Abps. Moore & Markham
	Conduct of French war	82–13	None	*Horsley**, Moss, Douglas, Warren, Courtenay, Abps. Moore & Markham
1795	Recall of Earl Fitzwilliam from Ireland	83–21	None	*Horsley*, Porteus, Moss, Barrington, Pretyman, Warren, Cornwallis, Manners-Sutton, Courtenay, Smallwell, Yorke
	Seditious Meetings Bill	57–14	None	*Horsley*, Porteus, Pretyman, Cornwallis, Courtenay, North, Stuart, Abp. Moore
1798	State of Ireland	51–18	None	*Horsley*, Cornwallis, Courtenay, North, Buckner
	Change of ministers	88–11	None	Porteus, Barrington, Cornwallis, Manners-Sutton, Courtenay, North, Yorke, Stuart, Bagot, Vernon, Cornewall, Abp. Moore
1801	Preliminaries of peace with France	94–10	*Horsley*	Porteus, Barrington, Manners-Sutton, Buckner, Murray, Abp. Moore

TABLE 2. *Continued*

Year	Issue	Overall majority (all peers excluding proxies)	Bishops in Opposition	Bishops with Government
1802	Definitive Treaty of Amiens	100–16	None	Porteus, Cornwallis, Manners-Sutton, North, Buckner, Murray, Beadon, Randolph, Knox, Abp. Moore
1804	Irish Militia Offer Bill	77–49	Pretyman, Madan	*Horsley*, Barrington, North, Randolph, Burgess, Fisher, E. Cleaver, Bennet, Abp. Moore
	Irish Militia Augmentation Bill	94–62	Pretyman, Vernon, Madan	*Horsley*, Barrington, Cornwallis, North, Beadon, Randolph, Burgess, Fisher, E. Cleaver, W. Beresford, Abp. Moore
1805	Defence of the country	127–52	W. Cleaver	Barrington, Abp. Manners-Sutton, Yorke, Randolph, Burgess, Fisher, Majendie, Dampier, Porter, Loftus, Abp. Moore

* The vote of the bishop is known in these cases; in the other cases it has been deduced.

the Addington ministry. His son Heneage, dedicating the posthumous edition of his Speeches to Lord Grenville, described the latter as 'the political leader to whom', with the exception of Windham, 'my father was most strongly attached'.[13] Grenville, Pitt's cousin and his leader in the House of Lords, was reluctant at first to oppose the ministry which succeeded Pitt's, but events drove him at length into full-scale opposition in union with Fox. Bishop Horsley was even more chary. He apologized to the House for assailing the preliminaries of the Peace: 'I ought perhaps to be diffident of my own

[13] Horsley, *Speeches*, i, p. i, Preface.

judgment, when it stands in opposition to the sentiments of those whose opinions I have long been in the habit of looking up to with respect and deference.'[14] He rarely attended Parliament in the next eight months, and did not vote against the ratification of the treaty in May 1802. When Grenville moved in to the kill of the Addington Government in April 1804 by attacking its Irish Militia Bills in the House of Lords, the bishop raised an objection to one of these, the Militia Offer Bill, which authorized withdrawal of militiamen from Ireland to Great Britain, on the ground that it might inflict further disabilities on the Irish Catholics. Grenville took up the matter, and proposed an amending clause.[15] After this was lost, however, Horsley did not follow Grenville into the division against either bill. Nor did he have anything to do with Lord King's motion for a Committee on the Defence of the Country backed by the leading Grenvilles when Pitt was in office once more in March 1805.

A cynic might affirm that he had been bought off with the lucrative see of St Asaph. Perhaps he was baited with it, but timetabling considerations show that his attitudes were shaped before the offer was made. He was not an independent but a king's friend, torn in his later years between loyalty to George III and his ministers and the demands of his conscience and of his party leader on the other. While the monarch remained in politics, no prelate of the Church of England, bound by his oaths and homage, could wholly repudiate him.

There were large differences, however, in the extent to which bishops took their parliamentary duties seriously. These were a function not only of their adhesion to the king's ministers, though they were not unrelated to that, but also of their sense of constitutional obligation, their seniority rating, the accessibility of their dioceses to the House of Lords, and the offices they held in that chamber. It seems to have been assumed that at least one bishop would be in attendance every day, to justify the heading in the Journal: 'Domini tam Spirituales quam Temporales Praesentes fuerint.' Attendance by a single bishop was a not uncommon occurrence, the duty falling with a less than fair incidence on the latest addition to the bench, but, except when business of great moment arose, it was unusual for eight or more bishops to be present at debates. Horsley's performance was quite outstanding. In the great majority of parliamentary sessions while he was eligible he was in his place in the Lords on about every alternate day of meeting from the beginning of the session until near its end. His persistence relative to that of his slacker brethren is shown by his appearances on days when reports from committees on private bills and other matters of minor importance held the floor, and when in

---

[14] *Parl. Hist.* xxxvi (1801–3), 178–83; cf. Peter Jupp, *Lord Grenville 1759–1834* (Oxford, 1985), 306–44.
[15] *Parl. Deb.*, 1st ser., ii (1804), 169–71.

consequence no more than four bishops were present. In 1792–3 he scored
33 such attendances, beaten only by the newly appointed bishop of Exeter,
who was winning his spurs and reached 46. The bishop of Bangor, who was
deputy lord chairman of committees, had 18 and the archbishop of York 11.
No other bishop raised more than 9. Horsley maintained his involvement in
parliamentary routine in 1797–8, though by then he was a senior bishop and
dean. Fifty-eight appearances on such occasions were recorded in his favour,
more than for anyone save the bishop of Bristol with 60. He was a new boy.
Most ranged downwards from 9.[16]

His role in the House was by no means passive. He contributed frequently
and at length to some of the most important debates of the time. Though
bishops did not usually speak in the House of Lords, he was in the habit of
intervening six, eight, or even sixteen times in a session by the middle 1790s.

Dr McCahill has shown that the behaviour of the king's friends in the
Upper Chamber was determined not so much by the exercise of Crown
patronage as by their conservatism of outlook.[17] Horsley can be fitted easily
into this mould. His political ideas were representative of a stage in the
evolution of High Churchmanship. Their roots must be sought in an apologetic, strong in the Church in the Restoration era, which emphasized the
divine right of kings and the concomitant duties of non-resistance and passive
obedience. Though the Revolution of 1688–9 gave every denial in practice to
this theory, it survived by an ingenious process of adaptation. Conservative
Anglicans who accepted the change of monarch argued like William Sherlock
in his *Case of Allegiance* (1691) that God himself had intervened to bring it
about, thus transferring the old sanctions to the new rulers. About the same
time, Sherlock, Peter Allix, Archbishop Sharp, and other like-minded thinkers
began to insist that passive obedience was owed not to the person but to the
office of the monarch and to extend it to Parliament as the high court of
England which declared the law and apportioned the Crown.[18] Thus while
indefeasible hereditary right ceased to be proclaimed except by the Jacobites
and Nonjurors,[19] an abstract dispute over passive obedience continued to
divide High Churchmen from Latitudinarian Whigs for a quarter of a century.
This was muted when the triumphant Whigs after 1714 borrowed the doctrine of providential right, and used it together with more secular arguments
to bolster the dull but stabilizing regime of the Hanoverian kings. Tories, if
they wished to be regarded as loyal, had first no option but to yield grudging

---

[16] *JHL*, daily attendance lists. For bp. of Bangor's position, see McCahill, *Order and Equipoise*,
95 and n. 1.

[17] Ibid. 153–67.

[18] G. M. Straka, *Anglican Reaction to the Revolution of 1688* (Madison, Wis., 1962), 70–3,
108–12; cf. J. P. Kenyon, *Revolution Principles: The Politics of Party 1689–1720* (Cambridge, 1977),
88–9.

[19] Straka, *Anglican Reaction* 107.

assent.[20] As J. C. D. Clark has shown, however, a refurbished doctrine of monarchy was trumpeted forth by Hutchinsonian divines from Oxford in the years before and after the accession of George III. Its origins lay, as Clark points out, in the earlier needs of a new opposition which wrestled with the implications of Bolingbroke's relatively innocuous *Patriot King*,[21] but centenaries also played their part in calling it forth, notably those of the royal martyrdom and the Restoration. The new preachers dipped into the dangerous political doctrines of the Nonjurors, Hickes and Leslie. Nathan Wetherell's sermon on 30 January 1755 was attacked by Kennicott for maintaining:

the justly-exploded doctrine of absolute passive obedience, and this in terms so extremely gross, as even to have out-Filmered Filmer: to maintain it to be the indispensable duty of all Christian subjects, under the worst of tyrants, to bow down in the dust or upon the block; and patiently to permit him to ravish from them religion, liberty, property, and life itself—and, at last, to tell the congregation, that no man could vindicate resistance in any case whatsoever, without giving up all regard for the Bible, and all pretension to common sense![22]

Preaching on the same occasion in 1761, George Horne did not hesitate to draw comparisons 'between our Lord and the royal martyr', and urged endeavours 'to eradicate out of the minds of men those diabolical principles of resistance to government in church and state, which brought his sacred head to the block' and 'an imitation of his godlike virtues'.[23] This was extravagant language, but it introduced no new principle, merely a change of emphasis induced by different circumstances. As Dr Clark observes, 'during George II's reign, the Hutchinsonians practised passive obedience towards a regime which, as George Horne believed, blocked their promotion. In 1760, that barrier was removed.'[24] The expectation that it would soon be removed had encouraged the 'outs' to look for relief of their condition to a fresh exercise of royal authority in the years when the old king's life slipped inexorably towards its close. The political High Churchmanship engendered at that time was further elaborated by Horne and others in sermons, charges, and discourses published during the next thirty years or more. Though it eulogized monarchy its chief concern was not with the form of government but with the divine sanction underlying it. Hence it was not always as illiberal as it seemed. While Locke's theory of government based on contract was repeatedly criticized by Horne, and Jones of Nayland taught in a tract published in 1776 'that

[20] H. T. Dickinson, 'The Eighteenth-Century Debate on the "Glorious Revolution"', *History* 61 (1976), 28–45; Clark, *English Society* 173–9.
[21] Ibid. 218–22; cf. 179–84.
[22] Benjamin Kennicott, *A Word to the Hutchinsonians* (1756), quoted from Clark, *English Society*, 219.
[23] Ibid. 222.
[24] Ibid. 219.

resistance to civil government asserted on principle, is nothing but the extra-
vagance and nonsense of designing writers',[25] all occasion for reform was not
necessarily dismissed by members of this school. Horne's lifelong friend,
Prebendary Berkeley, both extolled the virtues and admitted the faults of the
Hanoverian mixed system in a sermon preached at Cookham on the Fast Day,
1780:

> One of the most obvious excellencies of our constitution is, its due distribution of the
> legislative power among the several orders of the community, and the share of it into
> which the representatives of the people are admitted: representatives chosen by the
> people, and who ought to be freely and prudently chosen, on account of superior
> integrity and ability; if the people will sell their birthrights for a mess of election
> pottage, the people may thank themselves for all the real grievances which their own
> corruption, perjury and folly, have at any time brought upon themselves. If a perfect
> stranger can, by sending a merry andrew and a punchboard *punchinello* into a borough,
> and (notwithstanding the highest possible provisions of the legislature to prevent the
> people betraying their country), if such a wretch can be almost unanimously chosen, to
> represent the people of an English borough, let it be remembered from whence the
> horrid abuse originally springs; and let not the King or the nobles be blamed, when
> originally we, who choose the commons, are only and septennially in fault.[26]

Clark distinguishes between the Anglican divines from Oxford whose political
idiom was more concerned with 'dynastic titles, monarchical allegiance, and
divine sanctions' and those of Cambridge, who went on defending the constitutional regime which had developed under the first two Georges and
praised the liberty which it guaranteed. These too waxed increasingly defensive under the attacks on Church and Government which developed from the
later 1760s.[27]

   Horsley was a Cambridge man, but he had transferred to Oxford, and
occupied ideologically a middle position. His image as a reactionary royalist
and as 'the most powerful and articulate excoriator of French republicanism in
particular and change in general', to use Dr Soloway's phrase, is undeserved.
It is principally derived from his sermon before the Lords in Westminster
Abbey on the anniversary of King Charles I's 'martyrdom', 30 January 1793,
nine days after the execution of Louis XVI. The rhetoric and the historical
view breathed an extravagant royalism, but the tone was influenced by the
occasion: 'O my Country! Read the horror of thy own deed in this recent
heightened imitation! Lament and weep, that this black French treason should

---

[25] William Jones (of Nayland), *Discourse on the English Constitution* (1776) quoted from Clark,
English Society, 227.
[26] Berkeley, *Sermons*, no. ii, 27–37. The specific allusion is to the notoriously corrupt
Shaftesbury election of 1774. Sir L. Namier and J. Brooke, *The History of Parliament: The House of
Commons, 1754–1790* (1964), i. 271.
[27] Clark, *English Society*, 228.

have found its example, in the crime of thy unnatural sons.'[28] The simultaneous rising of the congregation at these words shows how much the preacher held their approval. But, when the content of his discourse is examined, the moderation of his opinions stands revealed. He began with an attack on Locke, denying that mankind ever existed in a state of nature, and affirming that, therefore, 'to build the authority of princes, or of the chief magistrate under whatever denomination, upon any compact or agreement between the individuals of a multitude living previously in the state of nature, is in truth to build a reality upon a fiction'.[29] This was no betrayal of eighteenth-century constitutional principles, for recent historians such as J. C. D. Clark and H. T. Dickinson have shown how little support there was for Locke's ideas, even against the supposedly outmoded patriarchalism of Filmer, in Britain throughout the eighteenth century.[30] Nor was he alone in withholding from citizens the right of resistance to governors, for Blackstone and other recognized authorities did so too.[31] It was in the derivation of governing authority from God that the conservative side of Horsley's message was displayed. Against the secular notion of origin in contract he proclaimed:

The plain truth is this. The manner in which, as we are informed upon the authority of God himself, God gave a beginning to the world, evidently leads to this conclusion, —namely that civil society, which always implies government, is the condition to which God originally destined man. Whence, the obligation on the citizen to submit to government is an immediate result from that first principle of religious duty which regards that man conform himself, as far as in him lies, with the will and purpose of his maker.

Nevertheless, he was careful to distance himself from Stuart concepts of the divine right of kings. Direct nomination of rulers or dynasties by God and 'endless indefeasible right' were dismissed as exploded. No greater sanctity was ascribed to hereditary monarchy than to any other form of established government.[32] Here he followed Hallifax, who in 1769 combated the doctrine that a Christian republic was a contradiction in terms.[33] In Bishop Horsley's sermon on King Charles's Day, passive obedience was enjoined as a universal obligation, but it was recognized that in Britain the monarch to whom it was owed was bound by 'a legal contract with the people', quite different from the theoretical original contract of the philosophers. It was expressed in the coronation oath, in Magna Carta, the Petition of Right, Habeas Corpus, the

---

[28] R. A. Soloway, *Prelates and People: Ecclesiastical Social Thought in England 1783–1852* (1969), 31–2.

[29] Horsley, *Sermons*, iii (1816), 293–321.

[30] Clark, *English Society*, chap. ii, *passim*; Dickinson, 'Eighteenth-Century Debate'. Cf. G. J. Schochet, *Patriarchalism in Political Thought* (Oxford, 1975).

[31] Dickinson, 'Eighteenth-Century Debate'.

[32] Horsley, *Sermons*, iii. 293–321.

[33] S. Hallifax, *Sermon before the House of Commons*, 30 Jan. 1769 (Cambridge, 1769).

Bill of Rights, and the Act of Settlement. Two provisions of the constitution answered for the king's performance of his side of the bargain—'the judicious partition of the legislative authority between the king and the two houses of Parliament' and 'the responsibility attaching upon the advisers and official servants of the Crown'.

What the bishop thought he had delivered was not a eulogy of divine-right monarchy but a defence of the existing constitution, 'its basis religion, its end liberty', against 'that god of the republican's idolatry the consent of the ungoverned millions of mankind'. As such it had some claim upon the respect of the vast majority of oligarchically minded politicians of the time, whether ministerialist or moderate Whig. But the form of the argument had a touch of old-fashioned Toryism which, in the savage conflicts over domestic order in the 1790s, could be used to present the author as a backwoodsman. Radical Whigs like Sheridan pounced on his call for passive obedience, and sought to equate him with Sacheverell.[34] This was no longer a serious charge now that the Glorious Revolution was beyond reversal. A more relevant indictment stemmed from the strength of his devotion to the monarchical principle. It cannot be denied that in his theory of the constitution the Crown held a paramount place. His 1793 sermon in Westminster Abbey postulated that it was the king who entered the contract with his people, while the 'principal means and safeguard of liberty' was 'the majesty of the sovereign'. For Horsley, the monarch was ever the touchstone of the constitution, his ultimate authority the proof against popular encroachment which he, like most Whig and Pittite parliamentarians, dreaded.

The fear was not surprising. During the 1790s Government in Britain was subjected to the most sustained pressures from outside Parliament since the restoration of the monarchy. Implied in this was a recognition that because of the smallness of the electorate and the very general use of patronage at elections, the representation of the people in the House of Commons worked badly. As a contemporary earl of Fife correctly judged, the origins of effective extra-parliamentary political organization dated from 'the Associated Reform in Yorkshire' in 1779–80,[35] but it was from the clash between a reinvigorated Anglican loyalism, which Burke and Horsley in their different ways stimulated, and a resurgent liberalism moving to celebrate the centenary of the Glorious Revolution, that revival sprang a decade afterwards. Professor Albert Goodwin has shown[36] that there was a continuity in the development of agitation for reform from the banquets of the London Revolution Society in 1788–9, to the self-renewal of the Society for Constitutional Information in December 1789 and the rise of the popular societies in London and the

[34] Clark, *English Society*, 233.
[35] Roger Wells, *Insurrection: The British Experience 1795–1803* (Gloucester, 1983), 1.
[36] Albert Goodwin, *The Friends of Liberty: The English Democratic Movement in the Age of the French Revolution* (1979), *passim*.

provinces in 1792. Class fissures did less to interrupt it than was once believed. Defiance of Government mounted. What they lost in 'respectability', they gained in defiance. According to Dr Clive Emsley there were more provincial prosecutions for seditious words in 1793 than in any other year during the decade. Scottish reformers called a Convention to Edinburgh in November. It was dominated by English delegates, who projected an English Convention for the following spring. A Committee of Secrecy appointed by Parliament described it as 'an open attempt to supersede the House of Commons in its representative capacity, and to assume to itself all the functions and powers of a national legislature'.[37] The idea of Convention had been mooted before in British Radical history. It could mean much or little. But the widespread dissemination of Paine's *Rights of Man* with its alternative political philosophy of popular sovereignty gave to the proposal on this occasion a sweeping significance. Moreover, as Dr Roger Wells observes, 'those activists who really did understand the fullest implications of democracy—a minority to be sure—were quite capable of linking democratic politics and popular grievances'.[38] Hence in the famine year 1795 the London Corresponding Society launched the soon to be familiar device of holding large open-air meetings to voice its plans for universal suffrage and annual Parliaments.[39]

It was these developments which caused His Majesty's Government, hitherto content to enforce the existing law against sedition, to approach Parliament for new powers. Habeas corpus was suspended by statute in 1794, but for less than a year in the first instance and only in cases involving treason and treasonable practices. In November 1795, following attacks on the royal coach as King George III travelled to and from Westminster for the opening of Parliament, two bills were introduced: one to render actions against the king and his heirs capital offences and to extend treason to cover incitement to hatred of the monarch, his heirs, his ministers, or the constitution, by speech or writing; the other to restrict public meetings to less than fifty persons unless a magistrate was notified well in advance, and to empower justices to control meetings and lecture halls. Because of the difficulty of enforcing them, the 'Two Acts' are no longer regarded by all historians as 'a new departure in English law'.[40] It must nevertheless be insisted that contemporaries in the country, Whigs, anti-war liberals, popular radicals, and many independents concurred in opposing them as an infringement of liberty.[41] Even in Parliament, where easy majorities were eventually secured, Pitt and Grenville

---

[37] Clive Emsley, 'Repression, "Terror" and the Rule of Law in England during the Decade of the French Revolution', *English Historical Review*, 100 (1985), 801–25.

[38] Wells, *Insurrection* 21.

[39] Goodwin, *Friends of Liberty* 372–3, 384–5.

[40] Cf. Emsley, 'Repression'.

[41] J. E. Cookson, *The Friends of Peace: Anti-War Liberalism in England, 1793–1815* (Cambridge, 1982), 123.

found it expedient to give them a very soft sell.[42] Bishop Horsley did much to counteract the good which this may have effected, for he was utterly indiscreet.

The trouble began on 11 November when the peers debated the clause of the Treasonable and Seditious Practices Bill which, as it stood, imposed a sentence of up to seven years' transportation for criticizing the 'established government, or constitution of the realm'. Lord Thurlow observed that under this men might be transported for mentioning that 'twenty acres of Land, at the foot of a hill called Old Sarum, sent two representatives to Parliament'. Horsley spoke in favour of the clause and of every part of the bill 'without going into any abstract questions about the borough of Old Sarum, or any other place'. At this point the Whig duke of Bedford intervened to trip him, urging that unless every borough were treated as a component part of the House of Commons and every law as a part of the constitution, a man might proceed from borough to borough and from county to county until he had proved that the whole system of representation in the House of Commons was corrupt. The bishop conceded the point, but instead of letting the matter drop he proceeded, by way of disclaiming any need to interfere with 'speculative and philosophical disquisitions', to explain that the bill was 'merely directed against those idle and seditious public meetings for the discussion of the laws where the people were not competent to decide upon them'. His further words were reported as follows by the *Parliamentary Register*: 'He was of the opinion, that assemblies of people, for the purpose of discussing public measures, were illegal, and calculated only to do mischief. He declared, that individuals had nothing to do with laws, except to obey them.' Cobbett's derivative *Parliamentary History* changed this to the more provocative: 'he did not know what the mass of the people in any country had to do with the laws but to obey them.' The first formulation is more likely to be correct, but in either case the bishop had played straight into the hands of the Opposition leaders, who aimed to present the clause and indeed the whole bill as a 'flagitious outrage on the liberty of the subject'. Bedford reminded him 'that the right of the people to assemble and discuss the laws, was the peculiar characteristic, and an essential part of the British Constitution', instancing meetings of shopkeepers for the repeal of the shop-tax.

Sensing that he had gone too far, Horsley agreed that any body of individuals who felt themselves to be oppressed by a law had a right to meet to represent their grievances to the legislature—he was thinking of trading interests—but it was too late to prevent the earl of Lauderdale, an opponent with whom he had crossed swords before, from likening his opinions to those of 'the Mufti . . . in the Turkish Divan'.[43] The Islamic figure still hovered over

---

[42] John Ehrman, *The Younger Pitt: The Reluctant Transition* (1983), 455–9.
[43] *Parl. Reg.*, 2nd ser., xlv (1795–6), 88–98; *Parl. Hist.* xxii (1795–7), 257–8.

the debate when Bedford and Lauderdale resumed the attack on the bill at its third reading on 13 November. Denying the alleged connection between the attack on the king and certain seditious meetings, the former taunted the bishop of Rochester with having changed his view of the rights of the people, as he had once attended a reform meeting in Southwark—it turned out to have been a parliamentary election which he attended about fourteen years earlier to serve the anti-Government candidate for personal reasons. He also taxed Grenville, the Leader of the House, with being a convert to the prelate's present opinions.

Horsley, who had cried loudly 'Hear, Hear' when the noble duke reminded the House of his avowal that 'the people' had nothing to do with the laws but to obey them, took a more cautious stance when he rose to reply. He reaffirmed that 'subjects' had the duty only to obey the laws, but conceded that they had the obligation to study them and a 'right to state their grievances, and by all lawful and constitutional measures, to endeavour to obtain a repeal of such laws as appear to them partial and oppressive'. But to say that 'under these restrictions' 'the individual' had nothing to do with the laws but to obey them was not to admit that the present bill was 'more calculated for the meridian of Constantinople than of Britain', for 'in that miserable and despotic country, the inhabitants are neither called to study nor to obey the laws, for, unhappy people, they have none!' 'The rule of our conduct as Britons', he averred, 'is to be found in the statute book of this kingdom.'[44]

Horsley had thus to some extent redeemed his mistake. By taking his stand upon the rule of law, he robbed the Whig charges against himself and Government of their most damaging thrust, the suggestion that the constitution was being dismantled and that the country was to be ruled by force.[45] He had nevertheless exposed himself to ridicule. A satirical squib, headed 'From an Ancient Horsleian Manuscript, found in the Cathedral of Rochester. Trial and Execution of the Grand Mufti', was drawn up for local circulation. Purporting to describe a demonstration which culminated in hanging the victim in effigy to a tree outside his cathedral, it contained many amusing but unflattering allusions to the bishop's habits and appearance—bull-like features, rotundity, blotchy skin, and fondness for the table and the wine-cellar.[46] Whether or not it was based on any real occurrence, which can at the most have been inconsiderable, the tract did him little harm.

The authoritarianism of his pronouncements became even more explicit in the years to come. He had declared war on the press in his speech on 13 November, rejoicing that the bill being debated would check its licentious-

---

[44] *Parl. Reg.*, 2nd ser., xlv (1795–6), 110–16.
[45] Emsley, 'Repression'.
[46] *Trial and Execution of the Grand Mufti* (?1795).

ness.[47] When the young earl of Oxford, finding that his motion for peace with France had not been entered in the Journals of the House of Lords, published his Protest in the *Oracle and Public Advertiser*, instead of entering it in the Journal, Horsley came down to the House on 30 March 1797 brandishing a copy of the offending print, and moved the reading of the standing order of November 1777, which forbade peers to publish the proceedings of the Upper House without leave of their Lordships on pain of high breach of privilege. Strictly he was right to do so, though Oxford could plead extenuating circumstances in that the Lord Chancellor had carried away his motion so that it could not be entered in the Journal. But the bishop in his attack fastened particularly on that portion of the publication which affirmed that 'the people of Great Britain have a right, and ought to be fairly and equally represented in that which, by its very name, is their House of Parliament'. This he regarded as 'Very audacious, and very unconstitutional language', for 'He conceived the Parliament to be the King's Parliament, and not the Parliament of the People.' The Marquis Townshend corrected him: 'He had always been taught to believe, that the Parliament was the Parliament of the Nation, of which the King formed only a component, though certainly the highest part.' But Horsley replied: 'It was "convened at the will and pleasure of the King: it was prorogued at his will; and it was dissolved when and so often as he thought proper." Could any thing be more strongly convincing that it was the King's Parliament?'[48] There is no reason to believe that he wished to confer on George III authority to rule without Parliament, just as it is inconceivable that he desired to reduce the people of England to the status of helots governed by laws which they had no share in making. But the name of Samuel Horsley must be added to those of other Anglican publicists who responded to the total threat of Painite democracy by falling back on personalized theories of government which they somehow managed to hold in tension with the eighteenth-century norms of limited monarchy. John Reeves, whose *Thoughts on the English Government* (1795) was quoted as maintaining that the 'Kingly Government may go on, in all its functions, without Lords or Commons' and was nearly convicted of seditious libel for these extreme words by action of the Younger Pitt's administration, nevertheless ended by issuing a justification in terms of 'Revolution Principles' knitting together 'hereditary monarchy' and 'its laws and government'.[49] Jonathan Boucher, another High Churchman, published sermons in 1797 displaying elements of a patriarchal theory of the State derived from Filmer, but he remained an essentially eighteenth-century conservative constitutionalist believing in the rule of law.[50] These and other

[47] *Parl. Reg.*, 2nd ser., xlv (1795–6), 113–15.
[48] Ibid., 3rd ser., iii (1796–7), 141–5.
[49] Quoted from Clark, *English Society*, 264–5.
[50] U. Y. Zimmer and A. H. Kelly, 'Jonathan Boucher: Constitutional Conservative', *Journal of American History*, 58 (1971–2), 897–922.

effusions exposed the High Church cause to clinging accusations from the Whigs that they upheld old-fashioned notions of *iure divino* monarchy.

Horsley's record on civil liberties was marked, moreover, by certain redeeming features. He believed that laws, even repressive laws against sedition, should be administered impartially and with regard to humanity. When the Seditious Meetings and Assemblies Bill was before the House of Lords on 12 December 1795, he supported an amendment by Lord Lauderdale to remove an ambiguity which might have allowed the Scottish judges to impose the death sentence for an offence which in England carried a £50 fine. 'He said, that in all cases where the penalty of death was inflicted, the law ought to be as explicit as possible, and that the life of a fellow creature should never be at the mercy of the folly, the ignorance or the iniquity of a Judge.'[51] The motion was lost by the firm opposition of the Government's legal experts. His impartiality was put to the test on 20 June 1799 when a further bill for suppressing seditious gatherings came up for its third reading. The earl of Radnor moved the omission of a clause which exempted lodges of Freemasons from its provisions. He mentioned that these administered secret oaths and referred by name to John Robison's *Proofs of a Conspiracy against all the Religions and Governments of Europe*, a work published in 1797, which indicted Continental Freemasons and Illuminati of a conspiracy to overthrow all Governments. The motion was largely designed to embarrass Horsley, who, though he was a devoted admirer of the opinions of Robison, a fellow mathematician and a Scot, was also a Freemason belonging to a branch which existed in Scotland. The bishop reacted honestly. Declaring his interest, he did his best to clear Freemasonry in Britain of the imputation of disloyalty or impiety. But he supported Radnor's amendment on the ground that doctrines of revolution and anarchy had been insidiously grafted on to the institution in Europe and especially in Germany and that the book published about two years earlier had proved the existence of no less than eight 'illuminated lodges' already in this country. The outcome of the debate was that the amendment was carried, but that Lord Grenville, not himself a Mason, then brought forward a procedure by which existing English lodges could obtain protection by making an annual declaration of self-limitation to Masonic purposes.[52]

The bishop's finest contribution to British politics, however, was his sustained participation in the campaign for the abolition of the slave trade. This has gone unrecognized in studies of the movement which have seized on Beilby Porteus as the one outstanding episcopal figure involved in it. Abolitionism has been seen as an Evangelical, Quaker, politically ambivalent, but largely Foxite enterprise, into which a furious High Churchman cannot

[51] *Parl. Reg.*, 2nd ser., xlv (1795–6), 178–9.
[52] *Parl. Reg.*, 3rd ser., ix (1799), 26–8.

easily be fitted. Drescher, it is true, has lately suggested a broader participation.[53] But Samuel Horsley's opposition to the trade cannot be explained by
any group activity; it was intensely personal. With Wilberforce, his relations
were almost uniformly bad, fouled by the latter's involvement in Bentham's
penitentiary scheme and his unwelcome enquiries into the books from the
Abbey Library which he wished to consult when writing his *Practical View*.
Wilberforce's behaviour was somewhat devious. He admitted to a desire to
conceal from the dean of Westminster the identity of the works which he
wanted to use, and followed his enquiry by asking the bishop of London,
Porteus, rather than Bishop Pretyman, dean of St Paul's, whether he might
draw upon the resources of the cathedral library instead. The incident illustrates the mistrust existing between Wilberforce and the High Church
prelates over his writing the aggressively Evangelical *Practical View*.[54] But the
slave trade was a different matter. Contemporaries assigned to Horsley the
role of a prime mover in the Lords. In March 1794 the duke of Clarence
(later King William IV), a firm opponent of abolition, alleged in debate that
the reason why the slave trade had not been brought forward previously that
session was from consideration to the bishop whose ill health had prevented
him from attending Parliament until that day.[55] It was true that he had made
only three earlier appearances since January.

His convictions followed a general change in the spirit of the age, which
Anstey has discerned in the later eighteenth century, entailing a shift to a
more generous attitude towards subject peoples. 'Nearly every school of
thought which dealt with ethical problems had, from about the middle of
the century, come up with specific condemnations of slavery sometimes
persuasively encapsulated in a corpus of moral or legal philosophy... Dr.
Johnson strongly opposed it; as did Rousseau whom Johnson detested.'[56]
Horsley may well have sharpened his hatred of the slave trade in the Doctor's
Essex Head Club. Other members of that circle—Boswell, Windham, and
Bennet Langton—joined Clarkson as he enlisted support in the preparations
for the assault.[57] But the bishop's thrust was deeper and more lasting. He had
an emotive commitment to the extirpation of the trade, which he denounced
to the House in 1804, in terms he ascribed to Stanhope, as 'a traffic... in
human tears and groans, in human flesh and blood, and carried on under
every criminal aggravation of cruelty, of chains, of murder'.[58] His case against
the African slave trade transcended the criteria of liberty, benevolence, and
happiness, which eighteenth-century philosophers such as Hutcheson and

[53] S. Drescher, *Capitalism and Anti-Slavery* (1986), 123–4.
[54] John Pollock, *Wilberforce* (Tring, 1986), 138, 146.
[55] *Parl. Reg.*, 2nd ser., xxxix (1794), 152–4
[56] R. Anstey, *The Atlantic Slave Trade and British Abolition 1760–1810* (1975), 94–5.
[57] Pollock, *Wilberforce*, 56; Anstey, *Atlantic Slave Trade* 250.
[58] *Parl. Deb.*, 1st ser., ii (1804), 929.

Montesquieu used against slavery. It bypassed the theological analogies drawn by Evangelicals,[59] and took root in a belief about the nature of man. Distinguishing more carefully than was usual in abolitionist polemic between the trade and the institution of slavery, which he professed it impolitic and even mischievous to attack,[60] he condemned the former roundly as an affront to human dignity. The argument was sufficiently close to the ideology of Tom Paine to require an explicit differentiation. Thus the bishop told the Upper House when speaking on Wilberforce's bill to suspend the trade in 1799:

My Lords, we who contend for the abolition, proceed upon no visionary notions of equality and imprescriptible rights of men. We strenuously uphold the gradations of civil society. But we do, indeed, my Lords, affirm, that those gradations, both ways, both ascending and descending, are limited. There is an exorbitance of power, to which no good king will aspire; and there is an extreme condition of subjection, to which man cannot, without injustice, be degraded. And this, we say, is the condition of the African carried away into slavery.[61]

It was the act of selling that clinched the degradation. In the closing paragraphs of an exceedingly lengthy speech Horsley turned to examine the validity of the scriptural arguments used to defend slavery. He admitted that the Bible contained no explicit prohibition of it, but countered with a warning that it would be 'extravagant and dangerous' to infer that what was not expressly reprobated in the Scriptures was sanctioned by them. That would be to convey religious sanction on the cruelties practised by King David against the Ammonites, 'when he put them under axes, and saws of iron, and harrows of iron, and made them pass through the brick-kilns', for these severities were not condemned in the telling. But the slave trade was a different matter. By an ingenious exegesis of 1 Timothy 1: 10 he claimed 'an express reprobation' of the traffic, in holy writ. Among the sins berated by the apostle, 'man-stealing', that is kidnapping and panyaring, was placed next to parricide, homicide, and sodomy. With the bishop's claim that this text outlawed one of the most productive modes of supplying the trade (that is slave-raiding by African chiefs) it is hard to disagree, but wishing to condemn the whole traffic (some of which consisted of bartering manpower obtained by native rulers through the tribute or taxation system, or sold by poorer peoples to their richer neighbours), he proceeded as follows:

The original word, for which the English Bible gives 'men-stealers', is ἀνδραποδιστὴς Our translators have taken the word in the restricted sense, which it bears in the Attic law; in which the δίκη ἀνδραποδισμοῦ was a criminal prosecution for the specific crime of kidnapping, the penalty of which was death. But

---

[59] Anstey, *Atlantic Slave Trade*, chaps. 4, 5.

[60] On 17 Apr. 1793 he said he 'only would avail himself of the arguments in favour of the abolition'. *Parl. Reg.*, 2nd ser., xxxvi (1793), 180.

[61] *Parl. Reg.*, 3rd ser., ix (1799), 538–57.

your Lordships know, that the phraseology of the Holy Scriptures, especially in the preceptive part, is a popular phraseology: and my noble and learned friend opposite me, very well knows, that ἀνδραποδιστὴς in its popular sense, is a person who 'deals in men', literally, a slave-trader.[62]

Wilberforce, not without warrant, thought the application 'ill-judged'.[63] It indicates fairly enough, however, the character of Horsley's objection to the trade—one which was raised on occasion by statesmen of varying politics. Fox quoted Burke that the slave trade was 'not a traffic in the labour of man but in the man himself'.[64] Stanhope asked the House in 1804: 'What was the slave trade? It was the going and seizing, or purchasing from those who had seized, a parcel of unhappy beings, over whom neither God nor nature gave us any control.'[65] To call it a 'trade in flesh and blood' was the deadliest of labels to fasten on the slave trade. It had the same devastating effect as was later to be inflicted on the Corn Laws by dubbing them 'the bread tax'.

Samuel Horsley was thrust to the centre of the stage just when abolitionist fortunes entered a long phase of adversity. By an arduous struggle dating from 1787 William Wilberforce, supported by the prime minister, had brought the House of Commons, at the price of compromise, to accept five years later a motion for gradual abolition of the slave trade which should reach completion on 1 January 1796.[66] The decision of the Lords, when the question reached them in May 1792, to take evidence before bar on the Commons' resolutions, was the first major setback, for it led to nothing but interminable delays. The bishop shared the responsibility for the move, persuaded by earlier speakers that it was the best means of preparing the House to discuss 'the grand point' of abolition. He took an active part in examining witnesses, endeavouring to bring before the House the truth of the case, of which he had himself no doubt.[67] Resistance to abolition was more formidable in the Upper even than in the Lower Chamber. As Anstey has shown, the obduracy of the peers stemmed not so much from the presence of West India interests as from aristocratic recoil from Jacobinism, a greater sensitivity to intra-imperial relationships in the aftermath of the American Revolution and a less able presentation of the abolition case than in the Commons.[68] The last of these factors was strongly affected by the balance of forces within the Younger Pitt's Government. Lord Grenville, who had been leader of the House of Lords

---

[62] Ibid. For the organization of the slave trade in Africa and the various methods of gathering the slaves see Anstey, *Atlantic Slave Trade*, chap. 3. Horsley showed no knowledge of the particulars given above in parenthesis, but he was aware that some slaves were not obtained by violent methods.

[63] Jebb, 146–52.

[64] *Parl. Deb.*, 1st ser., vii (1806), 581.

[65] Ibid., 1st ser., ii (1804), 927.

[66] Pollock, *Wilberforce*, 115–16.

[67] *Parl. Hist.* xxix (1791–2), 1355; *Parl. Reg.*, 2nd ser., xlv (1795–6), 224–6.

[68] *Atlantic Slave Trade*, 315–18.

since November 1790 was an able man, and had been convinced since 1787 'on every principle of humanity, justice or religion' that the British slave trade should be abolished and the slaves eventually liberated. Not until 1794–5, however, did he find his feet in the Government or possess sufficient authority to act independently of Henry Dundas, who became Secretary of State for War (and effectively the Colonies) in the former year, and urged the necessity of taking no action on the slave trade which would upset the Caribbean legislatures.[69]

All obstacles to abolition were exacerbated by the progress of Revolution and the outbreak of war with France. Especially damaging was the successful rising of the Negroes and mulattos in St Dominique and San Domingo, the French and Spanish colonies in the island of Haiti, in 1791. The bloody massacres of Europeans struck terror into the hearts of British West Indian colonists, and deepened fears of alienating them or of encouraging their own slaves to revolt.[70]

In these conditions it was an asset to the abolitionists to number in their ranks so stalwart an upholder of the established order as the preacher of the King Charles's Day sermon in Westminster Abbey. When, two months after the outbreak of war with France, the earl of Abingdon rose in the Lords to move the postponement of further investigation of the slave trade by the House for what might in practice have been for ever, he urged that the abolitionist movement was inspired by the new philosophy of the French Revolution, and that its supporters, who were Quakers and Dissenters, would, if not stopped, go on to carry parliamentary reform, confiscation of Church lands, abolition of the House of Lords and of the monarchy. The royal duke of Clarence followed by pronouncing Wilberforce to be either a fanatic or a hypocrite. The bishop of St Davids was well equipped to dispel such phantasmagoria. He

said, though neither a correspondent with Condorcet, an admirer of French republicanism, or a friend to fanatics, yet he conceived that, before war was declared against France, he might communicate by letter with a man of sense, talk familiarly with a Dissenter, and converse on philosophy, without losing an atom of that veneration he had for our mixed monarchical government, or forfeiting an iota of his firm allegiance to the King and his true friendship for the constitution. But it so happened that he had no correspondents in France, and that he detested from his heart the principle which it is now evident actuated this Rebellion. He was, however, a friend to the bill for abolishing the slave trade, and having read and studied the whole of the evidence on that subject, and in great measure made up his mind upon it, he should certainly give his negative to the motion made by the noble Earl.[71]

---

[69] Jupp, *Lord Grenville*, 74, 187; Anstey, *Atlantic Slave Trade*, 308; Pollock, *Wilberforce*, 124–5.
[70] John Ehrman, *The Younger Pitt: The Years of Acclaim*, 399–400; id., *Reluctant Transition*, 262–3.
[71] *Parl. Reg.*, 2nd ser., xxxv (1793), 153–63.

It was a speech full of good sense and moderation, which proceeded to defend the orthodox or Calvinist Dissenters from charges of disloyalty: very different in tone from the extravagant outburst against the Sunday Schools seven years later which historians often quote against him.

Finding the disposition of the House against him, Abingdon withdrew his motion, and the examination before bar proceeded on its leisurely course. It was Horsley, however, who, revising his earlier stand in the light of experience, took action to jolt it forward by moving on 10 March 1794 that the further hearing of counsel and taking of evidence on the slave trade should be referred to a committee upstairs. This was the tactic which had brought Wilberforce a qualified victory in the Commons. The motion was opposed by Clarence, who pointed out that the West India trade benefited the country by £24 million per year and found employment for 25,000 seamen. Abingdon, in strange contrast with modern evaluation, criticized Bishop Horsley as a philosopher of the Brissotine school, and although Grenville lent him support, his expediting proposal was defeated by 14 votes to 42. He had the mortification of seeing his old patron Lord Thurlow ranged against him, though over the years this had become a not unfamiliar experience.[72]

A further setback occurred two months later when he was obliged to turn against a bill prohibiting the carrying of slaves in British bottoms to the colonies of foreign powers which Wilberforce had carried through the Commons on the second attempt.[73] At first, it would seem, he had given the impression of favouring it, for Lord Abingdon, as usual in firm opposition, turning to the bench of bishops, had addressed himself particularly to 'the Right Reverend Prelate whose mind has been so readily made upon this occasion', inviting him to look at it again 'with his microscopic eye (for, as a man of science, a microscopic eye he must have)'. When Lord Grenville then moved the postponement of the bill for three months (virtually its rejection at that time of the session), Bishop Horsley had no option but to follow him. Habitual loyalty to the Government lead in the House of Lords, as well as a special relationship with Grenville which had already started to form on the basis of a commonly held reforming Anglicanism, deflected him from his real inclinations. He had the embarrassment of explaining to the House the difference between 'not particularly objecting to the bill' and agreeing with the motion to destroy it. More convincingly, he added that in present circumstances the bill would prove nugatory as it would do nothing to prevent slaves from being landed on the portion of St Domingo occupied by the British whence they could be easily transferred to the Spanish port.

Grenville and Horsley were both taunted with inconsistency with their general principles. The former excused himself by stating that the Foreign

[72] Ibid., 2nd ser., xxxix (1794), 151–6.
[73] Pollock, *Wilberforce*, 123–5.

Slave Bill was but a partial remedy of a particular branch of the trade.[74] The Government's case lacked consistency, as Pitt had supported the bill in the Commons.[75] It may perhaps be assumed that rising optimism as to gains which were being made by the British task force sent to capture the French West Indian islands and to complete the occupation of St Domingo overcame scruples against including the slave trade in the extended commerce which the prime minister hoped would accrue from these victories.[76] For some years to come, moreover, Dundas, the most powerful advocate of the blue water strategy for winning the war against Revolutionary France, urged with regard to the British possessions in the Caribbean that 'prohibition of the trade with Africa ... would throw them entirely into the power of the enemy'.[77]

The decade following 1794 was unfruitful for abolition in any form. The inquiry before the bar of the House of Lords petered out without achievement or regret, and with no attempt being made by Bishop Horsley to continue it. Its dilatory procedures had been chiefly valuable to the anti-abolitionists who now derided Horsley and Grenville for not moving to retain it.[78] The bishop nevertheless gave strong support to such proposals from the Lower House as found their way from time to time into the Lords. Henry Thornton's Slave Trade Limitation Bill of 1799 was a half-measure designed to prohibit the export of slaves only from that part of the African coast north of Cape Palmas (the Windward Coast). It was opposed with the excuse that the passage which it attacked was less harmful to the slaves than the voyage from the Leeward Coast, east of that point. At the second reading Bishop Horsley turned his 'microscopic eye' on the evidence presented by the Opposition at the examination before bar:

My Lords, Mr Robert Hume made several voyages from different parts of the coast of Africa to the West Indies; and he has given his account upon his oath, of the time of each voyage, the total of his cargo, and the number of the deaths in each.

My Lords, in the year 1792 Mr. Robert Hume made a voyage from the Windward Coast to Jamaica. He made it in thirty-three days. He shipped upon the coast of Africa two hundred and sixty-five slaves, and twenty-three died in the Middle Passage. Twenty-three, my Lords, out of two hundred and sixty-five, in thirty-three days; thirty-three days are, as nearly as may be, one eleventh of a year; and eleven times twenty-three, is two hundred and fifty-three: and this would have been his loss by death, had the passage lasted a whole year: two hundred and fifty-three out of two hundred and sixty-five, the man would have lost within a very few of his whole cargo.

Now, my Lords, your Lordships know, that the importation of slaves above the age of twenty-five is prohibited, in the West Indies, by the Colonial Laws. I must therefore

---

[74] *Parl. Reg.*, 2nd ser., xxxix (1794), 274–8.
[75] Pollock, *Wilberforce*, 125.
[76] Ehrman, *Reluctant Transition*, 355–6.
[77] Anstey, *Atlantic Slave Trade*, 314–15.
[78] *Parl. Reg.*, 2nd ser., xlv (1795–6), 224–6.

assume, that this cargo of Mr. Robert Hume's, and other cargoes, which I shall have occasion to mention, was composed of persons not above the age of twenty-five years. My Lords, in this town of London, the rate of mortality, by the most approved tables which all calculators use, at the age of twenty-five, is not more than seventeen in one thousand in the year. Out of 1,000 persons living, of the age of 25, 17 and no more die in the town of London in year. In Mr. Hume's ship 253, my Lords, out of 265.

The bishop then entered into a similar leisurely calculation from Hume's voyage from the Gold Coast to St Vincent in 1795, which led him to conclude that the passage from the Leeward Coast was far the healthier, though the rate of mortality remained much higher than among a similar age-group living in London, when both were expressed for the same annual period (24 out of 215 as against 17 out of 1,000).[79]

Samuel Horsley's peculiar strength in debates rested not so much on flights of oratory or skilful use of imagery, though he was a fair master of irony, as on the ability to marshal a weight of facts behind his arguments. Less common in eighteenth-century Parliaments than in those of the nineteenth, this skill was displayed not only in presenting statistics but in the engagement of the geographical knowledge which his involvement in the Royal Society's explorations had encouraged him to amass. This also he exhibited in his speech on the 1799 bill. Taking the complaint of the slavers that the measure would deprive them of their best slaves, he admitted the truth of it, but turned the argument back on those who used it. The slaves from the northern portions of the African coast were the best not only because they were the healthiest and strongest but because they were the fittest for field labour, the most tractable, docile, and submissive. This implied that they were the most civilized, yet the slave trade was defended on the pretence of rescuing Africans from barbarism.

The slaves, procured upon this windward coast, are not the natives of the coast itself; they are brought down from remote parts of the interior country. The witnesses have told your Lordships, that these people reckon their time by moons, and describe the time that they are travelling to the coast as 5, 6, 7, and sometimes 8 moons: and the witnesses guess, that their rate of travelling may be 15 miles per day. I will take six moons as the time of the journey, and I will suppose they travel only twelve miles per day: 12 miles per day, for six months together, makes a journey of 2,124 British miles: and so many British miles, upon the parallel of the middle latitude of the Windward Coast, make 31 degrees and a half of longitude; and 31 degrees of longitude, eastward from the middle of the Windward Coast, carry us into the very heart of Africa, in the broadest part: and throughout this long tract of country, the natives, by the evidence of the witnesses themselves, bear the marks of incipient civilisation. But, my Lords, by the relation of Mr. Park, on which I rely more than on the united testimony of all these witnesses, through the whole extent of this country, civilisation is much more than incipient. Through this very country the line of Mr. Park's journey lay. And, my Lords,

[79] *Parl. Reg.*, 3rd ser., ix (1799), 543–5.

you cannot travel half a day with Mr. Park, in the whole route from Pisania to the very extremity of that line, but you will find all the way the pleasing vestiges of a civilisation that has already made some progress, and is heightening every step you go the farther you get in-land from the coast; that is the farther you recede from the stage, on which the slave trade perpetrates its horrors.[80]

From this he proceeded to give detailed examples drawn from Mungo Park's recently published account of his explorations up the Gambia river to the banks of the Niger, to show that the habitat, economy, and manners of the Mandingo people, through whose territory Park had passed, was far from being the undifferentiated savagery so often ascribed to African tribes by Europeans of that and later periods. His comments were 'curious' and perceptive, though the prodigious length to which the speech ran sometimes provoked their Lordships to laughter which he stopped to rebuke solemnly. Occasionally be interjected points which Park had missed. Thus:

Your Lordships, I am sure, must recollect the affecting story of the return of the blacksmith of Kasson to his native village. (By the way, my Lords, I must ask, is this a character of savage manners, that a young man goes from his home to a distinct country to find profitable employment in a trade?).[81]

Thornton's bill was lost by seven votes, but the bishop also delivered what Anstey deemed a very able speech in support of the Slave Carrying Bill which failed by only a hair's breadth in the same year. He worked hard on Wilberforce's bill for suspending the slave trade, which passed the Commons in 1804, but was nevertheless defeated in the Lords.[82] Total abolition of the trade was eventually carried by a stratagem devised by James Stephen and agreed by Wilberforce with the heads of the Ministry of All the Talents. Opponents were first disarmed by a bill forbidding the importation of slaves into captured enemy colonies (which might have to be returned as part of a peace deal) and the fitting-out British ships to trade in slaves with foreign territories. This was accepted as a war measure. It was followed almost immediately, as the schemers intended, by a general Anti-Slave Trade Bill, which passed the Lords by an overwhelming majority early in 1807.[83] Horsley was dead before victory was achieved. But he did not hesitate to endorse the method. Speaking at the third reading of the Foreign Slave Bill on 16 May 1806,

The Bishop of St. Asaph said, that a noble lord had characterised the bill before their lordships as abolition in disguise. He was no friend to anything in disguise; but while he was in that house, he would by every means in his power, whether fair or foul,

---

[80] Ibid. 549–50.
[81] Ibid. 551.
[82] *Parl. Deb.*, 1st ser., ii (1804), 874, 929–30, 931.
[83] Pollock, *Wilberforce*, chap. xx, *passim*.

whether by open hostility, or secret stratagem, labour to destroy that infamous traffic, which was no less a disgrace to humanity, than it was destructive of the morals of the nation.[84]

Shortly afterwards, on 24 June that year, he was provoked by an attempt of Lord Westmorland to quote Scripture in its support, to affirm that slavery itself, not merely the selling into slavery, was an evil degrading to mankind, 'abominable', and contrary to the Christian religion. [85] Doubtless this was what he had long believed but deemed damaging to the cause of abolishing the slave trade to say. Only two years earlier he had assured the House of Lords that the latter 'would gradually produce all the amelioration in the state and condition of African slaves that was practicable, or indeed desirable, and that he looked to no farther consequences whatever'.[86] But there are evident grounds for believing that, had he belonged to the next generation he would have stood with Wilberforce, still disapproving of his theological principles, in applauding the emancipation which was carried in 1833.

Late eighteenth-century sensitivity to the needs of subject peoples found expression not only in the crusade against the slave trade, but in other imperial affairs, chiefly those of India. It cannot be said that Bishop Horsley was alive to all her needs. From his place in the House of Lords he opposed the efforts of the Clapham Sect Evangelicals to introduce clauses into the East India Company's Charter in 1793, authorizing the engagement of school-masters or missionaries to work among the native population. His hostility may have been partly due to the strong connections of members of his family with the East India Company, which resisted the well-meaning intrusion vigorously. He expressed it, however, in the familiar language of his own conservative political theology. 'He conceived the religion of a country to be connected with its government, and he did not think that any foreign state had a right to interfere with the government of another country, without an express commission from Heaven.'[87]

It was with reference to the character of British rule, however, that the bishop made his principal contribution to the discussion of Indian affairs. He was among the foremost champions of Warren Hastings at his impeachment. The proceedings against Hastings on sundry charges of corruption, oppression, and maladministration during his former tenure as Governor-General lasted for nine years, 1786–95. The trial itself, which opened with a flourish in Westminster Hall in February 1788, attended initially by 164 peers, occupied thirty-five days of parliamentary time that year, seventeen in 1789, fourteen in 1790, five in 1791, twenty-two in 1792, twenty-two in 1793, twenty-eight in

---

[84] *Parl. Deb.*, 1st ser., vii (1806), 231.
[85] Ibid. 808.
[86] Ibid., 1st ser., ii (1804), 931.
[87] *Parl. Reg.*, 2nd ser., xxxv (1793), 242–6.

1794, while the finalities in 1795 continued from January to April.[88] It generated twenty volumes of parliamentary reports, eleven folio volumes of evidence, and 3,000 pages of oratory from managers and counsel.[89] On some petty instigation from Philip Francis, a malicious colleague of Hastings in the Governor-General's council, the Whig Opposition leaders Fox, Burke, and Sheridan raised the issue to national importance in order to serve their own purposes. For Fox it was largely a matter of putting Pitt in the wrong as Hastings's employer, just as for Pitt it became important to side-step the manœuvre by associating himself to a limited extent with the indictment.[90] But as the party interest flagged and attendances fell, 'the possessed purpose' of Edmund Burke, urged forward by Francis, kept things going. For Burke it was not just a man who stood his trial, but a standard of colonial administration. Hastings seemed the embodiment of Company power which perpetrated injustice after injustice upon the natives of India. To remedy this he and Fox had proposed to vest control of India in a parliamentary commission but the present Government had come to power on the shipwreck of his plans. The exposure of Warren Hastings was designed to vindicate Burke's moral purpose. The trial, in the event, did nothing of the sort. Hastings emerged from it neither as an oppressor nor as a peculator, but as a reforming governor overwhelmed by growth problems and struggling to keep his ship afloat by expedients which, if not always consonant with the highest ethical ideals, were at least appropriate to the circumstances and often necessary to the survival of the British raj. If anything was vindicated it was not, to use Professor Ian Christie's brilliant phrase, Burke's 'armchair administrator's answer' of a commission of Parliament but the on-the-spot, practical touch of the British colonial service.[91]

Samuel Horsley used his legal training to prove it to the House. His commitment to Hastings was strong and complete. At the end of the impeachment process he was one of the eighteen peers who found him not guilty on any charge.[92] The reasons for this may only be conjectured. His stance was consistent with his inclination towards the king's Government, for Hastings enjoyed favour at court, and was upheld by Thurlow, the king's chancellor, who presided over the trial even after Pitt had forced him out of office, while Lord Grenville, the ministerial leader in the House of Lords took a lenient view of his conduct.[93] This, however, cannot have been the principal determinant of his attitude, for in broad political perspective the impeachment was scarcely an issue dividing Government from Opposition, at least in its later

---

[88] Keith Feiling, *Warren Hastings* (1954), 352.
[89] Ibid. 367.
[90] Ian. R. Christie, *Wars and Revolutions: Britain 1760–1815* (1982), 203–4.
[91] Ibid. 150–2; cf. Feiling, *Warren Hastings*, 367–9.
[92] *Parl. Reg.*, 2nd ser., xlii (1794–5), 399, 403.
[93] Ehrman, *Years of Acclaim*, 445, 446–7; Jupp, *Lord Grenville*, 50–2.

stages, when fear of revolution had driven Burke and Windham into Pitt's camp while other prominent impeachers, Sheridan and Philip Francis, stayed with Fox. By the time the bishop of Rochester made his principal exertion against them the managers, in Feiling's phrase, met 'coldly as enemies'.[94] Personal loyalty seems to have been more important. Hastings was a distinguished pupil of Westminster School. He was the foremost of a group of Old Westminsters serving in India towards the close of the eighteenth century who had donated a silver cup, hallmarked 1785–6, for presentation to the King's Scholars of the School. As it was inscribed with the names of the donors, headed by that of Warren Hastings, it was known as the Warren Hastings Cup. Horsley's idolized son Heneage was a Westminster boy during the years of the trial, and became himself a King's Scholar in 1791.[95] Neither as dean of Westminster nor as father of Heneage could the bishop allow the name of so eminent an alumnus to be dragged through the mire by the excited invective of Edmund Burke, even if the claim that he had himself attended the School cannot be made good. Similar considerations doubtless weighed with Archbishop Markham, formerly headmaster of Westminster, in giving a complete clearance to Hastings, though in his case a strong personal attachment can be shown to have existed.[96]

A sense of fairness withal led Bishop Horsley to take up the cause. This he displayed in the way in which he pleaded it. He had listened attentively to the long-drawn-out proceedings of the early 1790s, when on a comparatively small number of days in each session their Lordships trooped over from their usual meeting place to Westminster Hall to constitute themselves a high court of justice, examine witnesses called by Hastings's counsel in his defence, and subject them to interminable cross-examination on every point. He took copious notes of the evidence given, waiting for the opportunity to use them in Hastings's defence.[97]

This came when ex-Lord Chancellor Thurlow intervened on 26 February 1795 to propose that the process should be taken into a committee of the whole House and that a new procedure should be adopted to clarify the taking of decisions on the Commons' articles, which, he claimed, were loosely and inaccurately drawn. Each article should, where necessary, be broken down into the specific criminal facts which it alleged.[98] Under Thurlow's strong lead the committee went through the charges one by one, and finished its

---

[94] Feiling, *Warren Hastings*, 362.

[95] G. Russell Barker and A. H. Stenning, *The Record of Old Westminsters: A Biographical List of All Those who are known to have been Educated at Westminster School from the Earliest Times to 1927* (1928), i, pp. xv, 480.

[96] Markham's son served under Hastings in India. He attended the annual dinner which the governor used to give for fellow Old Westminsters out there. So, curiously, did young Burke. Feiling, *Warren Hastings*, 211, 258.

[97] *Parl. Reg.*, 2nd ser., xxxiii (1792), 507–10; xxxix (1794), 385–6; xlii (1794–5), 244–5.

[98] Ibid. xlii (1794–5), 163–6.

business in just over a month. Bishop Horsley spoke on five of the articles or charges, and appeared at his best. To the Benares charge, that Hastings had persecuted the zemindar Chait Sing by deposing him from his state in 1781, Horsley replied, with truth, that Chait had been a disloyal and disaffected subject who had violated all the conditions of his tenure. He spurned, however, the defence made by Lord Shelburne that the raja was worthy of less credit because he had 'no line of ancestry to be proud of, no honourable lineage to boast'. He could not agree 'that it was of any consequence to the merits of the cause, whether Cheyt Sing could boast of a long line of ancestry or not. Be he of ever so obscure origin, he was entitled to justice as an individual, much as any other man standing in the same relationship to the British Government in India.' Doubtless he recalled that he was not himself a nobleman bishop, but the sentiments were not less laudable for that. Shelburne had a more sensitive point when he argued that Hastings should have been tried for this action by Muhammadan judges and a Muhammadan jury, but Horsley's reply that a 'British subject was entitled by British laws, to be tried by a British jury and British judges, acting upon the principles of justice recognised and established under the British constitution' was more in line with the developing idea of imperial trusteeship.[99]

Coming on 17 March, his speech on the seizure of the treasures of the begums of Oudh also pleaded a moral justification. Spurning the technical defence of Hastings that he was not responsible at English law for an action committed by the nawab Asof-ud-Daulah at his instigation, he invoked Grotius and the *ius gentium* to show that 'Justice in the eye of reason and morality, was due to every individual, whether the subject of a despotic prince or a free Government.' He referred to his notes of previous evidence for proof that by Muhammadan law and custom only an eighth of the treasures of the nawab's mother were her own property; the remainder belonged to her son Asof. On this he built his case that the governor was fully warranted in compelling the nawab to recover his own belongings in order to pay off his debts to the East India Company. A subsidiary plea was that of necessity. The begums had forfeited their rights by their rebelliousness, and Hastings had saved India by the measure which he had adopted in Oudh after the treaty of Chunar.[100] This was only half the story. Here, as in Benares, Hastings's need for money to sustain the Company's military ventures was a principal factor leading him to actions which themselves disturbed the *status quo*.[101]

Six days later the House turned its attention to the more squalid accusations of corruption. Horsley spoke at length on the motion, 'that the Commons had made good the sixth article, in so far as related to the sum of two lakhs of

---

[99] Ibid. 203, 204–5.
[100] Ibid. 244–5.
[101] Christie, *Wars and Revolutions*, 125.

rupees corruptly received from Sadamund, the buxey of Rajah Cheyt Sing'. The bishop admitted contradictions in the accounts, but scarcely thought that if Hastings had written a wilful falsehood from Cheltenham as to the date of endorsement of bonds, he would have eagerly sent to Bengal for these very bonds, which the moment they appeared would convict him of misrepresentation; nor if he had retreated through fear from an original intention to convert them to his own use would he have failed to cover his traces by backdating the endorsements to the day of receiving them. On the following day (24 March), when the residue of the sixth article was considered, the bishop was able to turn from worldly wisdom to something closer to his own profession. He quoted two passages of Scripture to demonstrate that it was the custom of the East to bring presents to the ruling prince, so much so that not to bring them was a mark of 'acting disobediently and contumaciously'. The presents received by Warren Hastings from Kelleram, Nundoolol, and the vizier were thereby compared with the vessels of gold and silver, the garments and armour, the spices, horses, and mules brought to Solomon, while 'the children of Belial', who brought no presents to Saul were 'the Jacobins of those days'.

Bishop Horsley spoke once more in the committee—on the article 'Contracts and Allowances'. He fixed on the only allegation in this group on which he thought the smallest doubt to exist, namely the opium contract granted in 1781 without advertisement to Stephen Sulivan, son of the chairman of the Company, who promptly sold it before executing any part of it for 350,000 sicca rupees to a man who subsequently resold it at an enhanced profit. The bishop sounded distinctly uncomfortable in defending Hastings's conduct on this count. He was highly critical of the practice of bestowing contracts without throwing them open to competitive tender, and calculated that in this case it had robbed the East India Company of £14,900 a year for five years. He was obliged to bolster his argument with pleas based on the governor's services to the Company in general and in respect of securing this valuable branch of the revenue in particular.[102]

Here as in several other respects Horsley stood on the reforming side of British public life. The inference to be drawn from this study of his political behaviour is that he was far from being the 'mufti' of Whig-Radical mythology. His conservative opinions usually sounded more extreme than they actually were because of the vehement language in which he chose to express them. A continuator of the Anglican Tory tradition which had been adjusted to the facts of the Glorious Revolution, he kept within the framework of acceptable constitutional ideas which in a broad sense of the word were known as Whig. His hatred of the democracy which welled up around him in the closing decades of the eighteenth century can scarcely be denied. But he was an ardent friend of certain kinds of liberty and an advocate of good

[102] *Parl. Reg.*, 2nd ser., xlii (1794–5), 287–9, 311–13, 368–70.

government. Professor D. E. Ginter's doubts whether it is meaningful to regard the British propertied classes as being simply fused at the crisis of the French Revolution into a solid 'party of order'[103] can be extended if one adds to the residual radicalism and reform evident at loyalist meetings a disposition towards more limited change on the conservative side of the political nation.

[103] D. E. Ginter, 'The Loyalist Association Movement of 1792–93 and British Public Opinion', *Historical Journal*, 9 (1966), 179–89.

12

'Militant Here in Earth'

FOR thirteen of the eighteen years when Horsley was a bishop, England was at war with France. Moreover, it was a different kind of war from those which had punctuated the eighteenth century. In March 1792, preaching in the Quebec Chapel, Marylebone for the benefit of the Philanthropic Society, he could still credibly pronounce on developments since the rise of Christianity: 'From that time forward the cruelty of war has gradually declined till in the present age not only captives, among Christians, are treated with humanity, and conquered provinces governed with equity, but in the actual prosecution of a war, it is become a maxim to abstain from all unnecessary violence. Wanton depredations are rarely committed upon private property; and the individual is skreened, as much as possible, from the evil of the public quarrel.'[1] The contrast with hints published in *The Times* only six years later, for the defence of London against invasion, could scarcely have been sharper. The twelfth in the series ran: 'No quarter to be given the enemy when found in the actual attempt of invading the country whether in transports, gun-boats, or otherwise.'[2] The international conflict into which Britain was plunged on 1 February 1793 was total, so far as eighteenth-century conditions would permit, because it was basic and ideological. As Dr Clive Emsley has recently insisted, it was undertaken by the French as a nation in the spirit of a crusade: Brissot's 'crusade of universal freedom'.[3] England, though with an intermingling of opportunistic motives, responded with what even the sanguine Prime Minister Pitt confessed to be a war 'against armed opinions'. He was following Burke whose *Letters on a Regicide Peace* had affirmed in 1796 that 'it is with an armed doctrine that we are at war... It is a colossus which bestrides our channel... It has one foot on a foreign shore, the other upon the British soil.'[4]

The bishop of Rochester, likewise, supported the war for anti-Jacobin reasons, and waxed increasingly patriotic as it ran its course. At first he contented himself with following Lord Grenville's lead in the House of Lords. The Foreign Secretary's mind was moving slowly towards a policy of military

---

[1] Horsley, *The Abounding of Iniquity...A Sermon Preached on Sunday, the 25th of March, 1792* (1792), 8.
[2] *The Times*, 25 Apr. 1798.
[3] Clive Emsley, *British Society and the French Wars 1793–1815* (1979), 2–3.
[4] Quoted from Norman Gash, 'From the Origins to Sir Robert Peel', in Lord Butler (ed.), *The Conservatives* (1977), 28, 32.

collaboration with counter-revolutionary forces in and on the borders of France while stopping short of working, as Burke desired, for a restoration of the Bourbon dynasty.[5] When on 7 April 1794 Lord Stanhope intervened in the Lords to condemn a speech by Lord Mansfield on a former occasion proposing an engagement with French royalists for such an object, Grenville roundly condemned his language, and the Lord Chancellor moved to delete the offensive preamble to his motion. Stanhope nevertheless insisted on pressing it to a vote, and was placed in a minority of one, whereupon the words were on Lord Grenville's initiative expunged from the Journal of the House. Bishop Horsley spoke late in the debate. Without entering into the issues of Stanhope's objection, which turned on the impolicy of fomenting civil war in France, he condemned the noble earl for making a motion on a subject which had already passed on a former occasion, and gave his approbation to the action taken by the Lords.[6]

During the next three years, when Government flexed to the strain of financing the war and of regulating the food supply in such a way as to reduce the threat of a breakdown of internal order, Horsley gave it a not undiscriminating support in Parliament. In the 1795 Budget Pitt proposed a loan of £18 million and a set of duties on wines and spirits, tea, wood imports, life insurance, the insurance of ships' cargoes, and hair powder. The last of these was grounded not only on revenue considerations but also on the need to conserve the grain constituent after the disastrous harvest of 1794 had ushered in alarming food riots.[7] Horsley was nevertheless persuaded by Major-General Lord Mulgrave, to support him in a bid to exempt half-pay officers from the new excise. Mulgrave, who was one of Pitt's chief military advisers, had cajoled the episcopal bench by claiming to have voted for exemption of the poorer clergy. This brought the bishop into conflict with his customary leader Lord Grenville, who pointed out that half-pay officers could fight without hair powder, to which Richmond added that many of them had retired from the army. The question, which was decided in the negative, was one which divided supporters of the Pittite administration and could be argued either way for its bearing on the good conduct of the war.[8] To the Foxite opposition who disparaged the national endeavour, however, Horsley would lend no support. When in December 1795 the earl of Mansfield, then Lord President of the Council, proposed, as a means of confronting the more serious deficiency of wheat at the harvest of the current year, that their Lordships should enter into an engagement to restrict the consumption of wheaten bread by their families by one-third, the Whig duke of Bedford dismissed the plan as futile and inadequate. He wanted legislative action to

[5] Peter Jupp, *Lord Grenville 1759–1834* (Oxford, 1985), 177–8, 187.
[6] *Parl Reg.*, 2nd ser., xxxix (1794), 210–11.
[7] Emsley, *British Society*, 41–3, 49.
[8] *Parl. Reg.*, 2nd ser., xlii (1794–5), 451–3.

regulate the composition of the loaf to two-thirds wheat and the rest potatoes. Lord Hawkesbury, president of the Board of Trade, made clear that the Government was not ready for compulsion, but Lauderdale, another leading Whig, flatly opposed the planned voluntary engagement as being likely to discourage further exertions to remedy the scarcity. Sourly, he ascribed the scarcity to the war and the impolitic measures of England. Bishop Horsley sprang to the defence of Government policy while upholding the old interventionist argument against it. He denied that the shortage arose entirely from the present war. The remedy ought to be not to reduce the price of the scarce commodity but to lessen its consumption. So far ministers were right. He averred that the association of the peers would have an effect, but he doubted whether anything short of legislative enactments would be sufficient. Noble lords should sign the engagement to convince their servants that they must abide by it, but a total prohibition of the making of fine bread was the only practical means of causing the 'middling' and lower classes to substitute a coarser variant in their diet. The peers and their domestics could turn to 'various viands' but wheaten bread was the 'luxury' of the poorer sort who were not likely to purchase any other unless compelled to do so.[9] As Dr Stern has shown, Parliament was not prepared to go to this length, hampered as it was by a mass of obscure laws upholding the medieval assize of bread. Voluntary pledges to restrict consumption were signed by members of both Houses, and resolutions widely circulated. But legislation was kept to the permissive level. By the 36 George III, c. xxii, bakers were authorized to use every kind of grain, grain mixture, and potatoes as well as the wholemeal wheat flour to which the urban South had grown accustomed.[10]

In this matter Horsley had gone beyond the Government in his advocacy of emergency measures. On the issue of increasing taxation he supported it unequivocally. Pitt's most important fiscal innovation in 1796 was a duty on inheritances passing in collateral succession. It was to be levied on all legacies given as annuities, on a sliding scale varying with the distance of the inheritor from the deceased. Lord Lauderdale attacked the proposal at its second reading in the Lords on 14 April, maintaining that by taxing not consumable articles but 'the whole capital stock of the nation', it introduced a dangerous new principle. An aggressive Scottish Presbyterian as well as a Whig, he incorporated in his assault a proposal for a tax on translations to bishoprics and presentations to good livings in the Church levied during the first four years of tenure, the period fixed for a collateral succession duty on real estate which was also planned by the Government. This brought Horsley to his feet to defend the Church of England. In 'all scenes of commotion' in the history of the world, he said, 'the plunder of the Church was the first subject'.

[9] Ibid., 2nd ser., xlv (1795–6), 209–13.
[10] W. M. Stern, 'The Bread Crisis in Britain, 1795–96', *Economica* (May, 1964), 168–87.

Clergymen were taxed in the same manner as laymen, except that the residences of bishops and deans were exempt from parochial taxes. Lauderdale
then attacked 'the high tone and assumed importance' of the bishop's speeches,
and urged him not to misconstrue the utterances of others. Horsley replied by
imputing ignorance to the earl concerning special ecclesiastical taxation (first-
fruits, tenths, and various fees on presentation), adding that he would not have
expected him to complain of 'high tones and harsh expressions'. He and
Lauderdale always showed their worst sides to each other. Lord Grenville,
who had moved the passing of the tax, intervened to support the bishop of
Rochester's remarks about church property, and when Lauderdale renewed
his onslaught on the principle of the bill at the third reading that prelate
repaid the Foreign Secretary's indulgence by entering upon a general defence
of the measure. He set out to demolish the earl's hyperbolic remarks that
together with the corresponding duty on land the proposed tax 'went to sweep
all the property of the kingdom into the hands of the government'. Affecting
to have 'been at pains to make some calculations on the subject', he produced
the hypothesis, hardly more than an intelligent guess, that a piece of property
would 'descend in collateral succession eleven times in two hundred and
twenty years' on average, arguing loosely that this would be the time it would
take for the sum of £100 to be annihilated by the payment of tax at not more
than 6 per cent. He pointed out that the calculation would be 'a decreasing
series' as the sum remaining to be taxed would diminish with each levy, but
that in practice the remainders would either be consumed by their owners or
invested to offset the loss by taxation and perhaps grow. Lauderdale, a
political economist, could only retire, baffled by this ingenious display of
pseudo-science, which was not without point. The bill was accepted, though
the tax on real estate was abandoned by the prime minister.[11]

There was evidently a reciprocity in the day-to-day working of the alliance
of Church and State, but something stronger than that was needed to explain
Bishop Horsley's passionate reaction to the French invasion threat in 1797–8.
In most histories of the war written from the British angle this episode is
comparatively neglected. It is true that the greatest danger of invasion came in
1803–5, when Napoleon had established an autocratic control within France,
and France could rely on the firm support of her dependants.[12] On the earlier
occasion her plans to mount a direct assault on the island fortress were as
fickle as the Government of the Directory itself. Nevertheless, they did exist,
under the surveillance of Louis Lazare Hoche, still the most influential of the
French marshals and for a time minister of war.[13] An Army of England was
assembled, dispersed, and gathered again at Brest and other Channel ports,[14]

---

[11] *Parl. Reg.*, 2nd ser., xlv (1795–6), 258–71; cf. Emsley, *British Society*, 50.
[12] Ibid. 99.
[13] Georges Lefebvre, *The French Revolution from 1793 to 1799* (1967), 182.
[14] James Dugan, *The Great Mutiny* (1970), 418.

and reports reached England from an American traveller as early as October 1796 that the French were making 'a great number of gun-boats', fitted to carry 200 men apiece and equipped with wheels to enable them to be drawn on shore, and with a 24-pounder in the bow.[15] The first blows were struck in the following winter. They went badly astray. The amphibious expedition to disaffected Ireland, led by Hoche in person, was prevented from landing by quarrelling commanders and adverse winds at Christmas-time. On 18 February 1797 a large body of convicts of the Légion Noire under a former American rebel colonel sailed for Bristol with the objectives of raising an insurrection, intercepting commerce, and probably preparing the way for a further descent upon Ireland to assist the designs of Wolfe Tone. The transports got no further than Fishguard, and their occupants, after harassing a few Welsh farmsteads, surrendered to the county forces three days later. The chief significance of this incident lay in the panic which it aroused, extending to the City of London.[16] Samuel Horsley was sufficiently excited by it to pass on rumours even when he did not believe them. He wrote to his undergraduate son in March: 'If you have had the same reports in Oxford that have been spredde in London—of the escape of the French prisoners—of 2,000 more landed at Swansea & of the town of Carmarthen burnt down, you may rest assured there is not the least foundation for any one of them.' But throughout the year he watched the English naval victories at St Vincent and at Camperdown with an interest which stemmed from support of the Government as well as from pride of country. Admiral Duncan's worsting of the Dutch fleet in October was, he told Heneage, 'certainly one of the happiest events of the whole war, and comes very seasonable indeed for the minister'.[17]

It was in 1798 that a more urgent moralizing tone entered his commentary. Approving Pitt's revolutionary budget, excepting 'the trebling and quadrupling scheme', he observed: 'The nobles and the prelates must lay aside their robes, and take the sagum, rather than not crush the ambition of this execrable Republic.'[18] His advocacy of extreme measures became more marked, but he never lost sight of the need to preserve the sovereignty of Parliament. When Grenville moved in the House an address to the king signifying readiness to adopt the unconstitutional proposal to send the militia out of England to subdue the rebellion which had broken out in Ireland in May, Horsley urged that 'the legislature itself should by its own act, in times of great danger, suspend those particular restrictions of the laws which fetter the Executive Government in the exertions which the crisis may demand'.[19]

---

[15] James Greig (ed.), *The Farington Diary* (1923–8), i. *1793–1802*, 165–6.
[16] Dugan, *The Great Mutiny*, 40–55.
[17] HP 1767, fos. 114–15, 118–19, S. to H. Horsley, 3 Mar. and 22 Oct. 1797.
[18] Ibid. fos. 128–9, do. to do., [n.d.] 1797.
[19] Jebb, 146.

The sense of emergency was not confined to Ireland. After the Fructidor *coup* (4 September 1797) had strengthened the influence of the war party in the Directory, the Army of England was assembled for a landing on the south coast, and a patriotic loan was raised to support this expedition in the winter of the Year 6. It was to be repaid from the receipts of taxes to be levied on conquered English territory. April 1798 was the date set. On Bonaparte's advice (the Anglophobe Hoche having died prematurely in the preceding autumn) the invasion plan was laid aside by 'Ventose' in favour of glistering visions of conquest in Malta and Egypt.[20] But across the Channel feverish preparations to repel it continued into May. Initiatives for organizing the people into corps of armed volunteers sprang up from every side, from the High Sheriff of Dorset who wanted to base them on the posse comitatus, to the marquis of Buckingham who directed the Buckinghamshire quarter sessions to follow his lead. The Government lent encouragement in April with an Act authorizing the recruitment of armed associations,[21] while in London plans were advertised for erecting blockhouses in every square and barricades in every street, to be manned by the inhabitants who were to be supplied with hand-grenades and summoned to their posts by bells.[22] So widespread did the volunteering become that it interfered with the practice of ordinary vocations, and conscientious doubts arose among gentlemen, farmers, and manufacturers whether their services or those of their employees could be spared.[23] These extended to the clergy, normally immune from combative service, but now frequently impelled by Tory zeal to enrol. The archbishop of Canterbury called a meeting of bishops then in London to the Bounty Office on 28 April to give advice. It was attended by the two English primates and eleven other bishops. A wide difference of opinion was revealed, and the prelates failed to agree on a general letter to be sent to the clergy. As Samuel Denne, vicar of Wilmington, explained shortly afterwards to his friend Richard Gough the antiquary, the bishop of Rochester 'was singular in his opinion at first, and zealous in maintaining it, that his brethren ought forthwith to be trained to the use of arms', but he 'was with dignity answered by the Archbishop of York [Markham]'. Compromise resolutions were passed, and it was left to individual bishops to advise the pastors of their own dioceses. Archbishop Moore, who was under strong pressure from agitated clergymen, was insistent that this should be done as soon as might be convenient. The first resolution proclaimed that it would not conduce significantly to the defence of the kingdom, and would 'interfere with the proper duties of the profession' if the clergy accepted commissions in the army, enrolled in military corps, or were

---

[20] H. Martyn Lyons, *France under the Directory* (Cambridge, 1975), 201; cf. A. T. Mahan, *The Influence of Sea Power upon the French Revolution and Empire 1793–1812* (1892), i. 253.

[21] Emsley, *British Society*, 72–3.

[22] *The Times*, 25 Apr. 1798.

[23] Emsley, *British Society*, 73–4.

trained to the use of arms; the second allowed that 'in the case of actual invasion, or dangerous insurrection' it would be the duty of every clergymen 'to give his assistance in repelling both, in any way that the urgency of the case may require'. The archbishop and Bishop Horsley drew up printed circulars to their clergy which were published in the reviews; it is not clear whether any other bishops did so. The two were very different in tone. The primate's kept close to the wording of the resolutions, adding only that a particular service which the clergy could perform in an emergency was to 'be the instruments of maintaining internal harmony and subordination'.[24]

Horsley's pastoral to the Rochester clergy, issued from Westminster, was at once more practical and more spirited. It conveyed the text of the resolutions, but added some glosses of his own. These included hints for civil defence:

It is true, that even under the urgency of that extreme necessity, of invasion or insurrection, there will be many ways in which a clergyman may be useful, besides that of actual military service: In directing, for instance, and superintending the removal of the women and children, and of the old and infirm, to places of safety: in advising the method and pointing out the route of driving off the livestock: in overseeing the destruction of such things as cannot be removed, and would be serviceable to the enemy if they were to fall into their hands: and in many other very important, though indirect and collateral operations of defence, which it is impossible to enumerate.

But the letter began by proclaiming a crusade 'against an enemy, who threatens to come with a prodigious army, to depose our King, to plunder our property, to enslave our persons, and to overturn our altars; instigated, in addition to the common motives of ambition and revenge . . . by that desperate malignity, against the faith he has abandoned, which in all ages, has marked the horrible character of the vile apostate'—a clear allusion to Antichrist. Accepting that disorders and scandals would arise if the clergy were to accept military commission, or submit to be drilled in the ranks, he nevertheless proposed to speak out his own mind 'very plainly' and with the desire 'to be clearly and fully understood'. Defensive war was neither 'contrary to the general spirit of the morality of the Gospel' nor 'forbidden by any particular precept' nor 'discouraged by the example of the first Christians', who served in the armies of heathen sovereigns. The clergyman must decide his particular conduct in the light of the occasion when it arose, but his country had a right to his best services, even if these should be '(as in many instances will happen) to level the musquet or trail the pike'. 'Nor let him fear, that the sanctity of his character shall contract ought of stain, even in the moral strife against the enemies of his King and of his God.' To believe the contrary was a 'superstitious apprehension'.[25]

[24] LPL Moore Papers, v, fos. 116–21, Memorandum from Bounty Office; Jebb, 117–19; *Annual Register*, xl (1798), App. to Chr. 190–3.

[25] Ibid. 191–3.

The bishop's conviction that the needs of a nation in arms were to be preferred to the immunities of the clerical body was being simultaneously tested within his own family. On his return from the meeting of his fellow prelates in London he found a letter from his son, then an undergraduate at Christ Church, who was under pressure to join a corps for the defence of Oxford. Disturbed in mind about the principle of such an association, he called on Archbishop Moore, whose son Robert was a student of Christ Church. Robert Moore had not written to his father, but when Samuel Horsley showed the paper which he had received from Heneage to the primate, he found him, as he recounted, 'struck with it much in the sense I was'. He bustled back to Lambeth the following morning, sat with the archbishop until the post came, and when it brought nothing related to the Oxford plan, they both concluded that the business was not going on very rapidly. Heneage Horsley, however, was left in no doubt about the reasons for his father's dissent. The bishop wrote to him:

To pass by all the other objections ... I think it is ill considered with respect to its professed object. Admitting the Studentships are the estates of the students (tho' I hope most of them have estates of more consequence either in possession or expectation) how will their assembling at Oxford conduce to the defence of their estates, which lie in all parts of the kingdom. The notion that they shall all bind themselves to repair to Oxford in case of an invasion is perfect madness. Are the young men of family upon that event to be called from Kent, Sussex, Essex, and all the maritime counties, to Oxford, which of all places in the kingdom will be the least in danger? Will they not be of much more service with their friends & connections in their respective counties? I am astonish'd that the Dean should give his sanction to so wild a project.

There was good sense in this. Cambridge had 'taken wiser measures'. 'They enroll no undergraduates', he added, but 'give them the term upon the condition of military service in their respective counties'. There was also, however, an implied theory of Church–State relations, for Oxford in the eighteenth century was, *par excellence*, the theological department of the Church of England; yet Horsley warned his son against taking the oath to protect a particular place: 'in such a crisis you must be ready to serve where the King, not where the Vice-Chancellor shall require'.[26]

The bishop addressed to the dean of Christ Church, Dr Cyril Jackson, a letter 'in the most decided terms', stating explicitly that he would not consent to his son's being enrolled at Oxford. With characteristic high-handedness the young man—he was 22 years of age—was steered towards the Bromley association in Kent. His father made the application on his behalf to the recruiting officer, and instructed him to follow up the acceptance. The dean thought it 'unpardonable' that his brother of Westminster should have opened

[26] HP 1767, fos. 132–3, Horsley to H. Horsley, 30 Apr. 1798.

his mind to Heneage on the demerits of the University plan.[27] In High Church Oxford there was more support for Horsley's advocacy of arming than for his wish to merge the clerical exertion in that of the nation. By July nearly 500 men were enrolled in the University troops. They exercised daily in four divisions: St John's, Magdalen, Trinity, and New College, and thrice a week together in Tawntons Meadow. Cotter, late of New College, was colonel, the Vinerian Professor of All Souls, was lieutenant-colonel, and Barnes of Christ Church was major. On 2 July there was a grand field-day when the duke of Portland gave them their colours. John Randolph, soon to be bishop of Oxford, and a practical High Churchman, viewed this with interest and enthusiasm. He thought it a spectacle 'such as has never before been seen & probably will not be again'.[28]

The immediate crisis passed, but Bishop Horsley's enthusiasm for the war continued unabated during the next four years. His detestation of France and her Revolutionary principles showed through his theological writings, and influenced especially the charge which he delivered to the clergy of Rochester in 1800. When, after the ups and downs of the Second Coalition the new prime minister Henry Addington made peace with Napoleon at the beginning of one of the upswings in Britain's fortunes, the bishop spoke against the preliminaries of the settlement in the House of Lords on 3 November 1801. The terms were more favourable to France than to Britain, which surrendered all her wartime conquests except Trinidad and Ceylon. Both sides needed peace, Britain for financial reasons, and these were the conditions on which, in the view of the minister and his predecessor, she seemed most likely to obtain it. The Peace of Amiens was popular in the country, less uniformly so at Westminster.[29] H. H. Jebb concluded that Horsley could only have been acting from 'courage and far-seeing statesmanship', as he was 'opposing all his best friends and the ministry from which alone he could expect preferment'.[30] This was the image which the bishop tried to present of himself but it is misleading. Only sixteen peers eventually voted against the definitive treaty of Amiens but of these six were former Cabinet Ministers.[31] It had been touch and go whether George III, who liked the Peace as little as they did, would not at an earlier stage have turned out Addington. He was said to have been consulting with Windham and Rosslyn about a change of Government.[32] Of greater significance for Horsley was the fact that Grenville and Windham led the attack on the preliminaries, for these, on his son's admission, were his

[27] Ibid., fos. 134–5, 136–7, Horsley to H. Horsley, 5 and 17 May 1798.

[28] Bodl. Top. Oxon. d.354/2, fos. 33–4, 36–7, Randolph to Lambard, 20 June and 10 July 1798.

[29] Philip Ziegler, *Addington* (1965), 122–7.

[30] Jebb, 164–5.

[31] A. D. Harvey, *Britain in the Early Nineteenth Century* (1978), 127.

[32] Ziegler, *Addington*, 127.

closest political associates. It is hard, therefore, to accept Professor Sack's view that his presence in the ranks of opposition was 'by fluke'.[33]

His speech was nearer to Grenville's sentiments than to those of Windham. Like the former he attacked the terms of the Peace rather than the notion of concluding one. His case was markedly similar to that of the former Foreign Secretary, namely that it was little short of madness to throw away conquests, which, if the war might shortly be renewed, could be of strategic importance and provide useful bargaining counters.[34] France, the bishop pointed out, was 'possessed of a continental territory, which comprehends nothing less than the whole body of the ancient western empire'. 'This vast tract of territory', fenced on the one side by an impenetrable barrier of rivers, mountains, lakes, rocks, and forts, and bounded on the other by a length of sea coast from the mouth of the Texel to the harbour of Brest, was 'covered with a population far exceeding any thing that was spread over the same surface when it was subject to the Romans' and 'at the command and disposal of a government more energetic, more united, more prompt in execution, than the government of Rome was under any of her best emperors'. It would not be long before France, with 'the vast forests of timber' which 'clothe sides of the mountains' crowning the banks of the Rhine, would build up a navy able to exploit its coastline. British sea power could do nothing to deprive her of her Continental advantages, but 'for this very reason this country ought to have retained the acquisitions of her naval victories; which ... would have been in our hands a great drawback, as it were from the enemy's general strength'. Why, he asked ministers, by the cession of Minorca, Malta, and every island and every port in the Mediterranean and the Adriatic, had they ceded to France 'the absolute sovereignty of the Mediterranean'? Why had they given back to them West Indian islands, enriched on their own admission by the years of English occupation? Why had they given the French 'the key of re-admission to their Asiatic possessions' by yielding Pondicherry, which in a few years would render the British conquest of Mysore useless? So far it was a statesman's speech rather than a Churchman's, not uncharacteristic of the political grouping with which he was acting. But he added an ideological note, which not only brought him close to Windham, but disclosed an influence which went far towards explaining his intensified support of the war: 'My lords, what I dread as the worst consequence of this peace, is the revival of the spirit of Jacobinism in this country. My lords, in this country the spirit of Jacobinism is revived: we have already seen unequivocal symptoms of it.' He instanced sentiments which had been publicly avowed by persons of high standing that 'the terms of this peace are not bad enough for Great Britain—

---

[33] J. J. Sack, *The Grenvillites 1802–29* (1979), 57–8. But note his admirable analysis of the alignments on the peace issue.

[34] Jupp, *Lord Grenville*, 310–13.

not good enough for France', as 'the interests of mankind demand that France should be exalted and Great Britain humbled'.[35]

Total war presupposes in the belligerents a conviction of the utter rightness of their cause and an absolute denigration of the enemy. During the First World War of the twentieth century Germans became the Huns, while in the Second, Churchill's emphasis upon the 'evil' which we fought played a not inconsiderable part in sustaining morale. In the French Revolutionary and Napoleonic Wars that role was played by certain mythologies about the revolution which the Established Church did much to propagate. Two, in particular, were outstanding. They were intertwined. The first, which has the greater claim to be regarded as basic, was that the French Revolution resulted from a conspiracy of eighteenth-century *philosophes*, Freemasons, and Illuminati, working for the overthrow not just of the *ancien régime* in France, but of monarchy as an institution, of the Christian religion, and of propertied society. As Dr J. M. Roberts has shown, in a distinguished contribution to intellectual history, the myth of the influence of the secret societies was built up gradually during the eighteenth century, and especially during the second half of it, from criticisms of the secrecy of the Masons, which later developed into suspicion, or rather a set of inconsistent suspicions of subversive purposes. These were, as he is at pains to point out, 'nonsense', but they moved at the pace of 'nonsense on stilts', and after the exposure of Weishaupt's Bavarian Illuminati in 1785, a veritable panic about secret societies and sects spread through the states of Europe, so that when the French Revolution broke four years later, a ready-made explanation lay at hand which only needed to be applied by critics. The thesis was communicated to England in its most cogent shape by the *émigré* priest Augustin de Barruel in his *Mémoires pour servir a l'histoire du jacobinisme* published in 1797–8, and quickly translated into English, German, Italian, Spanish, Portuguese, and Dutch. Later in 1797 a Scottish mathematician John Robison produced a watered-down version of the theme entitled *Proofs of a Conspiracy against all the Religions and Governments of Europe, Carried On in the Secret Meetings of Freemasons, Illuminati and Reading Societies*, which went through five editions in two years.[36]

As Dr Roberts observes, the strength of the plot mythology was that 'it rested on the assumption of one great and general antithesis, Good versus Evil, Right versus Wrong'.[37] Hence arose an interpretation of the Revolution

[35] *Parl. Hist.* xxxvi (1801–3), 178–83.
[36] J. M. Roberts, *The Mythology of the Secret Societies* (1972), *passim*.
[37] Ibid. 203.

which invoked a supernatural power of evil. In Protestant England during the 1790s, where radical action was mainly open and explicit, the conspiracy myth of the origins of the French Revolution was not strong enough to pose a serious threat to the Freemasons. But from 1797 onwards into the opening years of the next century it emerged as a dominant theme in the writings of earnest churchmen. They were mainly High and conservative Churchmen, for Clapham-style Evangelicals reacted to events by appeals to personal holiness such as featured in William Wilberforce's *Practical View*. Dr R. A. Soloway's valuable summary mentions six outstanding contributions: Bishop Pretyman's sermon on Thanksgiving Day, 19 December 1797, and his charge to the clergy of Lincoln diocese, June and July 1800, Beilby Porteus's London visitation charge 1798–9, Horsley's second Rochester charge in 1800, and his sermon at the celebration of the Battle of Trafalgar in December 1805, and William Van Mildert's Boyle Lectures delivered in the church of St Mary-le-Bow in the years 1802–5.[38]

In these pronouncements, fanciful conspiratorial explanations blended with the second allegory, an apocalyptic view, derived from the study of Bible prophecies. Both, however, were nourished by contemporary events—the course of the war and the threat, or supposed threat, of insurrection. Most of the discourses made their appearance during what was for Britain the most trying phase of the conflict: a period when European allies were falling away and the danger of invasion was never far distant. In such times Churchmen, speaking on public occasions—clerical visitations or national thanksgivings—were expected not to give vent to their own fears but to deliver a message of reassurance, commitment, and hope. Orthodox eschatology served their purpose well, for in the premillennialist view at least, Antichrist came before the Second Coming of Christ and the Second Coming before the millennium. Conspiracy alone could be likewise used, as by Pretyman in 1797, to show that the plot was a divine instrument to achieve some ultimate good, as when the French Revolution destroyed 'the cruelty, the tyranny and the impiety of the Church of Rome'.[39]

The war, however, did not merely create an atmosphere receptive to the myths. Successive events unfolded their meaning. As Dr Roberts has written: 'From 1793 onwards, that power [France] was exporting revolution. First in Belgium and the prince-bishopric of Liège, the legislation of the Republic carried forward everywhere the benefits of secularisation and the Rights of Man. When the French armies broke into the Rhineland and Holland, and later Italy and Switzerland, they found sympathisers there who eagerly helped

---

[38] R. A. Soloway, *Prelates and People: Ecclesiastical Social Thought in England 1783–1852* (1969), 37–45. He also instances a later use of Barruel's and Robison's conspiracy theory in a sermon by Bishop Huntingford at the thanksgiving for the restoration of peace in 1814.

[39] Ibid. 38.

in setting up the new satellite republics with constitutions on the French model, and social and legal institutions to suit.' The 'unfolding pattern', which was the product of war as well as of internal developments in France, 'explains the near-hysterical state of shock of the European monarchies by the end of the first decade of the Revolution'. 'The scale and violence of the changes that men were called upon to account for soon seemed to exhaust all conventional and familiar categories of explanation. Some new dimension of understanding was needed.'[40] For Samuel Horsley, fascinated by biblical prophecy, the chief interest of the war lay in the assimilatìon of France to the old Roman Empire which persecuted the first Christians. He proclaimed in his charge to the clergy of Rochester diocese in 1800:

The countries against which their arms have been turned, either in the West or in the East, have been principally those which formed the body of the Roman Empire. Insomuch that in this odious French Republic, aping the manners, grasping the dominion, speaking to friends and to enemies the high vaunting language of antient Rome, we seem to behold the dreadful Apocalyptic Beast, which at the time of the desolation of the pagan whore exhibited in vision to St. John, had been, but was not, but was to be again, we seem, I say, to behold in the French Republic, this dreadful monster beginning to rise, in its antient form, out of the raging sea of anarchy and irreligion.[41]

Other features of the Revolutionary Wars which nourished millennialist speculation were the capture and subsequent deportation of the Pope, Pius VI—significant because in traditional Protestant exegesis the papacy had been identified with Antichrist—and Napoleon's invasion of the Ottoman dominions from 1798. This last event raised expectations in the minds of certain scholars, notably James Bicheno, a Dissenting minister, that the French might become the instruments of the restoration of the Jews to Palestine. In his *Signs of the Times* (1799) the expulsion of the Pope and his cardinals was the fifth vial of the Revelation; and the shaking of the Turkish Empire, perhaps, the sixth.[42]

Samuel Horsley's reputation has suffered much from his apocalyptic predictions. A private letter to his brother four days before he died, forecasting that Bonaparte would settle a considerable body of Jews in Palestine to open the door for a conquest of the Middle East as far as the Euphrates, and would then set himself up for the Messiah, was quoted by Jebb with the remark that it was 'not likely that his well-balanced mind, unless quite unhinged by illness should have adopted the millennialist and fatalistic ideas

[40] Ibid. 147–9.
[41] Horsley, *Rochester Charge 1800* (1800), 10–11.
[42] I owe this reference to Dr J. A. Oddy, who generously allowed me to read his unpublished Ph.D. thesis, 'Eschatological Prophecy in the English Theological Tradition *c.*1700–*c.*1840' (London, 1982).

which at that time were so prevalent'.[43] Dr Soloway has judged his 'strange predictions' to have been 'not simply the paranoic ramblings of a frightened old man'.[44] These assessments are anachronistic and severe. They proceed from an age when millennialist and apocalyptic speculation was confined to extreme Adventist sects of an ultra-Protestant character, whose opinions were viewed with the greatest reserve by the mainstream churches. In the eighteenth century, however, as Dr J. A. Oddy has shown,[45] such ideas were held in a respectable intellectual tradition, to which a massive output of commentaries, monographs, sermons, and tracts bears witness. In its English Protestant form shaped by Joseph Mead [Mede] (1586–1638), the Cambridge don and polymath, the prophecies of the book of Daniel and of Revelation were interpreted as part realized, part present, and part to come, but the millennium, the reign of Christ and his saints for a thousand years foretold in the twentieth chapter of Revelation, was firmly consigned to the future after the Second Coming of Christ. This teaching passed into the eighteenth-century mind modified but substantially maintained by the liberal intellects of Sir Isaac Newton and his successor in the Lucasian Chair of Mathematics in Cambridge, William Whiston. Later it came under heavy attack from Deists like Matthew Tindal and sceptics, but a move to reinstate it was perceptible in conservative Latitudinarian quarters from mid-century onwards. This was part of a broader return to orthodoxy. Bishop Thomas Newton, whose *Dissertation on the Prophecies* appeared in 1754–8, and Bishop William Warburton both saw the argument from prophecy as succeeding the testimony from miracles as the means of defending Christianity against its challengers. Warburton in 1768 established a Trust to provide lectures which would prove the truth of revealed religion from the completion of the Old and New Testament prophecies, especially those relating to the apostasy of papal Rome. Of the principal lecturers in the next twelve years, Bishops Hallifax, Hurd, and Bagot,[46] the first was Samuel Horsley's friend and consecrator, the second one of his patrons, the third his predecessor as bishop of St Asaph. Horsley did not himself lecture for the Trust, but so far from displaying eccentricity or mental decay, his interest in the fulfilment of biblical prophecy was one which he shared with earlier mathematicians of distinction, a fascination with number providing at least part of the link. It was also deeply rooted in his own branch of academic theology, the critical study of the Old Testament prophets. Moreover, it was fully consonant with his proclivities as a High Churchman, both in the general sense of being a rehabilitation of conservative and mystical divinity, and more particularly because he looked to

---

[43] Jebb, 223–8.
[44] Soloway, *Prelates and People*, 40.
[45] Oddy, 'Eschatological Prophecy'.
[46] Ibid. 7, 12–23, 35–44, 55–6.

patristics as a guide to the transactions of Antichrist. In a letter to Edward King published in 1799 he wrote:

I have an unfashionable partiality for the opinions of antiquity. I think there is ground in the prophecies for the notion of the early fathers that Palestine is the stage, in which Antichrist, in the height of his impiety, will perish. I am much inclined to assent to another opinion of the fathers; that a small band of the Jews will join Antichrist, and be active instruments of his persecutions. And I agree with you, that it is not unlikely, that this small part of the Jews will be settled in Jerusalem, under the protection of Antichrist.[47]

He approached the subject in a cautious, scholarly manner. The first evidence of his interest in eschatological prophecy antedated the French Revolution by nearly a decade. It was presented in four sermons on the Second Coming of Christ composed in 1780, but not published until after his death. These were directed against the minimizing rationalism of the age. Admitting that there was a time when 'mystical meanings were drawn by a certain caballistic alchymy, from the simplest expressions of holy writ', he urged that the pendulum had swung to the opposite extreme. 'In later ages, since we have seen the futility of those mystic expositions in which the school of Origen so delighted, we have been too apt to fall into the contrary error; and the same unwarrantable licence of figurative interpretation, which they employed to elevate ... the plainer parts of Scripture, has been used in modern times, in effect to lower the divine.' The specific error which he was combating was that of explaining away the expected Second Advent as having been already realized in the fall of Jerusalem in AD 70, by such figurative devices as identifying the 'eagles' of Matthew 24: 28 gathered round 'the carcase' with the eagles of Vespasian's legions.[48]

By the 1790s the climate had changed. The earthquake-like shock of the convulsions in Europe had induced a sense of living in the apocalyptic age. Responses were not confined to the popular millennialism of Richard Brothers and the Southcottians, with which the anti-democratic Horsley could be expected to have little rapport. They also extended to a crop of writings by middle-class intellectuals. Some of these authors were Dissenters, like James Bicheno and the Unitarian J. L. Towers, who wrote without sympathy for Catholicism and the *ancien régime*, regarding Antichrist as comprising the papacy and what they thought of as secular tyranny. Others were High or High-oriented Churchmen like William Jones of Nayland, Samuel Horsley,

---

[47] Horsley, *Critical Disquisitions on the Eighteenth Chapter of Isaiah, in a Letter to Edward King* (1799), 103.

[48] Horsley, *Sermons* (1810), i. 1–60. The four eschatological sermons are dated by the bishop in a letter to Thomas Witherby, 26 May 1804, as having been written about 20 years earlier. *Gent. Mag.*, 80/2 (1810), 158. A more precise dating—'composed seventeen years since'—was assigned by Horsley in an epistle to the author of 'Antichrist in the French convention', 4 July 1797. *British Magazine*, 5 (1834), 135.

and G. S. Faber, who, in taking up the theme, transferred the image of Antichrist to the spirit of the French Revolution. Another theme in this serious and animated debate was the prospect of the fulfilment of the promise to restore the Jews to their Palestinian home: Bicheno in 1800 devoted an entire book to the subject.[49]

Horsley entered the lists early in spring 1797, when he opened a private correspondence with the anonymous author of two pamphlets, one on 'The Second Advent', and the other, appearing about the end of the preceding year, entitled 'Antichrist in the French Convention'. Horsley's son Heneage, who published his father's letters in the *British Magazine* in 1834, believed the correspondent to be a layman. His identity is revealed in a note appended to Jocelyn Palmer's transcripts of the letters in August 1807 as C. Goring.[50] It is uncertain how much influence he exercised upon the bishop's subsequent thought, but though Heneage deemed the latter's expressions of assent to have proceeded mainly from natural politeness, the exchange was still in progress at least four years later.[51]

Another character with claim to have affected the development of Horsley's thinking concerning Old Testament prophecy was Edward King, a fellow of the Royal Society. But, as in the case of Goring, it was the sort of influence that proceeded from the rub of mind on mind rather than from the direct importation of ideas. Though the bishop had long been deeply engaged in the study of the prophetic parts of Scripture, it was a conversation with King that fixed his attention on the eighteenth chapter of Isaiah. In the Introduction and Commentary which he published in 1799 in reply to King's printed interpretation, he rejected the latter's suggestion that the French were designated as the instruments of Providence in the restoration of the Jewish people.[52] It was in the so-called *Critical Disquisitions on the Eighteenth Chapter of Isaiah, in a Letter to Edward King*, as well as in the *Charge . . . to the Clergy of [Rochester] Diocese* delivered in the following year, that the climax of the bishop's eschatological pronouncements was to be found. He was led to devise a High Church variant of what Dr Oddy has styled 'the great Protestant paradigm'.[53] His thesis had three distinct constituents. First, the Median method of interpreting prophecy was stood on its head. In the *Disquisition on the Prophetical Periods*, undated and first published in 1833, though perhaps written before the outbreak of the French Revolution,[54] it was laid down that the meaning of the events foretold should be established first, and the identity of the

---

[49] Oddy, 'Eschatalogical Prophecy', 57–66.

[50] LPL 2809, Palmer Transcripts of Original Letters, 18 Apr. 1797.

[51] Editorial comment on the printed correspondence mentions a letter written 'twelve years after the commencement of the French Revolution'. *British Magazine*, 5 (1834), 523.

[52] *Critical Disquisitions*, esp. 1–3, 15–17.

[53] 'Eschatological Prophecy'.

[54] That event is not mentioned in the discussion of 'the great mystic period of time, times, and half of a time' which looks back to the beginning of the 'atheistical philosophy' in France in 1726.

prophetic numbers deduced from these rather than that the numbers (which were shown to be mathematically unreliable) should provide the 'key to the sense'. Secondly, Mede's historic identification of the papacy with Antichrist was jettisoned in the same work, as 'that unwarrantable, monstrous supposition, that Christian Rome is Antichrist, and all who have at any time opposed her, however wild and fanatical in their application, saints'.[55]

The third characteristic was his view of eschatology. A study of the *Critical Disquisitions on the Eighteenth Chapter of Isaiah* (1799) reveals a more sophisticated understanding of the nature of Antichrist than was to be found in earlier writings on the subject. Antichrist was seen by Horsley as an emergent, evolving phenomenon, a sort of personification of God's judgement, which would reach its dreaded consummation only in the future, but was currently manifested in the Revolutionary excesses. Thus:

I fear, I see too clearly the rise, instead of the fall, of the Antichrist of the West. Or rather I fear, I see him rapidly advancing to full stature and ripe age. His rise, strictly speaking, the beginning of the monster, was in the apostolic age. For it were easy to trace the pedigree of French Philosophy, Jacobinism, and Bavarian Illumination, up to the first heresies. But it is now we see the *adolescence* of that man of sin, or rather of lawlessness, who is to throw off all the restraints of religion, morality, and custom, and undo the bonds of civil society.

The full Antichrist would be wholly different from anything known: 'That son of perdition, who shall be neither a Protestant, nor a Papist; neither Christian, Jew nor Heathen: who shall worship neither God, Angel nor Saint—who will neither supplicate the invisible Majesty of Heaven, nor fall down before an idol.'[56] The same reservations were to be found in the public pronouncement to his clergy in 1800. While conjuring up for his auditors 'the dreadful Apocalyptic Beast' apparent in the French Republic, his remarks about it were always related to the future. It was 'beginning to rise'. The democracy of apostate France was 'doing the work of Antichrist before he comes'.[57] He never subordinated his scholarship to the dictates of panic.

Horsley was not the only High Churchman to paint the Revolution with the stain of Antichrist. Jones of Nayland had done so less cautiously in a sermon of 1794. G. S. Faber, a High Church Evangelical, was to produce a generalized version of the new Tory exegesis, tender to Rome, hostile to Revolutionary France, in the year before Horsley's death.[58]

The value of this exegesis in strengthening determination to fight the enemy was apparent to all, even to those who helped to formulate it. It worked

---

[55] *British Magazine*, 4 (1833), 718–41.
[56] *Critical Disquisitions*, 105–6.
[57] *Rochester Charge 1800* (1800), 10–11.
[58] See Oddy, 'Eschatological Prophecy', 70–2, 84–90 for an assessment of these and other writers.

in two ways. Firstly by direct denigration of the French the British national cause was enhanced in righteousness. Thus Horsley in his second Rochester charge detailed the preparations of the French Republic for the reign of Antichrist:

The new government had no sooner renounced the faith, than they proceeded to a malignant persecution of it; and they used their utmost endeavours to excite similar persecutions, and an equal hatred of the clergy in other countries. We have seen them anticipating the work of Daniel's wilful king, by remarkably changing times and laws. They gave their Calendar a form entirely new, in purpose to obliterate the memory of the festivals of the Church. They openly renounce the first principles of morality, and they 'use no discretion in the pleasures of women', dishonouring not merely by the gallantries of private life, but even by their laws, the holy institution of marriage. The more effectually to wean men from Christianity, they have introduced something like the old pagan idolatry; much of the pomp and lascivousness of its rites.[59]

Secondly, under the bishop's direction the fatalistic theme of Antichrist was so handled as to prevent its being twisted by the anti-war movement into an instrument of pacifism. He addressed himself to this need in his Trafalgar Day sermon in December 1805:

At the commencement of the disordered state, which still subsists in Europe, when apprehensions were expressed by many—apprehensions, which are still entertained by those, who first expressed them,—that the great Antichrist is likely to arise out of the French revolution; it was argued by them, who were friends to the cause of France, 'To what purpose, is it then upon your own principles, to resist the French? Antichrist is to arise; he is to prevail; he is to exercise a wide dominion, and what human opposition can set aside the fixed designs of Providence?' Strange to tell, this argument took with many, who were not friends to the French cause, at least as to make them averse to the war with France.

He answered:

In the case of Antichrist . . . prophecy is explicit. So clearly as it is foretold, that he shall raise himself to power by successful War; so clearly it is foretold that war, fierce and furious war, waged upon him by the faithful, shall be, in part, the means of his downfall. So false is all the despicable cant of puritans about the unlawfulness of war.[60]

Horsley had always regarded prophecies as signs from Providence rather than as a blueprint of its intentions. The motif of Antichrist, so strongly iterated in the years of continuing endurance 1799–1800 was softened by him in his sermon after the victory at Trafalgar. Napoleon was assessed at St Asaph in terms of mingled execration and wonder—'a man whose undaunted spirit, and success in enterprise, might throw a lustre over the meanest birth'.

---

[59] *Rochester Charge 1800*, 10–11.
[60] *The Watchers and the Holy Ones: A Sermon Preached in the Cathedral Church of St. Asaph on . . . December 5, 1805* (1806), 25–6.

There was no attempt to read ultimate triumph in the signs of the times or to hint at impending disaster. It was all in the lap of the Almighty. 'What is called the fortune of war, by this unseen and mysterious cause, may be reversed in a moment.'[61] At that time it was a realistic assessment, with Austerlitz fought three days earlier and news of the loss of the British transports to come. It would be unsafe to generalize from a single example, but Horsley's development provides a hint that, like religious revivalism among the poor,[62] apocalyptic prophecy from on high flourished more mightily under national pressure than when conditions were eased.

The French Revolutionary and Napoleonic Wars had the effect of producing a shift in the balance of parties and groupings in the English Church. They worked in favour of those which assigned to Providence a major concern with the regeneration and protection of the civil community. The Evangelicals profited through their attachment to the idea of a righteous nation and a national faith, but failed to press home their advantage because their emphasis on individual conversions and personal righteousness divided English society between the sheep and the goats. It was the Old High Church, committed to an alliance or a more intimate union of Church and State that benefited most from the increased services of the clergy to the State called forth by the protracted hostilities.[63] Its traditionalist wing was also better equipped than most theologians of the Age of Reason to handle the emotional releases of a nation at war. The well-known lead taken by Joshua Watson, the Hackney Phalanx leader, in the work of Christian reconstruction in Europe after the battle of Leipzig is a measure of the enhanced importance of the school of Anglican divinity in which he had been reared.

---

[61] Ibid. 22.

[62] See E. P. Thompson, *The Making of the English Working Class* (1963), 388.

[63] This theme has been developed by Nancy U. Murray, 'The Influence of the French Revolution on the Church of England and its Rivals, 1789–1802', D.Phil. thesis (Oxford, 1975), using the Fast and Thanksgiving Day sermons for the 1790s and early 1800s.

13

Society and Social Reform

THE pessimism which seized the minds of the English upper classes at the end of the War of American Independence was not merely a response to defeat and national humiliation. It was evidence of social crisis, which had been unfolding during the preceding years. The marks of this have been listed by Geoffrey Best—the spread of Methodism and fanaticism, the progress of radical politics, the breakdown of law and order not only in the Gordon riots, unique in their ferocity in a capital city which was becoming notorious for its disturbances, but in the expansion of ordinary crime due to the 'antique decrepitude' of the machinery of police and administration.[1] Disorder also extended to the provinces. Wartime dislocation of overseas markets blended with a quickening industrialism and population growth to produce unemployment in Lancashire which issued in 1779 in a serious outbreak of Luddism directed especially against Arkwright's carding and roving machines. In anticipation of the more serious outbreaks of the early nineteenth century the larger workshops and factories suffered most.[2] Meanwhile, in the agricultural counties of the South, where lay the estates of the powerful, the spread of enclosures brought resentment to the dispossessed, and poor-rates rose from about £1½ million in 1776 to more than £2 million ten years later.[3] But it was the slackening of enclosures in the late 1770s and 1780s that most clearly betokened the economic problems of the landholders. They were not facing ruin but, as Professor E. L. Jones has pointed out, farm incomes were falling for parts of that period, landlords were finding difficulty in collecting rents, and the necessity of cutting back the costs of improvement was widely felt.[4] Professor F. M. L. Thompson has found corroborative evidence of declining expectations in a break in the yearly incidence of private estate acts in 1777, which was not reversed until 1792.[5]

This concatenation of adversities bringing reflections on the Industrial Revolution and what was later to be called 'the Condition-of-England question' released a flow of exertions to modernize English social institutions and to promote the welfare of the poor.[6] How far it was prompted by paternalism

---

[1] G. F. A. Best, *Temporal Pillars* (Cambridge, 1964), 137–9.
[2] John Stevenson, *Popular Disturbances in England 1700–1870* (1979), 117–18.
[3] Best, *Temporal Pillars*, 138–9.
[4] E. L. Jones, *Agriculture and Economic Growth in England 1650–1815* (1967), 42, 44.
[5] F. M. L. Thompson, *English Landed Society in the Nineteenth Century* (1963), 213–14.
[6] Best, *Temporal Pillars*, 139 ff.; U. Henriques, *Before the Welfare State* (1979), chap. i.

and how far by the need to impose social control is a question which cannot be answered, for paternalism, properly defined, did not exclude social control. As David Roberts has shown by a comparison of successive phases of the phenomenon from feudal times to the Victorian period, the duties of the paternalist superior were threefold—'ruling, guiding and helping'.[7] There can be little doubt, however, that the sincere if often misguided desire to help figured prominently among the objectives of social reformers in the 1780s at both the local and the parliamentary levels. When, rightly or wrongly, evil consequences were seen to have accrued from indiscriminate charity, paternalists turned for assistance to the other objectives, and their influence became harsher. Nevertheless, moral and religious considerations remained uppermost in their minds, and the earliest steps to reform social policy in the 1780s were taken in a generous spirit, and as part of a policy of church reform.

This chapter will be devoted to exploring how Bishop Samuel Horsley, outstandingly the advocate of the unity of the civil and ecclesiastical communities, interpreted the obligations of a Churchman to society.

A sympathetic concern for the problems of poverty may be generally inferred from the title of a manuscript found in his library at his death, namely 'A Plan for Preventing the Distresses of the Labouring Poor', though his chaplain was unable to identify the author of it.[8] It must be seen how far this was reflected in particular policies.

RECONSTRUCTION OF THE POOR LAW

The only provision by the State for the welfare of its citizens was made through the poor law, resting on the comprehensive statute of 1601 which laid the responsibility for implementing it on the parishes. For most of the eighteenth century the system was run on a loose rein. Except in the minority of parishes which had followed the 1696 Bristol City model of amalgamating to provide houses of industry where pauper labour could be made profitable, relieving policies were compounded of the independent decisions of parish officers, vestries, and Justices of the Peace which coincided from necessity rather than from overall direction. Chiefly, they consisted of various forms of outdoor relief—small weekly or fortnightly pensions, funeral expenses, apprenticeship fees, subsidizing of rents, etc.—granted to needy individuals in a neighbourly spirit. But there were also many abuses, principally connected with disputes between parishes over settlements and harsh treatment of migrating poor. In the later years of the century the poor-law authorities came

---

[7] David Roberts, *Paternalism in Early Victorian England* (1979), 4–5.
[8] LPL 2810, fos. 279–91, W. J. Palmer, 'Account of Horsley's Manuscripts'.

under pressure from intensifying rural unemployment and distress, a change which was reflected in a rise in the level of the poor-rate, slow from the 1770s and rapid during the French wars, 1793–1815.[9] Against this background a national debate on poor-law policy developed in the 1780s and continued for half a century.[10] Two basic standpoints were revealed. One was traditional and paternalistic. It looked back to the teachings of the early divines of the English Reformation, notably to Latimer and the sixteenth-century commonwealth school. Its unifying theme was the abiding responsibility of the rich to relieve the poor, which was regarded as a necessary condition of existence. This view was still promulgated by conservative Churchmen in the eighteenth century, by Atterbury, George Horne, Lewis Bagot, Horsley, and others, and remained strong enough (or perhaps regained sufficient strength) to influence the dominant course of legislation and magisterial action from Thomas Gilbert's Act of 1782 providing shelter for the orphans, sick, and aged poor to the Speenhamland decision of 1795, which built on earlier local precedents of outdoor relief for the able-bodied. But the conservatives had to confront a reforming lobby hostile to relief of the poor on both moral and economic grounds. Thriving on the puritan gospel of hard work, it emphasized the danger of encouraging improvidence and thus creating the very destitution which it was sought to alleviate. After a premature start in the first quarter of the century, these ideas regained their force with Joseph Townshend's *Dissertation on the Poor Laws* published in 1786. In this he demolished the case for intervening to raise standards of relief which would only reduce the willingness of the poor to persevere in the humble tasks which nature had assigned to them.[11] It laid the foundations of the early nineteenth-century abolitionist approach which looked to Malthus for inspiration, and encouraged Bentham and others to revive proposals for setting the poor to work for profit in workhouses.[12]

Horsley fought these inhuman trends in an idiom which was tellingly contemporary. In a sermon delivered in the year when Townshend's book appeared he used empirical and utilitarian arguments to defend traditional Christian charity against the encroachments of a gloomy determinism. Poverty was an inevitable consequence of human sinfulness, but Providence had not fixed the condition of each class. Hence men must strive so far as possible to eliminate it. Poverty existed whenever the individual's means of subsistence fell short of what was needed to enable him to fulfil the duties of the sphere which he was best able to fill to the advantage of the community. But

---

[9] Henriques, *Before the Welfare State*, 11–14, 19.

[10] J. R. Poynter, *Society and Pauperism: English Ideas on Poor Relief 1795–1834* (1969), *passim*.

[11] R. A. Soloway, *Prelates and People: Ecclesiastical Social Thought in England 1783–1852* (1969), 64–5.

[12] Henriques, *Before the Welfare State*, 23–4.

subsistence standards were not enough to measure need, for they did not take account of varying expectations. Poverty was to be found at all social levels. It obstructed the powers of the individual, rendering him not more miserable in himself than useless to the community, which for its own sake must free the captive from the chain in order to regain his services. The impotent poor were also entitled to relief according to the first idea of all civil association which was that of a union of the many to supply the wants of the infirm. Horsley was contemptuous of those who offered the poor a compensation in the next world for their sufferings in the present. But he was no advocate of unlimited relief. He saw dangers in removing the threat of impoverishment, which encouraged industrious activity and promoted class harmony, and did not believe that the poor could readily move from one rank to another and remain useful members of society. His was a middle path between benevolence and prudence not untypical of the best in late eighteenth-century thought. Characteristically Providence was invoked at almost every stage to harmonize the prescriptions.[13]

Horsley's generous conservatism showed in his opposition to the drive to reform the parochial machinery for administering the laws by concentrating power in the hands of the wealthier inhabitants. This movement achieved its most apparent successes in the passing of the Parish Vestry Act of 1818 and of Sturges Bourne's Select Vestry Act of 1819 which was described by Professor Finer as 'a rich man's reaction to democracy'.[14] But it was already at work in the metropolitan parishes before the bishop's death. In June 1805 he attempted in the House of Lords to obstruct a Poor Law Amendment Bill for the parish of St Pancras, which was designed to 'take the administration of such affairs from the vestry at large, the churchwardens, etc.' and to vest it in 'a select body ... of men; who styled themselves the guardians or directors of the poor'. The question had been in agitation since the end of 1803, when the Lords amended a bill to confer on the guardians despotic powers to control assessments and fill vacancies without producing vouchers and to appoint their own auditors. The wealthy inhabitants of St Pancras, who had promoted it, refused to accept the compromise, and moved to repeal the amendments. Horsley led the attack on them in the Upper Chamber, comparing their proposal witheringly with a recent bill to improve the art of chimney-sweeping which aimed 'to place more power in the hands of a select body of chimney sweeps'. His motion to abandon the committee on the Select Vestry Bill was defeated by 31 votes to 7. The Lord Chancellor (Eldon) warned of the confusion and 'numerous litigations' resulting from popular parochial elections, but whether the right answer was a concentration of authority in an oligarchy interested in holding down the rates is another matter.[15]

[13] Soloway, *Prelates and People,* 67–9, 75–7.
[14] S. E. Finer, *The Life and Times of Sir Edwin Chadwick* (1952), 42.
[15] *Parl. Deb.* v (1805), 240–2.

CHURCHES FOR THE POOR

The establishment of 'Free Churches' for the urban poor was a High Church initiative. In 1795 Charles Daubeny laid before the SPCK a plan for erecting a free church at Bath by public subscription. Horsley was present when the decision to subscribe £500 was taken, and he took the chair at a later meeting to appoint the Society's treasurers to the board of trustees. It was proposed in a prospectus that the whole area of the building should be benched for the free accommodation of the poor of Bath, and the galleries let at rents sufficient to defray the outgoings. The church, Christ Church, Walcot, was opened in 1798 with Daubeny as its minister.[16] The Bath example was followed in Birmingham in 1803, when a plan originating with Spencer Madan, the 'Church and King' rector of St Philip's, passed through Parliament.[17] In November 1806 J. J. Watson, vicar of Hackney, issued an address for the building of two chapels of ease in his vast parish. Except for the pews appropriated to the use of schools, sittings were to be free. The situation of the chapels was chosen with a view to their proximity to proposed building development and the numerous poor in their vicinity. Among the more prominent subscribers were the leaders of the Hackney Phalanx, and H. H. Norris became perpetual curate of the South Hackney chapel in 1810.[18]

PRISONERS AND SOCIAL OUTCASTS

From about the middle of the eighteenth century onwards there was a gathering interest in the welfare of what the Victorians were to style 'the perishing and dangerous classes': criminals and those whose way of life set them permanently athwart the law and the community. It was an outflow from the broader stream of philanthropy which had focused upon the establishment of voluntary hospitals in the first three decades of the Hanoverian era, and had then started to spread to the relief of victims of other kinds of misfortune: foundlings, sufferers from venereal diseases, prostitutes.[19] During the century there was a massive change in the form of the giving, from privately endowed trusts regulated by Chancery to organized groups of donors or benevolent societies which pursued well-defined objects of social improvement.[20] These

---

[16] SPCK Minutes, xxxi (1792–5), fos. 318–19, 349–50, 359–60, 362, 366–7, 370–1; xxxii (1796–9), fos. 326, 372; *OCM* 9 (1805), 59–66.

[17] W. W. Wilson (ed.), *A History of the Church of England Cemetery, Warstone Lane, Birmingham, together with a History of Christ Church, Birmingham* (Birmingham, 1900); Hamilton Baynes, *Two Centuries of Church Life 1715–1915: St. Philip's, Birmingham* (Birmingham, 1915), 45–6; Falconer Madan, *The Madan Family* (Oxford, 1933), 143.

[18] Shoreditch PL D/F/Tys, Hackney Papers, 'Address to the Inhabitants of Hackney', 20 Nov. 1806.

[19] David Owen, *English Philanthropy 1660–1960* (Oxford, 1965), chap. ii, *passim*.

[20] Richard Tompson, *The Charity Commission and the Age of Reform* (1979), 68–72.

were usually lay-centred, predominantly Low Church or moderationist, Quaker or Dissenting, and are conceived to have become before the close of the century outstandingly the preserve of the Evangelicals. Among the achievements of the latter E. M. Howse lists the Society for Bettering the Condition of the Poor, founded in 1796; John Thornton's Society for the Relief of Persons Imprisoned for Small Debts, which released 14,007 people in five years; John Venn's Society for Bettering the Condition of the Poor at Clapham; the Society for the Reform of Prison Discipline; the Indigent Blind Institution; the Foundling Hospital; and 'all sorts of sporadic charities: to provide support for war widows, distressed sailors, "suffering Germans", "Spanish Patriots", French Protestants, Russian sufferers, Lascars, "foreigners in distress", and the 'Refuge of the Destitute''.[21]

With men of sincerity, however, the unambiguous prescriptions of the Gospels transcended the barriers of ecclesiastical traditions. From 1688 to the birth of Tractarianism the Old High Church school never lacked contributors to practical philanthropy. A succession of figures—Robert Nelson, the Non-juring layman; William Stevens, renowned for his liberality to his friends; Samuel Glasse, the Hutchinsonian vicar of Wanstead, examined by the House of Commons for three days on houses of correction and spokesman for the Samaritan Society founded to assist the rehabilitation of poor patients discharged from the London Hospital;[22] John Bowdler; Joshua Watson of Hackney, organizer of famine relief in Germany after the battle of Leipzig[23]—testified to the truth that if, as Archbishop Tillotson remarked to Beveridge, 'Charity is above rubrics',[24] obedience to rubrics by no means precluded charity. Horsley may with warrant be added to the number. He could not be compared with the wealthy bankers and merchants of the Clapham Sect, who subscribed to more than fifteen societies, and gave away a quarter to two-thirds of their incomes to good causes.[25] But he preached charity sermons. The bodies which he was most prone to favour were those concerned with the morally degraded and persons exposed to the temptation of crime. On the whole they were different from the charities, like the Bettering Society,[26] patronized by the Evangelicals, less judgemental in their tone, and more national in their objectives. The Philanthropic Society, for whose benefit he preached in Quebec Chapel, Marylebone, on 25 March

[21] E. M. Howse, *Saints in Politics: The 'Clapham Sect' amd the Growth of Freedom* (1953), 124–5.

[22] Poyntz Letters, Glasse to Poyntz, 8 Apr. 1799; cf. Ibid., do. to do., 16 and 23 June 1797; Owen, *English Philanthropy*, 123.

[23] A. B. Webster, *Joshua Watson: The Story of a Layman, 1771–1855* (1954), 49–57.

[24] Owen, *English Philanthropy*, 13.

[25] Ibid. 93, citing figures compiled by Ford K. Brown.

[26] The Society for Bettering the Condition of the Poor, commonly called the Bettering Society, made moral worthiness, attendance at public worship, and willingness to train children in industrious habits conditions for the grant of relief. Soloway, *Prelates and People*, 79.

1792, had been established four years earlier to provide for young children at risk in London. It was described in an early address as a project to 'unite the purposes of charity with those of industry and police'. Pioneering the development of reformatory schools in collaboration with judges and magistrates was its principal achievement. Jeremiah (*sic*) Bentham and Dr. J. C. Lettsom, a Quaker founder of dispensaries, were members of the Committee.[27] Horsley in 1792 preached an optimistic sermon, supplying a Christian basis for its humanitarian purposes. The prophecies of future happiness contained in the books of Isaiah and Joel, referring as in Isaiah 12: 9 to a time 'when the earth shall be filled with the knowledge of the Lord, as the waters cover the sea', were applied to the improvement of manners since the first promulgation of Christianity in the world, namely the suppression of cruelty and barbarism by the growth of the 'philanthropic spirit', leaving only 'sins of indulgence and refinement'. [28] Another charity which he patronized was the Magdalen, founded in 1758 as a refuge for London prostitutes. Robert Dingley, a Russia merchant, and his partner Jonas Hanway were chiefly concerned in it, and although John Thornton, the Evangelical, was also involved, the Hospital's first chaplain William Dodd went out of his way to proclaim that the instigators were not 'moved by either of those two indelible marks of ill-breeding, methodism or enthusiasm'. Despite their moral failings the inmates were treated without the condescending discrimination sometimes exercised by Evangelicals against the undeserving poor. The object of the institution was to render them happy in themselves and useful to society. They were trained in manufactures of various kinds and, where practicable, placed in service or restored to their families.[29] Samuel Horsley's anniversary sermon in the chapel of the Magdalen Hospital on 22 April 1795 fitted this conception of non-puritan Christian philanthropy. Beginning with an affirmation that the future bliss of the saints would consist partly of 'certain exquisite sensations of delight ... produced by external objects acting upon corporeal organs', he delivered a panegyric upon the higher pleasures of the senses, art, music, and literature. Turning to the purity of Our Lord's life, he categorized evil thoughts, adulteries, and fornications as the defilements which humanity found the most difficult to escape. In this, the most relevant of Horsley's sermons to our present conditions, and also the best, he criticized the ostracism of fallen women both on the ground that it applied a double standard to male and female, and because it stood in the way of a return to virtue.[30]

With prison reform, properly understood, as a combined movement of

---

[27] Owen, *English Philanthropy*, 120–1, 120 n. 98.

[28] Horsley, *The Abounding of Iniquity ... A Sermon* (1792).

[29] B. Kirkman Gray, *A History of English Philanthropy* (1905), 163–5; Owen, *English Philanthropy*, 57–9.

[30] Horsley, *The Enjoyments of the Future Life ... A Sermon* (1795).

private philanthropy and official action dating from the 1770s,[31] the bishop had little to do. He is chiefly remembered for the obstruction which he offered as dean of Westminster to Jeremy Bentham's plans for building a penitentiary on the Panopticon design on land held by the Abbey in seigniory in Tothill Fields. For this he was much censured by Wilberforce, whose biographer John Pollock wrote: 'A prince of the Church had refused charity to prisoners.'[32] This judgement is unwarrantably curt. Professor Gertrude Himmelfarb has claimed that Bentham's high-sounding plan was 'a travesty of the model prison', amounting to little more than a private profit-making concern for employing convicts as cheap labour under contract with the Government on the wood-working machinery invented by his brother Samuel in Russia. In the end it was jettisoned by a parliamentary committee for not providing adequate safeguards against exploitation of prisoners and for neglecting their physical and moral welfare. Moreover, Horsley's resistance was but a brief phase in a struggle which continued for twenty years, and was bedevilled by obstruction and mismanagement on all sides.[33] There is evidence in the recently published *Correspondence of Jeremy Bentham* that opposition to the project, chiefly on environmental grounds, was at first stronger among the vestrymen of the Westminster parishes than with the dean and chapter of the Abbey, though nowhere was it more than faint.[34] The trouble began when Bentham, having heard from Wilberforce that the Treasury had approved the purchase of the site, and acting on Wilberforce's advice, took the negotiations with the dean and chapter into his own hands. His approach to Bishop Horsley by letter of 31 October 1796 was scarcely tactful. The bishop was informed that the Government already had powers of compulsory purchase under an Act of 1794, but an appeal was made to his better nature to co-operate in 'a foundation of so much importance to the public service'. At that time the land was used partly as a rubbish dump by the inhabitants of St Margaret's and St John's parishes, who also had rights of common pasture upon it, and partly as a cricket ground for the boys of Westminster School. There was an 'old and decay'd' poorhouse at the end of the waste. Horsley was assured by Bentham that compensation would be paid to those interested, including a 'minute compensation' to the dean and chapter for the loss of their unprofitable right. Horsley turned the application over to Dr Samuel Smith, one of the prebendaries, who had a connection with Bentham, and wrote twice to the prime minister to discover whether the Government was sincerely behind the plan. Bentham learned privately that 'if the Bishop is

---

[31] Henriques, *Before the Welfare State*, 161.

[32] John Pollock, *Wilberforce* (Tring 1986), 138.

[33] Gertrude Himmelfarb, 'The Haunted House of Jeremy Bentham', in ead. (ed.), *Victorian Minds* (1968), 32–81.

[34] J. R. Dinwiddy (ed.), *The Correspondence of Jeremy Bentham*, vi. *January 1798 to December 1801* (Oxford, 1984), esp. 86, 116.

fully impressed that Mr. Pitt really wishes it, it will be done—otherwise not'. Pitt was too busy to attend to the matter, but when George Rose, secretary to the Treasury, eventually gained his consent to a letter being sent to the dean of Westminster vaguely intimating approval, the chapter met on 16 November, with Bentham present, and agreed to treat on minimal concessions. The land at Tothill Fields was to be divided. Part was to go to the parishes for a new poorhouse, part to the dean and chapter for a cricket ground for the scholars, part to the chapter and the parishes jointly for building or other improvement. A mere six acres out of the eighty required was to be allocated to Panopticon, an area quite inadequate, thought Bentham, for the 2,700 prisoners he might be asked to accommodate. Horsley had expostulated against the scale of the proposal at the meeting—'So, then, you mean to make a Botany Bay of it?'[35]—and was working to curtail it to a size which Westminster could absorb.

Quite apart from the threat to property values in an area where the Abbey drew about one-fifth of its income,[36] and the discouragement to powerful developers such as the Grosvenor family,[37] it was not in the national interest to plant a colony of 2,000 or more otherwise transportable felons on the doorstep of Parliament which, if they broke out, they might besiege as had the 'No Popery' mob of 1780. Wilberforce hinted that the bishop's influence in the House of Lords made it unthinkable to coerce him by Act of Parliament.[38] Bentham tried to bribe him with a reallocation of the land at the expense of the parishes. He had been fed by Prebendary Smith with an improbable story that Horsley wanted an alliance against Pitt 'to see His Ministership eat a dish of humble pye'.[39] But the dean of Westminster, whatever his faults, was not venal, and Bentham was thrown back on what the Government would do to apply force. This amounted to very little. After some delay the law officers of the Crown decided that action must take the form of an Enclosure Bill for Tothill Fields requiring public notice to be given before it could be introduced. Unfortunately the Treasury solicitor published the notice in the press without prior intimation to the dean and without reference to the commitment to reserve portions of the land for interested parties. Bentham made a frantic effort to redeem the mistake by writing to Horsley to explain and apologize. But the bishop, feeling himself to have been betrayed, and confirmed in his suspicion that Bentham was not an accredited agent of the administration, abruptly refused him an interview.[40] It was effectively the end of all negotiation in that quarter, and Bentham finding himself abandoned by Long, the

---

[35] A. T. Milne (ed.), *The Correspondence of Jeremy Bentham*, v. *January 1794 to December 1797* (1981), 285, 289–93, 298–307.
[36] See above, p. 189.
[37] Dinwiddy (ed.), *Bentham*, pp. xxii–xxiii.
[38] Milne (ed.), *Bentham*, 309–10.
[39] Ibid. 315, 316–17.
[40] Dinwiddy (ed.), *Bentham*, pp. xix, 75–8, 88–9, 127.

junior secretary of the Treasury,[41] was thrown back on his own devices for forwarding the plan. In 1799 he arranged the purchase of an adjacent site at Millbank from the marquis of Salisbury, but still hankered after Tothill Fields. In 1801 the new Government drastically contracted the project,[42] which eventually foundered on the opposition of the strict upholders of the solitary confinement penitentiary against a profit-making prison.[43]

POPULAR EDUCATION

Since the middle of the seventeenth century, encouraged by the interest of the Commonwealth State in education, the provision of schools for the poor had established a principal claim on the philanthropy of the wealthy and middle classes. To serve the purpose for which they were intended such institutions had to be available free or at low fees, and must offer instruction of an elementary kind, capable of being absorbed by pupils who had neither the nature nor the domestic nurture to enable them to cope with the rigours of the traditional classical curriculum of the old grammar schools. As Miss M. G. Jones has shown, endowed 'English' schools, teaching religion and the three Rs, which were either attached to the grammar schools as preparatories or conducted independently of them, pointed the way forward. No fewer than 460 such were returned in the reports of the Charity Commissioners at the end of the seventeenth century. In terms of their function and personnel these cannot be sharply distinguished from the metropolitan charity schools and equivalent country schools, financed by public subscription, which emerged under the auspices of the SPCK mainly in the period 1700–25. Jones assumes the existence of 'a continuous movement for elementary education in the eighteenth century',[44] but although improvements continued to be made, recent research extending to the sampling of localities has revealed a patchy and uneven development for the middle years of the century followed by a marked tendency during the earlier decades of the Industrial Revolution for supplementary exertions such as the Sunday Schools in the 1780s, to be overwhelmed by the rise of the population and an increase in the quantity and intensity of child labour. Hence there is no undisputed evidence of an overall increase in literacy before 1820. A lately published study of the education of the poor in Kent, for so long Bishop Horsley's county, stretching forward to 1811, suggests that improving ratios of school provision in the rural areas offset a deteriorating situation in the towns. In a few of the more fortunate

---

[41] Ibid. 117.

[42] Ibid., pp. xxi–xxv.

[43] Henriques, *Before the Welfare State*, 165–6.

[44] M. G. Jones, *The Charity School Movement: A Study of Eighteenth Century Puritanism in Action* (Cambridge, 1938), 15–16, 27.

country parishes more than 50 per cent of poor children were enrolled in non-classical schools.[45]

Historians, especially Marxist historians, have assigned a prominent place to 'social control' as a motive for educating the poor. The emphasis is only partly justified. Social discipline, the inculcation of habits of industry, thrift, sobriety, and orderliness, featured as strongly as the teaching of Christian belief in the objectives of the first sponsors of the charity schools as well as in those of the founders of the later Sunday Schools. But this was not necessarily the same thing as the wilful subjection of one class to another. In an up-to-date history of the Sunday Schools addressed to their social significance Dr T. W. Laqueur has portrayed them as 'largely the creation of the working-class community', and has shown that, without noticeable tension, their pupils absorbed from teachers of their own social class skills and values which served them well in life, even in towns like Stockport, where the managers were drawn from among the employers of labour.[46] What perhaps needs most to be affirmed is the importance, declining though it was in the long term, of the religious impulse behind the eighteenth-century advances in elementary education. Until 1810, when secular liberals like Brougham, Whitbread, and James Mill took over the British and Foreign School Society,[47] the churches and especially the Church of England had almost a monopoly of the initiatives in any large schemes. In the English parochial charity schools the Anglican catechism formed the backbone of instruction.[48] The Sunday Schools varied in type. Large institutions in the North were often interdenominationally floated, though the Wesleyans, and afterwards the Church, were not slow to become separately and independently involved.[49] From rural Oxfordshire and its market towns, however, comes evidence that the schools were both founded and financed by the parish clergy.[50] Earnest High Churchmen were as forward in the movement as Evangelicals. Jones of Nayland announced in December 1783 that he had just composed an anthem for a Sunday School festival at the instigation of his fellow Hutchinsonian Dr Glasse, and looked to Charles Poyntz, another of that brotherhood, to arrange a visit of the Countess Spencer, 'a lady who shines so much as the patroness of Sunday Schools, that if we could have seen her here we should have thought it nearly

---

[45] R. Hume 'Educational Provision for the Kentish Poor, 1660–1811', *Southern History* (1982), cited from John Rule, *The Labouring Classes in Early Industrial England 1750–1850* (1986), 231–2. Dr Rule's work also provides a critical survey of the published assessments of literacy (Ibid. 234).

[46] T. W. Laqueur, *Religion amd Respectability: Sunday Schools and Working Class Culture 1780–1850* (1976), *passim*, esp. 61, 241.

[47] Henriques, *Before the Welfare State*, 205.

[48] Jones, *Charity School Movement*, 241.

[49] Ward, *Religion and Society* 13–16, 40–3.

[50] Diana McClatchey, *Oxfordshire Clergy 1777–1869* (Oxford, 1960), 147.

equal to an episcopal visitation'.[51] Oxfordshire clergy maintained day schools for the offspring of the poor or paid for the village children to be educated elsewhere. Such examples of private benevolence were by no means rare towards the close of the eighteenth century.[52]

At that time, however, opposition to the education of the masses was still to be encountered. Those who mounted it were the strongest advocates of social control. The early eighteenth-century writer who remarked, 'If a horse knew as much as a man, I should not like to be his rider', had his sentiments echoed in the House of Commons by an opponent of Whitbread's bill for the instruction of pauper children in 1807. The words of his speech have been often quoted. Schooling would teach the labouring classes 'to despise their lot, instead of making them good servants in agriculture and other laborious employments'; it would enable them 'to read seditious pamphlets, vicious books and publications against Christianity'. It would make them 'insolent to their superiors'.[53] As R. A. Soloway has shown, most of the bishops bearing office during the French Revolutionary epoch, whether High Church or Low, were sufficiently enlightened to recognize that for the sake of religion and good government some kind of popular education was necessary. The more adventurous among them—Barrington, John Douglas of Carlisle, and Richard Watson of Llandaff, theologically a curiously mixed bag—looked beyond private benevolence and the Sunday Schools to some kind of public system. Samuel Horsley, however, has been deemed a renegade on account of his association of the Sunday Schools with Jacobinism in 1800.[54] This is misleading and also unfortunate, in that his remarks have unduly stamped the contemporary High Church cause with the impress of extreme reaction.

Horsley was a firm advocate of popular education, especially in religion. Preaching for the SPCK, of which he was an assiduous patron, on 1 June 1793, he recalled the Society to its pristine purposes after a long period of diversion to the Indian mission and other concerns. His starting point was a changed theological perception—that 'the prophets describe the poor', the literal poor, not, as figuratively understood, the heathen world poor in religious knowledge, 'as especial objects of the divine mercy in the Christian dispensation'. The most effectual means of communicating the gospel to them, he urged, was 'by charitable provisions for the religious education of their children'. He excoriated the objection voiced against institutions for this purpose 'by a mean and dastardly policy imbibed in foreign climes' that 'by the advantages of a religious education, the poor may be raised above the laborious duties of his station, and his use in civil life be lost'. When the defensive intention of his argument is borne in mind, it is not surprising that

---

[51] Poyntz Letters, Jones to Poyntz, 8 Dec. 1783.
[52] McClatchey, *Oxfordshire Clergy*, 150–1.
[53] Quoted from Derek Fraser, *The Evolution of the British Welfare State* (1973), 72.
[54] Soloway, *Prelates and People*, 352–8, 363.

he fell over himself to subscribe to the conventional view that Christian instruction was quite compatible with civil subjection, and assigned only a minimal role to secular training, which should be kept, he held, to 'those first rudiments of . . . the trivial literature of their mother tongue, without which they would scarce be qualified to be subjects even of the lowest class of the free government under which they are born'.[55] Dismissively expressed, as much to reassure those clergy and lay backwoodsmen who still feared that any kind of education would make the labouring classes discontented, as to convey his own preferences, his curricular prescriptions hardly fell below the average practice of late eighteenth-century charity schools, which, as Jones has shown, continued to exclude the 'trivial literature' of children's books from the classroom, though *Mother Goose's Melody* and *The Tale of Goody Two-Shoes* were being replaced, as the century reached its close, by better fare like Hannah More's *Sacred Dramas for Children* and Mrs Trimmer's *Story of the Robins*.[56] If scarcely an educational prophet, Horsley at least defended the charity schools, and by implication the Sunday Schools also.

There is no reason to suppose that he changed his mind even under the stress of revolutionary war. The claim that he did so rests partly on his speech in the House of Lords on the Monastic Institutions Bill on 10 July 1800, and partly on his Rochester visitation charge published later that year. His reference in the former to some of the Protestant Dissenters 'in whose schools the doctrines of Jacobinism, sedition, and infidelity, were but too frequently inculcated' instanced as examples schools 'under the name of charity-schools, Sunday-schools, and schools to *enlighten* children in and about the metropolis'.[57] The bishop's language was ambiguous, and was not specifically directed against Sunday Schools. A report was nevertheless circulated at the time, which he ascribed to 'a misrepresentation in the public prints' that he had spoken 'with decided disapprobation' of all Sunday Schools. In the charge to the clergy of Rochester he gave unqualified denial to the claim: 'The report is false. I spoke of them, upon that occasion, as I have always spoken, and always shall speak, as institutions that may be very beneficial, or very pernicious, according as they are well or ill conducted, and according as they are placed in proper or improper hands.' Earlier in the charge he had specified more pointedly than before the types of school he was lambasting:

In many parts of the kingdom new conventicles have been opened in great number, and congregations formed of one knows not what denomination. The pastor is often, in appearance at least, an illiterate peasant or mechanic. The congregation is visited occasionally by preachers from a distance. Sunday-schools are opened in connection with these conventicles. There is much reason to suspect, that the expenses of these

---

[55] Horsley, *Sermons* (1810), i. 193–221.

[56] Jones, *Charity School Movement*, 83.

[57] *Parl. Reg.*, 3rd ser., xii (1800), 346–7 (10 July). See above, p. 110.

schools and conventicles are defrayed by associations formed in different places . . . It is very remarkable that these new congregations of non-descripts have been mostly formed, since the Jacobins have been laid under the restraint of those two salutary statutes, commonly known by the names of the Seditious [Meetings] and the Treason Bill. A circumstance which gives much ground for suspicion that sedition and atheism are the real objects of these institutions, rather than religion. Indeed in some places this is known to be the case. In one topic the teachers of all these congregations agree: abuse of the Established clergy, as negligent of their flocks, cold in their preaching, and destitute of the Spirit.[58]

It is evident from the above that the dispute was not about Sunday Schools or the merits of elementary education. It resulted from the stinging resentment of Churchmen, and particularly High Churchmen, of the itinerant evangelism which spread as a wave through the English villages in 1797–8, under the auspices of largely undenominational county associations, determined, as in Bedfordshire, to employ untrained lay agents to assist in the work.[59] The odium incurred by the associations rubbed off, as Professor W. R. Ward has shown, on the older undenominational Sunday Schools,[60] but evidence of serious political engagement is hard to find in either. Laqueur's investigations unearthed no political Sunday Schools before 1818 and very few afterwards.[61] Opponents of village evangelism noticed in the High Church *British Critic* laid their emphasis rather on the following of 'a wandering tribe of fanatical teachers, mostly taken from the lowest and most illiterate classes of society; among whom are to be found raving enthusiasts, pretending to divine impulses of various and extra-ordinary kinds, practising exorcisms, and many other sorts of impostures and delusions, and obtaining thereby an unlimited sway over the minds of the ignorant multitude'.[62] Contemporaries dubbed these activities 'Methodist', but usually distinguished them from official Methodism and Dissent. Even Horsley did not claim, as Ward supposes, 'that the expansion of non-Anglican Sunday Schools and conventicles since 1795 was the work of Jacobins', nor is it apparent that his charge was 'designed as a signal for legislation by the government'.[63] Though he mentioned the possibility that the legislature might take action to stem the growing evil, he insisted that his present concern was with the assistance which his auditors might offer in their 'proper character . . . of parish priests'. Among other remedial measures he urged them 'that you should, by all means in your

---

[58] Horsley, *Rochester Charge 1800* (1800), 19–21, 24–6.
[59] Ward, *Religion and Society*, 47–51.
[60] Ibid. 40–4.
[61] Laqueur, *Religion and Respectability*, 179–86, *passim*.
[62] Quoted from review of 'Report of the Clergy of a District in the Diocese of Lincoln (1800)', *British Critic* 15 (1800), 409–16. This epitomizes comments elsewhere in the journal in the early years of the 19th cent.
[63] Ward, *Religion and Society*, 41.

power, promote the establishment of Sunday-Schools in your respective parishes, and take the trouble to superintend the management of them'. Superintendence, however, meant leaving nothing to the discretion of a master or mistress, allowing no books to be introduced which they had not previously vetted, and confining the selection 'almost' to expositions of the Church catechism, psalters, prayer-books, Testaments, and Bibles, using the SPCK lists as a guide.[64] At that time it was only the exceptional Sunday School that strayed beyond those limits, though there was already an un-denominational school at Nottingham which taught writing on Sundays, and met on weeknights for instruction in arithmetic.[65]

SEX, MARRIAGE, AND DIVORCE

A sense of the conflict between traditional family values and an advancing licentiousness was present in England throughout the eighteenth century. In the early decades of the century it was linked to complaints of decay in the effectiveness of the old machinery of control, which was basically ecclesiastical. These found classical expression in the *Representation of the State of Religion* by the clergy in Convocation in 1711, which expatiated on blasphemous and scurrilous writings and the immoralities of the stage, and traced the origin of the evil to the Civil War, 'that long and unnatural rebellion which loosened all the bonds of discipline and order, and overturned the goodly frame of our ecclesiastical and civil constitution'.[66] Whether the weakening of clerical control of morality by the political revolutions of the seventeenth century was as immediate in its incidence or as important in its consequences as Atterbury and his associates affected to believe is a matter open to question. The late Gareth Bennett argued that the penitential discipline of the church courts, which was recovered at the Restoration, collapsed in the immediate aftermath of the Toleration Act.[67] Other evidence from the diocese which he used as his principal example, namely Exeter, seriously undermines this conclusion, for Arthur Warne's compact study of Devon points to an effective continuance of this jurisdiction down to 1787, when Parliament set a strict time limit for presentments.[68] Lawrence Stone writes of a 'collapse of business in the consistory courts' between 1680 and 1720, supporting his case with evidence from the archdeaconry of Chester and the dioceses of Lichfield and Exeter.[69] But the Chester correction book shows a massive survival of moral discipline through the deanery courts well into

---

[64] Horsley, *Rochester Charge 1800*, 21, 24–6.
[65] Laqueur, *Religion and Respectability*, 131.
[66] Bennett, *Tory Crisis*, 136–8.
[67] Ibid. 6–7, 14–15.
[68] Arthur Warne, *Church and Society in Eighteenth-Century Devon* (Newton Abbot, 1969), 76–9.
[69] Lawrence Stone, *Road to Divorce: England 1530–1987* (Oxford, 1990), 40–3.

the eighteenth century. One hundred and twelve presentments for sexual offences—fornication, adultery, bastardy, cohabitation, and incest—were made at the archdeacon of Richmond's visitation in October–November 1735. When the cases came before the rural dean's court held in the cathedral and other large churches in Lancashire and Cheshire in the following year, some kind of follow-up, usually the imposition of a penance, was recorded against fifty-three of them. In this extra-ordinary diocese an itinerant rural dean acted for the archdeacon in proceedings which were still operative but for the most part never came to the consistory. Twenty years later the system was in a state of decay. Though the number of presentments continued to rise, the proportion leading to recorded court apearances and sentencing fell away almost to nothing by the mid-1760s.[70] The chief importance of Stone's systematic exploration of statistics is not that it shows the inactivity of ecclesiastical moral police in the eighteenth century but that it reveals a significant revival of the competence of the church courts in marriage disputes from the 1760s onwards. Most of this was handled in the first instance by the London consistory court, which by the period from the 1770s to the 1840s had become 'the main conduit for matrimonial breakdown in the country'.[71] A probable corollary of this was the persistence of defamation (or 'words') cases, which constituted the mainbrace of the moral jurisdiction of the diocesan courts in the 1780s. Fifty-nine such actions were brought in the London consistory in 1780–3, compared with forty-three in 1743–6.[72] Cast mostly in a standard form, in which one woman accused another of abusing her falsely as a 'whore', they reflected the weakening position of women, largely married women of the middle classes, in the marriage partnership.

While the business of the canon law courts fell but slowly and unevenly away, Church control of personal morality was in other ways increased. From about 1750 onwards clergy were appointed in increasing numbers to the office of JP,[73] giving them coercive powers over putative fathers of bastard children. Most important of all, Lord Hardwicke's Marriages Act of 1753 made a wedding in an Anglican church after banns or special licence necessary to establish the validity of the ordinance for all but the minority of Englishmen.

Any deterioration of morals occurring during the century is likely to have arisen from pressures changing the habits of the population rather than from enfeeblement of the mechanisms of control. Parish register research conducted by the Cambridge Group for the History of Population and Social Structure and comparable work by Continental demographers have pointed to a European 'sexual revolution in the late eighteenth century' evident for

---

[70] Cheshire CRO EDV.1/122, 154, 167, dio. Chester Correction Books, 1735–6, 1755–6, 1765–6; also others in series.

[71] Stone, *Divorce*, 34–5, 43–4.

[72] Dio. London DL/C/170 & 179, Allegations, Libels, and Sentence Books.

[73] E. J. Evans, *The Contentious Tithe* (1976), 11.

England and Wales in sharply rising illegitimacy ratios from 1750 onwards.[74] This has been explained by Edward Shorter in terms of an emancipation of lower-class women from the traditional virtues of premarital chastity resulting from urbanization and the growth of opportunities for employment outside the home. This thesis does not fit the facts of economic geography. Moreover, the heavy incidence of pregnancy at the time of marriage occurring in between one-third and two-fifths of eighteenth-century weddings, renders it more convincing to ascribe the increase in bastardy to the non-fulfilment of expectations of matrimony consequent on the proletarianizing of the village community and movements of population than to rampant promiscuity.[75] Among the upper classes, however, there was an acceleration of the growth of divorce which is less easily exonerated.

A private Act of Parliament was the only means by which, for those wealthy enough to pay for it, the right to remarry might be obtained, as church courts administering canon law could grant no more than a separation, *a mensa et toro*, for adultery or cruelty. Lord Auckland gave figures from the House of Lords Journals in 1800. During the 130 years since Lord de Roos's marriage had been dissolved in 1670 on grounds of his wife's adultery, there had been 132 parliamentary divorces. Of these there were only eight in the first forty-five years; fifty in the next sixty years, and seventy-four in the last twenty-five years. In the four years immediately preceding the session of 1800 there were twenty-nine bills, excluding five which had been rejected, and in the last session alone, ten exclusive of two rejected.[76] His words bear testimony that formal divorce was becoming socially more acceptable, but should not be taken as proof of a deterioration of morals among the aristocracy and gentry. Literary evidence points in the opposite direction—to a retreat from the grossness depicted by Hogarth and John Gay in the first four decades of the eighteenth century and an advance of refinement and sensibility. It is told of the young Walter Scott that when he sent to his great-aunt, on her own strong insistence, the novels of Aphra Benn to provide her with reading matter in the 1790s, she returned them to him with the comment that it was 'a very odd thing' that 'I, an old woman of eighty and upwards, sitting alone, feel myself ashamed to read a book which, sixty years ago, I have heard read aloud for the amusement of large circles, consisting of the best and most creditable circles in London'.[77] Muriel Jaeger has reinforced the impression of a younger generation at the beginning of the nineteenth century critical of the morals of

---

[74] P. Laslett, K. Oosterveen, and R. M. Smith, *Bastardy and its Comparative History* (1980), esp. introduction by Peter Laslett, 1–68.

[75] Jeffrey Weeks, *Sex, Politics and Society: The Regulation of Sexuality since 1800* (1981), 61–7, discussing Shorter's arguments advanced in his *The Making of the Modern Family* (1976) and articles. Bridal pregnancy levels are examined by P. E. H. Hair, 'Bridal Pregnancy in Earlier Rural England', *Population Studies* 24 (1970), 59–70, and by John Rule, *Labouring Classes*, 196–8.

[76] *Parl. Reg.*, 3rd ser., xi. 607.

[77] Noel Perrin, *Dr. Bowdler's Legacy* (1969), 9.

its elders.[78] But perhaps that was just the point. Roy Porter has shown[79] that marriage among the landed and well-to-do classes changed its character accordingly, broadening from a stiff dynastic alliance, concerned with the transmission of property, into a closer personal union which, although it kept the woman in firm subordination to the man, conceded a little to love in the initial choice of partner, ensured by the 1780s that husband and wife were seen to go about together, and turned the mother into a focus of family life. By this process successful marriages became more successful, but unsuccessful ones more intolerable. Moreover, with improving taste *mésalliances* could less easily be circumvented by whoredom. A procedure was thus required by which changes of spouse could be regularized.

From about the end of the first decade of George III's reign, however, a reaction supervened. Concern about the growing number of petitions prompted conservative moral reformers to take action periodically to stem it. They feared that young married women were being tempted by seducers with the promise of remarriage after their husbands had divorced them, the spread of adultery being thereby encouraged. There were suspicions of fraud and false accusations to procure severances desired merely for reasons of incompatibility of temperament, and of collusion between the parties to a divorce. These were not groundless—Lawrence Stone has produced evidence of increasing collusion to procure divorce by mutual consent after 1750 and especially after 1780[80]—but the crusaders proposed a remedy which threatened to make things worse. In February 1771 Lord Athol brought forward a bill to restrain persons divorced for the crime of adultery from marrying the co-respondent and to declare the issue of such a marriage incapable of inheriting. It passed the House of Lords, but though Edmund Burke argued strongly in its favour, it was defeated in the Commons by the opposition of Fox, Beauchamp, and Wedderburn.[81] Shute Barrington, the High Church bishop of Llandaff, tried again in March 1779 with a like proposal designated 'an act for the more effectual discouragement of the crime of adultery'. It was admitted even by Charles James Fox that 'adultery was present to an alarming degree, and divorces more frequent than ever', a circumstance which Barrington ascribed to the total extinction of shame and to the invention of settlements and bonds which circumvented the legal disabilities of the divorced woman in respect of recovering her dowry and the interval allowed to her for remarriage. The episcopal bill was lost, like its predecessor, in the Lower House, where Fox stigmatized it as unfair to women, who would be prevented by its provisions from making the only

---

[78] Muriel Jaeger, *Before Victoria: Changing Standards of Behaviour 1787–1837* (1956), p. ix, and *passim*.

[79] Roy Porter, *English Society in the Eighteenth Century* (Harmondsworth, 1982), 40–5.

[80] Stone, *Divorce*, 328–32.

[81] *JHL* 33 (1770–3), p. 82; *Parl. Hist.* xvii (1771–4), 185–6.

atonement in their power, and would be driven to become common prostitutes. He averred that the ladies, being totally unrepresented in the House, were entitled to 'the most tender treatment, in cases where the sexes were to be distinguished'.[82]

The question was not raised again in general form for nineteen years, at the close of which the upturn in the trend of divorces recalled Parliament's attention to it. The rise was probably due to an intensification of factors previously operative, which Lord Westmorland summarized in 1801 as a mixture of 'the increased wealth of the country, which afforded a greater facility for making such applications' and 'a nicer sense of honour'.[83] Zealous patriots sensed a new influence: that of Revolutionary France where the Constituent Assembly introduced a form of civil divorce in 1792. Given the revulsion against the French Revolution in all but the most radical quarters, it is unlikely that this example had much positive effect on the marital behaviour of the English upper classes, but in the hands of old-fashioned High Churchmen and conservative peers especially, the denunciation of French immoralities became for a while an instrument of psychological warfare against the new Republic. It fitted easily into Horsley's apocalyptic obsessions. Among the characteristics of Daniel's Wilful King ascribed to the enemy in his Rochester charge in 1800 was that they 'use no discretion in the pleasures of women'.[84] In the following year, before the uneasy Peace of Amiens was concluded, H. H. Norris, the future leader of the Hackney Phalanx, preached a sermon in St John's, Hackney, which was later printed. Heavily inspired by the conspiratorial doctrines of Robison's *Proofs*, it advanced the theory that the devotees of Illuminism had resolved upon using women to further their purposes of disorganizing society. The discourse exhorted English women to avoid 'every fashion, which bears the smallest remembrance [*sic*] to those licentious habits, which apostate France has adopted, and we, alas! are too constantly importing'. The allusion, as the appendix to the printed edition shows, was to revealing classical dresses of the Directoire style, which had been attacked by Robison both as immodest and as suggestive of an admiration of Greek democracy.[85] It is not to be supposed that this feeling was cynically concocted to serve the needs of the national war effort. Rather did it furnish an example of what the sociologists have lately called 'moral panic', triggered on this occasion by the national emergency.[86]

The pivotal theme in the response was the parliamentary battle over Lord Auckland's Adultery Bill, in which Samuel Horsley emerged as a key figure.

[82] *Parl. Hist.* xx. 599.

[83] *Parl. Reg.*, 3rd ser., xiv (1801), 668.

[84] Horsley, *Rochester Charge 1800*, 10–11.

[85] H. H. Norris, 'The Influence of the Female Character upon Society...a Sermon...November 22, 1801' (1801).

[86] Weeks, *Sex, Politics and Society*, 14, citing Stan Cohen, *Folk Devils and Moral Panics*.

Its immediate cause was an unsavoury private action which came before the House of Lords on 2 March 1798, in which James Esten, a former ship's purser, who had deserted his actress wife in Dublin several years earlier, was suing for divorce on grounds of her adultery with the duke of Hamilton. Esten had been in financial distress, and Lord Auckland, a member of the Government, who was present at the second reading of the bill, expressed his suspicions of collusion between the parties, and to the accompaniment of a loud cry of 'Hear, hear' from the bishop of Rochester (Horsley) and others, announced that the House could not entertain such a case, which was 'better adapted to the proceedings for divorces before the municipality of Paris'. He gave his 'cool and deliberate' opinion that 'French immoralities' were 'the most dangerous mode of attack that the enemy could make', and that he dreaded them 'more than any other kind of invasion, whatever menaces might precede it, or whatever shape it might assume'. That old veteran in the field Shute Barrington, now bishop of Durham, supported him with a fanciful insinuation that the French rulers, unable to subdue us by force of arms, had turned to undermining the morals of our youth by sending over a troupe of indecent female dancers, whose appearances 'far out-shamed any thing of a similar nature that had ever been exhibited—he would not say, on any Christian theatre, but even upon the more licentious theatres of Athens and of Rome'. The Lord Chancellor, Loughborough, nevertheless, insisted on hearing counsel for the petitioner, but, when the bill was then rejected,[87] lost no time in bringing forward two amendments to the standing orders of the House of Lords to guide the House in dealing with future applications and to prevent collusive divorces. The first required an official copy of the previous proceedings for *a mensa et toro* separation in the ecclesiastical courts, which were a requisite preliminary to a request to the Lords for permission to remarry, to be delivered at the bar of the House; the second required the petitioner for the divorce to appear at the second reading of the bill, and be examined about the state of his marital relations. Bishop Horsley welcomed the Chancellor's explanation that no reflection on the church courts for letting through the Esten case was intended, and with his support and Barrington's the orders were adopted on 28 March.[88] When Lord Mulgrave, a supporter of the Government, tried to get them rescinded two years later on the ground that they clashed with the leading principles of English jurisprudence and the rules of evidence, which forbade the questioning of an individual on oath in points where he was deeply implicated, the ebullient bishop of Rochester was foremost in their defence. Expatiating on the 'wretched' French example, he observed that the lenient provisions of Divorce Bills 'were most strenuously supported by the admirers of Jacobinism'. In flat contradiction of what

---

[87] *JHL* 41 (1796–8), pp. 485–7; *Parl. Hist.*, xxxiii (1797–8), 1306–10.
[88] *Parl. Reg.*, 3rd ser., v. 482–5.

Mulgrave had said, he claimed that 'in nine or ten suits on the score of seduction or adultery, the parties had agreed to get rid of each other; and in most cases the seducer accommodated the husband with evidence for the purposes of the latter, which otherwise could not be obtained'. His observations showed that he did not at all recognize the legality of remarriage after divorce. There 'was no such thing in the law of England as divorce: the Courts below could not exceed a *mensa et thoro*: they could not dissolve any marriage that was not *ab initio* bad . . . At the bar of that House, the petitioner could only solicit a favour, and not claim the Act of Divorce as a right.'[89] This was a tenable but conservative view. Most peers would have recognized that the changing practice of the ecclesiastical courts and of the Upper House of the legislature in the late seventeenth and early eighteenth centuries had jointly established sufficient precedent for divorce inclusive of the right to remarry. But that was not really the issue. The right had been abused, or was widely believed to have been, and the question before the House was how to apply a corrective.

Auckland used the debate, on 21 March 1800, to gather support for the bill which he intended to introduce, reviving the idea of a ban on the inter-marriage of the offending parties. He wished to incorporate in it a provision to enable those who were not wealthy enough to afford a private Act of Parliament to engage in divorce proceedings. This enlightened suggestion did not materialize until 1857, when the Matrimonial Causes Act established secular courts and procedures which would make divorce available to the upper middle class.[90] Auckland's bill, when it was presented to the House of Lords on 2 April, though styled 'An Act for the More Effectual Prevention of the Crime of Adultery' was really a measure to discourage divorces by implementing on a general scale the prohibition of subsequent marriage between the guilty parties.[91] The bill was defended at its second reading by the princes of the Church, Porteus, the serious-minded bishop of London, Barrington, and Horsley against head-on opposition from the royal duke of Clarence, later King William IV. Clarence had set up house with the actress Dorothy Jordan, a woman with a past but not married to anyone else.[92] There is no reason to doubt the altruism of his objection to the unfairness of a measure which would prevent a man from rescuing a woman who had been turned out by her husband for her adultery with him. As he explained to the House, he would be placed in that position by the Royal Marriages Act 'if he should at any time incur the guilt of having seduced a married lady'. On the other side Porteus bolstered the case for deterrence with evidence from his own consistory court that the number of divorces sued for had of late years

---

[89] Ibid, xi (1800), 78–83 (21 Mar. 1800).
[90] Ibid. 83–6; cf. Weeks, *Sex, Politics and Society*, 24.
[91] Ibid. 171–2.
[92] P. Ziegler, *King William IV* (1973), chap. vi. *passim*.

increased enormously, to 198 in a very short period. Horsley made an ill-judged speech, referring to the law of the Commonwealth making adultery punishable by death and to precedents in Jewish and Roman history. Dissociating himself from this severity, Mulgrave seized the occasion to hold him up in the unusual guise of 'an advocate for the laws of the Commonwealth'. Clarence tore into his history when he seemed to imply that the last thirty years of the seventeenth century, including the reign of Charles II, were pure times compared with those of his present Majesty, though the bishop qualified his remarks. Clarence's adverse motion was lost by 11 votes to 30, and the bill passed its second reading.[93] But after the Lords committee on it had been postponed several times, Auckland replaced it on 16 May by a new bill. In its final form, this proposed to retain the prohibition of marriage between the guilty party and the co-respondent but to add a provision making adultery with a married woman under the care of her husband an indictable offence punishable by fine and imprisonment or either. Collusion by the husband, if proved to the court, was to deprive him of damages, and release the accused from the punishment.[94]

From insufficiency of manuscript evidence the reason for the change can only be conjectured. Auckland admitted that the original bill had been found to be very defective. He took the advice of the Scott family—Eldon, his son, and his brother Sir William, experts in the common and civil law—on Roman precedents for allowing the remarriage of divorced persons, though at what stage is uncertain. It is probable that Horsley had a considerable hand in the redrafting, for the new provisions followed his emphasis in the earlier debate on the punishment of adultery by law among the Jews and the Romans. Safeguards of a characteristically Horsleian kind to protect the jurisdiction of the courts ecclesiastical and temporal, were also built into the revised measure, and it was the bishop of Rochester who announced to the House that the changes had been made to avert the objection that the original bill was unequal 'because it went merely to punish the adultress, and not the seducer'.[95]

If this was their purpose the alterations did nothing to reduce the parliamentary opposition to the proposed legislation. Clarence assailed the new bill as fiercely as the old. He and other peers stigmatized it as a change in ancient law, and called for delay to allow it to be circulated and to permit the opinions of the best-informed authorities to be collected. Horsley replied that no more was proposed than to increase the penalties for an old crime, and urged that, as it did not differ in principle from its predecessor the new bill

[93] *Parl. Reg.*, 3rd ser., xi (1800), 185–202 (4 Apr. 1800).

[94] BL Add. MSS 34,455, Auckland Papers, xliv, fos. 293–4, printed copy of bill dated 26 May 1800; cf. *JHL* 42 (1798–1800), pp. 428, 435, 447, 505.

[95] *Parl. Reg.*, 3rd ser., xi (1800), 593, 670; BL Add. MSS 34,455 Auckland Papers, xiv, fos. 286–8, John Scott to Eldon, [n.d.] and endorsement.

might go straight into committee. To a greater extent than Auckland he was targeted by antagonists of the measure, indicating perhaps the belief that he was largely responsible for it. As the second reading on 19 May approached, the House of Lords was treated to the spectacle of a long and spirited attack by a future king of England on the position adopted by the venerable prelate. Clarence had gone to remarkable lengths to equip himself with ammunition from classical times—of Hipparete's divorce of her husband Alcibiades and Aemilius Paullus' divorce of his first wife Papyria—in a vain attempt to prove a right to remarry. The quaint resort to Roman precedents, also illustrated by the researches of John Scott, Jun., into the subject on behalf of his father Eldon,[96] shows the continuing importance of Roman civil law as a guide to matrimonial questions. A more piercing shaft in the duke's quiver was the discovery of the bishop's own sermon preached at the Magdalen in 1795 in which he had pleaded for Christian charity to the fallen female sinner. Clarence quoted it back to him at length across the floor of the House of Lords: the analogy between the pleasures of the senses and the joys of heaven, the double standard which laid the whole infamy of misconduct upon the woman, the obstacles which this placed to her return to virtue and even to the possibility of her repentance, 'unless it be such repentance as may be exercised by the terrified sinner in her last agonies! perishing in the open streets! under the merciless pelting of the elements! of cold and hunger, and a broken heart!' Horsley's reply when thus reminded of his own words was to draw the distinction between compassion for the poor prostitutes for whom he had been pleading then and the support of 'persons in an elevated life in a profligate breach of the marriage vow, when their education and duty ought to have restrained their depraved passions'.[97]

Despite its ominous title, 'An Act for the Punishment and More Effectual Prevention of the Crime of Adultery', the bill was regarded like its predecessor as a device for regulating divorce rather than a penal law imposing a code of morality on the entire community. Any ambiguity remaining on this score, and there was perhaps some in Horsley's mind, was removed by the three verbal amendments introduced by Lord Eldon, the Lord Chief Justice, at the committal proceedings on 21 May. It was ordered that the prosecution of an adulterer was to be by indictment not by information, that the right to initiate it should be confined to the offended husband or the offender's wife, and that the circumstances precluding a husband from bringing the indictment should be redefined.[98] Apart from a weakening of the overtones of sexual discrimination, in which Horsley to his credit played some part, the bill in its final form was a stiffened version of that which Auckland had first

---

[96] BL Add. MSS 34,455, xiv, fos. 286–8, Scott to Eldon [n.d.].
[97] *Parl. Reg.*, 3rd ser., xi (1801), 593–604.
[98] Ibid. 661–3.

introduced. At the decisive third reading on 23 May the bishop of Rochester rose to deliver the final answer to its critics.

A central issue in the debate was the role of the church courts and of civil and canon lawyers in the matrimonial process.[99] These were involved because the bill, while making a new misdemeanor of adultery, gave protection to the lower courts, ecclesiastical or temporal, in a jurisdiction which permitted the aggrieved husband to obtain a separation from the consistory and claim damages of the co-respondent in a common-law court for the same offence which he pursued in the Lords.[100] Earlier in the debate the earl of Carlisle, a Portland Whig, had attacked the 'monkish seclusion' of the practitioners in the ecclesiastical court which unfitted them for influence in the world of men, and had called for the cleansing of the 'Augean stable' renowned for its rapacity and delays. He had urged that the power to award damages encouraged the multiplication of divorce suits brought by avaricious spouses. Bishop Horsley followed Eldon in springing to the defence of the church courts. He resorted to history to prove that statute and the practice of the judges of the Court of King's Bench agreed in affirming 'that divines and canonists are the persons best qualified to judge of the crime of adultery—what is to be deemed adultery—what punishment should be applied to it'. He also claimed that justice was 'distributed with as much ability, and as much integrity, in their courts, as in any other court of law or equity in Great Britain'. The force with which his sentiments were delivered, as much as the content of them shows that behind the parliamentary quarrel over the Adultery Bill lay a still keen competition between the courts Christian and the high court of Parliament for the last word in the determination of marriage law. Eldon had invoked the powerful opinion of Lord Chancellor Thurlow that instead of conferring the power to grant final divorces on the House of Lords the ecclesiastical court should be empowered to confer divorce *a vinculo matrimonii*.[101]

Horsley would have had doubts about this solution. He was concerned not only with the competence of courts but with the divine law. His repeated claim was 'that the marriage of a divorced adultress with the adulterer is itself adultery by the law of God'. This was what was relevant to the proposed legislation. But the arguments which he used to support this implied the full Catholic doctrine of the indissolubility of marriage. He interpreted the Lord's words from Matthew 19: 3–9 strictly: 'By Christ's law, the man who puts away his wife, except for adultery, and marries another, commits adultery. And he who marries her, thus put away by Christ's law for adultery, the only cause of putting away under Christ's law, committeth adultery.' This

[99] Ibid. 699–713 (23 May 1800).
[100] BL Add. MSS 34,455, xliv, fos. 293–4, printed bill, 26 May 1800.
[101] *Parl. Hist.* xxxv (1800–1), 278–82; *Parl. Reg.*, 3rd ser., xi (1800), 699–700.

exposition he bolstered with the Pauline text, 1 Corinthians 7: 10–11, enjoining on the separated wife to 'remain unmarried, or be reconciled to her husband'.[102] It is small wonder that in an earlier debate Lord Mulgrave had understood him to assert 'that a woman divorced *a vinculo matrimonii*, commits adultery, let her marry whomsoever she will, whether her seducer or any other man'.[103] This was not the view of all High Churchmen. When the House was considering a private bill of divorce brought by George Taylor in 1801 against his wife who had been seduced by a clergyman, Horsley clashed openly with his colleague of Durham over the interpretation of Christ's injunction. Bishop Barrington maintained that the Lord was merely putting a gloss on the Mosaic law which permitted divorce. Rochester acknowledged the difference from his own view which was that Christ was pronouncing as an original legislator, restoring marriage to its pristine purity. Horsley urged that the opinion which he had expressed as to the Saviour's meaning, when speaking of adultery, was 'the concurring sentiment of the Greek and Latin churches from the time of Chrysostom down to the days of Luther'.[104]

The bishop was not called upon by the occasion to state whether he believed that absolute divorce was possible or not. He approached the subject as a lawyer, human and divine, not as a metaphysician. Nevertheless, reviewing the judgement of Archbishop Cranmer and his commissioners in the case of the divorce of the marquess of Northampton, 'that a marriage once dissolved was as though it had never been', he rejected it. The archbishop, he said, reasoned like a monk rather than a senator in that he reached a conclusion upon 'a great question of law and justice' upon 'a mere logical subtlety, applying abstract principles to a practical question, without due accommodation of them to the particular circumstances of the case'. On the practical question of whether to permit remarriage of separated partners his own view was conservative but pragmatical: 'I have sometimes thought, that it had been a happy thing for the public if no bill of divorce had ever passed. But I confess, that the notorious prevalence of adultery, in countries where divorce is by no means to be had, seems to prove the contrary.'[105]

His final speech helped to carry the bill through the Lords on 23 May by the narrow majority of 8 despite the strength of the aristocratic opposition headed by the Prince of Wales and five of the royal dukes. That the measure represented the mind of the late eighteenth-century Church is evident from the fact that the majority included the archbishop of Canterbury and nineteen other bishops from a bench of twenty-six.[106] Nothing showed more clearly Horsley's ability to command the support of his episcopal brethren in the

---

[102] *Parl. Reg.*, 3rd ser., xi (1800), 701, 705–6.
[103] Ibid. 626–31.
[104] Ibid. xiv (1801), 451–5.
[105] Ibid. xi (1800), 703, 709.
[106] Ibid. 715–16.

Upper House. When the bill foundered like its predecessors in the House of Commons notwithstanding Wilberforce's lead in its favour,[107] the bishop promised to bring forward a proposition of his own on the subject. There is no evidence that he followed this up, despite public encouragement from Lord Grenville to do so.[108] But he continued his vigilance over private Divorce Bills during the next two years, upholding the insertion of a specific clause to forbid intermarriage of the adulterers[109] and moving the rejection of a petition deficient in evidence of prior conviction for adultery in a common-law court.[110]

The Adultery Bill of 1800 was flawed by a wholly inadequate understanding of the causes of marital breakdown. Had it been enacted it would have set back the evolution of a sensitive code of divorce law, and would have intensified the oppression of married women. That it was contemplated is a sign of that harshness which historians have seen to enter into other aspects of English social policy about the turn of the century. Samuel Horsley made a more constructive contribution to the development of the marriage law in the closing years of his career by plugging the gaps in the operation of the system of regulation established by Lord Hardwicke's Act. That statute had failed to make regular provision for the solemnization of matrimony in certain churches and chapels where banns had not been called before its passing. This led to irregularities, especially in new churches. In the spring of 1804 Horsley carried two bills through Parliament—a general Act (44 George III, c. lxxvii) making good all marriages in unqualified chapels performed before 25 March 1805 provided that the registers were removed to the nearest parish church; and a local Act enabling the curate of Voelas chapel in his own diocese to publish banns after that date. The bishop devoted a good deal of his attention in his charge to the clergy of St Asaph in 1806 to warning them against neglecting the provisions of the Marriage Act. By that time the problem had been recognized as one of general concern, for the curates of some large parishes in the vicinity of the metropolis had been harshly reprimanded in the Court of Chancery for their inattention.[111]

MISCELLANEOUS MATTERS

To complete the available record, three further interventions indicative of Horsley's attitude towards social questions should be briefly mentioned. On

[107] *Parl. Hist.* xxxv (1800–1), 301–2. It was lost by 104 to 143 on the committal proceedings on 30 May. Ibid. 325.

[108] *Parl. Reg.*, 3rd ser., xii (1800), 283–4; xiv (1801), 450–1.

[109] In Taylor's Divorce Bill 1801, when the clause was moved by the marquis of Buckingham. Ibid., 3rd ser., xiv (1801), 450–2.

[110] In the case of Hoare's petition 1802. Ibid., 3rd ser., xvii (1802), 69–74.

[111] Horsley, *St. Asaph Charge 1806* (1806), 14–20.

17 July 1797 he gave qualified support to a bill to convert the existing Corporation of Surgeons into a College controlled by a committee of twenty-one, with power to examine candidates and to award diplomas costing £27. A learned and professional man himself, the bishop sympathized with this effort to raise surgery from a trade into a learned profession. It was, nevertheless, defeated by a ground-swell of meaner practitioners championed in the House by Lord Thurlow, who argued the case for army and navy surgeons.[112] Horsley also stood up to Government when exertions for economy in public expenditure trenched upon the observance of religious festivals. In June 1798 he spoke against a bill to reduce the number of holidays on religious festivals allotted by Parliament in Edward VI's reign to clerks in public offices from thirty-five to three exclusive of Sunday. The bishop protested that the observance of the holidays was 'essentially necessary to the due preservation of the established religion, against the inroads of Atheism'. Government spokesmen were concerned only to check abuses arising from the employment of deputies by clerks on such occasions, and readily agreed to substitute a more informal method of enforcing personal attendance.[113] During the last year of his life he fought a similar battle to retain holidays in the custom-house which, like modern bank holidays, restricted business in adjacent parts of the economy and for that reason fell under attack from the mercantile community. Horsley pleaded the case for four: the Epiphany, the Annunciation, the Ascension, and St John the Baptist's Day, but although the archbishop, Manners Sutton, proposed a compromise motion which would have kept the first of these, it was defeated.[114]

The conclusion to be drawn from this survey of his attitudes to social questions is that Horsley was a paternalist in the full meaning of the word. His outlook found room for genuine sympathy with the oppressed and even a 'bias towards the poor'. Not less strong, however, was his determination to combat secularization and to maintain the Church at the heart of community life. This, too, was relevant to the organic aspect of paternalism. As in early Victorian England, a paternalist 'saw the church as one of the central means of forming in the future a better society'.[115] It was a vision which came to be shared by the best Christians of all schools. But in the eighteenth century, when private benevolence fixed the limits of the finer impulses of most Latitudinarians and Evangelicals, doctrinal High Churchmen were alive to it most of all.

---

[112] *Parl. Reg.*, 3rd ser., iii (1796–7), 219–20, 227–31.
[113] Ibid., 3rd ser., vi (1798), 277–9, 351–2.
[114] A. W. Rowden, *The Primates of the Four Georges* (1916), 393–4.
[115] David Roberts, *Paternalism in Early Victoriam England* (1979), 52.

Finis

THERE could scarcely have been a sharper contrast than between Samuel Horsley's public career and his private life. In the first he was outstandingly able and effective but displayed to the world many of the more unpleasant qualities which attend success—a rough-tough fighting manner characteristic of the middle classes rather than a cultivated aristocracy, a sarcastic wit, and a tendency to talk down to audiences as if they were his students.

In private, however, he was a sensitive plant, emotionally dependent on diminishing home support and beset by a run of financial embarrassments, which, by his death, brought his affairs to such a state that, as his domestic chaplain, William Jocelyn Palmer, explained, 'there remained nothing which he could call his own'.[1] The loss of his young wife Mary in 1777 damaged him more than he showed, probably more than he recognized, at the time. His second marriage, to Sarah Wright, said to have been in service to his first wife, brought him a partner to whom he remained devoted and a good mother for his children, though perhaps a doubtful social asset. It is difficult to know quite what to make of Queen Charlotte's remark when she was presented at court referring to 'her ladylike bearing'.[2] But there can be no doubt that the breakdown of her health, which was apparent as early as 1786 in some sort of nervous disorder requiring sea-bathing treatment,[3] involved him in worry, absence from duty, and expense over a period of many years. By the end of the century her complaints had become very complicated and included dropsy which caused her to swell to a prodigious size. The doctors pronounced that it was not dangerous as the fluid was contained in a cyst and unlikely to affect the general system.[4] Nevertheless, when the couple went to Brighton in 1804 for the sake of Mrs Horsley's health, the visit had to be extended indefinitely, for she suffered a fresh attack.[5] On 2 April 1805 she died. Returning to London in a melancholy state, the bishop found a visit from his brother-in-law William Palmer a diversion from doing nothing but 'wander about from room to room and contemplate the solitude of my dreary house, relinquished by its best inhabitant'. He gave up his house in York Place and moved to Charles Street,[6] resuming his place in the House of Lords on 26 April. But

[1] LPL 2810, fos. 279–91, W. J. Palmer, 'An Account of Horsley's Manuscripts'.
[2] *DNB* xxvii. 383–6.
[3] HP 1768, fos. 147–50, E. to F. Horsley, 11 Nov. 1786.
[4] Ibid., fos. 82–7, A. to F. Horsley, 29 Dec. 1800.
[5] Ibid., fos. 103–4, A. to F. Horsley, 27 Feb. 1805.
[6] HP 1767, fos. 49, 50–1, Horsley to F. E. Horsley, 10 Apr. and 10 May 1805.

his real desire was to return to St Asaph, where disaster had befallen his family about the beginning of the year. The cause of the trouble was the misconduct of his son, the apple of his father's eye. The first intimation of this came when Heneage circularized his relatives informing them that he owed £4,000. According to Anne Horsley, the bishop's half-sister, whose letters gave details to her brother Francis in India, the entanglement was far worse than at first expected. Sister Mary Horsley's husband, William Palmer, a wealthy London merchant, undertook to sift the matter. After a great deal of work, he succeeded in arranging a settlement, but not before discovering that the liabilities amounted to some £13,000. Worse still, his creditors were pressing to have Heneage thrown into gaol. Allowing for some exaggeration on the part of Anne Horsley, outraged that her nephew had disgraced his father in his own diocese, it appears that he had raised money in St Asaph in ways which rendered him liable to arrest if he appeared there.[7] During the year he fled to Scotland,[8] where the Episcopal Church rewarded Bishop Horsley's past kindnesses by giving Heneage a chaplaincy at Dundee.[9]

The bishop, nevertheless, proceeded with his plans to go to St Asaph, as soon as the close of the business of a particularly heavy parliamentary session would permit. He installed himself at the episcopal palace with Heneage's wife Fanny and her two daughters, on whom he grew to dote.[10] Horsley's fondness for the company of children illustrates the tender side of his nature which was never far from the surface of the pompous exterior he presented to the world. More tellingly, it was reciprocated. Several years earlier, when Francis Horsley sent his family to England, his little son John spent some days at York Place with 'Uncle Bishop (of whom he is excessively fond)'. Aunt Elizabeth, who had custody of both the children, reported after her step-brother the bishop had stayed with them by himself 'that we have enjoyed this visit extremely & none of the party more than his nephew and niece. They are admirable playfellows & sometimes make a special noise together.'[11] At St Asaph he found a home, and the rest of the family rallied to his support in a way which, as Lord Selborne observed, was characteristic of them. William Jocelyn Palmer, his nephew, took up permanent residence there as bishop's chaplain. Jocelyn's father William Palmer and his mother Mary Horsley paid occasional visits—the first to interview creditors and the second to help with the domestic arrangements.[12] Fanny's prudence as a housekeeper had been

---

[7] HP 1768, fos. 106–8, 112–15, A. to F. Horsley, 1 Dec. 1805, 13 Mar. 1806.

[8] He was in Edinburgh by July 1805. HP 1767, fo. 52, Horsley to F. E. Horsley, 5 July 1805.

[9] J. Foster, *Alumni Oxonienses.*, 2nd ser., i. 694.

[10] HP 1767, fo. 53, Horsley to F. E. Horsley, 11 July 1805; HP 1768, fos. 112–15, A. to F. Horsley, 13 Mar. 1806.

[11] HP 1768, fos. 117–21, A. to F. Horsley, 7 Mar. 1804; Ibid., fos. 224–33, E. to F. Horsley, 5 Dec. 1802.

[12] HP 1767, fo. 52, Horsley to F. E. Horsley, 5 July 1805; HP 1768, fos. 106–8: A. to F. Horsley, 1 Dec. 1805.

called into question, and the bishop's peace of mind was disturbed by being required to compose quarrels in the family.[13]

Furthermore, at 72, he showed remarkable powers of recovery. In March 1806 he was quoted as saying: 'I never in my life was in such a wretched state of spirit: which makes me indolent to a shameful degree.'[14] By the middle of April, however, he was back in London, taking Fanny and the children with him. In the intervals of parliamentary business, he paid visits to several members of the family, proudly showing off the two little girls. But he was up and down. He found the session with its 'midnight revels in the House of Lords' unusually tiring, and there are indications in his letters that his health was giving trouble: a digestive complaint for which he was taking salts. It was severe enough for him to require excessively large doses. Nevertheless, there was no sign of long-term decline. He spoke at considerable length in the House on the slave trade on 25 June and 'was sometimes very energetic'.[15] At the end of the session he managed to preach in his old parish of St Mary, Newington before leaving for St Asaph to conduct the visitation. Death when it struck came suddenly, seemingly as the result of an infection. On 20 September he reached Brighton, where he had gone for a rest. On the 28th he walked with his daughter-in-law and grand-daughter to the Chapel Royal, and on the following day took a house 'in a retired situation', intending to spend the winter there. On 30 September he was taken ill, being affected by 'a slight complaint in his bowels' which 'brought on a mortification'. Early in the morning of 4 October, after only 'one day of pain', he died.[16]

On his death he was found to be insolvent. The elder Palmer obtained powers to administer his effects for the use and benefit of his creditors, who laid claim to everything. To Palmer's son, William Jocelyn, who remained at St Asaph, was left the task of preparing the bishop's fine library and mathematical instruments for sale, which took place by auction at Leigh and Sotheby's in the Strand, beginning on 4 May 1807 and lasting for nine days. In all, 1,932 books were disposed of, together with prints framed and glazed. When William Palmer had made his first dividend to the creditors, the latter gave their consent to the dispatch of the surviving manuscript material to Heneage Horsley. William Jocelyn sent him seventy-six parcels of this in one large box, including books with the bishop's most significant annotations which he had removed from the collection before sending it for sale.[17]

Though in public appearances were maintained to the end, to be sold up

[13] HP 1768, fos. 112–15, A. to F. Horsley, 13 Mar. 1806; HP 1767, fo. 74, Horsley to F. E. Horsley, [n.d.].

[14] HP 1768, fos. 112–15, A. to F. Horsley, 13 Mar. 1806.

[15] HP 1767, fos. 56, 62–3, 66–7, Horsley to F. E. Horsley, 14 Apr., 6 and 25 June 1806.

[16] *Gent. Mag.* 76 (1806), II, 987–90, 1057–9.

[17] LPL 2810, fos. 279–91, Palmer, 'Account of Horsley's Manuscripts'; 'Catalogue of the Entire and Very Valuable Library of the Late Rt. Rev Samuel Horsley, Lord Bishop of St. Asaph' (Sion College Library).

after death was a humiliating fate for a distinguished bishop and former dean of Westminster. Nevertheless, he cannot be entirely acquitted of blame for that outcome. There was substance in the remark of the great Victorian jurist, Lord Selborne, second son of Jocelyn Palmer, that 'of his private affairs' Bishop Horsley was 'unfortunately negligent'.[18] Already in difficulty when he went to St Asaph as bishop, since then he had doubtless contributed substantially to the repayment of Heneage's debts, as well as to support his son's family. He made some shift to redeem the situation before the end by adopting a rigid plan of economy, which extended even to items of clothing, and took out a life insurance for £5,000. According to the *Gentleman's Magazine* obituary notice, had he lived a few years longer, he would have enjoyed an income of £7,000 'by the operation of his prudent measures' but the journal also observed that the insurance ran out during his last illness, because he failed to renew it. Given the shortness of his illness this can only be seen as an avoidable oversight which ruined everything.[19]

RETROSPECT

When Horsley died his merit was at once recognized. In a commemorative sermon at St Mary, Newington on the Sunday after the funeral the preacher styled him 'that great luminary or shining light of the Protestant persuasion, the established English church'. The pulpit was occupied by the curate, the Revd Robert Dickinson, a friend and disciple, who did not scruple to treat him as a prophet, exhibiting the scriptural truths 'which could not have been thought of, had they not been revealed from heaven'.[20]

The mainstream view, expounded in a long obituary notice in the *Gentleman's Magazine*, was more discriminating. It paid a sincere tribute to his 'decisive victory' over the champion of materialism and philosophical necessity which gained him 'the respect and admiration of every friend to Christianity', though not without making an ironical reference to the further polemical exertions of 'this Prelatical Hercules' on behalf of the Established Church. It ranked him 'as a senator' in 'the first class'. His work as a diocesan bishop was admitted to have answered 'in a great measure' the 'expectations of eminent usefulness which his elevation to the mitre so generally excited'. Praise of his scholarship was in measured terms. 'No man of the age, perhaps, possessed more of what is generally understood by the idea of recondite learning', but his *magnum opus*, the edition of Newton's works, was criticized for its unhelpful commentary and rated below a Jesuit edition of the *Principia*.[21] This was unfair to him. Horsley was, indeed, a polymath, deeply read in both the

---

[18] Roundell Palmer, *Memorials*, i. *Family and Personal 1766–1865* (1896), 6.
[19] *Gent. Mag.* 76 (1806), II, 987–90.
[20] Ibid. 1057–9.
[21] Ibid. 987–90.

ancient and the modern writers, but he was also noteworthy as a mathematician and experimental scientist and as a biblical scholar.

Admiration of Horsley grew appreciably in the hundred years after his death. This was partly to be ascribed to the energetic devotion of his son Heneage, who sifted and prepared for the press the many manuscript commentaries, translations, and erudite sermons which the bishop had been too busy, and probably too much the perfectionist, to publish himself. A prelate who surveyed the material in its raw state described it as 'a mass of more important biblical criticism and research than has for many years made its appearance from the press'.[22] Having rescued the papers from his father's creditors, Heneage embarked on a programme of publication which took thirty-four years to complete. Two volumes of sermons in 1810, including the three powerful counter-naturalist discourses on eschatology opened a sequence which comprised commentaries on the historical and prophetical books of the Old Testament, the outpourings of years of patient study, and a critical revision of the traditional method of applying biblical prophecy inherited from Mede and Isaac Newton. The last was printed in Hugh James Rose's *British Magazine* as part of a bid to prop up Anglican morale in the crisis which struck the Established Church after the Reform Act. Unswerving in the determination to prove his father relevant for all time, in 1845 the younger Horsley published a letter to Sir C. E. Smith on the Maynooth grant, embodying the late bishop's opinion of that contentious endowment at an earlier stage.

There was no comparable relict of mathematical papers to set beside the legacy to theology. The impression to be derived from this and other evidence is that after he finished his work on Newton in 1785 Samuel Horsley started to wind down as a mathematician and to transfer his main studies to divinity. He never ceased to practise mathematics, and kept his scientific instruments to the end of his life.[23] But the three octavo volumes of practical mathematics for the use of students, ranging widely over Euclid's *Elements* and *Data*, the properties and projection of the sphere, spherical trigonometry, Archimedes on the mensuration of the circle, and the nature and use of logarithms, which were given to the world in 1801–3, have the appearance of being primarily didactic. They originated partly in the interest which he took in the education of his son at Oxford some years earlier. He wrote to him in 1797: 'For my own part I have been employ'd since you left me, in composing an elementary treatise of spherical trigonometry for your use, which I have just finished to my satisfaction. I know of no good treatise on the subject.'[24]

A factor more important than the editorial energies of Heneage Horsley in

---

[22] Horsley, *Sermons*, i (1810), pp. i–ix, Advertisement.
[23] See Appendix B for list of these from Sotheby's sale catalogue 1807.
[24] HP 1767, fos. 112–13, Horsley to H. Horsley, 1 Feb. 1797.

establishing the bishop's post-mortem reputation was the nineteenth century's growing respect for the style of Churchmanship which he represented. Except for Pusey, who cited him on 'non-resistance',[25] the Tractarian fathers largely ignored him, perhaps because his zeal for establishment interposed an impenetrable barrier between themselves and him. But with the upholders of Church principles, active under Hackney leadership before the Oxford Movement began and still expanding their influence after it had fallen, he gained lustre as the years passed. Esteem for him was at its height in the years between the later 1880s and the outbreak of the First World War, when church historians paid successive tributes. C. J. Abbey wrote in 1887: 'Samuel Horsley . . . is quite entitled to the name of a great bishop', recognizing among his distinctions 'a strong uncompromising belief in the doctrine which he professed and the Church to which he was attached'.[26] Overton and Relton, in 1906, acclaimed him as 'a giant'.[27] The way was open for his great-grandson Heneage Horsley Jebb to undertake the archivally daunting task of a book-length biography which, since 1909, has furnished historians with their main information about his career.

For most of the twentieth century, however, he has sustained an eclipse. The development of social history and the dominance within it of an aggressive left-wing critique of establishments after E. P. Thompson's *The Making of the English Working Classes* appeared in 1963, has created a climate highly unfavourable to Horsley's political ideas. He was a firm opponent of the English Jacobins and an outspoken supporter of the Younger Pitt's repressive legislation. Horsley and the leaders of Radicalism never understood one another. Taking Paine as his clue, he supposed them to be engaged in a plan to subject Parliament to the separate authority of the sovereign people and to level down the nation's institutions, which most of them neither intended nor desired. They in their turn ascribed to him un-English designs of oppression. His love of extravagant language exposed him to the charge. Speaking on the Surgeons Bill in 1797 he described democracy as 'a monster that ought to be unkenneled from its lurking places, and hunted down whenever it could be found'.[28] However mischievous such words could be in inciting loyalist violence, his personal convictions were those of a moderate Tory or conservative Whig —ideologies which were no longer so far apart as they had once been. He respected the law and the constitution, and was even prepared to support a liberal construction of it. On Fox's Libel Act of 1792, conferring upon juries the power to decide the criminality of a libel as well as the fact of it, he wrote to Lord Stanhope:

[25] Peter Nockles, in Perry Butler (ed.), *Pusey Rediscovered* (1983), 278.
[26] C. J. Abbey, *The English Church and its Bishops* (1887), ii. 263–4.
[27] *The English Church 1714–1800*, 256.
[28] *Parl. Reg.*, 3rd ser., iii (1796–7), 230.

tho' I confess I had my doubts about the necessity and the expediency of Mr. Fox's bill—about its necessity as asserting only what I conceived to be one of the first and most notorious principles of our criminal law—its expediency as declaring a general principle only in a particular instance—yet I never had the least doubt of the right of a jury to return the general verdict in opposition, if they tho't fit, to the judge's interpretation of the law, which by necessary consequence, involves a right to judge for themselves of the matter of law in its application to the particular case before them. And I perfectly agree with your Lordship that this right of juries is the great bulwark of our freedom.[29]

In recent years a reaction against the heroic interpretation of the French Revolutionary and Napoleonic phase in English Radicalism has taken root. Detailed researches by Albert Goodwin, John Dinwiddy, and M. I. Thomis have questioned the coherence of the movement,[30] while, viewing the conflict from the other side, H. T. Dickinson, J. C. D. Clark, Clive Emsley, and others have argued that the triumph of British conservatism stemmed more from success in the argument with its challengers than from naked repression. Against this background, interest in the political theory of English High Churchmen has started to develop. Separate studies, both of seminal importance, published in the mid-1980s, by Professor J. A. W. Gunn[31] and Dr Jonathan Clark,[32] have pointed to the survival of traditional and inherited ideas, associated more with Toryism than with Whiggery, into the forty-six years of Whig hegemony which followed the Hanoverian succession—'the spectre at the feast', as Gunn describes it—and to their resuscitation in more apparent strength after 1760. Clark's book displays strong sympathies with this tradition which he boldly credits with possessing 'the most intellectually powerful doctrine of the State' and shows marked appreciation of Samuel Horsley's role in shaping it.[33]

High Church political doctrine challenged the beliefs of late eighteenth-century Radicals at every point. Basically it was anti-Lockeian, as Horsley's sermon on King Charles' Day 1793 explicitly was. Divine right of kings was emphasized with unashamed bolstering from the cult of the martyr-king, and the duty of passive obedience was enjoined. Bishops in their yearly 'Martyrdom' sermons based these doctrines on scriptural texts, Romans 13: 1–7, 'the powers that be are ordained of God', and 1 Peter 2: 13–18, 'Submit yourselves to every ordinance of man for the Lord's sake: whether it

[29] Kent RO U.1590, C.57/2, Stanhope MSS, Horsley to Earl Stanhope, 27 Oct. 1792. I owe this reference to Dr Grayson Ditchfield.

[30] These issues remain, to a certain extent, in balance. See H. T. Dickinson, *British Radicalism and the French Revolution, 1789–1815* (Oxford, 1985).

[31] J. A. W. Gunn, *Beyond Liberty and Property: The Process of Self-Recognition in Eighteenth Century Political Thought* (Kingston and Montreal, 1983).

[32] Clark, *English Society*.

[33] Ibid. 247, 230–4. Edmund Burke is included with the High Churchmen, thus strengthening their claim to distinction.

be to the king, as supreme . . . ',[34] but the archaic patriarchalism of Sir Robert Filmer, deriving obligation to the State from the natural authority of our first parents, was still being taught, with appropriate modifications, by a little knot of Hutchinsonian High Churchmen—Horne, Stevens, and Jones of Nayland—after 1760.[35] Finally the creed was politico-theological, stressing the mutual dependence of religious and secular impulses and a theocratic union of Church and State.

Since Clark's *English Society* and its sequel, *Revolution and Rebellion*, made their appearance, the terrain of conservative political ideology in eighteenth-century England has been landscaped by Robert Hole in a book which sets out to refine one area of his analysis—the use of religious arguments in the whole political theory of the last seven decades of the unreformed Parliament. His chief contribution lies in showing the liberty which was allowed to theologians, Anglican and non-Anglican alike, in interpreting the loyalty texts of Holy Scripture. The limits of this tolerance were set by Horsley's patron Bishop Lowth in a sermon for 1767: 'Government in general is the ordinance of God, the particular form of government is the ordinance of man. The form of government, therefore, has not an absolute but only a relative goodness.'[36] Within those boundaries, which were necessary to ensure fidelity to the Glorious Revolution and the Hanoverian regime, the emphasis varied with the preacher's political and theological opinions. Thus, as Clark has shown, Horsley and the Cambridge expositors of 'orthodox political theology' were more moderate in their views than their Oxford counterparts.[37]

A feature of Hole's presentation, on which he lays much stress, is the change of emphasis in Christian political ideas under the influence of the French Revolution from abstract theorizing about the claims of the constitution in Church and State to the teaching of the social virtues and the underpinning of the same by religious sanctions and restraints. This transition is seen as a secularizing process, as it shifted the emphasis from proofs derived from revelation to an appeal to human reason. The Latitudinarian William Paley, whose *Principles of Moral and Political Philosophy* (1785) dismissed the Pauline and Petrine texts in favour of the maximization of happiness when prescribing on politics and society, stands out as the leading exemplar of the trend,[38] but Samuel Horsley is presented as a synthesizer of the old and new approaches.[39] There was indeed a utilitarian component in his later thought, as the reasoning of his Rochester charge of 1796 decisively

---

[34] R. Hole, *Pulpits, Politics and Public Order 1760–1832* (Cambridge, 1989), 12–13.
[35] Clark, *English Society*, 223, 227; Hole, *Pulpits, Politics*, 61.
[36] Ibid. 15.
[37] See above, p. 228.
[38] Hole, *Pulpits, Politics*, 73–82; cf. Clark, *English Society*, 234–5 for a different perception of the same change.
[39] Hole, *Pulpits, Politics*, 161–73, 214.

shows,[40] but it was concerned with means to ends not with the ends themselves, and is, therefore, secondary. Dr Hole's ambivalent reading of the manuscript essay 'Thoughts on Civil Government' overlooks the importance of the fact that in the bishop's view the legislator's problem to find 'a common measure of moral conduct universally applicable' for the happiness and welfare of the community,[41] had been solved already by divine intervention.[42] The 'Christological argument' was the governing one.

Dr Clark's demonstration that other groups, notably the Methodists and the Evangelicals, 'inherited almost intact the political theology of mainstream Anglicanism'[43] prompts the conclusion, strengthened by Hole's instructive comparisons of the political attitudes of divines of various schools within the Established Church and the similarities he finds in all orthodox Dissenting denominations and among the Roman Catholics,[44] that High Churchmanship cannot be defined in political terms alone. The political ideologies stemmed from something more fundamental: from human life-styles and from a religious outlook which embraced devotional practices and views of the supernatural which still mattered intensely to the eighteenth-century mind. In the last resort High Churchmanship was a kind of churchmanship and its revival in the second half of the eighteenth century a phenomenon in religion broadly conceived.

The problem, nevertheless, is to define it. During the eighteenth and early nineteenth centuries the name 'High Church' was given to at least five different levels of activity and understanding, linked only by an outstanding zeal for the Anglican establishment. The broadest meaning was that applied as early as 1705 in Evelyn's *Diary*, namely to denote 'a strong Church of England man in public life'.[45] In this loose sense, closely linked to Toryism in politics, most of the clergy remained High Church until the end of the period, and became actively so whenever legislation was threatened to reduce the privileges of the Established Church, as in the years 1787–90, when repeal of the tests was proposed. To dismiss this attachment as 'political' after the manner of W. J. Conybeare writing in the *Edinburgh Review* in 1853[46] is superficial; it was a shapeless atavistic loyalty to the Church in harness to the Crown capable of being shared by relatively uninstructed laymen. Among bishops, cathedral dignitaries, archdeacons, and even parish priests, High Churchmanship also meant a stiffness with regard to rubrics, articles of belief, canons, and statutes, and even an adherence to ancient ceremonies like

[40] See above, p. 150.
[41] Hole, *Pulpits, Politics*, 162.
[42] HP 1767, fos. 198–203.
[43] Hole, *Pulpits, Politics*, 235–47.
[44] Ibid. 21–9, 32–9, 112–15, 178–80, et al.
[45] G. Every, *The High Church Party, 1688–1718* (1956), 1.
[46] W. J. Conybeare, 'Church Parties', *Edinburgh Review*, 98 (1853), 273–342.

bowing to the altar, making the sign of the cross, wearing copes, and using incense, though such rites were always unusual and had mainly vanished by the accession of George III.[47] In the academic world it embraced conservatism regarding modes of learning which recalled the *Phalaris* controversy with Bentley, into which Atterbury was drawn at the end of the seventeenth century. As dean of Westminster, Samuel Horsley resisted innovations in the classical curriculum at Westminster School. He explained to Heneage:

I proposed an alteration of the Westr. Grammar. What I proposed and have still in contemplation is to restore the old Westminster Greek Grammar, which was in use in the School, till somebody that had more leisure than wit tho't of making it a didactic poem and so produced the Greek Grammar in hexameter verse, which is now us'd. The old Grammar of which I speak is fuller than the compendium, and yet not fuller than a Grammar ought to be for boys, very accurate in its rules, and very perspicacious.[48]

High Churchmen might still be discerned by their siding in the battle of the books. Thus the grammar school at Southampton kept by Richard Mant, the father of Bishop Mant, was renowned for its practice of the 'old and sound system', based on principle and a thorough grounding in grammar. Warden Huntingford of Winchester College, though himself a Whig, commented favourably upon it: 'I am convinced that an early habit of applying Grammar-Rules leads to accuracy and precision in reasoning at a more advanced age. The fashion of the day is superficial and unnatural prematurity; it is the bane of real knowledge & substantial ability.'[49]

Side by side with a temperamental aversion to change, which critics would have dismissed as mere prejudice, there was a serious and consistent High Church ideology handed down in the writings of Nonjurors such as Charles Leslie and Roger North and made more widely available in the Established Church during the first twenty years of George III's reign by the exertions of the Hutchinsonian divines, George Horne and Jones of Nayland. It had three interrelated facets. Firstly, the exaltation of State power by the recovery of certain attributes of divine-right monarchy. Secondly, the defence of the Church of England against Dissenters by the assertion of claims to apostolical succession. The third and most fundamental, however, was the protection and enhancement of the mysterious element in religion in opposition to the plainness of Latitudinarianism and the cold, mechanistic creed of the Arians and the Socinians.

Thus the High Church tradition of the later eighteenth and early nineteenth century still embodied a substantial element of seventeenth-century

[47] F. C. Mather, 'Georgian Churchmanship Reconsidered', *Journal of Ecclesiastical History*, 36 (1985), 255–83.
[48] HP 1767, fos. 110–11, Horsley to H. Horsley, 11 Nov. 1796.
[49] Sidmouth MSS 152 M/C 1792/F.21, G. I. Huntingford to H. Addington, 13 Apr. 1792.

Caroline divinity and devotion. Victorian writers like the satirist W. J. Conybeare, contributing to the *Edinburgh Review*, impressed by the éclat of the Oxford Movement, supposed that 'the true High Church theology' died out at the beginning of the eighteenth century, and did not revive until 1833.[50] Though specialized studies, notably by Richard Sharp and Peter Nockles, have already undermined it,[51] the view persists at the general level of historical writing that, while the 'High Church party' was powerful in the Church on the eve of the Tractarian revival,[52] it lingered only in a debased form, preoccupied with hunting Methodists and bolstering the unreformed constitution. Dr A. D. Harvey refers in a recent survey of British history in the early nineteenth century to the 'secular ideology embraced both by High Churchmen and by the comparatively indifferent'.[53] Some High Churchmen did adopt a mainly secular view, and were barely distinguishable from Tory politicians or from desiccated scholars fearful of 'enthusiasm'. Others, however, were of a warmer cast. They saw both Church and monarchy in a spiritual light, enjoined belief in apostolical succession, and dwelt in their sermons on the mysterious element in religion, on faith and sacraments, instead of on moral obligation alone.

These were never more than a substantial minority even among the bishops but the strength of their leadership, when the Church was believed to be in danger, qualified them to represent the larger number of 'Church and King' men. Contrary to what is commonly believed, the latter did not form a coherent party with a single distinct perception, but were drawn from differing theological groups and unattached individuals.

The Carolines had, nevertheless, been gaining strength since the 1750s, when George Horne and William Jones of Nayland set the course. But the adhesion of Samuel Horsley was attended by some remarkable advances in the 1780s. In a sequence of pronouncements from 1784 to 1792 Horsley familiarized the Church of his day with the doctrine of apostolical succession, rescuing it from becoming the exclusive property of the Nonjurors and slotting it into the apologetic of official Anglicanism.[54] By this action he performed a service to the Church of England comparable with that which was rendered to eighteenth-century executive monarchy by High Churchmen of the period who attached to it the Stuart attributes of divine right and passive obedience. On the practical level the assertiveness and independence of the clergy started to rise. A new emphasis could be detected in the working of the Church–State partnership when the Younger Pitt handed to the

---

[50] Conybeare, 'Church Parties'.

[51] See esp. G. Rowell (ed.), *Tradition Renewed* (1986), chaps. i and ii.

[52] B. G. Worrall, *The Making of the Modern Church: Christianity in England since 1800* (1988), 10–11.

[53] A. D. Harvey, *Britain in the Early Nineteenth Century* (1978), 107.

[54] See above, pp. 60–2, 128–9, 203–4.

bishops responsibility for deciding whether the Dissenting application for repeal of the Test and Corporation Acts in 1787 should be opposed. 'The Bishops all together lead Mr Pitt', it was later observed to Lady Hesketh,[55] and although the remark exaggerated their unanimity, it showed surprise, and pointed the contrast with the situation in the 1730s, when Walpole managed the conflicting demands of Church and Dissent on this question by his own perception of his parliamentary needs.[56] On the later occasion 'Church power' found a vigorous embodiment in the part played by clergymen and lay Anglicans in organizing public opinion in opposition to repeal, and in the uncommon zeal shown by individual bishops and other ecclesiastics who used their diocesan charges and published sermons to undermine the theology of its Unitarian supporters.[57]

English High Churchmanship also benefited from events abroad. The successful rebellion in America was a defeat for episcopacy as well as for the Crown. Hence the raising of subscriptions in aid of the distressed Loyalist clergy[58] and the flight of some of the most active supporters of episcopacy in their number to Britain lent encouragement to the cause. More importantly perhaps, the first halting steps to plant churches of the Anglican communion in territories outside the authority of the British Crown appealed to notions of primitive order never banished from High Church breasts. The consecration of Samuel Seabury as bishop of Connecticut by the Nonjuring bishops of Scotland, effected with the connivance of the Church of England in 1784, led to closer relations between parties in the English Church and the English and Scottish Nonjurors later in the decade.[59] After the defeat of Fox's motion for the repeal of the Test and Corporation Acts in 1790, there was a turning away from the basically political establishment and civil rights issues which commanded the scene in the first thirty years of George III's reign[60] to those which involved, implicitly at least, the nature of Anglicanism as a religious system. The battle to protect the Scottish Episcopalians from penal legislation was a return to the aspirations of the High Church Tories of Anne's reign.[61] The relief of the English Catholics in 1791 and the subsequent conjunction of Horsley with the anti-Cisalpine party to protect the French *émigré* clergy raised questions of doctrine which divided Anglicans from Anglicans.[62] The

[55] John Ehrman, *The Younger Pitt: The Reluctant Transition* (1983), 67.

[56] T. F. J. Kendrick, 'Sir Robert Walpole, the Old Whigs and the Bishops, 1733–1736: A Study in Eighteenth Century Parliamentary Politics', *Historical Journal*, 11 (1968), 421–45; S. Taylor, 'Sir Robert Walpole, the Church of England and the Quakers' Tithe Bill of 1736', *Historical Journal*, 28 (1985), 51–77.

[57] See above, pp. 62, 77–80, 83.

[58] G. M. Ditchfield, 'The House of Lords in the Age of the American Revolution', in Clyve Jones (ed.), *A Pillar of the Constitution: The House of Lords in British Politics 1640–1784* (1989), 235.

[59] See above, p. 122.

[60] Hole, *Pulpits, Politics*, 53.

[61] See above, chap. 7.

[62] See above, chap. 6.

path lay open to the re-emergence in the first twenty years of the nineteenth century of the two-party strife which had severed the Church of England a hundred years earlier on the basis of a new alignment of forces: High Church versus Evangelical instead of High Church versus Latitudinarian.

In fine the Georgian Church cannot be identified with any single school or mood of churchmanship. Under the first two Hanoverian monarchs Latitudinarianism attracted the limelight, as it accorded with the aspirations of the secular world, its need of a reasonable and orderly evolution, of political stability, economic prosperity, and liberation of the mind. Leading ideas, however, are not necessarily dominant ideas, as the conservative hold of the past and loyalty to its institutions is often stronger in the overall view than enthusiasm for change. This was a continuing limitation on their outreach, and the balance was tipped more decisively against the optimism of the forward-looking when the ongoing Enlightenment lost faith in its own values. This was partly the result of its self-criticism as displayed in the scepticism of David Hume, whose *Philosophical Essays concerning Human Understanding* appeared in 1748, and partly a consequence of a series of disasters. The catastrophic earthquake in Lisbon in 1755 and the carnage of the Seven Years War shook even Voltaire out of the already tenuous optimism which he had inherited from Pope and led him to round on the 'best of all possible worlds' theory of Leibniz. From this crisis of the intellect in which belief in the reasonableness of the universe was shaken, Latitudinarianism, as it had been understood since Newton's day, never recovered. Hume did not jettison his robust Scottish common sense, a quality which Horsley shared, but religious developments after his time accorded a larger role to the virtues which he had extolled: feeling, experience, and faith. Not only was there an inrush of raw, emotional, and mysterious energy through High Church channels as well as through Methodism. From the heart of the Enlightenment intelligentsia itself came a retreat from advanced positions which had brought tragedy and therefore disillusionment. As Geoffrey Scott has lately shown in an illuminating article,[63] Bishop Charles Walmsley, the English vicar apostolic as he later became, was reckoned an innovator in the first half of the eighteenth century and a hardened reactionary at its end. When he was made prior of a Benedictine monastery in Paris in 1749, he had developed an enthusiasm for mathematics and astronomy, and became active in a philosophical debating club established in the house, publishing papers to demonstrate Newton's conclusions. He became, however, disappointed with the progress of the European Enlightenment, and was increasingly alarmed from the 1780s onwards by the treatment of the religious orders by the Commission des Reguliers, by the suppression of the Jesuits, and by Emperor Joseph II's

---

[63] '"The Times are Fast Approaching"—Bishop Charles Walmsley, O.S.B. (1722–97) as Prophet', *Journal of Ecclesiastical History*, 36 (1985), 590–604.

asperities against the Church in the Habsburg lands in the 1780s. He fell back upon apocalyptic prophecy, and as vicar of the Western District he was one of the chief opponents of the English Cisalpine Catholics. The parallel with Samuel Horsley is instructive. Though never a *philosophe*, the latter belonged in the 1770s to the world of *belles-lettres* and scientific curiosity, collaborating in the Royal Society with world-famous luminaries and philosophers, Henry Cavendish and Benjamin Franklin, and planning to republish Voltaire's History. In the following decade, under the influence of personal tragedy, professional frustration, and humiliation of both Church and nation, he became disturbed and aggressive. The controversy with Priestley was his first blow against the spirit of the age. He emerged as a traditional High Churchman and an expounder of the prophecies. It needed only the Revolutionary upheaval in Europe to make him see the same Voltaire, whose work he had reservedly praised, as the persevering author of a conspiracy to extirpate the very name of Christianity.

Samuel Horsley was not a reactionary, though his sharp manner and sarcastic remarks sometimes caused him to be regarded as such. He was a conservative constitutionalist of mixed Whig and Tory pedigree, but of a type now comfortably accommodated among the supporters of George III's Governments. His churchmanship contained a paradox. No one believed more firmly than he did in the principle of establishment and the union of Church and State in a single society under the King's Majesty, but the independent spiritual authority of the Church's episcopal ministry also found no more eloquent advocate than he. The dichotomy was becoming increasingly difficult to sustain as encounters with non-established episcopal churches outside England pressed themselves upon the attention. It cannot be said that Horsley's efforts to uphold it were convincing at either the theoretical or the practical level. Of greater significance for the future of the Church of England after his death was his revaluation of High Churchmanship in spiritual terms, which came into its own only when the revolutionary changes in the Church–State relationship in 1828–32 prepared the way for the Tractarians to redraw the map. In this respect too his career was prophetic.

Appendix A

SPCK Distributions of Books
1790–1820

Packets of Books Sent to Subscribing and Corresponding Members, 1790–1809

Year	Bibles	New Testaments and Psalters	Common Prayer Books	Other Bound Books	Small Tracts	Total
1790	5,567	7,310	9,790	9,294	69,038	100,999
1791	4,915	7,240	8,819	10,372	64,699	95,045
1792	4,835	7,575	9,851	10,729	64,637	97,357
1793	4,938	8,215	10,373	11,697	75,058	107,281
1794	4,639	9,023	9,765	9,022	67,438	99,887
1795	4,960	9,846	9,589	12,467	72,868	109,730
1796	6,085	9,132	9,861	10,199	68,956	104,233
1797	5,721	8,775	9,399	10,606	66,691	101,192
1798	5,572	7,521	10,658	14,395	82,559	120,705
1799	5,890	8,873	10,058	17,435	89,739	131,995
1800	7,090	9,984	10,740	14,509	95,248	137,571
1801	7,291	9,958	12,895	14,710	96,354	141,208
1802	7,809	9,970	13,515	18,640	98,766	148,700
1803	7,958	10,520	14,230	19,243	103,658	155,609
1804	8,360	11,044	15,418	19,856	108,776	163,454
1805	8,490	11,466	16,096	20,460	112,440	168,952
1806	8,881	12,072	17,029	21,480	118,044	177,506
1807	8,476	12,930	17,867	19,572	120,157	179,002
1808	—	—	—	—	—	—
1809	8,760	12,540	19,060	19,440	120,236	180,036

Distributions to Members, 1811–1820 (excluding Free Distributions)

Year	Bibles	New Testaments and Psalters	Common Prayer Books	Other Bound Books	Small Tracts	Total
1811	12,657	21,971	29,752	38,024	215,175	317,577
1812	19,880	43,671	45,730	41,913	426,713	577,907
1813	24,890	40,310	52,106	46,350	480,357	644,013
1814	26,250	45,470	63,380	49,864	545,631	730,595
1815	24,471	38,406	66,048	55,554	788,387	972,866
1816	23,484	53,457	87,530	52,430	730,650	947,551
1817	29,852	53,723	86,558	60,330	835,140	1,065,603

Distributions to Members, 1811–1820 (excluding Free Distributions)

Year	Bibles	New Testaments and Psalters	Common Prayer Books	Other Bound Books	Small Tracts	Total
1818	32,036	53,803	91,589	74,617	912,300	1,164,345
1819	31,756	53,653	87,884	76,203	940,014	1,189,510
1820	31,983	45,455	84,975	74,904	821,044	1,058,361

Note: The above analysis is based on the printed *Annual Reports* of the SPCK. Owing to the problems of establishing comparability, the figures cannot be presented as a continuous series. From 1811 onwards the *Reports* supply additional information of gratuitous distributions to missions and from 1813 of instructional manuals on the Sacrament, Confirmation, the Catechism, etc. to Sunday Schools. For a similar reason this cannot be included in the table, but the large annual increases from 1811 to 1816 strengthen the impression of mounting exertion within the Society. The following aggregates show this trend at its peak:

1815	219,752
1816	262,448

CHURCH HO... LIBRARY
... F
NOR...ON NN6 0QE

BOOK No _ _ _ _ _ _ _

CLASS No _ _ _ _ _ _ _

DATE added _ _ _ _ _ _ _

Appendix B

List of Horsley's Scientific Instruments, Reprinted from Sotheby's Catalogue of the Sale of his Library, 4 May 1807 (Sion College Library)

INSTRUMENTS

1934 A case of instruments and a pith-ball electrometer

1935 A case of drawing-instruments, a 12 inch brass diagonal scale, and a protractor

1936 A 12 inch box sector, a 2 feet rule, and a pair of dividers

1937 A beam compass with two spare beams, and a 6 inch brass sector

1938 An 18 inch rolling parallel ruler, and a 12 inch ditto

1939 A 1 foot plated achromatic telescope, and a 12 inch rolling parallel ruler

1940 A two pole measuring tape, and an ivory rolling protractor

1941 A 6 inch brass circular protractor, *by Dolland*

1942 A 30 inch Robertson's improved sliding gunter, with adjusting screw

1943 A ditto—ditto

1944 A set of hydrostatic money-scales in a case

1945 A 2 feet 3 achromatic pocket-telescope, with a portable folding-stand, *by Jones*

1946 A 3 inch improved pocket brass box sextant, *by Jones*

1947 A 5 inch brass sextant with portable brass pillar, *by Berge*

1948 A magazine case of 6 inch silver drawing-instruments

1949 A 10 inch brass astronomical quadrant on pillar and foot

1950 A 6 inch theodolite with vertical arch, telescope and staves, *by Nairne and Blunt*

1951 A portable 4 inch equatorial instrument, *by Adams*

1952 An 18 inch reflecting telescope with rack-work motions in a case

1953 An excellent 30 inch achromatic telescope in brass on a stand, with astronomical eye-piece, &c. *by Ramsden*, in a mahogany case

1954 A pair of 18 inch Globes in claw frames, compasses, &c. *by G. Adams*

1955 *A complete 3 feet inflecting Telescope, with rack and motions, and divided object glass, micrometer, by James Short in mahogany case*

1956 An excellent 8 Day regulator, with an improved pendulum, *by Ellicott*, in a mahogany Case

1957 An excellent 2 feet astronomical Quadrant on a brass pillar and stand, *by Bird*

Bibliographical Notes

1. The Horsley Papers

The fate of Bishop Horsley's personal papers was described by Jocelyn Palmer, his domestic chaplain, who acted as his literary executor. 'The Bishop on his death bed', he wrote, 'earnestly requested that his correspondence with his private friends & with his relations particularly might be destroyed. This was accordingly done; and the papers [which] were preserved seemed only to contain matters of literary curiosity.' How much was lost by this must remain in doubt. A prelate of modest means, with no family seat, who was translated from one end of the country to the other, who at one stage held two official residences at once, and who for much of his career travelled backwards and forwards twice a year between remote Welsh dioceses and the House of Lords, cannot have been tempted to keep more paper than he needed. He gave no thought to the needs of a biographer, his sole concern being to ensure that his unpublished writings on theology, political theory, and general literature passed to his son for his own profit.

The Horsley Papers in Lambeth Palace Library form a small collection of manuscripts mounted in three volumes. Of these, the first (MS 1767) contains a few surviving letters to the Bishop, chiefly of a formal character. This compilation seems to have belonged to Heneage, for it includes letters of some interest from the Bishop to himself and his wife and the transcripts which he made of some of his father's writings, as well as later miscellaneous items. It was used by his grandson H. H. Jebb in writing a biography of Bishop Horsley in 1909, and deposited by 'H. H.'s' daughter Eglantyne Jebb in 1960.

The second and third volumes (MSS 1768 and 1769) consist of family letters to Francis Horsley, the Bishop's half-brother, a newspaper proprietor in India. They are from sisters and nieces in England, and in between the chatter they cast light on Samuel Horsley's career and character. Though also given by Miss Jebb in 1960 they do not appear to have been used by her father in writing his biography.

These collections are supplemented by the Papers of Roundell Palmer, first Earl of Selborne (second son of William Jocelyn), deposited at Lambeth Palace from 1962. They include further Horsley letters (MSS 1890–3) and bound volumes of notes and transcripts of the Bishop's writings made by his chaplain (MSS 2809–10).

2. Other Manuscript Collections

Surprisingly few letters from Samuel Horsley are to be found in the archives of his distinguished friends, notably William Windham and Lord Grenville. It is just possible that these were weeded in response to the appeal for 'correspondence' made by Heneage in the preface to the 1810 edition of his father's *Sermons*, when he was thinking of writing a biographical account. No material from these sources appears to have survived in the Horsley Papers, which show that by the end of the Bishop's life, Windham was negotiating with him through an intermediary.

The most useful collections searched for this book are listed below under the repositories in which they are located:

Aberdeen, King's College
  D.18, Skinner (Boucher) Correspondence.
Bodleian Library
  Add. MSS D.30, Nonjuror Papers.
  MSS Eng. Misc. *c.*690, W. J. Palmer Correspondence 1794–1852.
  MSS Eng. Misc. d.156–7, Mark Noble Collection.
  MSS Top. Oxon. d.353–6, Randolph–Lambard Correspondence.
Borthwick Institute, York
  Archdeacon's Visitation 1790, Citations.
British Library
  Add. MSS 46,689–90, 48,866, Berkeley, Misc.
  Add. MSS 39,311–12, Berkeley Correspondence.
  Add. MSS 5824, 5828, Wm. Cole.
  Add. MSS 34,455–6, Auckland.
  Egerton MSS 2185–6, Bishop Douglas.
  Add. MSS 35,649, Hardwicke.
  Add. MSS 37,848, 37,854, Windham.
  Add. MSS 46,136, Wordsworth.
  BL Althorp Papers, Letters of the Revd Charles Poyntz (recently transferred from Althorp).
Cambridge University Library
  Add. MSS 7886–7, Frend.
Chester Record Office
  EDV/7, Dio., Visitation Articles 1778, 1804.
  EDV/1, Dio., Correction Books.
  EDV/2, Dio., Archdeaconry of Chester, Call Book 1789.
Chetham's Library, Manchester
  A.3, J. Clowes, Memoirs.
City of London, Guildhall Library
  MS 9557, London Diocese Book 1770–*c.*1812.
  Pa. St Giles, Cripplegate, Registers.
  Pa. St Margaret, Lothbury, Vestry Minutes.
Corporation of London Record Office
  Marriages, Births, and Burials Tax, Assessment 1695.
  Common Council Journals.
Devon Record Office
  152.M, Sidmouth Papers.
Drapers' Hall, London
  Draper's Company Archives.
East Sussex Record Office
  Locker Lampson: Sec. I, Park, Locker, Watson Correspondence.
            A.I, B.1, 2, 3, and 5, Boucher Letters.

Greater London Record Office
D/LC 170, 179, London Consistory, Allegations, Libels, and Sentences 1743–6, 1780–3.
Hertfordshire Record Office
Pa. Broxbourne, Registers.
Pa. Ware, Registers.
Kent Record Office
MSS U.1590, Stanhope Papers.
MSS DRa/VB2, Rochester Dio., Archdeacon's Visitation Books 1781–1811.
Lambeth Palace Library
Fulham Papers, London Visitation Articles 1778, 1815.
Archbishop Secker's Visitation Articles 1759–61.
Canterbury Speculum 1758–68.
Archbishop's Act Books and Institution Act Books.
Archbishop Moore's Papers, vols. i–ix.
MSS 2103–5, Porteus Notebooks (1788–1809)
Lichfield Joint Record Office
B/V/5, Visitation Returns 1772.
Lincoln Record Office
Speculum 1788–92.
Magdalen College, Oxford
Horne Letters.
Papers of Martin Routh.
Manchester Central Reference Library
MSS f.1790/1, Repeal of Test and Corporation Acts 1790, documents.
National Library of Scotland
Acc. 4796, Fettercairn Papers.
Catalogued MSS 589, St Asaph tithe letter.
National Library of Wales
MSS 5456–7, Thomas Morgan's Diary.
MSS 22, 131.C, Lewis Evans Letters.
MSS 6203.E, Gilbertson Papers (Isaac Williams).
MSS 13145.A, Scrap Book.
St Davids Diocesan and Capitular Records, esp. SD.Ch./B.8, SD.Ch./Accts., SD.Ch.Misc., SD. Misc., SD/ERA, SD/QA.
MSS 9145.F, Rural Deans' Visitation Returns 1809 (photocopies).
Welsh Church Commissioners/Group 3/79–82, St Asaph Rentals.
MSS 12,415–23, Lloyd of Wigfair.
MSS 1448–1707, Leeswood Hall.
MSS 10,854, Frondirion.
St Asaph Diocesan Records, esp. Visitation Questionnaires (SA/QA) and Diocese Books (SA/MB).
Public Record Office
Probate of Wills, Prorogative Court of Canterbury.
30/8, Chatham Papers.
Royal Society Archives
Journal Book 1771–85.

Minutes of Council 1769–82.
Minutes of General Meetings.
Miscellaneous Manuscripts.
Rochester Diocesan Registry
  Bishop's Court Muniments 1790–1814.
Scottish Record Office
  'Episcopal Chest' Papers.
  Bishop Jolly Kist Papers.
Shoreditch District Library
  D/F/Tys, Tyssen Transcripts, Hackney Church Papers.
  St Mary, Stoke Newington, Vestry Minute Book 1784–1819.
Sion College, London
  Court Registers, C and D.
Society for Promoting Christian Knowledge (SPCK)
  Minutes of General Meetings and Committees.
Southampton University Library
  Wellington Papers.
Southwark Public Library
  St Mary, Newington, Parish Vestry Books.
United Society for the Propagation of the Gospel
  SPG Journals and Committee Books.
  Boxes of Misc. Letters and Papers, 18th and 19th centuries.
Westminster Abbey, Chapter Office and Muniment Room
  Chapter Act Books.
  Mun. 33,824–32, Treasurer's Accounts.
  Mun. 33,550–63, Receiver General's Accounts.
  Mun. 34,093–34,101, Steward's Accounts.
  Miscellaneous Papers.
Westminster, Archbishopric of, Archives
  MSS A Ser., xliii, xliv, Bishop Douglass's Papers (1792–3).
  III and IIIB, Further Correspondence, 1799–1800.
  Bishop Douglass's Diary, ii, 1800–12.
Dr Williams's Library, London
  Odgers MSS.
Westminster Public Library
  St Martin-in-the-Fields, Registers, Poor Rate and Highway Rate Books.
  St Margaret, Westminster, Poor Rate Book.

3. Abstract of Original Printed Sources

It is impracticable to list all the printed primary sources used in the preparation of this book. Those cited in the text are described in the footnotes. The principal published works of Samuel Horsley are set out in the printed Catalogue of the British Library under his name. In all instances the place of publication is London unless otherwise stated.

(*a*) *Published Sermons* are the main source of information for the theology, the tone, and the political theory of English High Churchmanship. Horsley is well served by three collections, published by his son:

HORSLEY, SAMUEL, *Sermons*, ed. H. Horsley, 2 vols. (Dundee, 1810); 3rd edn., 3 vols. (Dundee, 1812); new edn., 3 vols. (1816)

as well as by sermons on particular themes published separately. Other collections of sermons by mid and later eighteenth-century High Churchmen include:

BERKELEY, ELIZE (ed.), *Sermons by the Late Rev. George Berkeley* (1799).
CROFT, G., *Sermons by the Late Rev. George Croft* (Birmingham, 1811).
HORNE, G., *Sixteen Sermons on Various Subjects and Occasions* (Oxford, 1793).
HURD, RICHARD, *Sermons Preached at Lincolns Inn, between the Years 1765 and 1776* (1785).
JONES, WILLIAM (of Nayland), *Three Dissertations on Life and Death* (1771).
RIDLEY, GLOSTER, *The Christian Passover in Four Sermons . . . Revised and Enlarged by the Rev. Thomas Hopkins* (Dublin, 1770). Originally *Four Sermons* (1736).
SECKER, THOMAS, *Sermons* (Dublin, 1772).

To these may be added individual sermons by William Cleaver, Samuel Hallifax, H. H. Norris, and others, noting especially the 30 January sermons before the House of Lords, the *Hutchins Sermons on the Liturgy of the Church of England*, and the *Warburton Lectures on the Prophecies*, preached as sermons in Lincoln's Inn Chapel.

(*b*) *Visitation Charges.* Bishops and archdeacons, at their visitations issued Charges to their clergy, which were afterwards published. Though these too sometimes expounded general theological issues, they were more concerned than were sermons with the practical problems facing the Church at the time. Horsley's Charges as a diocesan bishop were gathered together in *Charges of Samuel Horsley* (Dundee, 1813) and also published separately, as was his *Charge to the Clergy of the Archdeaconry of St. Albans at a Visitation Holden May 22d. 1783* (1783).

(*c*) *Parliamentary Proceedings*
Journal of the House of Commons
Journal of the House of Lords
For a record of debates in the House of Lords, reliance has been mainly placed upon Almon and Debrett, *The Parliamentary Register, 1774–1803*, 83 vols. (1775–1804). Cited as *Parl. Reg.* This has been supplemented in places by William Cobbett's *Parliamentary History of England from . . . 1066 to . . . 1803*, 36 vols. (London, 1806–20). Cited as *Parl. Hist.* It has been replaced after 1803 by *Cobbett's Parliamentary Debates, 1803–1812*. Cited as *Parl. Deb.* None of these contain *verbatim* reports of speeches, and the volumes *Speeches in Parliament of Samuel Horsley*, ed. H. Horsley, 2 vols. (Dundee, 1813) have been used to elucidate points which reporters have missed, though, being a collection compiled from notes or drafts, it represents what the speaker intended to say rather than what he said.

(*d*) *Books, Reports, and Shorter Treatises*
An Authentic Narrative of the Dissentions and Debates in the Royal Society (1784).
BELSHAM, T. (ed.), *Priestley's Tracts in Controversy with Bishop Horsley* (1815).
Biographical List of the Members of the Club of Nobody's Friends (1885).
BRAYLEY, E. W., *The History and Antiquities of the Abbey Church of St Peter Westminster* (1818).
CHALMERS, ALEXANDER (ed.), *The General Biographical Dictionary* (1812–17).

Commissioners for the Redemption of the Land Tax on Church and Corporation Estates, *Repts.*, PP 1810 (325) ix; 1812–13 (71) v.

DANSEY, WILLIAM, *Horae Decanicae Rurales* (1844).

Ecclesiastical Revenues Commission, Reports PP 1835 (54) xxii, 1835 [67] xxii, 1836 (86) xxxvi.

FORTESCUE, J. (ed.), *The Correspondence of King George the Third, 1760–1783* (1927).

GREIG, JOHN (ed.), *The Farington Diary* (1923–8).

HEYWOOD, SAMUEL, *High Church Politics* (1792).

HORSLEY, SAMUEL, *Critical Disquisitions on the 18th Chapter of Isaiah in a Letter to Edward King* (1799).

—— 'Disquisitions on the Prophetical Periods', *British Magazine*, 4 (1833).

—— 'To the Author of Antichrist in the French Convention', *British Magazine*, 5 and 6 (1834).

HORSLEY, SAMUEL (attrib.), *An Apology for the Liturgy and Clergy of the Church of England* (1790).

—— *Review of the Case of the Protestant Dissenters* (1790).

JOHNSON, SAMUEL, LL D, *Works*, viii, 'A New Journey to the Western Islands of Scotland' (new edn., 1816).

JONES, WILLIAM (of Nayland), *Letters to the Rev. Dr. Priestley* (Bath, 1787).

—— *The Works of George Horne, with Memoirs of his Life, Studies and Writings*, 6 vols. (1809).

MACAULEY, J. S., and GREAVES, R. W. (eds.), *The Autobiography of Thomas Secker, Archbishop of Canterbury* (Lawrence Kan., 1988).

MASERES, F., *The Moderate Reformer* (1791).

MILNER, JOHN, *The History, Civil and Ecclesiastical, and Survey of the Antiquities of Winchester* (Winchester, 1798–1801).

—— *Letters to a Prebendary* (Winchester, 1800).

PETRE, *Letter from the Rt. Hon. Lord Petre to the Rt. Reverend Dr. Samuel Horsley, Bishop of St Davids* (1790).

PRENTICE, ARCHIBALD, *Historical Sketches and Personal Recollections of Manchester*, intro. by Donald Read (1970).

RENAUD, F., and RAINES, F. R. (eds.), *The Fellows of the Collegiate Church of Manchester,* ii (Chetham Society Remains, NS 23; Manchester, 1891).

Returns on the Residence of the Beneficed Clergy, PP 1809 (234), ix.

RUTT, J. T. (ed.), *The Theological and Miscellaneous Works of Joseph Priestley* (1832).

STEVENS, WILLIAM, *A Short Account of the Life and Writings of the Rev. William Jones, M. A., F.R.S.* (1801).

TAYLOR, R. V., *Biographia Leodiensis* (Leeds, 1865).

TOMLINSON, J. (ed.), *Additional Grenville Papers, 1763–65* (Manchester, 1962).

(*e*) *High Church Periodicals*. Organs of the press with leanings to a High Church theology were:

Critical Review (1756–1817)
British Critic (1793–1843)
Anti-Jacobin Review and Magazine (1791–1821)
Orthodox Churchman's Magazine (1801–8)
The Christian Remembrancer (1819–40)

4. Horsley Biography

JEBB, HENEAGE HORSLEY, *A Great Bishop of One Hundred Years Ago: Being a Sketch of the Life of Samuel Horsley, LL. D., Bishop of St. David's, Rochester and St. Asaph, and Dean of Westminster* (1909).

SELECTED SECONDARY SOURCES

Short List of Recent Works on or Closely Related to Eighteenth-Century High Churchmanship

This list does not include important modern works on contingent themes such as Latitudinarianism, Evangelicalism, Roman Catholicism, and Dissent, nor does it extend to the rich periodical literature which is growing up round the subject (for which items see footnotes). It is intended merely as a guide for the general reader to titles of central importance published mainly during the last twenty years.

BENNETT, GARETH V., *The Tory Crisis in Church and State, 1688–1730* (Oxford, 1975).

CLARK, J. C. D., *English Society 1688–1832)* (Cambridge, 1985).

COLLEY, LINDA, *In Definance of Oligarchy: The Tory Party, 1714–60* (Cambridge, 1982).

CRUICKSHANKS, E. (ed.), *Ideology and Conspiracy: Aspects of Jacobinism, 1688–1759* (Edinburgh, 1982), esp. for an important essay by Mark Goldie.

GUNN, J. A. W., *Beyond Liberty and Property* (Kingston and Montreal, 1983).

HOLE, ROBERT, *Pulpits, Politics and Public Order in England, 1760–1832* (Cambridge, 1989).

NORMAN, E. R., *Church and Society in England, 1770–1970* (Oxford, 1976).

ROWELL, GEOFFREY (ed.), *Tradition Renewed: The Oxford Movement Conference Papers* (1986), for notable essays by Richard Sharp and Peter Nockles.

WARD, W. R., *Georgian Oxford* (Oxford, 1958).

—— *Religion and Society in England 1790–1850* (1972).

Unpublished Theses Consulted in the Preparation of this Book

MURRAY, NANCY U., 'The Influence of the French Revolution on the Church of England and its Rivals, 1789–1802' (D.Phil., Oxford, 1975).

ODDY, JOHN A., 'Eschatological Prophecy in the English Theological Tradition, *c.*1700–*c.*1840' (Ph.D., London, 1982).

Index